Second Edition

THE INTERNATIONAL MONEY MARKET

D1447171

GUNTER DUFEY
University of Michigan

IAN H. GIDDY
New York University

PRENTICE HALL INTERNATIONAL, INC.

Library of Congress Cataloging-in-Publication Data

Dufey, Gunter.
    The International money market / Gunter Dufey, Ian H. Giddy. —
2nd ed.
    p.   cm.
    Includes bibliographical references and index.
    ISBN 0–13–095407–1
    1. Euro-dollar market.   2. Euro-bond market.   3. International
finance.   I. Giddy, Ian H.   II. Title.
HG3897.D83   1994
332.4'5—dc20   93-40621
                                           CIP

HG
3897
.D83
1994

To our parents

Acquisition Editor   Leah Jewell
Production Editor   Maureen Wilson
Copy Editor   Sally Ann Bailey
Prepress Buyer   Patrice Fraccio
Editorial Assistant   Eileen Deguzman

Printed in the United States of America
10 9 8 7 6 5 4 3 2 1

ISBN 0-13-095407-1

Prentice-Hall International (UK) Limited, *London*
Prentice-Hall of Australia Pty. Limited, *Sydney*
Prentice-Hall Canada Inc., *Toronto*
Prentice-Hall Hispanoamericana, S.A., *Mexico*
Prentice-Hall of India Private Limited, *New Delhi*
Prentice-Hall of Japan, Inc., *Tokyo*
Simon & Schuster Asia Pte. Ltd., *Singapore*

CONTENTS

iii

PREFACE

This book is about the money markets, domestic and international, that are used by multinational corporations, government agencies, and banks in the conduct of their business. The book seeks to explain how these markets work both by reference to basic principles of finance and by means of applications of interest to bankers, financial regulators, and students of the financial world. As we stated in the preface to the first edition:

> The Euromarkets, as they are popularly termed, do not exist in isolation. They parallel and are rooted both in domestic markets and in the traditional international financial markets. As such they are of interest not only in their own right, but also as the link between different national financial markets. The nature of these linkages, and of those that exist between the Eurocurrency markets and their domestic counterparts, forms a major theme of this book.

As a second edition, this text borrows heavily from the first version. Many of the fundamental concepts remain valid today. On the other hand, the international money market is a phenomenon that nurtures change and innovation, and the book reflects this fact. The market's evolution has affected financial intermediaries, and the markets in which they compete, on a global scale.

One change has been the integration of the offshore and onshore banking markets. In the first edition, we argued in favor of regarding the external market as a segment of the broad money market for claims denominated in a particular currency; this has now become a well-accepted fact. The key interest rate of the Eurocurrency market, LIBOR[1], has been adopted as *the* benchmark rate for domestic as well as international floating-rate instruments. It is also the principal pricing index in the huge market for money-market derivative instruments such as Eurodollar futures, options, and swaps.

A second evolution has been the liberalization by almost all industrialized countries of domestic money and banking markets. This liberalization is due in no small part to the competitive effect of the international money market. Along the same lines, the incipient trend of fifteen years ago toward securitization in U.S. markets has now become a global phenomenon: securities markets have now become the dominant competitor to financial intermediaries. Accordingly we have paid a great deal more attention to the markets for Eurocommerical paper, medium-term notes, and the like. The effect of these markets on banks themselves has been in part competitive, but also in part symbiotic. As the range of financial instruments available to borrowers and savers has broadened, so have banks' capabilities. A few have become more like investment banks, performing underwriting and distribution of securities to investors rather than lending money themselves. Many have developed skills in risk management instruments, such as options, swaps, and more complex derivatives.

Today, all successful participants in the international money market must have a far more sophisticated understanding of financial risks, and of the tools

[1]The London Interbank Offered Rate.

to manage them, than was once the case. There has been a notable shift of expertise and market power away from banks and toward corporations. The latter increasingly issue commercial paper, bonds, and medium-term notes, and manage their financial risks internally. Some have created finance subsidiaries that have become powerful financial service firms in their own right. The asset-liability management task in commercial banks has become more complex as the variety of products, both on and off their balance sheets, proliferates.

The changes in the markets and banking institutions have required changes in the way financial regulators approach their tasks. The preoccupation is no longer one of monetary control; inflation, it has become clear, can be reined in despite the growth of offshore markets. Today, regulators' predominant concern is systemic risk in the money markets, risk which stems from the soundness or otherwise of individual institutions. All public officials concerned with the financial system must have an understanding of the instruments and institutions of the international money market, as well as of macroeconomic and monetary phenomena.

Those familiar with our earlier book will find that while many fundamental features of the markets remain unchanged, the book now offers a much more thorough treatment of domestic money markets (Chapter 2), of money-market derivatives (Chapter 4), of prudential and capital-adequacy regulation (Chapter 7), and of international bank funding and lending techniques (Chapters 5 and 6). In short, the book strives to give the reader an up-to-date view of a market that is central to most modern financial decisions.

The bulk of the work is designed to enable readers familiar with the principles of financial markets to acquire a comprehensive knowledge about the function and functioning of the international money market. Because some readers may wish to learn about only one particular issue, we have sought to make each chapter largely self-sufficient.

In the task of writing this edition we have benefited greatly from the advice and counsel of colleagues and acquaintances in the financial community. Helpful advice on particular issues was given to us by Professors Richard Herring (University of Pennsylvania), Richard Levich (New York University), Arvind Jain (Concordia University), Thomas Featherstone (University of Alabama), Robert Connolly (University of North Carolina at Chapel Hill), Lee Remmers (INSEAD), and others. Robert McCauley of the Federal Reserve Bank of New York gave us incisive comments, and we have drawn upon discussions with individuals at a number of banks and securities houses: notably Chase, Chemical Bank, Bank of Boston, Credit Suisse, CSFB, Royal Bank of Canada, Bank of America, Deutsche Bank, Drexel Burnham Lambert, Merrill Lynch, JP Morgan, and Korea Exchange Bank. We are grateful to Joanne Ripple and Janet Sarkos for typing and organizing much of the manuscript.

This has been a challenging and satisfying task, but we are aware that there is always room for improvement of content or clarity. Accordingly, we invite our readers to send us suggestions and comments.

Gunter Dufey
University of Michigan

Ian H. Giddy
New York University

Chapter One

THE EURODOLLAR MARKET AND ITS LINKAGES

Contents: *Introduction   Some Background   Terms and Concepts   Why an Offshore Market?   Eurocurrency Markets and Institutions   Illustration of a Eurobank's Operations   The Eurobond Market   Other External Markets Conclusion   Selected References   Appendix 1-A: Are Eurodollars Money? Appendix 1-B: Eurodollar Growth: A Closer Look*

INTRODUCTION

London, Paris, Zurich; Singapore, Hong Kong, Tokyo; New York and islands of the Caribbean—these are some of the centers of the international money market (see Figure 1-1). These markets have often been identified by the prefix "Euro-," reflecting the geographical location of their beginnings, but this is quite misleading. Indeed, as we shall see, these markets are outside, or parallel to, the traditional markets based in national financial centers. As such, they have developed a competitiveness and resilience that have earned them a central place in private and even public international finance. Their significance lies in the fact that these external financial markets differ in regulation, institutional structure, and interest rate determination, and in the way in which funds reach the market and are made available to borrowers.

International financial transactions—that is, the exchange of financial claims between countries—have grown even faster than international trade and direct investment. But while international lending and borrowing per se is almost as old as international trade itself, the decades of the 1970s and 1980s were characterized by a unique phenomenon that has altered both the

1

FIGURE 1-1. Centers of the International Money Market.

nature and the volume of international financial transactions. This phenomenon is the emergence of external financial markets that have to a great extent displaced the traditional international and domestic capital markets.

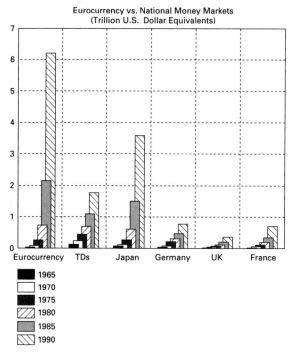

FIGURE 1-2. The Eurocurrency Market. The growth of the Eurocurrency market has outstripped those of all the major domestic money markets. *(International Financial Statistics.)*

By the 1990s, huge integrated markets for bank deposits and loans denominated in major currencies followed the sun around the globe every working day, linking various national financial markets in the process.

Although the measurement and comparison of the size of financial markets pose technical issues that are beyond the purview of this introduction, Figure 1-2 suggests that by 1990 the Euromarkets had become larger than all but the U.S. domestic financial market (and even this exception is subject to dispute).

The size of external, or Euro-, financial markets is matched only by the aura of mystery and controversy they have generated. The growth of the largest segment of these markets, the Eurodollar market, for example, has been attributed alternatively to U.S. balance-of-payments deficits, a "bookkeeper's pen," international interest rate differentials, plain uncertainty, and for those who revel in international intrigue, the financial machinations of the Russians.

What are the wider ramifications of these markets? They have been blamed for worldwide inflation and disorder in foreign exchange markets. The existence and growth of the Euromarkets have, according to some critics, undermined the power of central banks to defend the integrity of their respective national currencies. Finally, it has been implied that self-respecting bankers, normally sworn to conservative and sound lending practices, when operating in these markets suddenly begin to put their entrusted funds into the most questionable loans at rates similar to those charged by governmental agencies to flood victims, drought-stricken farmers, and indigent home buyers.

On the other hand, defenders of these markets claim that they have contributed significantly to the spectacular growth in world trade and investment, that business firms engaged in international operations could hardly function without the financial flexibility offered by these markets, and that they are a real blessing to growing countries that must raise funds for development. The markets have been given credit for "recycling" efficiently and with a minimum of disruptive effects the huge volume of funds transferred by the oil-importing countries to the members of the Organization of Petroleum Exporting Countries (OPEC) cartel in the 1970s, and Japan's surpluses in the 1980s and 1990s.

All this has raised many questions regarding the nature, the effect, and the detailed workings of these markets. There is no shortage of literature; different interpretations abound, and many aspects of the market have been extensively analyzed. Given the nature of the subject matter and the volume of the literature available, the reader will find few ideas that are absolutely new. We believe that almost all the issues arising in the context of the Euromarkets can be resolved by reference to relatively few concepts. As a result, the major intention of this book is to enable the reader to apply these concepts to such issues as "What determines interest rates in the Euromarkets?" "What determines the growth, and therefore the availability, of funds?" "How do bankers operating in the Eurodollar market obtain funds, and how do they put them to use profitably?" And, "what are the justifications for, and possibilities of, governmental control or regulation of these markets?" Seeking answers to these questions, we encounter many core issues in international finance, far beyond the bounds of the international money market itself. It is these issues that describe the true agenda of this book; ultimately, they are those that would be considered by a financial executive contemplating the use of these markets, and by others aiming to understand the markets' role in the world economy.

SOME BACKGROUND

International lending and borrowing is almost as old as international trade, and certain metropolitan areas with well-developed financial markets have provided credit and investment facilities for residents of other countries for many centuries. Indeed, there are reports that in the 1920s and 1930s banks in Europe bid aggressively for foreign currency deposits.[1] We would argue, however, that this phenomenon did not represent a Eurocurrency market but simply traditional foreign funding of domestic loans. External markets for foreign currency deposits and loans had their beginnings in London in the late 1950s and since then have grown rapidly, spread around the world, and spawned other external financial markets, such as the Eurobond and Eurocommercial paper market.

The widespread use of the dollar as a vehicle currency for making payments in international transactions, the easing of exchange restrictions in major European countries as a consequence of U.S. balance-of-payments deficits, and the general growth in European business after the formation of the Common Market in 1958 all contributed to the need for an external money market. A further stimulus was the sterling crisis in 1957, which led to the tightening of British exchange restrictions. These controls prevented London-based banks from financing third-country trade in sterling, and the Bank of England encouraged the use of dollars for this purpose.

Nevertheless, the use of Eurodollar facilities grew quite slowly at first, as international businessmen gradually learned of their existence, advantages, and risks. The takeoff stage did not occur until the mid-1960s. This fact has led many to assume that the market grew as a result of the imposition of controls on capital outflows from the United States in that period. To reduce the U.S. balance-of-payments deficit, the American authorities imposed restraints on foreign portfolio investment in 1963 (the interest equalization tax), on U.S. bank lending abroad in 1965 (the Voluntary Foreign Credit Restraint Program), and on U.S.-financed foreign direct investment in 1965 (the Office of Foreign Direct Investment Guidelines). However, these restrictions obvi-

---

[1] Paul Einzig, *The Eurodollar System*, 5th ed. (New York: St. Martin's Press, 1970), introductory chapter.

THE INTERNATIONAL MONEY MARKET

The **International Money Market** consists of the Eurodollar market and the other money markets to which it is linked. Prime among these are the other Eurocurrency markets—EuroDeutsche marks, Euroyen, French francs, and so forth; Chapter Three will show in detail how these markets are bound to one another through the spot and forward foreign exchange markets. Each Eurocurrency sector is in turn linked by back-and-forth flows to its home money markets and to financial conditions in that market, unless those ties are weakened by exchange restrictions. Finally, the Eurodollar market, which is a market for bank deposits and loans, operates hand-in-hand with the markets for direct financing—the Eurocommercial paper and Eurobond markets.

---

ously could not have been a major reason for the growth of externally inter-mediated funds, for the market has continued to survive and grow since the dismantling of the U.S. controls in January 1974. Those who are interested can read more on this in Appendix 1-B.

TERMS AND CONCEPTS

Both the terminology and the concepts pertaining to the international money market reflect the confusion surrounding this phenomenon. The frequently used term "Eurocurrency market(s)" itself gives rise to at least two misleading associations: (1) it implies that it is a market for foreign currencies similar or closely related to the foreign exchange market, and (2) the term implies either that the market is located in Europe or that it deals primarily in European currencies. Neither is true. *The Eurocurrency market is simply a market for bank time deposits and loans denominated in a currency other than that of the country in which the bank is located.* The international money market consists of the Eurocurrency market and its linkages to the major domestic money markets. This is illustrated in Figure 1-3.

Let us put this into context. How can financial markets be classified? We begin with the distinction between markets for **means of payments** (money) and markets for **credit** (the use of funds over time).

In a modern economy, money in the sense of the means of payment is of a strictly national character: it is produced by a national government, which carefully guards its prerogative to do so. Its acceptability is ensured by "legal tender" laws. Such laws give national money the power to discharge debt legally. But this ability is strictly limited by a nation's borders. Thus the exchange of national monies is necessary to effect payments in another

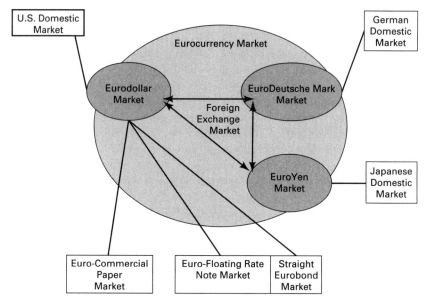

FIGURE 1-3. Eurocurrency Market Linkages. Each Eurocurrency market is tied to each other through the foreign exchange market, and each is linked to its home market.

country. This is the rationale for the **market for foreign exchange**, the market in which different national means of payments are traded.

In contrast to the foreign exchange market, **credit markets** deal in the allocation of claims over time. The saver, whose income exceeds his use of funds in a particular period, makes the additional output that he has created (earned) temporarily available to the (ultimate) investor, whose need for funds is greater than the resources available during that period. For credit to be extended or received, money is not necessary, although it definitely facilitates the transfer of purchasing power.

Our scheme for classifying credit markets, shown in Figure 1-4, is different from the usual distinction between money and capital markets, according to which the maturity of the instruments involved is the major distinguishing criterion. Instead, we ask how and where the process of transferring funds from savers to investors is effected.

First, savers can meet the needs of borrowers in one of two ways. They can get together directly, as when savers purchase the securities *issued* by ultimate borrowers (those who use the funds to invest in real assets). Markets for equities, bonds, and commercial paper would fall largely in this category. Alternatively, savers can invest in the obligations of *financial intermediaries*, which in turn lend the funds to those who purchase goods and services for consumption or investment. The primary distinction between the two channels is that in direct financing, the saver is confronted directly

I. MARKETS FOR MEANS OF PAYMENT
EXAMPLE: THE FOREIGN EXCHANGE MARKET

II. MARKETS FOR CREDIT

	National Domestic	International "Foreign"	"Euro"
Direct			
Intermediated			
	Internal		External

FIGURE 1-4. Classification of Financial Markets. International markets include "foreign" markets (issues by nonresidents in a domestic market) and "Euro-" markets (outside of the country of the currency).

with the credit risk of the issuer, while in financial intermediation a financial institution interjects itself between users and providers of funds. Any analysis of the sector of the credit market dominated by financial intermediaries must, of course, be very much concerned with these institutions themselves (their policies, financial condition, and regulatory environment) in addition to those factors governing suppliers and users of funds directly.[2]

Our second categorization concerns the location, or *jurisdiction*, where funds are exchanged. Normally, saving-investment transfers take place in a nation's domestic financial market. However, most financial markets have links abroad: domestic investors purchase foreign securities, and domestic banks make loans to foreign residents. Similarly, foreign residents may issue securities or deposit funds with domestic banks. These are the traditional forms of international financial transactions.

Before the existence of the Euromarkets, all international finance was of this kind. The key feature of traditional foreign lending and borrowing is that all *transactions are directly subject to the rules, usances, and institutional arrangements of the respective national markets*. Most important, these transactions are subject to public policy pertinent to (foreign) transactions in the domestic market. To illustrate, when savers purchase securities in a foreign market, they do so according to the rules, market practices, and the regula-

---

[2] Those with a penchant for precision may wish to add an additional category, "guaranteed funds," where savers and investors get together *directly*, but where claims are guaranteed by a third party. The banker's acceptance market fits this category. However, this segment is not important for the purposes of our discussion.

tory precepts which govern such transactions in that particular market. The same applies to those who place their funds with foreign financial intermediaries. Likewise, foreign borrowers who wish to issue securities in a domestic market must follow the rules and regulations of this market—and often these rules simply say "no." And the borrower who approaches a foreign financial institution for a loan borrows at rates and conditions imposed by the financial institutions of that country and is directly affected by the public authorities' policy toward lending to foreign residents.

Enter the Euromarkets. During the past 25 years market mechanisms have developed that remove international (and even national) borrowing and lending from the jurisdiction and influence of national authorities. This is done simply by locating the market for credit denominated in a particular currency *outside* the country of that currency. The markets for dollar-denominated loans, deposits, and bonds in Europe, for example, are not subject to U.S. banking or securities regulations. We refer to these markets as "Euro," or more properly "external," to indicate that they are distinct from the domestic or national financial systems. Thus the essence of this classification criterion is the absence (or presence), and the nature, of regulation. Differences in interest rates, practices, and terms that exist between domestic and external markets arise primarily from the extent to which regulatory constraints can be avoided.

We can now be more precise about the concept of the "international money market" that forms the focus of this book. The core of this market is clearly the Eurocurrency market, where funds are intermediated outside the country of the currency in which the funds are denominated, or outside the immediate regulatory environment governing domestic and foreign transactions. Thus the Eurocurrency market comprises financial institutions that compete for dollar (time) deposits and make dollar loans outside the United States, financial institutions outside Switzerland that bid for Swiss franc deposits and make loans in this or another currency (but not the currency of the country in which they operate), and so forth.

The Eurocurrency markets[3] are closely linked to the respective national markets through international (or "foreign") transactions. These linkages manifest themselves in interest rate relationships or the relative availability of funds, and are very much affected by public policy and regulation. Close ties also exist between intermediated and direct credit segments of the external market—between the Eurocurrency market (the dominant segment) and the Eurobond and Eurocommercial paper markets, for example. Finally, both segments of the Euromarkets have linkages to the national markets for bonds, debentures, commercial paper, and so forth.

We define the international money market, then, as the Eurocurrency market

---

[3] The term is used in its plural form whenever we wish to emphasize that the Eurocurrency market consists of various segments, distinguished by currency of denomination.

and its linkages with other segments of national markets for credit. Although the workings of the Eurocurrency market are intricately interwoven with those of the foreign exchange market, the latter does not constitute part of the international money market, because it is not a market for credit.

We do not find the traditional differentiation between money and capital markets very useful. Clearly, the linkages between markets are strongest when the maturity of the claims and nature of the securities are similar. In other words, the relationship between national equity markets and the Eurocurrency market is much less direct than, for example, the relationship between the Eurocurrency market and a national market for certificates of deposits (CDs). For clarity's sake, we shall focus in our analysis on the latter relationship (between equivalent onshore and offshore markets). The former relationships follow from the term structure of interest rates and the risk-return relation in each domestic financial market.

In Figure 1-5 we illustrate the flow of funds through the Euromarket, using the United States as an example. Before the Euromarket began to function, the international flow of bank deposits and bank credit went directly to foreign markets, usually through domestic banks that made loans to foreign banks or foreign borrowers. With the advent of external (or "Euro-") intermediation, these markets have not only become the conduit for most international flows, they also captured a large proportion of flows that used to be intermediated within national bank markets. Readers will observe that funds always originate from, and end up in, national financial or nonfinancial sectors.

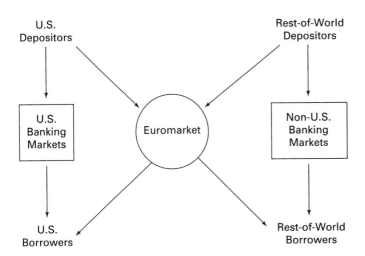

FIGURE 1-5. National and International Financial Intermediation. The Euromarket stands between and brings together borrowers and lenders from different national markets.

"ENTREPÔT" FINANCIAL INTERMEDIATION

Many financial systems are dominated by a few banks, and the development of an open and free money market is not in their interest. Governments frequently contribute to this situation. The banks are often partially or wholly owned by the government, which uses its influence to allocate credit. In addition, the government, seeking to provide its own agencies and industry with low-cost funds, keeps deposit rates low. Since the availability of alternative instruments would allow savers to withdraw their funds from bank time deposits and place them in markets where rates are competitively determined, both the banks and the government have an interest in preventing the development of a broader, competitive money market.

Where interest ceilings and other conditions make domestic bank time deposits unattractive, financial investors will seek alternative channels. That countries have been able to sustain economic growth without a well-developed domestic money market testifies in part to the success of the international financial system that integrated the domestic, foreign, and external money markets. It is possible for the foreign sector of one country's money market to serve as the financial intermediation sector for a number of other countries. It has been suggested that the foreign money markets of New York and London, for example, have become both the destination and the source of funds from the same developing countries. This **entrepôt** function is now performed to a large extent by the Eurocurrency markets for developing and developed countries alike.

In the following sections we shall pursue further the concept of a money market and the functions performed by individual money markets, and then look in detail at the institutions that perform the task of financial intermediation in the international money market.

WHY AN OFFSHORE MARKET?

The imminent demise of the Euromarket, or segments of it, has been announced at various times over the past two decades. Here are three conditions that in our view are necessary but not (individually) sufficient for the market for external deposits and loans to thrive:

- Foreign-based entities must possess the freedom to maintain and transfer demand deposit balances in, say, New York; that is, there should be no restrictions on nonresident inpayments, outpayments, and transfers. This condition has existed for the United States at least since World War II.

- Eurobanks must be able to offer external deposits and loans at competitive rates in a convenient location. While the absence of reserve requirements and the like made Eurobanks potentially competitive with their U.S. counterparts, the widespread currency restrictions during the decade following World War II eliminated most suitable locations outside the United States.
- There must be a demand for external currency deposits and loans. In other words, non-Eurobank entities must be willing and able to place dollar funds with banks outside the United States and to employ dollar funds borrowed from such banks. Prior to the restoration of convertibility of major European currencies in 1957, this ability was lacking for most non-U.S. depositors and lenders.

Thus the birth of the Eurodollar market in the late 1950s was not accidental. The rising U.S. balance-of-payments deficits at the time showed up as surpluses in the current accounts of European countries' balance of payments. And along with it, they relaxed their exchange controls either completely or, at least, sufficiently to permit their financial institutions and corporations to enter into financial transactions abroad. This, then, removed the obstacle that prevented fundamental conditions from becoming effective: *Eurobanks have a competitive advantage in financial intermediation resulting from the disadvantage of banks operating in their respective national markets.*

What, specifically, are the manifestations of this disadvantage? The relevant factors are based almost exclusively on governmental rules and regulations and can be summarized in general form as follows:

1. Regulations which influence credit allocation decisions of financial intermediaries.
2. Regulations which burden financial intermediaries with special costs; this factor includes, but is not restricted to, special assessments and taxes.
3. Rules and regulations which limit interest rates on deposits or assets.
4. Regulations which force intermediaries to maintain reserves which yield less than the market return for funds of such riskiness.
5. All other rules, regulations, and practices that restrict competition among banks in one way or another, or that tolerate the existence of private banking cartels.

Let us examine these points in turn. First, virtually all jurisdictions compel banks to book assets that—strictly in terms of risk and return—they would rather not have. In a U.S. context one must count the loans to and securities issued by many municipalities, local school boards, and even some states. Since banks are considered social tools, they must also provide home financing in all parts of their community, regardless of risks ("antiredlining provisions") and give preference to loans and mortgages in the local community (Community Reinvestment Act). In return, banks have enjoyed some protection from the entry of competitors, although this protection is increasingly eroding. Since the costs of credit allocation are in the nature of opportunity costs, they show up only in larger gross interest spreads. Nevertheless, they are real and often underestimated because they are "built into" the system.

In the second category are such items as Federal Deposit Insurance Corporation (FDIC) assessments as well as state and local taxes: income-, franchise-, business-, and real estate taxes are all burdens on banks that operate in a national market. In many countries, banks are limited in what they can pay on deposits and charge on loans. And while the United States as well as some other industrialized countries have relaxed or eliminated such restrictions, interest rate controls still exist on short-term deposits, and state laws limit lending rates under usury laws. There are no such restrictions in offshore centers.

In virtually all countries, banks must hold minimum reserve requirements in interest-free accounts with the central bank or, alternatively, invest a substantial proportion of their assets in government securities to facilitate the management of the money supply and credit conditions. While the merits of such policies will be analyzed later, there is no doubt that financial institutions incur a cost that their offshore competitors escape. The final point comprises all other cost factors which give offshore banks a financial advantage in competition with domestic banks in attracting (dollar-denominated) time deposits and dollar-denominated loans. The factors enumerated here apply, of course, not only to the United States and the Eurodollar market. They all must be judged within the specific context of the regulatory environment in each national market. For example, the asset structure of banks can be influenced by regulation in very many different ways. What matters are not only *existing* rules, regulations, and political pressures, but also those that are *expected* to be imposed at some time in the future. Such rules and regulations are in response to certain actions or inactions by financial institutions, with the aim of getting them to deviate in their asset/liability decisions from positions they might consider optimal solely on the basis of return and risk considerations. Specifics, of course, differ from country to country.[4]

Once the competitive advantage of Eurobanks is understood, the ques-

---

[4] It is also worth noting that not all regulations involve a competitive disadvantage for banks. For example, regulations promoting disclosure of financial conditions, and those activities of the supervisory authorities that further the safety of the institutions, will definitely contribute to the attraction of banks in a jurisdiction, be it in a national market or "offshore." But these are the exceptions. By and large, rules and regulations tend to be a costly burden on financial intermediaries; to the extent that banks operate in the external market, they effectively avoid most of these regulations and are therefore able to outcompete banks in the national markets.

tion as to the reasons for the existence of external financial intermediation tends to "flip": what requires explanation is the phenomenon that not all large (dollar) deposits and loans have been shifted to the books of offshore banks! A partial answer is that depositors and even certain borrowers perceive Eurodollar facilities to be more risky than domestic facilities. The reasons for concerns lies in the following contingencies:

1. Intervention by the authorities of the jurisdictions where the Eurobanks operate ("sovereign risk")
2. Restriction of nonresident convertibility by the countries whose currency is used to denominate external financial claims
3. Refusal of central banks refusing to function as lenders of last resort
4. Susceptibility of Eurocurrency transactions to exchange controls, because such transactions are "international" from a legal point of view

While the precise analysis of the foundations for these concerns and their seriousness must await our discussion of certain public policy issues, it is obvious that such considerations cause borrowers to be concerned about the timely availability of funds under previously negotiated lines of credit and depositors to worry about the safety and liquidity of their assets. This perception of risk helps explain the relative pricing of Eurodollar deposits.

EUROCURRENCY MARKETS AND INSTITUTIONS

The Eurocurrency, or external, money market, the major segment of which is the Eurodollar market, consists of banks that accept deposits and make loans in foreign currencies. Although the Eurocurrency market is closely tied to the foreign exchange market (almost all Eurobanks also deal in foreign exchange), it is useful to remind ourselves that the two markets are quite distinct in function. In the foreign exchange market, one currency is exchanged for another; in the Eurocurrency market, deposits are accepted and loans are granted, usually in the same currency.

The function of external financial intermediation is performed by specific financial institutions, usually referred to as Eurobanks. What, precisely is a Eurobank?

A textbook definition would be: *a **Eurobank** is a financial intermediary that simultaneously bids for time deposits and makes loans in a currency, or currencies, other than that of the country in which it is located.*

Figure 1-6 illustrates the Eurobank concept by the simplified example of a U.S.-based bank that has a branch in London. The business of the total bank is functionally disaggregated to show the various types of commercial banking activities one must distinguish to analyze transactions in the international money markets.

U.S. Bank

1. Dollar reserves Dollar cash	Dollar demand deposits and similar liabilities	*Traditional domestic commercial banking*
2. Dollar reserves Dollar loans and investments	Dollar time deposits and similar liabilities	*Domestic financial intermediation*
3. Dollar reserves Foreign loans and investment in dollars or other currencies	Dollar time deposits and similar liabilities	*International department*
4. Dollar reserves Foreign currency assets	Foreign currency deposits in United States	*International department*
5. Sterling reserves Sterling loans and investments	Sterling time deposits	*London branch*
6. Loans and investments in dollars, German marks, Swiss francs, etc.	Time deposits in dollars, German marks, Swiss francs, etc.	*Eurocurrency business*

FIGURE 1-6. Categories of International Banking.

The first four segments show the bank's activities in the United States, the last two the business carried out by the London branch. The first segment represents that part of the business funded by demand deposits—both domestically and foreign owned—that serve as means of payments to their owners. The remainder of the bank's balance sheet represents a purely financial intermediation function, in which the bank borrows from various depositors and invests the funds in earning assets.

Segment 3 represents traditional foreign lending and borrowing. The next segment of our bank's balance sheet, part 4, reflects deposits and assets that are allocated to the bank's international banking facility, or IBF. Such a "facility," which is only a set of segmented books in an existing bank, is not only free of reserve requirements but is in other respects also treated as an offshore bank by the U.S. authorities. Thus, IBFs are like a little bit of London in America.[5]

Moving to London proper, we find the bank's foreign branch doing

[5] IBFs cannot accept deposits from nonbank U.S. residents; they require a special declaration from the foreign subsidiaries of U.S. corporations that funds are linked to international purposes, deposits provided by nonresident nonbanks must have a maturity of at least two days, and so forth. Still, for regulatory purposes, IBFs can be considered to be "outside" the United States.

some business that is not really external intermediation. In segment 5 the branch is engaged in the domestic (or foreign) business of the host country, being subject to regulation and acting like any other bank or financial intermediary in that country. Only to the extent that the London branch engages in financial intermediation with funds denominated in currencies other than sterling does it perform Eurocurrency activities. Note that such transactions may be undertaken with British residents or with nonresidents. In practice, some countries impose controls to ensure that the bulk of Eurobanking business is with nonresidents.

Not all Eurocurrency business is done by branches or affiliates of U.S. banks, of course. For example, most major British banks are active in this business, in addition to their domestic and traditional "foreign" sterling transactions. Banks headquartered in other countries similarly carry out external intermediation. Relatively few institutions make external business their only business. Those that do are almost exclusively "consortium banks," which are really special-purpose joint ventures owned by a limited number of major commercial banks, often based in different countries. For conceptual purposes, these banks can be regarded as the jointly owned Eurocurrency "departments" of major banks which, for strategic as well as regulatory reasons, have been set up as legally independent financial enterprises.

To summarize, the term "Eurobank" denotes a function more than it does an institution. Although the legal form and organizational structure cannot always be disregarded for the purpose of economic analysis, we shall call all sections, departments, branches, or parts of financial institutions engaged in external intermediation as defined earlier Eurobanks.

EUROBANK

Assets	Liabilities
Working balance in U.S. bank	Due to other Eurobanks
Deposits in other Eurobanks	Due to nonbank private depositors
Loans to U.S. banks	Due to domestic banks
Loans to other national banks	Due to central banks
Loans to central banks	Due to governments
Loans to governments and private nonbank corporations	Equity

FIGURE 1-7. Stylized Eurobank Balance Sheet. Dollar assets and liabilities only.

Let us take a closer look at this Eurocurrency business proper. Figure 1-7 provides a schematic picture of the balance sheet of a Eurobank. The dollar-denominated assets and liabilities may be vis-à-vis a variety of financial and nonfinancial entities; typically, the major portion would involve claims between banks. In other words, the interbank market accounts for the majority of Eurocurrency assets and liabilities. The distinction between interbank and nonbank deposits is an important one to which we shall return shortly.

Thus a Eurodollar deposit is simply a time deposit, denominated in dollars, in a bank located outside the United States, or an IBF. A Eurodollar loan is a dollar-denominated loan made by a bank or branch of a bank situated outside the United States. Apart from their location, Eurodollar deposits and Eurodollar loans are virtually identical in nature to the corresponding time deposits and loans of conventional banks in the United States; indeed, corporate treasurers and the money managers of banks readily switch back and forth between the two markets. The important distinction between the external and the domestic financial market lies not in the overt nature of deposits and loans but rather in the fact that *Eurocurrency banking is not subject to domestic banking regulation, such as reserve requirements and interest rate restrictions.* This enables Eurobanks to operate more efficiently, cheaply, and competitively than their domestic counterparts and to attract intermediation business out of the domestic and into the external money market. Competitiveness and the absence of regulation, in other words, is the secret of the Euromarket's success.

Thus the market operates only in those currencies, such as the U.S. dollar and Deutsche mark, that are relatively freely convertible into other currencies, and Eurobanks are located only in those countries that refrain from regulating foreign currency banking activities. For example, there is no Eurobanking in Albania (yet). Most countries do not feel the need to regulate Eurocurrency banking activities, since these do not directly affect domestic monetary conditions, and they like the earnings that such activities generate. The Bank of England, for example, traditionally has a hands-off policy with regard to nonsterling banking in London, particularly as long as it involves nonresidents as borrowers and depositors.

The absence of reserve requirements and regulations enables Eurobanks to offer slightly better terms to both borrowers and lenders. Therefore Eurodollar deposit rates are somewhat higher, and effective lending rates a little lower, than they are in the U.S. money market. (In the absence of controls, arbitrage ensures that external money market rates and domestic rates remain closely aligned.) One might therefore ask, why do not all, or most, borrowers and depositors shift their business into the Eurocurrency market? One reason is simply the existence of exchange controls: many governments make it difficult for depositors to invest abroad, and a few restrict foreign borrowing by domestic companies. Another is the inconvenience and cost involved with maintaining balances or borrowing facilities in a foreign

FINANCIAL INTERMEDIATION*

Financial markets and financial intermediaries form the link between lenders and borrowers. Lenders or investors usually seek to allocate funds to investments with the highest yield, minimum risk, and maximum liquidity. Borrowers, on the other hand, generally seek low-cost loans with the flexibility and repayment schedule that matches their needs for funds. Borrowers represent a wide range of credit risks and types of securities issued, which are often difficult for the individual investor to evaluate. And while borrowers tend to seek long-term funds or credit commitments, lenders usually want shorter-term, liquid investments. Where no mechanism exists to reconcile these conflicting objectives, it is unlikely that many suppliers of funds will be found whose requirements match the needs of the borrowers. Real investments will, as a result, be largely self-financed.

Borrowers' and lenders' needs may be reconciled either through direct financial markets or through financial intermediaries. Direct financial markets require brokers, who serve as go-betweens between buyers and sellers of securities, and secondary markets, where instruments once issued can be bought or sold before maturity. But lenders are still subject to the credit risk of the borrowers and dependent on conditions in the secondary market for liquidity.

Financial intermediaries bridge the borrower-lender gap by creating markets in two types of securities: one type for lenders and another for borrowers. In other words, financial intermediaries invest in claims of borrowers and tailor these claims to the borrowers' needs, while issuing liabilities on themselves tailored to the maturity and liquidity needs of investors.

Of course, the financial intermediary charges a fee for this service, represented by the difference between deposit and lending rates. But in a competitive financial system, this fee may be quite small, simply because the financial institution, by pooling large groups of depositors and borrowers, can dramatically reduce the uncertainties involved in direct financial transactions. In other words, the pooling of depositors' funds and of loans enables the borrower to obtain the flexibility and maturity that he needs and the lender the liquidity and safety that he seeks. Financial intermediaries thus perform risk, maturity, and liquidity transformation.

The following elaborates on the functions of financial intermediaries.

Reduction of Risk Through Loan Diversification. By taking a large pool of funds and investing it in a diverse, relatively independent portfolio of loans, a financial intermediary can achieve a far more effi-

*This box draws in part on Chapter 5 of Paul F. Smith, *Economics of Financial Institutions and Markets* (Homewood, IL: Richard D. Irwin, 1971).

cient diversification of credit risks than individual lenders could achieve alone. By averaging the portfolio's risk over a large number of borrowers, the financial intermediary reduces the probability of an extreme loan loss to a negligible amount. As long as losses or loans are independent, the proportion of bad loans becomes statistically predictable within narrow limits and can be regarded as a cost of doing business; all depositors share this cost in the form of slightly lower interest rates.

Thus the pooling of funds by a financial intermediary results in a number of benefits to borrowers and lenders and adds greatly to the efficiency of any financial system by reducing individuals' risks, providing liquidity, and facilitating the allocation of funds to their most productive uses. In addition, by applying economies of scale arising from the division of labor and specialization in credit evaluation, a well-developed and competitive system of intermediaries may significantly reduce the costs of transferring funds from savers to investors in real assets. And, finally, the more diverse, numerous, and specialized the financial institutions dealing with one another are, the more rapidly and efficiently will depositors' funds be pooled and allocated to productive borrowers.

Transformation of Maturity. Financial intermediaries have traditionally been maturity mismatchers: they have taken short-term deposits and invested in longer-term assets, on the supposition—perhaps mistaken—that in the long run the yield on long-term securities exceeds that on short-term securities. Because some institutions were injured by persistently high short-term interest rates during the 1970s, however, the question of the appropriate maturity-transforming role of banklike intermediaries is open. Maturity mismatching is now done in a more calculating fashion, as will be seen in Chapter Four.

Provision of Liquidity Through the Pooling of Funds. Depositors in banks and thrift institutions who want liquidity expect that these institutions will have sufficient funds to enable anyone to withdraw deposits at maturity. Because inflows and outflows occur every day, banks are only concerned with the net flow of funds. If fluctuation in depositors' balances are largely independent and random, total net flows will diminish proportionally as the number of accounts increases. This means that banks need to keep only a small proportion of the maturing assets in cash or liquid securities. As long as they obtain funds from a large number of relatively independent sources, the statistical stability of net flows assures depositors of a high degree of liquidity, even though most of the banks' assets may consist of illiquid loans.

country. The market is largely a wholesale market and deals in sums of $1 million or more,[6] and Eurobanks prefer to lend to large, well-known corporations, banks, or governments. In addition, many potential borrowers and depositors are as yet unfamiliar with the character and techniques of the Euromarkets and fear the risk of ill-defined controls and "crisis." A major purpose of this book is to identify and examine these risks to permit both borrowers and depositors to assess risk and opportunities more accurately.

ILLUSTRATION OF A EUROBANK'S OPERATIONS

The rate at which the Eurocurrency markets have grown is evidence that many corporations and governments have learned to employ the facilities of the external markets as readily as they do the domestic banking system. It may be instructive to illustrate the mechanics of the market by tracing through the steps in the creation of a Eurodollar deposit, of interbank deposits between Eurobanks, and of a Eurodollar loan to a corporation.

First, let us suppose that Shapiro and Son, a Los Angeles–based publishing firm, decides that the extra $1/_2$ of 1 percent that it can earn on a Eurodollar deposit warrants shifting $1 million out of its Los Angeles bank time deposit (Figure 1-8) and into a time deposit with a Eurobank in London. The first set of T-accounts here represents this transaction.

Shapiro and Son first obtains a claim on a demand deposit from its bank upon maturity of the time deposit and then acquires ownership of a time deposit in First Eurobank, London, by transferring ownership (payment) of the demand deposit in the U.S. bank to London (Figure 1-9). A Eurodollar deposit has been created, substituting for an equivalent time deposit in a U.S. bank. To repay the time deposit, of course, the Los Angeles bank would have to reduce its loans by roughly $1 million.

Back to First Eurobank, whose dollar deposit dealer has realized that he would be foolish to leave idle funds in a U.S. bank. If he does not immediately have a commercial borrower or government to which he can loan the funds, First Eurobank's dealer will "place" the $1 million in the Eurodollar interbank market. In other words, he will deposit the funds in some other Eurobank. (First Eurobank may also keep some portion of the $1 million in a U.S. bank as a working balance, but this portion is likely to be so small that we can neglect it until Chapters Two and Five.) The resulting situation is shown in Figure 1-10.

We should perhaps emphasize that what has crossed the Atlantic to find a European home is not a demand deposit but rather an interest-bear-

---

[6] In the 1980s, however, banks began to offer Eurodollar certificates of deposit ((called "London dollar CDs") denominated in amounts as small as $5,000 or $10,000.

UNITED STATES
U.S. BANK

	$1 million demand deposit $1 million time deposit due to Shapiro

FIGURE 1-8. Mechanics of the Market. Initial situation— Shapiro's time deposit sits in a U.S. bank.

ing time deposit, although with a maturity that may be as short as one day ("overnight"). Despite their name, Eurobanks do not perform one of the prime functions of banks—that is, they do not offer checking accounts. The Euromarket has no particular competitive advantage in the payments transfer function of banks, which continues to be done through the domestic payments system of each currency of denomination in the Euromarket. Indeed Eurobanks have the disadvantage of not having *direct* access to the central bank. What Eurobanks do best is pure financial intermediation—taking fixed-term deposits and making loans.

The reader will have noticed that the role of the demand deposits held in U.S. banks is simply that of transferring funds from one party to another. Nobody holds on to these balances for very long; indeed New York's Clearing House Interbank Payment System, known as CHIPS, enables banks throughout the world to initiate and settle transfers of dollars within a matter of hours, with no loss of interest as a result of idle overnight balances.

UNITED STATES		LONDON	
U.S. BANK		FIRST EUROBANK	
	$1 million demand deposit due to First Eurobank	$1 million demand deposit in U.S. Bank	$1 million Eurodollar time deposit due to Shapiro

FIGURE 1-9. Mechanics of the Market. After a shift of funds into the Eurobank, a Eurodollar deposit has been created, substituting for the U.S. time deposit.

UNITED STATES U.S. BANK		LONDON FIRST EUROBANK	
	$1 million demand deposit due to Second Eurobank	$1 million Eurodollar deposit in Second Eurobank	$1 million Eurodollar time deposit due to Shapiro

SECOND EUROBANK	
$1 million demand deposit in U.S. Bank	$1 million Eurodollar time deposit due to First Eurobank

FIGURE 1-10. Mechanics of the Market. Redeposit of funds in another Eurobank.

If Second Eurobank cannot immediately use the funds to make a loan, it will redeposit them in the interbank market. This process of redepositing may proceed through several Eurobanks before the $1 million finds its way to a final borrower. At each stage the next bank will have to pay a slightly higher rate than the previous bank paid. However, the margins involved in the interbank market are very small, of the order of $1/_8$ of 1 percent. As a general rule, larger, better-known banks will receive initial deposits while smaller or less creditworthy banks will have to bid for deposits in the interbank market (i.e., will borrow from better-known banks).

This interbank redepositing of an initial Eurodollar deposit merely involves the passing of funds from bank to bank; it does not add to the final extension of credit in the financial markets. Only when the $1 million is lent to, say, a corporation or a government is credit effectively extended. So when we seek to evaluate the credit-granting capacity of the Eurodollar market, we net out interbank deposits.

The final step occurs when a Eurobank needs the funds to lend to a borrower. For the sake of simplicity, let us assume that Second Eurobank uses the funds to make a loan to Lessard S.A., a French perfume manufacturer. Second Eurobank would make the loan by drawing on its newly acquired balance in a U.S. bank and giving ownership of $1 million to Lessard. In all likelihood, Lessard would be drawing down on a previously made commitment from Second Eurobank and will use the funds immediately to make payments. Immediately after the loan is made, however, the position would be as shown in Figure 1-11.

	UNITED STATES U.S. BANK
	$1 million demand deposit due to Lessard

LONDON FIRST EUROBANK	
$1 million Eurodollar deposit in Second Eurobank	$1 million Eurodollar time deposit due to Shapiro

SECOND EUROBANK	
$1 million loan to Lessard	$1 million Eurodollar time deposit due to First Eurobank

LESSARD S.A.	
$1 million loan demand deposit in U.S. bank	$1 million due to Second Eurobank

FIGURE 1-11. Mechanics of the Market. Funds are loaned to a final borrower.

Loans made by Eurobanks are, in principle, quite similar to larger loans made domestically by U.S. banks. Borrowers can and do obtain very large amounts by borrowing from a "syndicate" of banks from different countries when the amount needed is greater than one Eurobank is willing to provide, and often have the option of borrowing in any of several currencies. Euroloans may be short term, for working capital or trade financing, or have maturities as long as 10 years. The latter would be designated as medium-term Eurocredits, although conceptually they are no different from their short-term counterparts. When a Eurocurrency loan or commitment has a maturity of more than 6 months, the interest rate is usually set on a "roll-over" basis: at the start of each 3- or 6-month period, it is reset at a fixed amount, say, 1 percent, above the prevailing London interbank offer rate.

The upshot of this process is simply a shift from domestic to external financial intermediation. It is, however, by no means an automatic process, for *three conditions* have to exist before such a sequence of transactions can occur. First, Eurodollar deposit interest rates must be high enough, relative to domestic rates, for Shapiro and Son to shift their funds to the Eurobank. Second, Eurodollar loan rates must be low enough to induce Lessard S.A. to borrow from Second Eurobank rather than, say, from a U.S. bank. And, third, the spread between Eurodollar deposit and loan rates must be sufficient to enable the Eurobanks to borrow and lend profitably. In addition, borrowers, depositors, and banks must have relatively free access to the market. *Only if these conditions are present will the market continue to exist and grow along with the expansion of credit in general.*

THE EUROBOND MARKET

The rapid growth of external financial markets has created its own myths. One of them is reflected in the term "Eurodollar bond market." Strictly speaking, there is no such thing. What does exist is a market for Eurobonds, a substantial number of which is denominated in U.S. dollars, the remainder in other currencies. These are debt securities issued in a way so as to escape restrictions prevailing in national bond markets. Eurobonds are quite distinct from Eurodollars, since bond markets enable final borrowers to issue securities in investors directly, whereas financial intermediation in the Eurodollar market allows investors to hold short-term claims on Eurobanks who "transform" deposits into (often longer-term, riskier) loans to final borrowers. In the Eurobond market, no intermediaries intervene between borrower and lender (except during the underwriting and distribution process). Eurobonds represent direct claims on corporations, governments, or governmental entities and therefore are in most respects very much like domestic bonds.

Traditional foreign bonds are issued in a particular country by a foreign borrower, in the currency of that country. The Eurobond market, in contrast, is "external": like the Eurodollar market, it is not tied to any particular location and thereby, to a certain extent, escapes the norms and regulations that restrict the access of foreign issuers to individual national markets.

Even countries with the most liberal regulatory philosophy limit the access of foreign borrowers who wish to raise funds by issuing securities. Such restrictions, which can easily be enforced, are usually rationalized on one or more of the following grounds:

- to protect the balance of payments from "excessive" capital outflows
- to preserve scarce capital resources for domestic borrowers
- to protect domestic investors from risky securities

On the other hand, most countries find it difficult, for political or simply practical reasons, to prevent individual investors from taking their funds outside their country of residence to purchase securities abroad.

Internationally operating investment banks have exploited this discrepancy in regulation by developing issuing techniques that, in effect, circumvent restrictions on foreign issuers in national markets. These techniques usually involve some or all of the following:

- Eurobond issues are given the form of private placements rather than broadly advertised in public markets.

- Eurobonds are placed through syndicates made up of issuing houses and banks in many countries who sell the bonds, often to nonresident investors.[7]

- Eurobonds are sold principally in countries other than that of the currency in which they are denominated.

- The bond issues are structured in such a way that interest is not subject to withholding taxes.

Conceptually, Eurobonds are in fact a little difficult to pin down and are less amenable to clear-cut definition than Eurodollars. For example, most, but not all, Eurobonds are issued by entities domiciled outside of the country of the currency—but this is a feature shared with traditional foreign bonds and is by no means universal. The important aspect is the combination of issue and placement techniques that free the bonds of withholding taxes and other restrictions which would reduce their attraction to internationally mobile investors. This will cause the price and yield of such a bond to follow other Eurobonds rather than domestic bonds or traditional foreign bonds issued in a (protected) national market.

Eurobond investors are typically not subject to taxation, because their country of residence does not tax foreign income until repatriated, or because they simply choose not to declare interest income, or because as institutional investors (pension funds of international institutions and corporations, offshore (captive) insurance companies, international mutual funds, central banks), they have tax-free status in their respective jurisdiction. Thus Eurobonds must be issued free of withholding tax to be competitive. While government issuers and their entities typically exempt themselves from their national withholding tax on interest paid to nonresidents, private corporate issuers must form a special finance subsidiary in one of the few jurisdictions that do not levy a withholding tax. The Netherlands Antilles have served as the preferred jurisdiction where such captive finance companies (or "NV's," for short) are incorporated.[8] Not only does the government in the capital of Curaçao refrain from imposing a withhold-

---

[7] Nonresident accounts are held by, say, French investors in Switzerland, Belgian and Dutch investors in Luxembourg, and African investors in the United Kingdom. These nonresident accounts are exempt from exchange and capital controls imposed by the host country on its own residents.

[8] They are known as NVs because that is an abbreviation for the Dutch term for public corporation. U.S. corporations have all but ceased to use NVs since the U.S. withholding tax on corporate bonds was effectively abolished (in July 1984) and the treaty with the Netherlands Antilles was revised. Suitable locations other than the Netherlands Antilles include Luxembourg and suitable U.S. states, primarily Delaware, that register so-called 80/20 corporations, a designation derived from an Internal Revenue Service rule that if more than 80 percent of such a corporation's income comes from abroad, no U.S. withholding tax is due.

ing tax, it also maintains an extensive network of bilateral tax treaties. One of those is in force with the United States, stipulating a zero withholding tax rate on interest paid from a U.S. source to an NV—provided certain conditions are met. The treaty permits corporations to use the funds raised via a Eurobond issue in the United States, without being subject to the withholding tax when interest is paid to the NV.

The U.S. withholding tax is one factor that inhibits arbitrage between the U.S. domestic market and the Eurobond market on the part of foreign private investors (foreign central monetary institutions are exempt from the U.S. withholding tax). When the U.S. withholding tax on both new corporate and government bonds was reduced to zero in July 1984, it became apparent that this was not the only barrier keeping foreign investors away from U.S. domestic securities. The provisions of the Tax Equity and Fiscal Responsibility Act (TEFRA) of 1982 do not permit the issuance of securities in bearer form. Since most private investors either do not declare interest income and/or hold foreign securities in contravention to (existing or anticipated) exchange control laws, they object to having their identity revealed abroad, especially if the country in question has little regard for the investors' desire to privacy. Thus it is possible for Eurobonds (denominated in U.S. dollars) to yield considerably less than domestic bonds, simply because investors outside the United States who wish to hold dollar-denominated paper from U.S.-based issuers find domestic bonds unattractive.

Inward arbitrage by foreign issuers is also limited. Compliance with Securities and Exchange Commission (SEC) registration and disclosure requirements are not only cumbersome and expensive, but would compel foreign corporations to reveal information that is politically sensitive in their home country. The restriction imposed by state laws on U.S. institutional investors, such as bank trust funds, insurance companies, and pension funds, against including foreign securities in their portfolios represent another obstacle to inward arbitrage. And since institutional investors dominate the demand for taxable fixed interest securities in the U.S. market, discrimination against foreign paper effectively limited access to the U.S. market by foreign investors.

Not only are there barriers to arbitrage between the U.S. domestic and the Eurobond market (similar barriers segment other major bond markets from their offshore parallel markets),[9] but it appears that the institutional investors that tend to dominate the U.S. market are influenced by somewhat different factors than the private individuals who play a significant role in the demand for Eurobonds. In particular, private Eurobond investors who take up a substantial proportion of many Eurobonds seem to be less influenced by formal credit ratings, but tend to look more to name recognition.

---

[9] For details on controls, see Organization for Economic Co-operation and Development, *Experience with Controls on International Portfolio Operations in Shares and Bonds* (Paris: OECD, 1980).

WHAT IS A EUROBOND?

Eurobonds differ from domestic bonds principally because they are:

- Issued in bearer form
- Issued outside the jurisdiction of the government in whose currency the bond is denominated; and
- Free of withholding tax.

FIGURE 1-12.   Characteristics that Differentiate the Eurobond Market.

Thus companies that are "household names" sell particularly well. Private investors also have a much stronger aversion to long-term maturities, and they seem to be more sensitive to currency expectations, when compared to professional U.S. portfolio managers whose fiduciary obligations are measured in nominal returns. It is not surprising, therefore, to find periods when U.S. issuers can raise medium-term funds for up to two percentage points less than in the domestic market (although higher issuing costs, necessary because of the "retail distribution," reduce the net yield advantage).

The Eurobond market has expanded quite rapidly, as shown in Figure 1-12. By comparison, its new-issue volume exceeds by far that of bonds issued in traditional national markets, and in terms of issue volume only the bond markets of major countries yield a higher volume. Figure 1-13 indicates the dominance of the major currencies—U.S. dollars, German marks, and Japanese yen—in the denomination of Eurobond issues. The increase in volume of bonds has been in part stimulated and paralleled by the growth in secondary market trading.[10]

In a fundamental sense, the Eurobond market performs the same function as is performed by the external money market: funds are gathered internationally, denominated in a variety of currencies, and made available to borrowers from various countries largely without being influenced by national authorities.[11] These features set it apart from both domestic bond markets and traditional foreign bond markets.

In summary, the external bond market, like the external money market, exists to avoid the regulation, control, and allocational influence of national authorities. Again, as with the Eurocurrency market, however, its existence depends on the willingness of governments to enable investors and borrow-

---

[10] For details see Gunter Dufey and Ian H. Giddy, *The Evolution of Instruments and Techniques in International Financial Markets* (Tilburg: S.U.E.R.F., 1981), pp. 17–22.

[11] Some governments such as Switzerland and Japan exert informal pressure on international issuing houses and banks to refrain from using their currencies to denominate Eurobond issues without explicit permission.

EUROBONDS

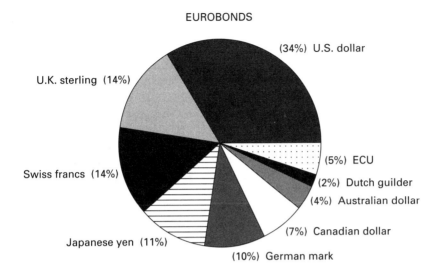

FIGURE 1-13. Currency Breakdown of New Issues in the International Bond Market Shows Dominance of the Dollar But Growing Importance of the ECU. Based on percent of Eurobond new issue volume in 1989.

ers to move across borders. As long as these conditions remain, and as long as governments continue to direct credit allocation and interest rates in domestic money and capital markets, the sophisticated institutional framework that both markets have developed gives reason to believe that the Euromarkets will retain their important role in financing the growth of the world economy.

OTHER EXTERNAL MARKETS

Eurobonds are not the only securities issued directly by borrowers in the external market. The 1980s saw a burgeoning market for Eurocommercial paper (ECP) and Euronotes in London. As in the huge domestic U.S. CP market, corporations began to issue short-term promissory notes which were placed by specialized investment banks and securities houses. These financial institutions also began to make a secondary market in this paper.

Such securities represent unsecured short-term bearer debt, typically sold by a corporation to money market investors. For high-quality borrowers such as large corporations and governments, it has proved to be among the least expensive form of short-term paper available and has to a large extent replaced bank borrowing for these entities. Because the market taps a different group of investors and is free of U.S. disclosure requirements and investor constraints (such as the need for a "rating"), many borrowers use the Eurocommercial paper market in lieu of the large U.S. domestic commercial paper market. To assure borrowers access to this relatively inexpensive form of credit, some Euronote facilities are backed by an underwriting commitment on the part of a group of commercial banks—an agreement to provide the borrower with credit if its commercial paper proves expensive or unavailable. These are known as Revolving Underwritten Facilities (RUFs) or Note Issuance Facilities (NIFs).

The success of the distribution method in the commercial paper market has led to its extension into longer and longer maturities. The medium- and long-term counterpart of the Eurocommercial paper market is called the medium-term note market. Medium-term notes are issued continuously on an "on-demand" basis in smallish amounts, rather than in the form of large, underwritten, widely distributed bond issues. The medium-term note has now become a serious rival to U.S. and Euro corporate bonds. These instruments and others are described in more detail in Chapters Four and Five.

The relative lack of constraints in the Euromarkets make them a fertile field for financial innovation, and some of the innovations have a tendency to blur the distinction between intermediated and direct channels of the flow of funds. These trends notwithstanding, it must be pointed out that the external debt markets and the Eurocurrency market can exist in and by themselves—although they support each other in the sense that an efficient money market will make bond operations easier, and the availability of the market for medium-term, fixed-rate securities permits financial intermediaries (and their clients) to obtain funds with greater stability than standard deposits. Floating-rate bonds have further blurred the distinction between intermediated and direct markets. While the presence of an intermediation function or the lack thereof still distinguishes markets and channels, from an issuer's point of view particularly, the distinction has become blurred.

Occasionally, one encounters the term "Euroequities." Upon closer examination, however, the term is seen to be devoid of meaning. Bonds issued by the same borrower can be differentiated from one another by the choice of legal entity—that is, the issuer, by underwriting and placement techniques, and the like. This is not possible with equity, which must ultimately be a claim against the profits of the enterprise as a whole. The term has usually been used to denote issues of U.S. corporate stocks placed with European investors, but these are simply new issues of corporate shares placed with investors outside the issuer's home market. Ultimately, therefore, these equities are no different from the shares held or traded by domestic investors.

CONCLUSION

In this chapter we have shown the significance of the international money market, attempted to clarify a few basic concepts and tried to illustrate the simple mechanics of the market. In the following chapters we shall analyze in detail the determination of interest rates, the use of derivative instruments such as forward rate agreements (FRAs) and swaps in the Euromarkets, market practices and institutions, and issues of public policy. Appendix 1-B to this chapter seeks to clarify the factors underlying the market's growth.

Despite its name, the Eurocurrency market is not confined to Europe, nor is it a market for currencies. It is the market for time deposits denominated in various currencies where the intermediary bank is located in a jurisdiction outside the country of the currency. Free of national restrictions and regulatory costs such as reserve requirements, the market has flourished in the past 20 years, to the point where it is now the primary conduit for international banking. This chapter has sought to show why this is the case, specifying the conditions that allow the market to thrive. We have also introduced the reader to the Euromarket activities of international banks and contrasted the intermediated market (bank deposits and loans) with the direct markets such as Eurobonds, Eurocommercial paper, and Euro medium-term notes. The theme throughout has been that national markets, via the Euromarket, are partially but imperfectly linked, and that the Euromarkets are able to exploit regulations and imperfections by separating the currency of denomination from the country of jurisdiction. This idea of separating and reconstituting the features of financial instruments will prove to be a common refrain throughout this book.

SELECTED REFERENCES

Bank for International Settlements, *Annual Reports*. Basle: BIS, various years.

Dobbs-Higginson, M. S., *Investment Manual for Fixed Income Securities in the International and Major Credit Markets*. London: Credit Suisse First Boston, 1982.

Euromoney Corporate Finance, Supplement, "Guide to International Commercial Paper," January 1993.

Euromoney Corporate Finance, Supplement, "The Corporate Debt Market Manual," January 1993.

Giddy, Ian H., *Global Financial Markets*. Lexington, MA: D.C. Heath, 1994.

Lomax, David F., and P. Gutmann, *The Euromarkets and International Financial Policies*. New York: John Wiley and Sons, 1981.

Dufey, Gunter, and Ian H. Giddy, *The Evolution of Instruments and Techniques in International Financial Markets*. Tilburg: S.U.E.R.F., 1981.

Einzig, Paul, *The Eurodollar System*, 2nd ed. New York: St. Martin's Press, 1970.

Organization for Economic Co-operation and Development, *Experience with Controls on International Portfolio Operations in Shares and Bonds*. Paris: OECD, 1980.

APPENDIX 1-A
Are Eurodollars Money?

The simple answer is "no," at least not in the narrowly defined sense. Eurobanks issue time deposits, not the kind of deposits that can be used to write checks on. Eurobanks and their customers alike use the domestic banking system to make payments. Thus Eurodollars are *not* a means of payment.

Let us explore this a little further. The concept of "money" has two interpretations. First, money can be regarded as a means of exchange used for purchases. Second, it can be viewed as consisting of various short-term assets held in anticipation of spending. Only currency and checking accounts serve the former function, while the second can be served by a wide variety of money market instruments, such as short-term certificates of deposit, savings deposits, commercial paper, and, of course, Eurodollar deposits. All these have a degree of liquidity, or what some call "money-ness." In this respect, therefore, Eurodollar deposits, like time deposits in U.S. banks and savings and loan institutions, can be regarded as "near-money."[1]

On the other hand, what counts for policy purposes is the central bank's ability to control the "money supply," whatever it is, and for this purpose the Eurodollar market is fundamentally different from the domestic money supply. As we shall see in Appendix 1-B, an injection of new money into a "demand deposit plus currency" money supply can expand by some multiple of the original amount added. But a time deposit system cannot, for each institution has to compete with each other institution for deposits by paying interest, and this interest has to come from putting the funds to work productively.

---

[1] Theories of money along these lines were first espoused in John G. Gurley and Edward S. Shaw, "Financial Intermediaries and the Savings-Investment Process," *Journal of Finance*, May 1956, pp. 257–266, and in James Tobin, "Commercial Banks as Creators of 'Money,' " in Deane Carson, ed., *Banking and Monetary Studies* (Homewood, IL: Richard D. Irwin, 1963).

The Eurodollar market may be regarded as directly analogous to a system of domestic nonbank intermediaries such as savings banks. Eurobanks, like savings banks, compete with other financial intermediaries by paying interest to attract deposits and make loans. Domestic banks do not usually pay interest on demand deposits; instead they provide payments services— to the public, to savings banks, and to Eurobanks. So why do Eurobanks use, but not provide, checking accounts?

Elementary banking theory stipulates that financial institutions—just like individuals and nonfinancial firms—retain a proportion of their assets in the form of cash balances to meet possible outflows of funds. For a bank with a fairly volatile deposit base, these balances contribute to the liquidity of the bank and, in general, larger balances are needed to support a greater volume of deposits. This theory, however, must be tailored to Eurobanks which represent a very special subgroup of financial institutions.

Let's begin with a glance at some technical details. When a Eurobank has negotiated a U.S. dollar (time) deposit, it will receive the funds from the depositor by way of a transfer in the ownership of a demand deposit in a bank in the United States: this transfer is effected by check or, more frequently, by "wire" (telex, or a message via SWIFT, which is a cooperative international communication system for banks). This message instructs the U.S. correspondent bank to debit the depositor's account and credit the account of the Eurobank. If the Eurobank does not have its demand deposit account within the same bank as the depositor, there will be a transfer of funds within the U.S. clearing system.

The largest New York banks, plus some others, are the settling members of the Clearing House Interbank Payment System. They, in turn, settle for the other members who number over 100; they all belong to the New York banking community, consisting mainly of the Edge Act subsidiaries of regional U.S. banks and the foreign banks operating in New York. With this very efficient clearing system they dominate the business of offering dollar payment facilities to banks throughout the world, for whatever purposes—not only for the clearing of Eurodollar transactions. After they have cleared transactions among themselves through the CHIPS system, they settle their remaining net debits position via the "Fed wire," a communications process by which the Federal Reserve System is instructed to debit and credit the accounts that these banks maintain at the Federal Reserve Bank of New York. These accounts are, of course, the reserves of the banks which link them to ultimate dollar money, that is, the monetary liabilities of the Fed.[2]

---

[2]For a detailed overview of the U.S. payment systems, especially with respect to the possibility of systemic risk, see *Federal Reserve Bulletin*, "A Primer on the Settlement of Payments in the United States," November 1991.

The reason why these technical details are not trivial is that they provide the key to the answer of a fundamental question: Why don't banks outside the United States offer (true) demand deposit facilities in U.S. dollars?[3] The essence of the explanation is that it is too costly and too risky for banks outside the United States to offer demand deposit facilities, that is, dollar means of payments. First, it is very difficult to compete with the CHIPS system in terms of cost per transaction. Further, from a worldwide perspective, the CHIPS system has the longest business hours: it accepts transactions until 4:30 P.M. U.S. East Coast time (and Fed Wire transfers can be made until 6:00 P.M.), a period when any dollar clearing system abroad would long be closed. The most important competitive factor, however, is that the banks abroad do not have direct access to ultimate money, that is, Federal Reserve Bank liabilities. On the other hand, member banks, while compelled to maintain minimum reserve requirements, do have considerable flexibility in managing their liquid balances. Reserve requirements must be achieved in terms of an average daily balance during the week running from Thursday through the following Wednesday. A bank may also be 2 percent short on its requirements.

Most important, member banks have access to (relatively inexpensive) Federal Reserve credit in case their cash balance should prove to be insufficient due to unanticipated outpayments. In contrast, banks offering dollar demand deposits without direct access to the Fed would either have to hold relatively large demand balances in New York to avoid ever being unable to settle or they would have to obtain access to liquid balances indirectly via Fed member banks, made available to them at equal or lower costs than to Fed member banks themselves.

It is not surprising to find the U.S. member banks, particularly those who run the efficient CHIPS dollar (pre)clearing system, outcompete all other banks. The same applies, of course, analogously to banks in other currency systems. Thus no bank situated outside of Canada can effectively offer Canadian dollar checking facilities, nor can Deutsche mark sight deposits be offered competitively outside of Germany, and the same is true with respect to other countries. This explains, in turn, why the shortest maturity for Eurodollar deposits is the overnight, that is, one-day, time deposit. At the beginning of every deposit when it is accepted and when it is returned at maturity, a payment takes place through the dollar clearing system. The same applies to loans, when the loan proceeds are paid to the borrower and when the borrower makes payment of interest and principal to the

---

[3] Some banks outside of the United States offer U.S. dollar checking accounts. Close inspection of the checks or experience with the collection process will reveal that they are always payable in the United States at the U.S. bank where the foreign bank holds its own demand deposit account. Indeed the check is simply a payment order against that account.

Eurobank. As Eurobanks accept many deposits every day and book and repay assets every day, they support a very heavy volume of payments, and this activity goes through the cash, or "working," or "clearing" balances, which are all names for the same thing, that is, demand deposit accounts in New York. What ultimately determines the size of a bank's working balance?

As with all financial intermediaries, the ideal position for a Eurobank is to match its payments (receipts of deposits and loan repayments) and disbursements (for loans and maturing deposits) each day. This minimizes the need to keep nonearning assets. But there are two reasons for a Eurobank to hold positive balances in New York accounts. One is related to the difficulty encountered by Eurobanks in perfectly matching in- and outpayments during each day. This is because there is a degree of uncertainty associated with the offers of funds for deposits as well as with loan demand and investment opportunities. The precautionary demand for liquid balances, discussed in detail shortly, is essentially based on this uncertainty. The other reason stems from the need to compensate U.S. banks for handling the many transfers on their books which occur every day. Maintaining interest-free demand balances is the traditional manner of compensating banks for this service, especially in the United States, but also elsewhere. Of course, the same balance can serve both precautionary purposes and for compensation. Indeed, the same balance serves not only for clearing Eurodollar credit transactions, but also for foreign exchange transactions, including payments for ordinary exports and imports.

We can now draw some conclusions: Eurodollars are not means of payments; what Eurobanks offer are time deposit facilities. Money, in the narrow sense, is only found onshore; what is offshore is credit; that is, loans by depositors to Eurobanks who, in turn rent funds for the use by borrowers for profit. Thus Eurodollars are not money except in the broad sense of providing liquidity. Only in a system where the liabilities of the financial intermediaries also serve as the means of payment can there be "multiple expansion" of total bank assets (credit). This leads us to the next appendix, where we show how Eurobanks, like nonbank financial intermediaries, have to rely on their ability to attract deposits away from other financial intermediaries to expand credit.

APPENDIX 1-B
Eurodollar Growth: A Closer Look

SOME QUESTIONS ABOUT THE GROWTH
OF THE EURODOLLAR MARKET

While we shall enter the debate on the public policy implications in Chapter Six, questions about the growth of external financial intermediation are of major importance to financial institutions planning to exploit opportunities in international financial markets and to business firms that are developing a global approach to funding. Thus there are many reasons to ask: What is the source of the past growth of the market? Can borrowers rely on it to provide a continually increasing supply of funds? Or does the present size represent a precarious "pyramid" of credit that could undergo a massive contraction at any time? That the Eurocurrency market's growth outpaced that of most national money markets for two decades was noted at the beginning of this chapter. What determines this growth? In the past, many writers and casual market observers have related Eurodollar deposits with U.S. balance-of-payments deficits and the corresponding accumulation of dollar balances by foreign residents. Conversely, some attribute the market's growth to capital controls intended to stop certain forms of international capital flows. Others see Eurodollar expansion as occurring through multiple credit creation, exactly as in a country's commercial banking system.

This appendix is designed to assist the interested reader in sorting out fact from myth in the many statements that have appeared and will appear concerning the expanding role of the Eurodollar market in the world economy. We shall argue that far from being "precarious," the expansion of Eurodollars represents the highly efficient response of international banks to the desires of investors for high-yielding safe and liquid investment, and the needs of businesses (and governments) for low-cost funds with a high degree of availability. Contrary to a widespread belief, the Eurodollar market is not caused by the U.S. balance-of-payments deficits, and the future growth of the Eurodollar market does not depend on a continuation of the U.S. balance-of-payments deficits. The connection between the two is tenuous at best. More important, the process of multiple credit creation is an inappropriate model to explain the growth of Eurodollars, nor is there any identifiable multiplier relationship between new deposits in the market and final credit extended.

Instead, as we shall see, the Eurodollar market grows in a quite unremarkable and uncomplicated fashion: by providing inexpensive and efficient financial intermediation, it attracts some depositors and borrowers away from purely domestic financial intermediaries. In other words, it grows primarily as it substitutes for domestic credit intermediation. As a result, we shall argue, the Eurodollar market is not by itself a major cause of global inflation. Before treating these somewhat complex issues, however, one point of common confusion must be clarified.

When talking about an expansion of credit granted in the Eurodollar system, we mean bank loans to ultimate borrowers—the end users of credit, such as corporations and governments. Not included is interbank depositing, sometimes called "pyramiding" (a most misleading term). A foreign bank that receives a dollar deposit will usually not lend the funds directly to a final borrower but will pass part or all of the funds directly to a second Eurobank. The latter may then redeposit the funds at a marginally higher rate in yet a third Eurobank, and so forth. In fact, a large proportion of the transactions in the Eurodollar system are interbank deposits, as is suggested by Figure 1B-1.

This lending and re-lending may continue through a chain of several banks serving as intermediaries between the original depositor and final

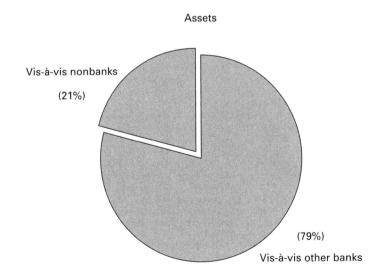

FIGURE 1B-1. Interbank Business of Eurobanks.

borrower. The chaining serves to achieve rapid and efficient allocation of funds and is possible because of the very narrow profit margins involved (as little as $^1/_{32}$ of 1 percent on an interbank placement). Of course, interbank redepositing is limited by the rather narrow total spread between loan and deposit rates. The important point is that the chaining of bank deposits clearly does not in itself build up the total outstanding credit to end users and therefore should be netted out when one is comparing the stock of Eurocurrency deposits with domestic time deposits. Thus to use "net size" data to measure the market's growth is justified only on the assumption that these data grow in line with nonbank deposits or assets.

WHY DO EUROCURRENCIES GROW?

In the body of Chapter One we enumerated the competitive factors giving the external market its *raison d'être*. However, the data (see Table 1B-1) indicate that Eurodollar deposits, for example, have grown much more rapidly than comparable domestic deposits over many years.

With a given competitive advantage of the Eurobanks, one would expect simply a "shift" of a proportion of the total credit intermediation activities into the external market, but after the competitive equilibrium between the internal and external market segments had been reached, the market would grow at a rate in line with that of the respective national market. Such a simple version of the substitution theory, however, is at variance with the data in Table 1B-1. To explain the disproportionate growth of the

TABLE 1B-1. Growth Rates of "Onshore" Versus "Offshore" Markets for Time Deposits (TDs), 1965–1990 (Billions of Dollar Equivalents)*

End of Period	Eurocurrency Market (net)	U.S. Bank TDs	Japan TDs	Germany TDs	U.K. TDs	France TDs
1965	17	151	42	30	18	4
1970	65	226	92	69	20	20
1975	255	437	247	183	46	77
1980	730	462	677	286	104	149
1985	1,675†	901	1,086	309	62	265
1990	u	p1,315	d2,793	a701	t165	e489

*Comparative data such as these are to be used cautiously, because they do not show the structure of the money market. Whereas time deposits are essentially the only financial asset in the Eurocurrency market, in a number of national markets, especially those in the United States and United Kingdom, a large volume of available money market instruments serve functions similar to time deposits. On the other hand, many small "savings deposits" are not equivalent to the competitive market in large deposits found in the Eurocurrency market. Thus if one considers only large, negotiable time deposits (in the United States, CDs) as truly equivalent, the Eurodollar portion of the Eurocurrency market is much larger than its domestic equivalent.

†*International Banking and Financial Market Developments*, Bank for International Settlements, Monetary and Economic Department. Basle, February 1992.

Source: Eurocurrency market: Morgan Guaranty Trust, *World Financial Markets*, various issues, and Bank for International Settlements, *Annual Reports*, various issues; national markets: International Monetary Fund, *International Financial Statistics*, various issues.

Eurocurrency market one must, therefore, search for "dynamic" factors, that is, those that cause change in the static, competitive equilibrium, thus explaining the relatively regular pattern of growth over time.

One set of factors that could cause change in the growth rate of the Eurodollar market are changes in the cost factors in the domestic market. Obviously, if costs rise gradually over time, one would expect a steady shift of deposits and loans offshore. An increase in reserve requirements would, for example, shift the competitive balance. While reserve requirements have been changed, the changes were by no means steadily upward. And even the direction has not been clear; while under the Depository Institutions Deregulation and Monetary Control Act of 1980, the reach of reserve requirements has been expanded to all institutions offering current account facilities, the rates have been decreased.

Closely related to reserve requirements is the level of interest rates: a rise in interest rates would cause the cost of (constant) reserve requirements to be higher; for a given, noninterest-bearing legal reserve requirement of, say, 5 percent, the opportunity cost for the financial institution is 50 basis points. When interest rates double to 20 percent, a bank in the domestic market can pay a full 1 percentage point less on deposits compared to its competitors in the offshore market. While interest rates did increase during much of the decades of the 1960s and 1970s, the rise was not smooth, nor did it continue in the 1980s.

A more plausible explanation for the persistently higher growth rates may be found by analyzing changes in risk perceptions. Relative to changes in cost, such changes are much more diffused among market participants, and they do not occur abruptly—except during occasional crises. Analysis of domestic versus offshore deposit rate differentials shows that prior to 1975 risk perception dominated.[1] They came down steadily to become mainly dominated by cost factors (reserve requirements, FDIC assessments) thereafter. This reduction in the risk differential can only be due to a gradual reassessment by market participants of the risk factors enumerated above. Once depositors at the margin charge fewer basis points for the risk than banks value the cost associated with taking domestic deposits, changes in risk perception show up purely as market growth; deposit rate differentials will remain constant, determined by cost differences.

THE SUPPLY AND DEMAND APPROACH

The factors influencing the size of the Eurodollar market can be examined by returning to the supply and demand framework discussed earlier in this chapter. We can express the notion that the demand for Eurodollar deposits

---

[1] See Ian H. Giddy, "Why Eurodollars Grow," *Columbia Journal of World Business*, Fall 1979, pp. 54-60.

(by banks) equals the supply of Eurodollar deposits (by depositors) more graphically by reference to the supply and demand curves in Figure 1B-2.

First, the demand for Eurodollar deposit funds by Eurobanks can be expressed as a function of the demand for Eurodollar loans by borrowers. The lower the interest rate relative to the U.S. rate, the greater the demand for Eurodollar loans. However, as long as virtually all Eurodollar borrowers have access to credit in the U.S. market, it follows that whenever the Eurodollar loan rate rises above the U.S. loan rate, all demand for Euroloans will virtually disappear as borrowers shift to the U.S. market. Hence at the point where the Eurodollar loan rate equals the U.S. loan rate, the demand curve for Eurodollar loans tends to be flat (perfectly elastic).

The depositors' supply curve for Eurodollar deposits is even more easily derived. As Eurodollar deposit rates rise relative to U.S. rates, more depositors are attracted to the market and the supply of deposits increases, as in Figure 1B-2. If Eurodollar rates drop below U.S. rates, however, almost no funds will remain in the Eurodollar market; depositors will shift their deposits back to U.S. banks. At the point where the Eurodollar deposit rate equals the U.S. rate, the supply of Eurodollar deposits becomes flat (perfectly elastic).

Figure 1B-2 enables us to see that the Eurodollar deposit rate (relative to U.S. rates) and the quantity of Eurodollar deposits are determined by the intersection of the supply and demand curves. That is, the Eurodollar mar-

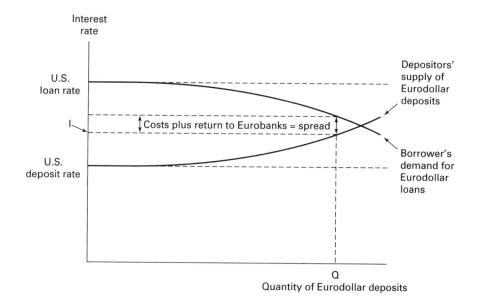

FIGURE 1B-2. Supply and Demand for Eurodollar Deposits.

ket's equilibrium size is Q, and the market can expand only if the Eurobanks' demand curve or depositors' supply curve, or both, shift rightward. What might cause such shifts?

When total dollar credit has expanded (perhaps as a result of the U.S. monetary authorities expanding the money supply, or a greater velocity of money), the supply of deposits in the U.S. and Eurodollar markets tends to expand and Q shifts to the right. If loan demand is unchanged, interest rates in U.S. and Eurodollar markets tend to decline. If this were the only factor operating, the Eurodollar market would grow at approximately the same rate as the U.S. credit market.

We know that the Eurodollar market has grown more rapidly than the corresponding U.S. credit market as a result of the increased relative attractiveness of the Eurodollar market to (Euro-) banks, depositors, and borrowers. In our demand and supply framework, their increased attractiveness is reflected in (1) a (modest) decrease in required spreads by Eurobanks due to the entry of new competitors, (2) a gradual shift of the Eurodeposit demand curve to the right, and/or (3) an equivalent shift of the Eurobanks' supply of Eurodollar loans. The slope (elasticities) of the demand and supply curves reflects the risk perceptions held by depositors and borrowers in terms of interest differentials: at any given time, Eurodeposits and credit lines are considered risky by transactors for a variety of reasons, which were enumerated in the main chapter. A change in risk perceptions, then, will manifest itself in a shift in demand or supply curves, respectively.

Changes in risk perceptions may also affect the slope of the demand and supply schedules. At one extreme, there will always be transactors commanding quantities of funds who will not venture offshore, for example, public employee pension funds under state regulation. At the other extreme, there may be borrowers and depositors who are very concerned about a U.S. sovereign risk, such as, Soviet bloc countries. The former will always keep their funds in the domestic market regardless of the differential between onshore and offshore rates; the latter will keep their dollar-denominated credit facilities and deposits offshore as long as some (non-U.S.) bank will offer reasonably priced, efficient dollar facilities. Between those extremes are segments of the market whose willingness to do more or less business offshore relative to onshore for a given interest differential depends on constantly shifting considerations, such as taxes, competitors' behavior, and regulatory changes.[2]

The demand and supply framework, then, permits us to arrive at the following generalizations about the growth (or decline) of the Eurodollar market: *ceteris paribus*, the Eurodollar market will grow (shrink) whenever:

---

[2] For example, different interpretations of the "prudent man" rule for fiduciary funds may cause a change in the elasticity of the demand for offshore deposits.

1. The difference between domestic deposit and lending rates increases (decreases).
2. Depositors and/or borrowers become more (less) sensitive to small interest rate differences between the internal and the external market.
3. The spread required by Eurobanks for providing external intermediation services decreases (increases).

Conceptually, this structural framework is quite complete and, in principle, should be useful for prediction. For practical purposes, demand and supply schedules are difficult to estimate, and most of the determinants of the respective elasticities and those that cause shifts in the schedules are difficult to measure.

THE FAMOUS EURODOLLAR MULTIPLIER

From the very beginning, the growth of the Eurodollar market has been accompanied by a debate between those who saw the phenomenon as one of financial intermediation drifting offshore and those who viewed the Eurodollar market as analogous to a commercial banking system. Quite naturally, this latter view has led to a search for the nature and size of the Eurodollar multiplier.

In a conventional banking system, an increase or decrease in the banking system's reserve base (reserves held with the central bank) will lead to a multiplied expansion or contraction of bank credit. In the case of the United States, as in most other countries, the total "base" of the banking system consists not only of reserves held at the Fed, but also of currency. A given change in this base leads to a much larger change in the volume of deposits that are built on the base. This may be illustrated using the traditional multiplier formula for the domestic money supply:

$$\text{Multiplier} = \frac{\text{Money supply}}{\text{Monetary base}}$$

$$= \frac{\text{Commercial bank deposits plus currency}}{\text{Bank reserves plus currency}}$$

$$= \frac{1}{\text{Proportion of money supply held as reserves plus currency}}$$

The domestic multiplier can thus be found if one knows (1) the total money supply and (2) the base of the money supply, bank reserves (essentially central bank liabilities to commercial banks), plus currency. It has been argued that if an equivalent base can be found for Eurodollar expansion, which bears some fixed relationship to the reserve base, one can predict Eurodollar credit expansion and thus the growth of the market.

Several concepts of a multiplier have been discussed in the literature. The first is the conventional money multiplier concept that appears in textbooks on money and banking.[3] This is the most common notion and so warrants examination. A banking system that receives additional reserves can produce credit by some multiple of the new reserves (deposits with the central bank); this multiple equals the reciprocal of the reserve ratio (plus, strictly speaking, the proportion of loans converted into currency). Hence the term "multiplier" is appropriate to a nation's banking system. Whether it is to a subsystem of nonbank financial intermediaries such as Eurobanks is quite a different matter.

A second concept of the Eurodollar multiplier is derived from the first. It takes the total assets of Eurobanks divided by their demand deposits claims on U.S. banks as the multiplier.[4] Since such deposits are essentially the cash balances or reserve base of the Eurodollar system, the ratio of total credit to reserves might be regarded as the Eurodollar credit multiplier. In fact, however, Eurobanks' demand deposits in the United States are held because of the liabilities of Eurobanks. The causation runs from the total volume of Eurodollar credit to the relative size of the reserve base, not vice versa, as the term "credit multiplier" implies. Thus, in the case of nonbank intermediaries whose liabilities are held for their liquidity and yield characteristics, the reciprocal of the reserve ratio has little meaning.

The third concept of a multiplier is what one might call the **marginal multiplier**. This marginal multiplier for the Eurodollar market (k_{ED}) shows the relationship between an increase in the demand deposits held in the United States by Eurobanks (DD_{US}) and the resulting change in total Eurodollar deposits (ED):

$$ED = k_{ED}DD_{US}$$

Standard money and banking textbooks[5] show that k is a function of (1) the reserve ratio of banks and (2) the proportion of the public's total liquid

---

[3] John J. Makin, "Identifying a Reserve Base for the Eurodollar System," *Journal of Finance*, June 1973, pp. 609–617.

[4] See, for example, George C. Kaufman, *The U.S. Financial System: Money, Markets, and Institutions*, 5th ed. (Englewood Cliffs, NJ: Prentice Hall, 1992), Chapters 25 and 29. Studies of the Eurodollar market employing this concept include Boyden E. Lee, "The Eurodollar Multiplier," *Journal of Finance*, September 1973, pp. 867–874, and Michele Fratianni and Paulo Savona, "Eurodollar Creation: Comments on Professor Machlup's Propositions and Developments," *Banca Nazionale del Lavoro—Quarterly Review*, June 1971, pp. 13–22.

[5] See Kaufman, *The U.S. Financial System*.

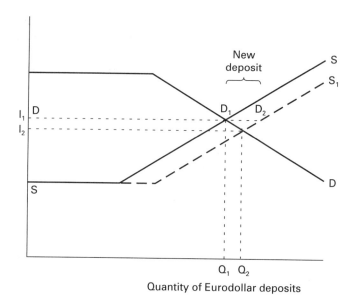

$$\text{Marginal multiplier} = \frac{\text{Final expansion}}{\text{New deposit}}$$

$$= \frac{Q_2 - Q_1}{D_2 - D_1} \text{, which is between 0 and 1.}$$

FIGURE 1B-3. The Eurodollar Multiplier in a Supply-Demand Framework.

assets held as the particular kind of deposits (in this case Eurodollar deposits). The first, we have noted, bears little relation to changes in Eurodollar deposits; the second will vary continuously with changing economic conditions. Since Eurodollars are held as alternatives to such a wide range of short-term securities, the relative holdings of which are subject to so many influences, it is unlikely that it will be possible to find a meaningful or stable value for the multiplier k_{ED}.

We may conclude this section by combining the demand and supply framework introduced earlier with the concept of the marginal multiplier, to capture the elusive Eurodollar multiplier.[6] Instead of assuming that some fixed "leakage" ratio determines the size of the multiplier, we shall employ supply and demand curves to show that the value of the marginal multiplier depends on the interest elasticities of the supply of, and demand for, Eurodollars.

Figure 1B-3 is a stylized version of Figure 1B-2. It depicts the effect of an

---

[6] This view is best exemplified in John Hewson and Eisuke Sakakibara, "The Eurodollar Deposit Multiplier: A Portfolio Approach," *IMF Staff Papers*, July 1974, pp. 307–328.

initial new deposit $(D_2 - D_1)$ on total deposit expansion in the Eurodollar market $(Q_2 - Q_1)$.

The Eurodollar supply and demand curves intersect initially at D_1: total deposits are Q_1 and the interest rate is I_1. Assume now that a new deposit is made in the Eurodollar market, perhaps by the government of an oil-exporting country that prefers not to leave all its dollar-denominated funds in the United States. What is the impact on total Eurodollar deposits and credit?

The marginal multiplier is the ratio of the final change in the size of the market to the amount of an exogenous inflow of funds. The initial exogenous deposit is $D_2 - D_1$, which is reflected in a rightward shift of the supply curve from SS to SS_1. This deposit, however, has the effect of reducing interest rates somewhat (e.g., from I_1 to I_2). As a result, some depositors shift their funds back to the United States, and the final deposit expansion is only $Q_2 - Q_1$.

The "multiplier," $(Q_2 - Q_1)(D_2 - D_1)$, is clearly between zero and 1. The size of the multiplier at any particular time depends on the slopes of these curves.[7] In general, as long as neither the deposit demand curve nor the deposit supply curve are perfectly elastic, the multiplier will be less than 1.

ANOTHER MYTH: THE EURODOLLAR MARKET AND THE U.S. BALANCE-OF-PAYMENTS DEFICITS

The early years of growth in the Eurodollar market coincided with mounting U.S. balance-of-payments deficits.[8] The deficit has continued intermittently since the late 1950s, despite the efforts of the U.S. government to control the outflow of capital at times. The annual deficits led to a considerable buildup of dollar balances held in the United States by foreign central banks. It also permitted foreign individuals, corporations, and banks to increase more easily balances of liquid dollar assets which they desired. Since the Eurodollar market has been viewed as "dollar deposits held abroad," it is not surprising that many assumed a direct causal relationship

---

[7] The interested reader may wish to consider the cases where one or another curve is intersected in its perfectly elastic region. First, if the upward-sloping supply curve intersects a perfectly elastic (flat) demand curve, $D_2 - D_1 = Q_2 - Q_1$ and the multiplier becomes 1. On the other hand, if a downward-sloping demand curve intersects a perfectly elastic demand curve, $Q_2 - Q_1 = 0$ and the multiplier is zero. If the Eurodollar deposit rates drop at all, deposits flow back to the U.S. market.

[8] We use the term "balance-of-payments deficit" rather loosely, since none of the usual measures are acceptable, particularly in a world of floating exchange rates. In most cases we refer to the official settlements deficit, the most common definition, which is the net value of trade, transfers, and capital flows between a country and private nonresidents during a particular period.

between the continued U.S. balance-of-payments deficit and the growth of dollar deposits outside the United States.

The notion is reinforced by the manner in which the creation of Eurodollars is usually explained. Foreign banks, it is said, accept dollar deposits from individuals and companies abroad that have received payment in dollars for exports to the United States. These deposits are Eurodollars. This statement, although correct as far as it goes, describes a rather incomplete sequence of events. The fact that foreigners have earned dollars by exporting to the United States does not mean that they must invest those dollars in the Eurodollar market; on the contrary, the normal practice would be to sell the dollars in the foreign exchange market. In fact, deposits made in the Eurodollar market are quite independent of foreigners' export earnings, which (1) are not necessarily invested in dollar assets and (2) even if they are held in dollar assets, are not necessarily held in the Eurodollar market. Indeed, most of the funds deposited in Eurobanks are probably obtained in the foreign exchange market by individuals and institutions who may or may not be involved in trade with the United States, but who have investible funds in one currency or another. Indeed, U.S. residents must make the very same choice as foreigners: to invest dollar balances in a domestic bank "onshore," or in a Eurobank offshore.

From a more formal perspective, the argument linking the growth of the Eurodollar market and the U.S. balance-of-payments deficit ignores the fact that Eurodollars are liabilities of banks outside the United States. The owners of these (time) deposits may be U.S. residents or foreign residents. The accumulated U.S. balance-of-payments deficits, on the other hand, show up as liabilities of financial institutions in the United States to foreign residents, both official and private.

Indeed, we can easily show how a rather large Eurodollar market can get started, irrespective of the state of the U.S. balance of payments. Assume that the domestic French money market is very inefficient, with wide spreads between borrowing and lending rates. It is entirely possible that those in France with excess funds will convert them in the foreign exchange market into dollars and invest these dollar funds with, say, London Eurobanks (and probably cover them through forward sales of dollars to hedge the exchange risk) while French borrowers take up dollar-denominated loans and convert the proceeds into French francs (again covering the exchange risk through a forward purchase of dollars). The only possible effect on the U.S. balance-of-payments occurs when and if foreign banks increase their (demand) balances in New York as a result of the increased volume of dollar payments necessitated by these deposit and loan activities. The effect of these balances will be discussed shortly; it is, however, extremely small, relative to the growth of the Eurodollar market created in this fashion.

A rather persuasive piece of evidence is the fact that despite the persistent balance-of-payments surpluses of countries like Germany and Switzerland, the German mark– and Swiss franc–denominated portions of the Eurocurrency market have grown apace with the dollar-denominated portion. Finally, in a world of generally floating exchange rates, the demand for and supply of dollars by foreigners have only the most tenuous connection with balance-of-payments surpluses or deficits.

One can sum up this discussion by saying that a continuing U.S. balance-of-payments deficit neither provides an assurance of, nor constitutes a necessary condition for, the growth in the availability of Eurodollars. Although a U.S. deficit certainly does increase the volume of dollars held by nonresidents, there is no reason to suppose that those particular foreigners would want to place their surplus funds in the Eurodollar market. The relevant questions are (1) whether economic entities have funds that they wish to invest temporarily, (2) whether they wish to invest them in U.S. dollar-denominated assets, and (3) whether they wish to invest them in the domestic or in the external dollar market. The status of the U.S. balance of payments has little bearing on the answers to any of these questions.

There are some minor but important qualifications to this conclusion. Although the expansion of the Eurodollar market is in no way dependent on the U.S. balance-of-payments deficit, the deficit may have contributed indirectly to the market's growth in several ways:

1. The U.S. capital control program, whose possible effect on the growth of the market was noted previously, was the result of the U.S. balance-of-payments deficits.

2. The U.S. deficits also allowed a number of European countries to run surpluses, which means that European governments were able to reduce their restrictions on international financial transactions.

3. The money supply abroad was probably greater than if those countries had been in deficit, unless foreign governments completely sterilized their net capital inflows. And as the world monetary supply increased, so did financial markets, both the domestic and external ones.

4. Many governments that held (larger) dollar reserves stemming from surpluses have placed funds in the Eurodollar market. Since the 1973 rise in oil prices, which has contributed to the U.S. deficits, the oil-producing countries have placed substantial sums in the Eurodollar market. As in the case of private depositors, however, both European and OPEC governments chose to invest their dollars in the international money market because of its liquidity and attractive yields, instead of in the domestic U.S. market.

While the U.S. balance of payments has little or no effect on the growth of the Eurodollar market, it may be that the reverse is true: that the existence and growth of the Eurodollar market has a positive or negative effect on the U.S. balance of payments or on the international strength of the dollar. One writer has argued, for example, that the Eurodollar system is itself responsible for some flows of capital pulsing from one nation to another. These capital flows eventually affect the national supply and demand for goods and services including, naturally, the national supply and demand for exports and imports. Thus the Eurobanking system helps in several ways to propel some nations toward balance-of-payments surpluses and others toward balance-of-payments deficits.[9]

Let us examine this proposition. First, is it likely that the existence of the Eurodollar market has increased the international demand for dollars? If it has, such increased demand would be reflected either in a stronger U.S. balance of payments (i.e., a smaller deficit) or in a rise in the dollar in the foreign exchange markets. This could result if the advantages of the market (higher interest rates, freedom from regulation) relative to the U.S. money market attracted funds from foreign currencies that would not have been invested in dollars in the absence of the market. Perhaps this is the case. However, the very features of the market that attract depositors also attract borrowers—lower borrowing rates, as well as higher deposit rates. Narrower spreads between loan and deposit rates imply corresponding U.S. rates, and along with fewer regulatory constraints, this means that the demand for dollar loans may increase just as much as the demand for dollar deposits. Hence any net purchases of dollars by new depositors are probably offset by sales of dollars for foreign currencies by new borrowers.

What of the effect of the Eurodollar market on U.S. exports and imports? By providing more efficient intermediation in both an operational and an allocational sense, the existence of the market may mean that more dollar credit is available to foreigners, who may use it to purchase U.S. exports. On the other hand, they may just as easily use the funds elsewhere—by selling the dollars in the foreign exchange market. More efficient credit intermediation may also increase the ability of U.S. residents to import. The effect of the Eurodollar market on the U.S. balance of trade, then, is indeterminate.

Similar reasoning applies to the argument that the existence of an efficient market for dollar deposits and loans easily accessible to foreigners may strengthen the attraction of the dollar as a currency to maintain working balances. In the 1960s this argument may have carried some weight, but since that time the analogous growth of external markets in virtually all major currencies has probably neutralized any competitive advantage of the dollar in this respect. Because the U.S. money market has traditionally been much

---

[9] Jane S. Little, *Euro-dollars: The Money Market Gypsies* (New York: Harper & Row, 1975), p. 172.

more efficient than the markets of, say, Germany, Switzerland, or Japan, the growth of the Eurocurrency market improved nondollar money markets relatively more than the U.S. markets. In any case, the effect is marginal when compared to other factors that govern the U.S. balance of payments, such as changes in exports and imports and capital flows caused by changes in relative (effective) interest rates.

SUMMARY

This appendix examined the nature and causes of the growth of the international money market. Much of the discussion was devoted to refuting the commonly held beliefs that the Eurodollar market results from U.S. balance-of-payments deficits or from the U.S. capital controls, from interbank pyramiding, or from some internal multiple credit creation process. We showed that in most respects Eurodollars are not directly comparable to the domestic money supply but instead are time deposits similar to those offered by nonbank financial intermediaries such as savings and loan associations in the United States.

The final sections explored concepts of credit creation and the size and existence of a Eurodollar multiplier; we argued that the supply and demand for Eurodollars is simply a function of the competitiveness of the external money market relative to the internal market, as reflected in interest rates.

SELECTED REFERENCES

Aliber, Robert Z., "Exchange Risk, Political Risk, and Investor Demand for External Currency Deposits," *Journal of Money, Credit and Banking*, May 1975, pp. 162–179.

Aliber, Robert Z., "Monetary Aspects of Offshore Markets," *Columbia Journal of World Business*, Fall 1979, pp. 10–11.

Aliber, Robert Z., "The Integration of the Offshore and Domestic Banking System," *Journal of Monetary Economics*, Vol. 6, 1980, pp. 518–520.

Dufey, Gunter, and Ian H. Giddy, "The Unique Risks of Eurodollars," *Journal of Commercial Bank Lending*, June 1978, pp. 50–61.

Einzig, Paul, *The Eurodollar System*, 5th ed. New York: St. Martin's Press, 1970.

Fratianni, Michele, and Paulo Savona, "Eurodollar Creation: Comments on Professor Machlup's Propositions and Developments," *Banca Nazionale del Lavoro—Quarterly Review*, June 1971, pp. 13–22.

Ghesquiere, H. "The Causes of Growth of the Eurodollar Market," *IMF*, DM/80/19, Washington D.C. March 7, 1980.

Giddy, Ian H., "Why Eurodollars Grow," *Columbia Journal of World Business*, Fall 1979, pp. 54–60.

Heller, H. Robert, "Why the Market Is Demand Determined," *Euromoney*, February 1979, pp. 41–47.

Herring, Richard J., and Richard C. Marston, *National Monetary Policies and International Financial Markets*. Amsterdam: North Holland, 1977.

Hewson, John, and Eisuke Sakakibara, "The Eurodollar Deposit Multiplier: A Portfolio Approach," *IMF Staff Papers*, July 1974, pp. 307–328.

Kaufman, George C., *The U.S. Financial System: Money, Markets, and Institutions*, 5th ed. Englewood Cliffs, NJ: Prentice Hall, 1992.

Kenen, Peter B., "The Role of the Dollar as an International Currency," Occasional Paper No. 13. New York: Group of Thirty, 1983.

Lee, Boyden E., "The Eurodollar Multiplier," *Journal of Finance*, September 1973, pp. 867–874.

Little, Jane S., *Euro-dollars: The Money Market Gypsies*. New York: Harper & Row, 1975.

Mahajan, Vuay, and Eitan Muller, "Innovation Diffusion and New Product Growth Models in Marketing," *Journal of Marketing*, Fall 1979, pp. 55–68.

Makin, John H., "Demand and Supply Functions for Stocks of Eurodollar Deposits: An Empirical Study," *The Review of Economics and Statistics*, November 1972, pp. 381–391.

Makin, John H., "Identifying a Reserve Base for the Eurodollar System," *Journal of Finance*, June 1973, pp. 609–617.

Mayer, Helmut, "Some Theoretical Problems Relating to the Eurodollar Market," International Finance Section, Essays in International Finance, No. 79, Princeton University, Princeton, NJ, 1970.

Meulendyke, Ann-Marie, "Causes and Consequences of the Eurodollar Expansion," Federal Reserve Bank of New York, Research Paper No. 7503, March 1975.

Mills, Rodney H., Jr., "Structural Change in the Eurodollar Market: Evidence from a Two Equation Model," Board of Governors of the Federal Reserve System (Washington, D.C.), Discussion Paper No. 33, November 1, 1973.

Morgan Guaranty Trust Company, "Life at a Bank's Money Desk," *Morgan Guaranty Survey*, November 1981, pp. 11–15.

Swoboda, Alexander K., *Credit Creation in the Euromarket: Alternative Theories and Implications for Control*. Group of Thirty, New York, NY 1980.

Throop, Adrian W., "Eurobanking and World Inflation," *Voice* (Federal Reserve Bank of Dallas), August 1979, pp. 8–23.

Wallich, Henry C., "Why the Euromarket Needs Restraint," *Columbia Journal of World Business*, Fall 1979, p. 17.

Willms, Manfred, "Money Creation in the Euro-Currency Market," *Weltwirtschaftliches Archiv*, Vol. 112, 1976, pp. 201–230.

Chapter Two

DOMESTIC MONEY MARKETS

Contents: *Introduction: The Eurocurrency Market and Domestic Money Markets*
A Framework for Understanding Domestic Money Markets, Their Similarities and
Differences   The United States   Canada   The United Kingdom   Germany
Japan   Developing Countries   Conclusions   Selected References

INTRODUCTION: THE EUROCURRENCY
MARKET AND DOMESTIC MONEY MARKETS

The Eurocurrency market is, we have argued, a segment of the broader money market in each currency. In this chapter we return to the roots of the major Eurocurrency markets and see how the external markets, spawned by regulatory and efficiency problems in their home countries, have in turn influenced the domestic money markets, many of which have become increasingly diverse and competitive.

The relationship between each Eurocurrency market and its domestic counterpart can be described as a process of controlled evolution. During the 1960s and 1970s, the major currencies gained a sufficient degree of non-resident convertibility that a Eurocurrency segment was able to arise. The Eurocurrency segment of the money market thrived and grew because domestic money markets were hobbled by outdated regulations such as interest rate controls and by oligopolistic pricing practices such as lending tied to compensating balances and slow-to-adjust prime rates. The easing of capital controls that followed the move to floating exchange rates in the 1970s allowed depositors and borrowers to shift their business to the external market, which offered more attractive rates and conditions.

49

By the late 1970s and early 1980s the authorities of the United States, Germany, the United Kingdom, and other countries were forced to acknowledge the success of Eurocurrency-based wholesale banking. They began to ease the more burdensome and unnecessary of regulations and to lower reserve requirements and other taxlike burdens. Japan, France, and other countries encouraged the growth of the domestic money market and of innovative banking practices to attract some of the lost banking business back home. The 1980s and 1990s, therefore, have seen a resurgence of domestic money markets. Today, Euromarket instruments represent simply part of a spectrum of financial claims available in the money market of a particular currency, claims that are distinguished by risk, cost, and liquidity just like domestic money market instruments. Nevertheless, domestic money markets are and will remain important tools to implement two forms of government policy—monetary policy and the allocation of credit—and so important differences will persist not only between different domestic markets, but also between domestic markets and their external segments.

The objective of this chapter is to explain the structure of the money market of a major industrial country (and some developing ones), a structure that will enable the reader to ask the right questions when investigating one of the major money markets. We do this by providing first the economic and regulatory framework for money markets in general, and then by expanding on this framework through identifying the highlights and distinguishing features of the money markets of several major countries: the United States, Canada, the United Kingdom, Germany, Japan, and some emerging markets. It is evident that our coverage is not comprehensive: we have omitted the money markets of such important industrial countries as France, Belgium, and the Netherlands, for example. Moreover, some of the facts related here will no doubt become out of date. Our goal, therefore, is to offer a useful framework for analysis for the reader seeking some perspective before conducting factual research of his or her own.

A FRAMEWORK FOR UNDERSTANDING DOMESTIC MONEY MARKETS, THEIR SIMILARITIES AND DIFFERENCES

The **money market** of a country consists of the market for instruments and means of lending (or investing) and borrowing funds for relatively short periods, typically regarded as from one day to one year. Such means and instruments include short-term bank loans, Treasury bills, bank certificates of deposit, commercial paper, banker's acceptances and repurchase agreements, and other short-term asset-backed claims.

As a key element of the financial system of a country, the money market plays a crucial *private economic role*: that of reconciling the cash imbalances of economic entities (individuals, firms, and government agencies) that come about because of uncertainty in the timing of cash receipts and disbursements. (This contrasts with the capital market, where funds are made available by savers to borrowers for longer-term investment purposes.) A well-functioning money market can perform these functions very efficiently if borrowing-lending spreads (or bid-offer spreads for traded instruments) are small (**operational efficiency**), and if funds are lent to those who can make most productive use of them (**allocational efficiency**). Both borrowers and lenders prefer to meet their short-term needs without bearing the liquidity risk or interest rate risk that characterize longer-term instruments, and money market instruments allow this. Thus the money market sets a market interest rate that balances cash management needs and sets different rates for different uses that balances their risks and potential for productive use.

The money market sets prices for financial claims that simultaneously balances the relative value of money *over time* and *across countries*. Through the term structure of interest rates, short-term interest rates are linked to long-term rates by the market's expectations about future long-term rates. Through foreign exchange swap contracts—simultaneous spot purchase and forward sale of a foreign currency—the interest rate in one currency is linked to the equivalent rate in another currency.[1] These and related phenomena are addressed in Chapter Three, *Eurocurrency Interest Rates*.

At the same time, domestic money markets everywhere play a key role in the implementation of *public economic policies*. These policies are of three kinds:

1. The money market, along with the bond market, is used to *finance the government deficit*.
2. The transmission of **monetary policy** including **exchange rate policy** is typically conducted through the money market, either through banks or through freely traded money market instruments.
3. The government uses the institutions of the money market to influence **credit allocation** toward favored uses in the economy.

These three important public policy functions of the money market mean that the domestic money market is likely to be subject to substantial government influence. Deficit financing may mean that there is an imbal-

---

[1] Indeed in some countries the most important domestic money market instrument is a foreign currency deposit converted into a domestic currency deposit by means of a foreign exchange swap. Thus in some countries such as Switzerland, foreign exchange swaps are regarded as money market instruments in and of themselves.

ance between supply and demand in certain segments of the maturity spectrum, which can result in a "kink" in the Treasury yield curve in some countries. The conduct of monetary policy and retention of special influence usually implies protection of the privileged positions of certain financial institutions, such as the primary dealers in the United States and the discount houses in London. And the legal or moral suasion that governments exert over their banks and other financial institutions to allocate credit to favored sectors can produce distortions in the domestic sector that are not present in the external sector of a money market.

To summarize so far, the observer of a money market can begin by asking two questions: (1) How *efficiently* does the money market perform its private economic role of balancing the cash needs of investors and borrowers, and (2) what does the *government* demand of the money market to serve its public policy objectives?

In answering these questions, the reader will discover that there are two fundamentally different structures for money markets around the world. The first, exemplified by the United States, is *securities market dominated*: most short-term funds are channeled through markets for traded instruments such as Treasury bills and commercial paper. The second is *bank dominated*: the bulk of short-term investments are placed in bank deposits or equivalent instruments such as banker's acceptances, and most short-term funding is in the form of bank loans. The German system is an example of this structure.

Another way of understanding a money market is by identifying the **risk and liquidity structure** of money market instruments. Ranked roughly from least to most risky and illiquid, these are (1) government securities, (2) bank deposit instruments, and (3) corporate liabilities. A fourth category, asset-backed securities, can fall anywhere in the spectrum, depending on the quality of the assets and other features. Table 2–1 lists typical money market instruments in each of these categories.

A final feature of modern money markets is the **derivative instruments** sector. All important money markets nowadays have futures and options markets in the key money market instruments such as Treasury bills. Most

TABLE 2-1 Money Market Instruments.

Type	Examples
Government securities	Treasury bills, government agency notes, municipal notes
Bank liabilities	Time deposits, certificates of deposit and deposit notes, banker's acceptances, repurchase agreements
Corporate liabilities	Commercial paper, money market preferred stock
Asset-backed securities	Commercial paper backed by accounts receivable

have corresponding markets in over-the-counter, that is, private, contracts to fix or hedge money market interest rates, such as forward rate agreements (FRAs) and interest rate caps. These derivative markets differ widely in their liquidity, and one can obtain interesting insights into the money market as a whole by noting the number of traded contracts and volume of contracts outstanding or "open interest" in the futures and options contracts in local money market instruments. As we shall see, the authorities of some countries regard these instruments with suspicion, viewing them as engines of speculation rather than as useful hedging tools that contribute to the depth and diversity of the financial sector.

THE UNITED STATES

While the U.S. money market falls decisively into the category of free market–dominated systems as opposed to bank-based ones, the U.S. Federal Reserve ("Fed") and the large banks in cities like Chicago, San Francisco, and especially New York, known as "money center banks," are among the market's most important players. The Fed uses the U.S. money market as its instrument for the implementation of monetary policy, and the banks use the market to make the most efficient use of reserves held at the Fed in excess of those required or to meet shortfalls. The distinguishing feature of the U.S. money market is the degree to which the market is used by nonfinancial organizations, such as industrial corporations and municipal, state, and federal government units, both as a source of funds and as a repository for cash. Another dimension has been the pioneering of (indirect) individual investor use of the market, via **money market mutual funds** that invest in wholesale instruments, such as those described shortly, and sell shares to the public in $1 denominations. Indeed, the growth of money market mutual funds, which provide individual investors and small business firms with returns that are typically just less than 50 BP below "wholesale" rates for money market instruments, has had considerable impact not only on the competition for retail deposits, but it has generated substantial demand for money market instruments, especially commercial paper. Some prominent instruments and their principal users are listed in Table 2–2.

The Federal Reserve Bank of New York, acting on behalf of the Federal Reserve Board in Washington, implements monetary policy by daily **open market operations** in the U.S. money market. When the Fed wants to inject money into the system, it will buy Treasury bills from a group of authorized banks and securities firms, "primary dealers," or lend money under repurchase agreements, buying securities today while agreeing to resell them at a certain price at a later date. When the Fed wants to tighten money, reducing the money supply and raising interest rates at the margin, it will sell Treasury bills or do "reverse repos," that is, sell money market paper while agreeing to buy it back at a fixed price. Alternatively, banks may borrow

TABLE 2-2   Prominent Money Market Instruments and Principal Functions.

Instrument	Principal Functions
Federal funds	Interbank lending
Discount window advances	Bank borrowing from the Federal Reserve system, usually only when private sources not easily available
Negotiable certificates of deposit	Bank deposits taken from the public; negotiable CDs are large denomination wholesale money market instruments
Repurchase agreements	Securities dealers, banks, thrift institutions, nonfinancial corporations, governments use these to obtain short-term (usually overnight) loans backed by securities
Treasury bills	Short-term debt of the U.S. government
Municipal notes	Short-term state and local government obligations
Commercial paper	Unsecured negotiable notes issued by nonfinancial and financial businesses
Banker's acceptances	Tradable notes issued by banks when they "accept" or guarantee trade-related obligations of nonfinancial corporations
Federal agency discount notes and coupon securities	Short-term claims issued by Farm Credit System, Federal Home Loan Banks, Federal National Mortgage Association
Futures contracts	On organized exchanges, dealers, banks, and individuals trade on contracts for future delivery (or cash equivalent) of instruments including some of those described above
Futures options	Exchange-traded rights to buy or sell futures contracts
Forward rate agreements	Over-the-counter contracts to hedge interest rates on instruments such as some described above

money from the Fed on a collateralized basis through the central bank's lending facility, the **discount window.** By controlling the supply of money or reserves that banks hold, the Fed has a direct influence on the Federal funds rate that institutions pay in the market to borrow and lend reserves and an indirect influence on all other money market rates.

The fundamental attitude of the U.S. authorities is one of a suspicious *laissez-faire*: the guiding principle is to leave the markets alone except when instability, fraud, or loose banking practices are likely to upset the politicians or cause the public to lose confidence. If a suspicious practice occurs, the authorities intervene forcefully. But since the United States is a country that has great respect for the rule of law rather than the institutional influence of the regulators, abuses do occur right under the noses of the authorities from time to time. The use of commercial paper by securities firms' holding companies, the Treasury auction process, and the repo market have all had their crises and have spawned legislative response in Washington. By and large, however, the bank supervisors are concerned with bank soundness, the Securities and Exchange Commission focuses on public disclosure and transparency, the Treasury is worried with financing the government deficit, and the Federal Reserve is concerned with stable markets in which to conduct monetary policy. As long as these concerns are satisfied, the U.S. government has little concern with the operation of the money market. Most of all the market is not called upon to play a significant role in credit allocation, as is the case in some countries.[2]

The **Treasury bill** market is the world's biggest of its kind, and is widely used as the benchmark for short-term dollar-denominated instruments as it is effectively free of default risk.[3] The T-bill is also regarded as the most liquid of securities. A measure of the liquidity of a financial asset is the spread between the bid price and the asked price quoted by market makers. In recent years the bid-asked spread on actively traded bills has been only two to four basis points, which is lower than for any other money market instrument.[4] As a result, they normally bear the lowest interest rate at a given maturity. Treasury bills are issued and traded at a discount from par. They are sold at regularly scheduled auctions held by the Federal Reserve Bank of New York. On the day of the auction, a competitive bidder states the quantity of bills desired and the price he is willing to pay for each quantity.[5] After filling noncompetitive orders, the Treasury allocates the remainder to those competitive bidders submitting the highest offers, ranging downward from the highest bid until the total amount offered is allocated. The "stop-out price" is the lowest price, or highest yield, at which bills are awarded.

Bank **time deposits** (TDs) and **certificates of deposit** (CDs) have to a large extent atrophied in the United States, as their Eurodollar counterparts

[2] Even the United States is not free from such attempts to allocate credit. One example is the Community Reinvestment Act, an instance of legislative credit allocation focusing on the banking industry.

[3] Even if the U.S. government's credit standing were to deteriorate, they could always print new money to pay off Treasury bills, and would do so rather than default. So while T-bills are free of credit risk, there is no guarantee that their value in terms of purchasing power will hold.

[4] The more volatile are interest rates, the greater is the risk taken by a dealer "making a market," that is, quoting a bid and an asked price. Hence bid-asked spreads tend to rise during periods of increased interest rate volatility.

[5] Investors can also make "noncompetitive bids," indicating the quantity of bills desired and agreeing to pay the weighted-average price of accepted competitive bids.

have substituted for the domestic market. The reason is that conventional bank TDs and CDs are subject to reserve requirements, an issue that is explored at length in Chapter One. Instead, the wholesale interbank market in the United States is the market for **Federal funds**, which means short-term interbank loans of money that is immediately available as deposits in the Federal Reserve System. Fed funds are not subject to reserve requirements.

Banker's acceptances (BAs) are in effect a means of bank financing, although they take the form of tradable paper much like CDs. Indeed in the United States, BAs substitute to an extent for negotiable CDs as a bank-backed tradable instrument. A banker's acceptance is created when a bank supports a corporate trade obligation (a "trade bill") by accepting responsibility for repaying the note, often after having issued a letter of credit to assure both parties' performance. While BAs reflect the accepting bank's credit standing, when that particular institution or the whole banking sector is under pressure, BAs can yield less than CDs, reflecting the fact that they are "two name" paper.

The principal form of funding for securities dealers is the **repurchase agreement**, or repo. A standard repurchase agreement involves the acquisition of immediately available funds through the sale of securities with a simultaneous commitment to repurchase the same securities on a certain date in the future. The repo is commonly regarded as a short-term (often overnight) loan that is collateralized with Treasury bills or bonds or other government obligations. Under an overnight repurchase agreement, a dealer borrows funds from a bank by selling it a security, which the dealer repurchases the next day at a price agreed upon in advance. A reverse repo is the mirror image of a repo. Securities dealers handle a huge volume of transactions of this kind with the Federal Reserve. In addition to banks and dealers, corporations, institutional investors, and government agencies are also major users of the repo market, both as borrowers and as lenders.

In some repurchase agreements, the agreed-upon repurchase price is set above the initial sale price by an amount that reflects the interest rate. More typically, however, the repurchase price is set equal to the initial sale price plus a negotiated rate of interest to be paid on the settlement date by the borrower. Repo interest rates are straight "add-on" rates calculated on an "actual/360" days basis. The amount of securities required as collateral for a given amount of cash loaned is the cash amount plus a "haircut" or margin, ranging from 1 to 5 percent, to reduce the lender's exposure to market risk, principally interest rate risk, affecting the value of the collateral. The collateral is valued at current market price plus accrued interest. Since most repos involve Treasury and federal agency securities that are maintained in book-entry form, the transfer of ownership of the collateral can be done efficiently at the same time as the transfer of funds. Since the costs can mount for many transactors, some lenders prefer to protect their ownership claims by using safekeeping arrangements. The most popular of these is the "triparty repo" in which a custodian becomes a direct participant in the transaction with the borrower and the lender. The clearer-custodian ensures that exchanges of collateral and funds occur simultaneously and that appropriate operational controls are in place to safeguard the investor's ownership interest in the underlying collateral during the term of the agreement. Such an arrangement is now provided by the international securities clearing house, Euroclear.

In the United States, **commercial paper** (CP) has become the principal means of short-term financing for nonfinancial and financial corporations, and as such now has an amount outstanding exceeding every other money market instrument except Treasury bills. Commercial paper is simply an unsecured short-term corporate promissory note. The CP market is unique in that it substitutes for bank lending and yet is highly dependent on commercial banks. In order to be marketable and to earn a top rating from the rating agencies, U.S. commercial paper must be supported by a liquidity line from a commercial bank. This "back-up line" as it is called, does not guarantee the *creditworthiness* of the issuer. That guarantee is provided by a standby letter of credit. Instead, the back-up line assures the investor that under normal circumstances, the issuer will have access to short-term credit that could be used to repay the commercial paper if for some reason the commercial paper market proves inaccessible.[6] Although corporations must pay a fee for this line, strong credits can usually raise money less expensively than by borrowing from banks. Even weaker credits have been able to issue commercial paper, either with a letter of credit or by issuing **collateralized commercial paper.** The latter employs Treasury or agency securities, or increasingly accounts receivable, with sufficient overcollateralization, to earn a top credit rating. The technique consists of selling the assets to a special purpose vehicle, such as a trust, which issues commercial paper. This insulates the investor from the fortunes of the sponsoring company or financial institution.

Corporations issue commercial paper under a **commercial paper program**, an arrangement with a group of banks that is set up in advance and that provides the master documentation and paperwork for future issues. Once the program is in place, paper is continuously offered. If and when the firm requires funds, or as is often the case, when an investor wants to place money for a short period, new paper is issued under the program (see box). The paper is issued at a discount and pays par at maturity. Maturities can last one day or up to 270 days, the maximum maturity to escape SEC regis-

---

[6] A standard backup line of credit can be withdrawn by the bank in response to a significant change in the company's financial condition; "committed" back-up lines provide a greater degree of assurance—for a fee.

Commercial Paper Placement

Issuers sell commercial paper to the institutional investor public through **dealers**. Issuance occurs more or less as follows:

> When a company issues commercial paper through a dealer, early in the day the treasurer of the company tells the dealer how much paper the company wants to sell and in what maturities. The dealer contacts prospective customers to determine the rate at which he will be able to sell the paper. On the basis of this information the dealer determines the rate at which he will buy the paper from the issuer. He also relays the issuer any special requests for paper in specific quantities and maturities, but the issuer makes the final decision on these matters. The trade is usually settled the afternoon of the same day. The dealer resells the paper to investors as quickly as possible; only 5 to 10 percent of paper bought is taken into inventory. The dealer finances any paper held in inventory either with overnight repurchase agreements or with secured call loans from banks.

Source: Timothy D. Rowe, "Commercial Paper," in Federal Reserve Bank of Richmond, *Instruments of the Money Market*.

tration requirements; however, most mature in 1 to 3 months. Money market funds are the largest investors, and the market is dominated by institutional investors such as bank trust departments, pension funds, and insurance companies as well as mutual funds.

Many instruments of both the money and the capital market are *tax driven*. Treasury bills are exempt from state and local tax, and **municipal notes** are exempt from federal tax, so both are extensively used by individual investors in tax brackets where the lower yield is offset by the tax benefit. Some money market mutual funds specialize in RANs (revenue anticipation notes), TANs (tax anticipation notes), and other short-term state and local government obligations. Municipal issuers also use tax-exempt commercial paper and variable-rate demand or put obligations. The latter are floating-rate notes with a feature known as a demand option which gives the investor the right to tender the instrument to the issuer or a designated party on a specified number of days' notice at a price equal to the face amount plus accrued interest. Most of these securities are in the portfolios of tax-exempt money market funds.

An innovative form of tax-driven money market paper is **money market preferred stock**, which substitutes for commercial paper for some issuers. This paper, which is short-term debt masquerading as equity, offers corporate investors a significant tax benefit: inter-company dividends are taxed at a favored rate in some countries. Therefore, the after-tax return to corporate investors can be quite attractive. Since dividends are not tax deductible, they are issued only by corporations that cannot use the tax shelter that interest payments provide.

Discussion of the U.S. money market would be incomplete without mention of the role of futures, options, and FRAs. Hedging instruments such as these have become an essential part of the toolkit of all banks and dealers, and of most issuing and investing participants in the money market. The exchange-traded and over-the-counter (OTC) **derivatives markets** in the United States are perhaps the best developed in the world. By far the most actively traded contracts in the world are the Eurodollar futures and Treasury bond futures contracts traded on the International Monetary Market (IMM) of the Chicago Mercantile Exchange, where options on futures contracts are also widely used for hedging. Many banks offer the over-the-counter equivalents of interest rate futures, namely, FRAs. These are explored in detail in Chapter Four.

CANADA

To the unsophisticated observer Canada often looks like a smaller version of the United States. In a superficial way, this holds also for the Canadian money market. However upon closer inspection one detects significant differences. Some differences in the Canadian market relative to the U.S. market result from the smaller size of the market and the higher concentration among the financial institutions, which makes liquidity constraints more acute. Also, there are significant differences with respect to liquidity management by the Bank of Canada. Effective in late 1991 the Bank moved toward a system of zero required reserves. Instead of restricting borrowing from the central bank by moral suasion, price incentives trigger the money market responses by direct clearers (which comprise both banks and deposit taking nonbank financial institutions) in the face of changes in the supply of settlement balances, i.e., high powered money.[7] Last, but not least there are substantial regulatory differences, especially with respect to **banker's acceptance** market, which in Canada has become a major vehicle to avoid regulatory costs of the banking system.

As in other Anglo-Saxon countries, the **Treasury bill** (T-bill) market represents the core of the money market. All levels of government in Canada have run substantial deficits on a fairly regular basis. Accordingly, the Bank of Canada, as the agent of the federal government, sells discounted T-bills during Treasury auctions on Tuesdays of every week. Any bank or

---

[7] For a detailed account of Bank of Canada operating practices, see Donna Howard, "The Evolution of Routine Bank of Canada Advances to Direct Clearers," *Bank of Canada Review*, October 1992, pp. 3–22.

investment dealer (the Canadian term for investment banks) that is on the list of primary distributors of Government of Canada marketable securities is eligible to bid. Other investors have to put in their order through one of these primary distributors. Bills are issued in maturities of 91 days, 182 days, and 364 days.

While chartered banks hold a major portion of Treasury bills as part of their required secondary reserves (eliminated in 1992) bought in auction, other financial institutions, corporations, pension funds, and so on, even out their different liquidity needs by purchasing and selling T-bills between themselves and money market dealers on a daily basis. Minimum trading units are C$250,000. There is an active "when-issued" market, a forward market linking the new-issue market with the secondary market in a smooth fashion.[8]

Apart from the federal government, the Canadian provinces issue 3-month **provincial treasury bills** as well as shorter-term cash management promissory notes. Often this is done on a less regular, or "tap," basis. Even Canadian municipalities will occasionally use the money market to cover short-term financing needs, mostly for less than 90 days. Denominations are C$100,000 and less, and debt issues originate by tenders to investment dealers or through private placements. This public market resembles the United States closely, except that volumes are smaller, players are fewer, and market liquidity is therefore somewhat less. Further, certain constitutional issues, especially the possibility of Quebec declaring independence, raise questions of credit risk even on securities by the federal government itself.

As far as bank-issued securities are concerned, Canadian-chartered banks originally offered traditional time deposits only. Later they came under pressure from nonbank intermediaries such as acceptance companies and large industrial enterprises competing for short-term funds. As a consequence, there is now a Canadian CD market, where paper known as **chartered bank CDs** or **chartered bank bearer deposit notes (BDNs)** are available from 30 days to 1 year. Minimum denominations are usually $100,000. These securities trade on a discount basis and in most cases are issued directly by the banks to their customers rather than distributed by investment dealers. Chartered banks also issue bearer-form term notes and CDs in smaller denominations, ranging from $5,000 to $100,000, or even higher in registered form. Chartered banks also issue U.S. dollar deposit notes; essentially these notes are akin to Eurodollar CDs.

---

[8] For a thorough analysis of this market, see D. Graham Pugh, "The When-Issued Market for Government of Canada Treasury Bills: A Technical Note," *Bank of Canada Review*, November 1992, pp. 4–22.

There is an active market for **wholesale deposits** in amounts above $100,000. These are denominated in U.S. dollars outright, or they are so-called swapped deposits, that is, covered with a forward exchange contract into Canadian dollar deposits,

Introduced only in 1962, the market for **banker's acceptances** has become huge. These are bills of exchange or commercial drafts, that is, written orders to pay, drawn up by nonbank borrowers for payment on a specific date. Each of these notes is then accepted, that is, "guaranteed," at maturity by the borrower's bank.[9] Thus BAs represent two-name paper. Once the acceptance has been obtained, the drawer can present what is now a banker's acceptance to a money market dealer or the bank for sale. The latter will bid for the acceptance on a discounted basis. The normal terms are 30 to 364 days, although exceptions are possible. BAs have to be issued against security as defined in the Bank of Canada Act, but that definition is much broader than it is in the United States. The bank's acceptance is provided in return for a stamping fee (elsewhere known as a BA commission), the bank's reward for taking on the default risk. BAs come in round denominations of $100,000 as well as $500,000 and $1 million.

The banker's acceptance market in Canada is in some respects a direct substitute for the external market. By accepting drafts and creating BAs, banks avoid the intermediation costs such as reserve requirements, and, until recently, the contingent obligations created did not count against bank capital requirements. Thus, the BA rate in Canada substitutes for the London interbank offered rate (LIBOR) in the U.S. dollar market, and there even exists a futures market for BAs on the Montreal Exchange. This futures market in turn allows the larger Canadian banks, as well as some foreign banks to create efficient over-the-counter markets for all kinds of interest rate management products such as FRAs and swaps, paying a fixed rate against the 90-day or 180-day BA rate, and the usual options-type products, such as caps and floors.

Just as in the United States, finance companies, both captive and independent, play an important role in the Canadian market. They obtain a large part of their funds from the sale of short-term promissory notes which are known as "finance" or "**acceptance paper**." These short-term securities are much more akin to CP than bankers' acceptances because they represent only one-name paper, although it is sometimes secured by specific assets such as receivables. In other cases, however, the backing is simply the general credit of the issuer.

---

[9] Technically speaking, an acceptance is better than a guarantee, since the bank is the first obligor, while the bank is only the second obligor under a guarantee.

Finally, there is a relatively small Canadian **commercial paper (CP)** market,[10] rated by one or two of Canada's rating agencies (i.e., the Canadian Bond Rating Service and Dominion Bond Rating Service). As in other areas, the CP market developed because of the price of chartered bank prime loans to better industrial credits. CP is issued in either discount or interest-bearing form and can be made available both in bearer as well as registered form. With no SEC registration serving as a constraint, terms can vary from a few days to a year, and offerings are usually restricted to $100,000 and higher. As in the United States, CP is backed by the general credit of the issuing corporation and implicitly by an unused line of credit at the issuer's bank. A special version is available in the form of demand paper that can be cashed in on 24-hour notice by the investor. The return on such paper is higher than the prevailing overnight rates and is normally slightly below 30-day prime finance company paper. Because of Canada's close economic relations with the United States and the important role played by Canadian subsidiaries of U.S.-based multinationals, "U.S. pay CP" (i.e., commercial paper denominated in U.S. dollars) has been available as an alternative in Canada for many years. Since most of these multicurrency programs are backed up by a parent company guarantee, they provide further avenues to integrate the foreign exchange markets in Canadian and U.S. dollars.

Because of the fact that dividends received by a Canadian corporation from another corporation are 100 percent exempt from taxation, **Dutch auction preferred shares** have caught on very quickly in Canada. Like "money market preferred" in the United States this instrument pays something called a "dividend." However, the size of the dividend is established periodically at an auction through investors' bids that are unrelated to the earnings of the issuer, but rather determined by market yields on tax-free money market instruments.

Canadian government securities, as in the United States, have been stripped, and the short coupons are traded in the market as so-called residuals, competing directly with Treasury bills.

Last, but not least, the Canadian market just started experimenting with securitization, although these efforts are several years behind equivalent activities in the U.S. market. What seems to work best so far are special-purpose finance subsidiaries that purchase receivable, and obtain credit enhancement, thereby reaching a standing that allows them access to the commercial paper market financing. The reason why this development has lagged behind similar developments in the United States is a factor that affects other money market activities in Canada: the position of the banks is

---

[10] For a detailed account of Canada's CP market, see: Peter Marchart, "Canadian Commercial Paper," in *Guide to International Commercial Paper, Euromoney Corporate Finance*, Supplement, January 1993.

much stronger as their intermediation function is less hampered by regulation and legally imposed fragmented structures.[11]

THE UNITED KINGDOM

London's success as a global financial center is based in no small part on the reputation its domestic market enjoys, a reputation for being open, competitive, sound, and liquid. The City, as the financial community is called, has always encouraged a high level of professional competence, and Britain is fortunate that the same can, by and large, be said of the regulatory authorities. The U.K. regulators, notably the Bank of England, have employed a modestly paternalistic, but by no means dirigistic, approach, trying instead to ensure that their regulations merely reflect best market practice. In Britain the central bank, the **Bank of England**, conducts monetary policy and supervises the banks. In addition, it is the instrument for financing government deficits and is under the control of Her Majesty's Treasury. Thus the Old Lady is forced to wear three hats, not all of which can be carried very elegantly at the same time. Observers have frequently advocated some devolution of these roles, particularly giving the Bank of England the degree of independence from government pressures that characterizes the Bundesbank or the U.S. Federal Reserve.

In most domestic money markets the dominant player is the central bank, and the United Kingdom is no exception. The Bank of England intervenes daily in the money market to balance the supply of and demand for funds. If government inflows exceed outflows, for example, there will be a shortage of cash in the private market, so the Bank will invite offers of eligible paper (Treasury bills, local authority obligations, and banker's acceptances) from the **discount houses**, either for outright sale or on a repurchase agreement basis. The discount houses are specialists in secured money and short-term paper trading. The discount houses, an institution peculiar to the London money market, are officially-sanctioned intermediaries through which the Bank of England implements its monetary policy.[12] *It is the allocation of privileged positions to certain classes of financial institutions such as the London discount houses that distinguishes even the fairest of national money markets from the indiscriminate Eurocurrency market.*

Commercial banks deal with each other in the **interbank market** for

---

[11] In particular, Canadian banks never were subject to any restriction against nationwide banking.

[12] In days gone by, directors of discount houses wearing a top hat called on the senior money man at a clearing bank to borrow monies with which to finance their book. To some extent that is still done, although the "book" is now a computer and demand is now communicated by telephone. Personal visits are more for the purpose of information gathering.

deposits, but collectively they meet an overall shortage or surplus by calling money from or lending to the discount houses or by trading in paper with them. The interbank market is a market in unsecured deposits, whereas money placed with the discount houses is secured by Treasury bills or other instruments. Deposits by banks with the discount houses are regarded by the Bank of England as first-class liquidity and enjoy a low risk weighting (of 0.1) in the calculation of banks' risk asset weightings for capital adequacy purposes. Interbank deposits' weighting is 0.2.

As in most "market-oriented" financial systems, **Treasury bills** lie at the core of the money market. In the United Kingdom, Treasury bonds ("gilts") provide the government with the bulk of its financing, and Treasury bills are the vehicle for the government's residual borrowing. They are issued at a discount to their face value, rounded to fractions (1/16ths or 1/32nds). They are considered absolutely safe and as having first-class liquidity by the bank and building society[13] supervisors, and their yields are usually slightly lower than other similar investments, although not as much as in some other countries, perhaps because issues have tended to be smaller. They can be sold at any time in their life for settlement the same day. Ninety-one-day and 182-day U.K. Treasury bills are sold by the Bank of England at a weekly tender auction and actually issued on any day of the following week, at the choice of the successful bidder. The Bank announces the lowest accepted bid, and the percentage allotment of applications at that price. Higher bids are allotted in full. More than half of outstanding Treasury bills are held by commercial banks and building societies, mainly to meet liquidity requirements imposed by the supervisors.

The principal form of financing for banks is **time deposits** or their negotiable variant, **bank certificates of deposit**. There is a huge interbank market for time deposits encompassing about 400 domestic and foreign banks, but nonbank investors favor tradable CDs. Negotiable CDs can be issued by both commercial banks and building societies, but the investor community's preference for readily marketable instruments ensures that the majority of CDs are issued by the most creditworthy institutions. Prime, that is, newly issued, CDs are either issued directly to a depositor or sold through a money market broker, who charges a small commission for the service of introducing buyer to seller. Active buyers will compare rates on prime CDs with yields offered on secondary CDs by brokers and by discount houses. The latter run substantial portfolios for their own investment purposes and, as with Treasury bills and banker's acceptances, act as the central market

---

[13] In the United Kingdom, "building societies" are the retail savings institutions whose principal business is taking retail deposits and making home mortgage loans.

makers in CDs, making firm two-way prices and creating a liquid market for both holders and issuers.

For many investors, however, **banker's acceptances** have more appeal as a short-term investment. While the bare trade bill of exchange has largely been superseded by the more convenient bank loan or overdraft, a substantial volume of trade is still financed through the bankers acceptance, under which a bank accepts (or promises to pay upon presentation of correct documents) a bill drawn by its customer. The popularity of banker's acceptances in the U.K. investment community can be attributed to low credit risk, to supervisory approval, and most of all to excellent liquidity. A holder of BAs can always sell them to the discount houses, who have a constant appetite for first-class bills, and it is one of their obligations to bid for bills at all times. Nearly all bank-accepted bills are eligible for rediscount at the Bank of England or can be pledged by the houses when borrowing from the Bank. As is the case elsewhere, BAs are traded at a discount from the face value.

A long-established instrument in the United States, **commercial paper** was only introduced in the United Kingdom in the mid-1980s. Sterling CP quickly gained favor as a financing instrument among corporate treasurers, although as in the bank market, there is sharp discrimination between top credits and others, with some companies finding themselves excluded from the market in times of recession and heightened concerns about credit risk. Most paper is issued for short periods between one week and one month, and is usually placed with nonbank investors through a bank dealer and issuing agent. Banks and discount houses hold little SCP, for the yield is too low in relation to the capital, liquidity, and special deposit requirements that apply to banks, building societies, and discount houses.

Since the 1980s the **derivatives markets** for money market instruments have come to be an integral part of the London money market, as has occurred in most of the major money markets. The London International Financial Futures Exchange, or **LIFFE**, is the world's second most active, after the Chicago market. While much of the activity is in nonsterling instruments such as Eurodollars, banks and other money market participants make frequent use of the futures and options contracts on sterling bank deposits, Treasury bills, and gilts. There is also a well-developed over-the-counter market in sterling FRAs and swaps.

Finally, we should mention that money market instruments denominated in pounds sterling, especially bank deposits, enjoy a very close relationship through covered interest arbitrage with their nonsterling equivalents. This is because much of the international money market is centered in London, and because domestic instruments are free of withholding tax and exchange controls. It means that events in the foreign exchange market, such as strains in the pound sterling's relationship with the European Monetary System, are directly felt throughout London's money market.

GERMANY

For a country that in terms of output of goods and services represents the third largest economy and whose currency is second only to the U.S. dollar in world financial markets, Germany has an odd money market: opportunities for households, business firms, and even public enterprises to even out their short-term liquidity surpluses and deficits are extremely limited. And even treasury managers of financial institutions have at their disposition far fewer opportunities to manage their liquidity positions than their colleagues responsible for funds management in Anglo-Saxon institutions.

In sharp contrast, the monetary policy of Germany's central bank, the Bundesbank, can be conducted via a wide variety of instruments and techniques on the short-term end of fixed income markets.[14] Monetary policy for some time has been conducted largely through weekly repo auctions (*Pensionsgeschäfte*) with a 14 day duration, implemented as volume or price tenders for Central Bank reserves. Minimum reserve requirements play a crucial role in the Bundesbank's monetary management, and one cannot understand that institution's resistance to innovation in the money market without being aware of the judgment arrived at by key executives in that institution that a tighter linkage between central bank reserves, that is, high-powered money, and liquidity available to households, business firms, and public entities is well worth the cost and inconvenience to nonbanks of having fewer opportunities for cash management.

In this respect the interest of the Bundesbank and those of the traditional financial institutions are perfectly aligned. New instruments and techniques in the money market would only increase competition for funds for banks already confronted by fierce competition for business loans and hampered by terrific overhead expenses for branches, personnel, technology, and regulatory compliance; they are strongly opposed to new instruments and techniques on the fund-raising side of the business that would make life even more difficult.

The Bundesbank is also aware of the importance of not paying interest on reserves, forcing banks to minimize balances, thus further taking away any possible slack between high-powered money and liquidity in the econ-

---

[14] It is true, the Bundesbank has been active occasionally in the markets for longer-term government and agency securities (the federal postal service, including Telekom; the federal railway system; the privatization agency Treuhandanstalt; and a number of government-owned financial institutions), the purpose there is largely to prevent excessive price/yield fluctuations in narrow markets (*Marktpflege*).

omy. It goes without saying that the Bundesbank interest is in tune with that of the federal Finance Ministry as the Bundesbank surpluses represent an important source of revenue for the federal budget.

Repo transactions have become an efficient means for the Bundesbank to fine-tune liquidity. This is particularly important when rapid changes in domestic liquidity conditions occur. These are often caused by the ebb and tide of foreign exchange transactions which are reflected immediately in the increase or decrease of high-powered money, because of the Bundesbank's need to intervene in the quasi–fixed exchange rate system of the European Community. In contrast, more traditional techniques of the Bundesbank have lost importance. Like some other Central Banks, the Bundesbank stands ready to buy back from commercial banks eligible trade acceptances at the **discount rate**. However every financial institution has an individual maximum ceiling for such transactions, known as the **rediscount quota**. Set at 100 to 300 (max.) basis points above the refinancing rate is the **Lombard rate**, which is yet another refinancing facility that allows banks opportunities to obtain additional liquidity for a period of up to 3 months by pledging paper fulfilling certain quality criteria.

Each of these tools can be modified, and at times the Bundesbank has done exactly that: minimum reserves have been changed, although infrequently. The direction of adjustment has been downward as the Bundesbank has become conscious of the competitive effect of such reserve requirements when an efficient external market exists. A significant adjustment took place in early 1993, when reserve requirements on time and savings deposits were lowered to 2 percent, while they were left for current accounts (30 days and less) at up to 12.1 percent. Rediscount facilities can be expanded or curtailed, and "special" Lombard facilities have been offered at times. Beyond these tools, the Bundesbank can and does use foreign exchange forwards, so-called swaps, to provide markets with liquidity or to withdraw liquidity at a given maturity of the forward. Also, repos with same day settlement (Schnelltender) have been utilized.

Apart from buying short-term money market paper, especially Treasury bills, the Bundesbank can issue to the banks, and on rare occasion even to nonbanks, **discountable bills** (Bundesbank bills). As a rule, they mature in 3 days. In years past, some varieties could be discounted at the Bundesbank prior to maturity. Actually, the Bundesbank does not issue such paper directly: the Treasury of the federal government is obliged to make available short-term paper, up to a limit, upon request of the central bank.

Finally, the Bundesbank can use funds in government accounts with the banking system to influence liquidity.

An important interbank market for funds exists in Germany, one whose rates (influenced by the Bundesbank's repo transactions) fluctuate typically somewhere between the discount and the Lombard rate. At times market rates can and do break through these barriers when internal or external events trigger such large transaction volumes that quantitative restrictions come into play. Like the U.S. Fed funds market, interbank deposits are not subject to reserve requirements; thus the market is very active. It was reorganized in the late 1980s to compete more effectively with the EuroDM market, resulting, among other things, in a reference rate FIBOR (Frankfurt interbank offered rate). Trading in short-term paper, Treasury discount paper (*U-Schatze*), or acceptances is rare.

For nonbanks, the German money market offers few opportunities to even out liquidity imbalances. Borrowers for short-term funds essentially have only the (expensive) overdraft facilities of the banks. Trade can be financed through the acceptance market under limited conditions similar to those prevailing in the United States. Of course, there is always the Euromarket which larger German companies use extensively.

For those companies that have excess funds to invest for short periods, the alternatives were not much better—until the early 1990s. The banks offer time deposits (*Festgeld*) and, since 1986, negotiable CDs. However, the CD market has never taken off because of the turnover tax (removed in February 1991) and minimum reserve requirements, a cost that prevents the banks from offering competitive CD rates. Eurocommercial paper or other U.S. dollar money market instruments covered with a foreign exchange swap into Deutsche marks are probably the next best alternatives, although the compounding of both money market as well as foreign exchange transactions costs allow this opportunity only for very large transactions. For individuals, even high-net-worth individuals, there is only *Festgeld*. Money market funds are not permitted in the Federal Republic because of Bundesbank opposition.[15]

Retail investors have access to another variety of bill which is specifically designed for retail investors, so-called **financing notes** (*Finanzierungsschätze*). Such notes, however, carry maturities of either one or two years and are nonnegotiable.

With gradual liberalization resulting from external competition, a market for commercial paper did not start until 1991, when the Bundesbank gave up its opposition. German commercial paper comes in denominations of $DM^1/_2$ million and the market has grown quite rapidly, being supplied not only by German corporations, but also by prime non-German multinationals who, since mid-1992, do not need to have a German issuing entity (subsidiary) anymore. Further, CP has been issued by a number of government

---

[15] For the German retail investor, DM money market funds are available only in Luxembourg and Switzerland. The closest vehicles in the German market are "near money market funds." However, the money market funds offshore or onshore cannot compare with those in the United States; sales charges of up to 1 percent and costly as well as cumbersome redemption features limit the usefulness for cash management of such vehicles for private individuals and small-business firms.

agencies, notably the Treuhand, whose CP has become the benchmark issue due to the Treuhand's credit standing and the large issue volume.

However, like other markets, the German market is in transition. Two factors provide the impetus for change. First, the cost of German reunification has brought tremendous stress on public budgets, increasing the need for on- and off-budget financing. Second, EC economic integration compels Germany to align its regulatory framework to the directives of the EC and this opens the German market to new instruments and techniques. The major effects on the money market has been a somewhat greater supply of short-term Treasury bills and federal agencies. Treasury discount paper is available to investors by competitive tender or private placement in minimum denominations of DM100,000.

In February 1993, the Bundesbank issued DM 25 billion of Bundesbank-Liquiditätspapiere (called "Bulis") to offset liquidity faced by the reduction of reserve requirements on time and savings deposits. Because of higher credit standing and perhaps greater liquidity, they traded around approximately 37–47 BPs under FIBOR rates of equivalent maturities. More interesting is the reaction of some banks to offer marketable, short-term CDs to offer clients competitive money market investment opportunities.[16] Whether this phenomenon represents the beginning of a trend remains to be seen.

As for derivatives, while the German derivatives exchange (DTB) does not offer a short-term interest rate contract as of mid 1993, EuroDM futures are available on LIFFE in London and on the Paris exchange, the Matif. Options on 90-day EuroDeutsche marks are also available. On that basis, four or five German banks have developed an active over-the-counter market for swaps, caps, floors, and similar derivatives.

For the German retail investor, only DM "quasi"-money market funds in Luxembourg and Switzerland are available. The closest vehicles in the German market are "near money market funds" (without checking privileges). However, the money market funds offshore or onshore cannot compare with those in the United States; sales charges of up to 1 percent and costly as well as cumbersome redemption features limit the usefulness for cash management of such vehicles for private individuals and small-business firms.

JAPAN

For at least the past 30 years, discussions of Japan's financial markets in general, and the money market in particular, have been dominated by two themes: **internationalization** and **liberalization**. This is still the case, except

[16] Deutsche Bundesbank, Auszüge aus Presseartikeln, March 5, 1993, No. 17, p. 4.

that in conformance with current fashion, the word "internationalization" has now been replaced by "globalization." By the same token, every major and not-so-major publication dealing with the analysis of these markets contains an appendix with an extensive timetable of various liberalization measures.[17] What all this really means is that, while significant steps toward liberalization have been taken, there are still restrictions that are a puzzle for the naive observer and are simply classified as Oriental mystiques. The essence is a precarious co-existence of regulated and nonregulated markets to which concepts such as market mechanisms and efficiency are applied at some risk.

To understand Japanese financial markets, one has to be aware that the real miracle is that liberalization has progressed as far as it has. A fundamental facet of the Japanese political economy is that financial markets are considered too important to be left to the free play of market forces. On the danger of doing injustice to a complex system, it is nevertheless useful to focus on certain of its salient characteristics. Deeply ingrained beliefs in the scarcity of resources, together with high population density and a long history of frequent man-made as well as natural calamities, have convinced the Japanese that society has to be well regulated and ordered in order to avoid the alternative of chaos and destruction. Based on Confucian values, wise leaders set policy, implemented by a well-educated and pervasive bureaucracy, that is usually honest (unlike the politicians) and, at times, even efficient.

Destructive conflict among major interest groups is to be avoided by all means; no group with sufficient power to raise a major ruckus can be ignored or run over in a roughshod fashion. Consensus is achieved through negotiations, give and take, and various factions are persuaded and bribed to agree to compromise in a lengthy process. Often, the compromise consists of the status quo being preserved with only minor cosmetic changes.

Foreign pressure plays a special influence in this process. It would be wrong to credit outside forces as being at the root of all significant changes in Japan's financial markets, such as the introduction of new financial instruments or general liberalization of financial markets. However, when outside pressures coincide with significant domestic interests, change often does occur more swiftly.[18]

These general characteristics certainly apply to the Japanese money

---

[17] For an example, see Masahiko Takeda and Philip Turner, "The Liberalization of Japan's Financial Markets: Some Major Themes," *BIS Economic Papers*, No. 34 (Basle: Bank for International Settlements, November 1992), pp. 99–121.

[18] See Adreas R. Prindl, *Japanese Finance: A Guide to Banking in Japan* (New York: John Wiley and Sons, 1981), and Frances McCall Rosenbluth, *Financial Politics in Contemporary Japan* (Ithaca, NY: Studies of the East Asian Institute, Cornell University Press, 1989).

market. Historically speaking, the **call market**, established approximately in 1902, and the **bill discount market**, which originated in 1971, have been the primary markets by which Japan's financial institutions even out excess and deficit liquidity among themselves. These markets have also been used by the Bank of Japan to affect the money supply.

The market for **call money** is very similar to the U.S. Fed funds market with one exception. For many years, beginning after the 1927 banking crisis, call money transactions were collateralized. Noncollateralized call market transactions, however, have been expanding quite rapidly during the 1980s, and by the end of 1991 the average annual volume of unsecured call transactions exceeded that of collateralized transactions.[19]

More important, for many years interest rates for call money have been set under the guidance of the Bank of Japan with little regard to market rates, largely by compelling transactors to go through special brokers (*tanshi*) whose quotes were guided closely by the monetary authorities. And while the system of *direct* guidance of tanshi rates was officially abolished in the mid-1980s, the guiding hand of the Bank of Japan on money rates is still evidenced by the low variance of daily changes in market rates.

The **bill discount market**, based on commercial bills (*tegata*), played a similar role in financing trade. Like the market for call money, however, the market is strictly interbank, with participation limited to various financial institutions, including nonbank financial institutions such as insurance companies, credit cooperatives, and others. Nonbank financial institutions, smaller banks, and credit unions are active in the money market, primarily as suppliers of funds; city banks and long-term credit banks tend to have structurally a shortage of funds.

By way of a footnote, besides intervention in the call and *tegata* markets, the Bank of Japan has also engaged at times in *direct lending* through the discount window. For many years this policy led to a condition of so-called "overloan" where Japanese banks booked commercial loan volumes exceeding their deposits, funded by such direct loans from the Bank of Japan. This phenomenon has led to all kinds of theories about the uniqueness of the Japanese system. With the benefit of hindsight, it was largely due to the fact that interest rates on the deposit side as well as on the lending side were controlled, and the banking sector was starved for funds. This condition allowed the authorities to keep very close controls on the quantity of money in the economy and also permitted the government to direct scarce funds into favored industries.

All of this, of course, changed in the early 1980s: capital markets devel-

[19] Tomoko Fujii, "A Primer on Yen Fixed-Income Markets" (Tokyo: Salomon Brothers, June 1992).

oped, large firms went to the Euromarkets, interest regulation was circumvented and subsequently relaxed, and banks were finally glad to have customers desiring loans.

During 1979, under some pressure from the United States as well as certain Japanese banking institutions, the Ministry of Finance permitted the issuance of **certificates of deposit**. Originally, this activity was curtailed by maturity restrictions as well as minimum size limits (¥100 million), but the rules were changed in 1988 to ¥50 million and have become lower since. Over the years, particularly since the 1988 money market reform, yields on 3-month CDs have become the representative domestic open market interest rate. CD rates in turn have become the base to compute rates on **money market certificates (MMCs)** for individual investors and have turned out to become the base for the short-term prime rate. CDs, however, have never played a role matching their potential, largely because of transactions taxes, and the secondary market for these instruments has therefore remained poor. Instead, corporations use large-scale (nonnegotiable) time deposits which are directly negotiated with the banks.

It is characteristic for the Japanese market in a way that T-bills, the backbone of most other money markets in industrialized countries, have come on the scene relatively late. It was not until early 1986 that the Ministry of Finance (MoF) started to issue 6-month bills, and 3-month instruments were not introduced until September 1989.

Besides **Treasury bills**, the Ministry of Finance has also been issuing so-called **financing bills (FBs)**. These are used for central government cash management purposes only, as opposed to a way to raise funds systematically for the government in the short-term markets. Since 1982, the Bank of Japan has occasionally been reselling FBs to money brokers to soak up liquidity. FBs are issued in discount form with an initial maturity of approximately 60 days.

The next step in the development of the Japanese money market occurred in November 1987 when the issue of **yen commercial paper (¥CP)** was permitted. Issuers are corporations that obtain a credit rating from at least two rating institutions. By 1991 approximately 700 firms had qualified for CP issuance, and in 1988 foreign companies were permitted to issue "Samurai CP"; Dow Chemical Company was the first company to take advantage of this opportunity. Banks and nonbank financial institutions are not permitted, however, to issue such securities.

Securities houses have been permitted by the MoF to issue CP since April 1990. Securities companies raise funds for financing inventories through the collateralized interbank market. Other nonbank institutions may be admitted to the market later.

The evolution of the CP market is a classic example of how financial reform works in Japan. During the early 1980s a strong domestic constituency, namely, corporations, threatened to move their short-term fund raising abroad if they were not given permission to issue CP in Japan. Banks were opposed as they hated to see their best customers leave their captive lending business and corporate CP become competitive with CDs as well as time deposits. U.S. negotiators had pushed Japan to further liberalize their financial markets to remove "structural impediments" to free markets and open competition beyond trade in goods and services. In a complex process that lasted several years,[20] the CP market was opened by giving CP a legal form, the equivalent of bills. Both securities companies and banks become CP dealers, whereby the latter, got a foot into the securities business. For a while, after the introduction, competition between various institutions for CP business was so keen that CP rates were below time deposit rates. Obviously, many corporations took advantage of this *hara-kiri* market.

The secondary market for CP has not developed very well because of transactions taxes. Instead, paper is traded in the form of repurchase agreements.

The *gensaki* **market** is actually a very old market: it represents a typical market phenomenon in response to restrictions. In the past nonbanks, that is, corporations, had only the banks to rely on for adjusting liquidity, which was not too bad as long as Japan was rapidly growing and virtually all corporations were in a borrowing position. This situation, however, began to change in the 1970s and 1980s when successful corporations began to accumulate large cash balances in spite of their extensive investment programs. With no short-term paper available (except trade receivables), the inventive Japanese began to develop a short-term market out of longer-term securities by selling (buying) and simultaneously repurchasing (selling) the securities for different points in time. The difference in price, of course, represented the interest implied in these repolike transactions. The market developed particularly during periods when the discrepancy between (controlled) deposit rates and market rates became significant.

The specific type of securities used for these repo transactions has changed. For many periods in the 1970s and early 1980s, the market used the medium-term bonds issued by the long-term credit institutions. However, there is nothing magic about these securities; some long-term government bonds, and currently even money market paper with limited liquidity such as CDs, T-bills, and CP, is traded on the basis of *gensaki* agreements. In fact, all money market instruments are now traded in this market, with CD gensaki being most liquid and the interest rate in this market substituting as *the* money market indicator.

By law, such repo transactions can have maturities of up to 1 year, but in

---

[20] For details see Ulrike Schaede, "The Introduction of Commercial Paper (CP): A Case Study in the Liberalization of the Japanese Financial Market," *Center for Japanese Studies Occasional Papers*, Philipps-Universität Marburg, 1988.

reality most deals are done for maturities with less than 2 months. Japanese securities companies were originally very active, using this method to finance their bond inventories necessary for trading operations; corporations joined later. Indeed, the market differentiates by counterparty: *jiko gensaki* means an agreement negotiated by the securities company intermediating between its clients for its own account, while a repo negotiated between a securities company and an industrial corporation is known as *itaku gensaki*. These two types serve the purpose of providing funds for securities companies and corporations, respectively. A third type of agreement that is know as *jiki gensaki* is negotiated directly between a borrower and an investor, with the securities company acting not as principal but merely as broker.

Nonresidents have been allowed to participate in the *gensaki* market only since 1979. Tax issues have to be carefully monitored, which is why taxable investors use gensaki agreements that are timed in such a way that coupon dates fall outside the agreement for the taxable party; a tax-exempt investor owns the securities during coupon dates. This technique is known in other markets as "coupon washing." A transfer tax of 0.03 percent, however, applies. When using government bonds, an additional 0.01 percent is payable; CD *gensaki* transactions, however, do not involve a transfer tax which explains their popularity.

Asset-backed securities are being discussed in Japan in the early 1990s, but no consensus has been reached among the various parties concerned, and there are also legal/regulatory issues as yet unresolved.

There are, however, Euroyen futures contracts traded on the Tokyo International Financial Futures Exchange since June 1989. Since October of that year the Singapore International Money Exchange (SIMEX) has traded 3-month Euroyen futures. Options on Euroyen futures started to trade during 1992.

A good indicator of the functioning of the money market is a comparison of the differentials among rates of different instruments such as CDs, commercial bills, Euroyen, and others. A graph of such rates shows that toward the end of 1988 a substantial change occurred in the Japanese money market as rate discrepancies among these instruments became reduced to a few basis points. Prior to that period differences of up to 100 basis points, representing quantitative restrictions rather than credit or liquidity differentials, were visible.[21]

A **banker's acceptance** market was promoted by the authorities in 1985, but it disappeared because of various transactions taxes and better money market alternatives.

---

[21] See Tomoko Fujii, "A Primer on Yen Fixed-Income Markets," Salomon Brothers, June 1992, Figure 6, p. 9.

Given the history and the cultural context, Japan's money market has come a long way. A recent review by a Japanese observer mentions three remaining problems with respect to the Japanese money market.[22] First, there is a shortage of Treasury bills and financing bills; this is because the Treasury does not issue enough short-term paper relative to longer-term fixed-rate bonds. Second, market participants, including regulators, have not made up their minds regarding the need, or lack thereof, for collateralizing transactions. It must not be forgotten that the stability of the Japanese financial system is of post–World War II origin. Prior to that time, the Japanese system had to endure a number of financial crises and crashes, and even in the modern period there were several accidents that almost happened. Third, nonbank participants are again affected by the lack of treasury bills and financing bills. This pushes them into privately issued money market paper such as CDs and CP, where credit risk is always a factor. Participants in the money market are particularly risk averse—institutions seek not to maximize return but to assure liquidity and the availability of funds.

A secondary market that really meets the requirements of the Japanese economy has been prevented from developing by, for example, the Ministry of Finance's practice of issuing FBs at below-market rates to limit government interest costs, and by vexing tax problems. For example, the gains from the redemption of discount Treasury bills and Financing bills are subject to an 18 percent withholding tax. This levy is deductible for taxable corporations and refunded to tax-exempt corporations either at redemption or at time of purchase, with respect to foreign central banks and other official institutions with tax-exempt status in Japan.[23]

Turning to the individual investor, high-net-worth individuals now can choose from a variety of instruments as shown, for example, by the weekly personal investment column published in *Nikkei*. The competition for deposit funds is keen, and sharp consumers (in Japan this means housewives who control the family's funds) can get decent rates on term funds. But regulatory distortions and institutional quirks remain. For example, the Postal Savings System effectively offers savings deposits which guarantee a fixed rate that allow for withdrawal of funds by depositors without penalty. There is a whole range of time deposit facilities: small and large money trust accounts, medium-term bond funds offered by investment companies, as well as trust fund accounts by trust banks that serve a similar function. However, when it comes to the "real thing," that is, money market mutual

---

[22] Kenzo Yamamoto, *Capital Markets and Financial Services in Japan: Regulation and Practice* (Tokyo: Japan Securities Research Institute, 1992).

[23] Interestingly, the reason given why individuals are not permitted to purchase Treasury bills or FBs is the difficulty of tax collection.

funds that allow for check writing or, in Japan, the issuance of bank transfer orders, legal restrictions do not permit such vehicles. Instead, the average investor is relegated to a savings account that pays, with luck, 1 percent per annum.

DEVELOPING COUNTRIES[24]

Analysis of the money markets of developing countries is necessarily different from those of developed countries; after all, they are still developing. Let us begin, therefore, by providing a general picture of the development phase of a money market and of the structure of interest rates in different segments of the market. We can then turn to cases of money market conditions in several developing countries such as Indonesia and Korea and finally draw some conclusions about causes and remedies for underdeveloped money markets.

In those developing countries where a money market exists, it plays a different role from that in the industrial countries with well-developed securities markets. Most developing countries rely much more on banks than on markets for the allocation of short-term credit, so it should not be surprising that the first semblance of a money market is often the **interbank market** for deposits. Banks in developing countries are often seen as semi-public institutions since they serve most of the functions of a money and capital market. Banks themselves also serve much more important functions in both monetary policy and credit allocation. Often they are required to make loans to favored sectors at below-market interest rates (see box on banking in China). In turn, their market position may be sheltered from foreign competition and from financial innovation, or troubled creditors may be bailed out by government subsidies. In fact in many developing countries, the principal banks are state owned.

Some countries have actively promoted the development of a domestic money market, mainly because the government has recognized that the money market, particularly the market for Treasury bills, can be very helpful in the implementation of monetary policy. The government of a developing country typically creates a *primary market* by distributing money market instruments through compulsory assignment to banks and other financial institutions. But as a rule, low transaction volumes of these instruments indicate that the *secondary market* remains in its infancy often caused by the very fact that new issue rates are "off market."

Indeed, the major constraints on money market development in devel-

---

[24] The authors are grateful to Mr. Park Soonpoong, who made many helpful suggestions about this section.

BANK LENDING IN CHINA

The early 1990s saw rapid growth of private banks in China, in response to enormous demand for credit on the part of nonfavored businesses. Until the mid-1980s, all banks were state owned. Their lending practices were the very antithesis of prudence. If a factor was in decline, manufacturing pink sofas or something else that faced weak demand, then that would be sufficient reason to extend a loan so that the factory could meet its payroll. It did not matter whether the factory could repay the loan; the important thing was to avoid labor unrest. It helped if the factory manager had cultivated good *guanxi* (connections) with government officials and offered "samples" to lending officers. Because state banks were all chock full of bad loans that were rolled over when they became due, no one was ever disciplined for adding one more irrational loan to the pile.

Source: "Pushing the Limits in Chinese Banking," *The New York Times*, February 7, 1993.

oping countries are restrictions on interest rates. The monetary and regulatory framework is used not only for its traditional functions, but also for the twin goals of lowering the cost of public borrowing and rationing domestic credit. Obviously, this gives considerable power to the government and its bureaucracy to channel cheap credit resources to a limited group of chosen industries ostensibly to promote industrial growth, generate scarce foreign exchange, or serve the present government's interests in other ways. This means that interest rates paid on deposits and charged for loans are unlikely to reflect the risks of these instruments. In many cases, real interest rates in regulated financial institutions are negative, providing opportunities for political corruption and incentives for criminal, personal enrichment of decision makers.

There is little room for an efficient money market in this context. In a free market the return will reflect the riskiness of the instrument, and interest rates in advanced countries' money markets will tend to be lower than commercial loan rates because the latter are riskier and less liquid. In a restricted money market the opposite is often true. So, if the government of such a developing country were to permit an open money market to compete freely with banks, the result would be severe disintermediation, and the government's power to ration credit would be profoundly weakened.

As one might expect the result is that in some countries, huge informal or "curb" money markets develop. Rapid economic growth coupled with subsidized and rationed credit creates a chronic shortage of capital, and to many companies what matters is the availability rather than the cost of funds. As a consequence, interest rates in curb markets are much higher than those charged by regulated institutions.[25]

In addition, effective rates charged by regulated banks may in fact be much higher than nominal rates, if the restrictions apply to nominal rates only. In Saudi Arabia, where Islamic *shari'a* laws restrict loan rates, banks offer loans at a discount from face and charge ongoing administrative fees to substitute for interest. Japanese banks have traditionally demanded that loan customers maintain a considerable amount of interest-free compensating balances. As a result Japanese banks retained considerable autonomy in controlling the effective interest rate level, circumventing nominal interest rate controls. In Korea, commercial banks are prohibited from requiring compensating balances; and while this prohibition had been on the books for many years, it has been honored more in the breach than in the observance. At times, however, the Korean authorities have enforced this rule; during those periods, the banks' autonomy in loan pricing has been severely restricted.[26] Korea's curb market is huge, and, as described in the accompanying box, its money market has been rife with distorted interest rates.

In sum, restrictions on either nominal or effective interest rates often produce unattractive real interest rates to savers, particularly where (as in many developing countries) inflation is rife. This creates distortions, promotes informal markets and self-financing by companies, and impedes the development of a money market. Further, although interest rate distortions constitute a major feature of financial markets in developing countries, the root of the problem is an absence of economic democracy, a political economy of what economists term *financial repression*. Political decisions that ration credit and favor a limited group of industries not only suppress financial market development but also may cause a critical shortfall of capital and inhibit real economic development. Worse, they often lead to capital flight as one avenue for savers to obtain adequate returns. Capital flight in turn necessitates foreign exchange controls, which carry with them their

---

[25] The fact that many countries with repressed financial markets were able to achieve impressive growth rates on the real sector of the economy is in part explained by the availability of parallel markets, i.e., the domestic curb market for small enterprises, and the offshore market for large business firms. These operate effectively in an environment of "dual" financial markets. See Gunter Dufey, "Banking in the Asia Pacific Area," in *Asia Pacific Dynamics*, R. Moxon, J.F. Truitt, and T. Roehl (eds.) Greenwich, CT: JAI Press, 1983.

[26] Korean academics criticize this restriction on the basis that it has kept Korean commercial banks from cultivating a capability for assessing customers' creditworthiness as well as from charging an effective rate based on that assessment. They argue that even though politically dictated credit rationing is the most critical cause of huge problem loans at Korea's commercial banks, the banks' incapability of assessing credit contributes to bad loan problems. They support their argument with evidence that compensating balances required by American banks have assisted banks in monitoring customers' credit. This interference appears to stretch that argument considerably.

THE KOREAN MONEY MARKET: AN EXAMPLE OF A DISTORTED
INTEREST RATE STRUCTURE

Korea's financial market is a segmented one, and interest rates vary accordingly. The first segment is deposit and loan rates at banks: these are constrained to low levels—below 10 percent—by government regulation. The second is the nonbank financial institutions (NBFIs). Contrary to the situation faced by commercial banks, they can control effective interest rates, although the government has frequently sought to prevent this. NBFIs lend to companies by underwriting commercial paper, but when they do, they may simultaneously require the issuing company to buy paper issued by the NBFI. Such paper pays a rate only slightly higher than commercial bank deposit rates. Official interest rates for CP ranged around 12–14 percent in the late 1980s, whereas effective interest rates fluctuated in a wide range centering around 17–19 percent. The third segment is the market for notes issued by the central bank, monetary stabilization bonds (MSBs), issued to absorb cash created by Korea's trade surplus in the late 1980s as well as excess liquidity generated after inflation, wage settlements, and government spending programs. MSBs were issued and traded publicly and could be bought by individual investors directly or through trust funds at commercial banks. The burgeoning supply drove secondary market yields up, frequently above 16 percent. Being risk free and offering yields much higher than commercial bank deposit *and* loan rates, MSBs created a huge crowding-out effect, undermining bank intermediation as well as the development of other money market instruments. Finally, interest rates in the informal curb market ranged between 2.5 and 3 percent a month, roughly 30–40 percent per annum.

own set of costs, distortions, and a corrosive effect on respect for laws and regulations.

Some argue that financial repression also constrains the central bank's monetary policy effectiveness and hence its ability to contain inflation.[27] Open market operations are far less likely to be distorted by credit allocation influences than are administrative controls. Using the money market for monetary policy both contributes to and depends on an efficient money market. The traditional instruments for the implementation of monetary policy in developing countries have been (1) commercial bank reserve

---

[27] See Robert F. Emery, *The Money Markets of Developing East Asia* (New York: Praeger, 1991).

requirements or liquidity ratios, (2) central bank discount policy, and (3) the use of various direct controls such as ceilings on the amount of commercial bank credit expansion. As their economies' need for freer financial markets has grown, however, a number of governments have employed open market operations in money market instruments, such as Treasury bills and notes issued by the central bank to achieve their monetary policy objectives. Not all such efforts have proved successful: in Indonesia, for example, the distortions in the money market produced yields that did not reflect market conditions, and open market operations have not had the desired effect.

It is difficult to generalize about the money markets of developing countries, as each reflects its country's political economy. The situation in Indonesia illustrates the fact that one has to go beyond a description of the instruments of the money market to understand how the market works. Unlike many developing countries, Indonesia has a substantial market in commercial paper, or SBPU. SBPUs are promissory notes endorsed by a bank or nonbank financial institution, and can be rediscounted at the central bank, Bank Indonesia. However the market for short-term obligations of Bank Indonesia, central bank certificates (SBIs), has remained undeveloped and artificial as a result of the central bank's control of the interest rate on SBIs. Bank Indonesia did this by mandating a cutoff rate for SBIs, that is, a maximum yield that banks and other purchasers of SBIs could receive and a rate that has generally been below other money market rates. This has made the paper unattractive to banks and forced the central bank to resort to administrative measures to control liquidity.

In some countries, such as Taiwan, where a current account surplus has translated into excessive monetary growth and inflation as the central bank purchases foreign exchange inflows, in order to prevent the currency from appreciating, the government has created special issues of central bank bills to sell to the market to absorb the overabundance of liquidity. These operations promoted money market liquidity and certainly prevented higher inflation in Taiwan. Yet from the point of view of money market development, allowing yields to be determined by supply and demand seems to be far more important than ensuring the questionable objective of depressing the value of the currency providing benefits to the export sector of the economy.

The Treasury bill market in the Philippines provides a good example of how a money market can thrive even in an inflationary economy, as long as real rates are free to find their own levels. The Philippine government first issued Treasury bills in 1966. Currently the Treasury bill market constitutes a major component of the Manila money market and has a turnover roughly equal to that of the interbank market. Open market operations in the Treasury bill market now constitutes the principal instrument for the conduct of monetary policy by the Philippine central bank. Not only does this contribute to a healthy financial market, but it provides the great bulk of domestic government debt financing. Last, but not least, it has permitted the country to remove all foreign exchange restrictions (1992), improving the economic management of a country afflicted by natural as well as man-made disasters.

In Korea, the evolution of a money market is constrained by the absence of a deep Treasury bill market as well as the interest rate distortions noted earlier. Volume is low because issuance has been sporadic, and although there is some trading of Treasury bills in a secondary market, the central bank does not support it through consistent open market operations because monetary policy is chiefly implemented via the central bank discount window. The market is further undermined by the lack of competitive bidding for the bills in the primary market. Instead, the issue system is administered by the Bank of Korea, with the paper being issued at yields that are unattractive relative to other returns available in the financial markets. The bulk of the traded money market consists of Monetary Stabilization Bonds (MSBs), issued by the central bank and traded on a discount basis, with maturities mainly under one year. MSBs are issued by public offerings and allocated administratively to banks and other financial institutions, who must then hold them or sell them in the secondary market. These allocations were a principal means of getting the vast supply of MSBs absorbed into the market.[28] Unlike Treasury bills, MSBs are issued purely for the purpose of reducing the rate of growth of the money supply, in effect sterilizing the inflow of funds from Korea's export boom. To forestall inflation the Bank of Korea issued huge amounts of MSBs in the late 1980s, crowding out the private sector and producing frequent disruptions of the money market.

Several lessons can be learned from the experience of these developing countries. First, a direct cause of money market underdevelopment is the absence of reasonable effective interest rates paid and charged by financial institutions. The cause of this is not simply that they have not had time to develop the instruments, institutions, and skills of advanced economies, but rather that the political-economic context is one of financial repression, where it is contrary to the government officials' interests to allow free, market-determined interest rates to prevail.

On the other hand, if some financial institutions are able to find ways to charge and pay reasonable effective real interest rates, the deleterious effects of interest rate controls may be muted. The money market can be very flexi-

---

[28] For example, trust funds at commercial banks have been forced to include monetary stabilization bonds in their portfolios. In some kinds of funds, the proportion of required MSBs exceeds 80 percent of their total portfolio. Ironically these funds have benefited in that many individual investors who did not have easy access to large-denomination money market instruments shifted their money from bank deposits paying under 10 percent to trust funds who were able to pay around 13 percent, thanks to the high yields on MSBs.

ble in adapting to changing macroeconomic conditions, allowing economic growth to occur even in the presence of high inflation. In fact in some inflationary economies, the money market has been forced to assume the functions of a capital market. Turkey and Brazil have experienced a decade or more of inflation and even hyperinflation accompanied by solid economic growth, thanks in part to the resilience of their money markets. Inflation discourages investors from holding long-term fixed-rate instruments, which forces the government to follow one or more of three courses. One is simply to issue short-term securities, as in the Philippines. Another, long the practice in Brazil, is to index government bonds to the inflation rate, or rather a so-called "monetary correction" factor. The third is to issue floating-rate notes, where the rate is somehow tied to the yield on Treasury bills. The government of Turkey, fearing the vicious cycle effect of inflation indexation, has chosen this path.

As the financial regime in a developing country becomes liberalized, administrative controls no longer suffice for effective monetary policy. A money market that grows simultaneously with credit allocation imposed on financial institutions can produce severe disintermediation, undermining the effectiveness of traditional monetary policy tools such as the discount window or credit ceilings. Open market operations require a deep primary *and* secondary money market, one that should be able to stand on its own and not be totally dependent on central bank operations. This means allowing and encouraging market makers to quote a two-way price. The rate set in both the primary and the secondary market should be determined by supply and demand rather than by government fiat.

In summary, a viable money market in a developing country, or anywhere, must go beyond the interbank market. It must include Treasury bills or some other form of government short-term obligations, which should be traded in an active two-way market by banks and/or other financial institutions. Central bank open market operations in the Treasury bill market or in repurchase agreements provide a sign of a well-supported market, as long as the interest rate for the instrument is market determined rather than foisted on the banks by the government. As the market develops, regulated institutions' rates converge with those in the curb market and in the market for short-term government instruments, and distortions in the interest rate structure are gradually corrected. Domestic financial institutions rely less on special protections against competitive pressures, learn to discriminate among credit risks, and gain other efficiencies that render them more able to fend for themselves in the international money market.

CONCLUSIONS

The thumbnail sketches of domestic money markets provided here reveal many similarities—but the differences are even more striking. The similarities stem from the fact that the money market in each country performs three basic functions. The first is the evening out of liquidity imbalances of different financial institutions and different sectors of the economy. The second is its role as a focus for control of aggregate liquidity by the central bank. The third is acting as a vehicle for the government to direct resources to favored uses, those with political as well as economic priority.

The problem is that the central bank officials, the political interest groups that make up the government, and the banks and companies who use the market, may all have different priorities. When these clash, the organization and functioning of the money market are affected, and the more it is distorted, the more it deviates from the "pure" sort of price-based allocation one finds in the international money market. Thus despite the considerable liberalization of capital flows and of domestic regulations that has occurred in the 1980s and 1990s, one finds plenty of evidence that even the major domestic money markets are restricted and incomplete. For example, when the Irish currency and money markets were under pressure in early 1993, the government undertook a "smear" campaign against unpatriotic currency speculators, prompting one journalist to remark:

> In many ways the Department of Finance dislikes the whole idea of government instruments like gilts being the subject of grubby market trading. To them, gilts are Exchequer funding; to the brokers they are just a way to make a living, sometimes a very good one. One can imagine how the official mind feels about the national currency being treated as a kind of super bookie's shop.[29]

It should not surprise the reader to learn that Ireland, like many countries, makes it difficult for money market traders to short government securities by borrowing them under repurchase agreements.

Let us develop the conflicting interests theme with illustrations from the material presented in this chapter. The central bank is the single most important factor in most money markets, and that institution's foremost concern is usually the effectiveness of monetary control. It is no easy task to maintain price stability and to keep the path of *actual* output close to that of *potential* economic growth, and in all countries this task is made more difficult because political interest groups' desire for easy credit clashes with the central bank's obligation to keep inflation from rising. Volumes have been written about the technical implementation of monetary policy, but few would dispute the statement that if central bankers had their choice, they would prefer a simple money market with few instruments in order to maintain as tight a linkage as possible between what they can control (*high-powered money*) and liquidity available to the public. It is no surprise there-

---

[29] Brendan Keenan, "Conspiracies and That 'Blackmail,' " *Sunday Independent*, January 24, 1993, p. 16.

fore to learn that central banks' natural reaction to the introduction of any new instrument or technique is negative, if the instrument threatens to loosen the linkage between central bank credit and liquid financial resources.

Central bankers' responsibilities extend beyond price-level control. The bankers are typically charged with the prevention of widespread defaults on financial institutions and a breakdown of the banking system as a result of financial panics or liquidity crises. This explains their role as "lender of last resort." In playing this role, however, the central bank cannot easily distinguish between rescuing the financial system and rescuing individual financial institutions. All panics start with the illiquidity of one particular bank. Hence the government is obliged to monitor, regulate, and supervise individual banks, and one difference between countries is how they allocate this responsibility—whether prudential supervision is done purely by the central bank or in part by a separate agency.

Government intervention is in part a function of the fact that investors in the money market have a very low tolerance for default risk, since money market instruments are "near cash" and so problems of liquidity or repayment can have a direct effect on businesses' ability to meet payrolls and other financial commitments. Consider the ongoing official concern about the stability of the market for derivative instruments and the risks banks take in this business. Derivatives have become such an integral part of some domestic money markets that any measures taken to restrict banks' activities in derivatives will be felt by all other money market participants. Some regulations designed to reduce default risk, such as collateralization rules in Japan, conflict with the central bank's interest in having a smoothly functioning, liquid money market to fine-tune monetary policy.

All central banks are bureaucracies with their own agendas, and not simply high-minded implementors of monetary policy. They seek power and a constituency and are inclined to aggrandize their aegis while fending off blame for the inevitable mistakes that occur in such a difficult field. They seek the tools to implement policy speedily, resist "loopholes" that give investors and borrowers choices, and attribute inflation to the budget deficit rather than to monetary policy. Their power on paper may be represented by a set of laws and regulations; but knowing that it is not possible in the innovative world of finance to design rules covering all contingencies, they seek "flexibility"—meaning personal discretion—in administering the financial system. The Bank of England has long stressed that bankers in London should follow well-accepted practices of good banking (as defined by the Bank of England, of course), in addition to following the letter of the law.

The informal, personal approach to money market supervision employed by some central banks may be illustrated by an anecdote. At a dinner party, the governor of the Reserve Bank of Australia remarked to the president of the Federal Reserve Bank of San Francisco that the implementation of policy in his country was not difficult despite financial market liberalization. The governor would simply invite the heads of the five major banks for lunch and the resulting informal consensus was sufficient to determine effectively the behavior of the institutions. After a pause, the president of the San Francisco Fed replied that if he were to try this method of policy implementation, it would be necessary to throw a banquet for roughly 4,000 people, reflecting the number of independent financial institutions in the Seventh District alone.

One result of central banks' desire to exert discretionary power is that *quantitative restrictions*, such as assigned discount facilities, rather than pricing are the preferred means of exerting influence. Quotalike rules have the same economic shortcomings as do quotas in international trade, yet central banks use them in countries as disparate as Germany and Venezuela. Offering below-market rates to a chosen few at the discount window gives the central bank power over institutions while also providing the government the opportunity to steer credit toward favored purposes such as exports that generate hard currency and jobs, designated industries such as prestigious high-technology plants, and ethnic businesses. Another example: requiring mutual funds to hold government bonds may make them safer, but not coincidentally it helps finance the public debt. Similarly reserve requirements may help the central bank control the money supply, but it also happens to give that institution free deposits with which to earn a profit by investing them in interest-bearing securities.

Another result is that the *monetary* authorities in developed as well as developing countries often welcome, indeed insist upon, *supervisory* power over banks. Since bank supervision depends to a large extent on judgments about the quality of assets producing uncertain future cash flows, much discretion is given to examiners. Bankers who fear adverse judgments about their condition are much more likely to pay heed to a central bank governor's wishes than those who know that all the central bank can do is operate at arm's length in the competitive money market.

Our survey supports the notion that when central banks seek power to get banks to do something they might not otherwise do, there is a quid pro quo. Once a group of financial institutions have established themselves and adapted to a given regulatory regime, they may grumble about being hamstrung, but that does not necessarily mean that they would welcome totally free competition. New instruments and techniques tend to disturb the status quo by bringing in new competitors and exerting pressure or lending spreads. Bankers therefore often form complex alliances and find common ground with the authorities in keeping competitive threats at bay. In Germany, for example, mutual funds can only buy securities that are traded on exchanges. But money market paper does not qualify as securities, so money market mutual funds have never gotten off the ground. This pleases the Bundesbank for reasons of monetary control effectiveness as well as the banks who fear (rightly) that money market mutual funds would simply enhance competition for depositors' money. Another illustration is the Japanese money market, which is based on a segmented system of financial institutions, facilitating the ability of the government to channel capital to favored sectors of the economy.

Of course domestic financial markets do not exist in a vacuum, and external market influences among other things make financial market development a dynamic process. Financial innovations, the Eurocurrency market, and gains in transactions and communications technology have forced many countries to liberalize their domestic money markets. Nevertheless the existence of central bank and other country-specific interests, and the inherent conflicts between the varied purposes that the money market is supposed to serve, virtually guarantee continuing discrepancies and distortions in domestic money markets—the very conditions under which external markets thrive.

SELECTED REFERENCES

Deutsche Bundesbank, *Die Deutsche Bundesbank: Geldpolitische Aufgaben und Instrumente*, 5.Auflage. Sonderdrucke der Deutschen Bundesbank Nr. 7, 1990 printing.

Dufey, Gunter, "Banking in the Asia Pacific Area." In *Asia Pacific Dynamics*, R. Moxen, J.F. Truitt and T. Roehl (eds.). Greenwich, CT: JAI Press, 1983.

Emery, Robert F., *The Money Markets of Developing East Asia*. New York: Praeger, 1991.

Euromoney, *The 1992 Guide to European Money Markets*, Supplement to *Euromoney*, September 1992.

Federal Reserve Bank of Richmond, *Instruments of the Money Market*, updated periodically.

Frankel, Allen B., and Paul B. Morgan, "A Primer on the Japanese Banking System," International Finance Discussion Paper No. 419, Board of Governors of the Federal Reserve System, Washington, D.C., December 1991.

Fujii, Tomoko, "A Primer on Yen Fixed-Income Markets." Tokyo: Salomon Brothers, June 1992.

Herrmann, Armin, *Die Geldmarktgeschäfte*. Frankfurt: Fritz Knapp Verlag, 1980.

Howard, Donna, "The Evolution of Routine Bank of Canada Advances to Direct Clearers," *Bank of Canada Review*, October 1992, pp. 3–22.

Issing, Otmar, *Einführung in die Geldpolitik*, 4.Auflage. Munich: Verlag Vahlen, 1992.

Japan Securities Research Institute, *Capital Markets and Financial Services in Japan: Regulation and Practice*. Tokyo: Japan Securities Research Institute, 1992.

Jochimsen, Reimut, "Der deutsche Geldmarkt im Wandel der Zeit," Deutsche Bundesbank, Frankfurt a.M., *Auszüge aus Presseartikeln*. June 1992.

Keenan, Brendan, "Conspiracies and that 'Blackmail', " *Sunday Independent*, January 24, 1993, p. 16.

Marchant, Peter, "Canadian Commercial Paper," in Guide to International Commercial Paper, *Euromoney Corporate Finance*, Supplement, January 1993.

"Off the Mark," *Risk*, Vol. 5, No. 7, July–August 1992.

Prindl, Adreas R., *Japanese Finance: A Guide to Banking in Japan*. New York: John Wiley and Sons, 1981.

Pugh, D. Graham, "The When-Issued Market for Government of Canada Treasury Bills: A Technical Note," *Bank of Canada Review*, November 1992, pp. 4–22.

RBC Dominion Securities, "A Guide to the Money Market in Canada."

Rosenbluth, Frances McCall, *Financial Politics in Contemporary Japan*. Ithaca, NY: Studies of the East Asian Institute, Cornell University Press, 1989.

Schaede, Ulrike, "The Introduction of Commercial Paper (CP): A Case Study in the Liberalization of the Japanese Financial Market," Center for Japanese Studies Occasional Papers. Marburg, Germany: Philipps-Universität Marburg, 1988.

Skully, Michael T., ed., *Financial Institutions and Markets in Southeast Asia*. New York: St. Martin's Press, 1989.

Staley, Sally J., *International Bond Manual: Japanese Yen*, 2nd ed. New York: Salomon Brothers, 1984.

Stigum, Marcia. *The Money Market*, 3rd ed. Homewood: Dow-Jones-Irwin, 1990.

Takeda, Masahiko and Philip Turner, "The Liberalisation of Japan's Financial Markets: Some Major Themes," *BIS Economic Papers*, No. 34, pp. 99-121. Basle: Bank for International Settlements, November 1992.

Wilson, J.S.G., *The London Money Markets*, SUERF Papers on Monetary Policy and Financial Systems. Tilburg: S.U.E.R.F., 1989.

Yamamoto, Kenzo, *Capital Markets and Financial Services in Japan: Regulation and Practice*. Tokyo: Japan Securities Research Institute, 1992.

Chapter Three

EUROCURRENCY INTEREST RATES*

THE TWO KINDS OF RATE LINKAGES

This chapter attempts to provide two things essential to an understanding of international interest rates: first, an analysis that identifies and integrates the determinants of Eurocurrency interest rates, and second, a framework that enables the borrower or lender of funds (a) to compare interest rates in the domestic and external money markets and (b) in the external markets themselves to compare interest rates on funds denominated in dollars, French francs, German marks, and so forth.

---

*A version of his chapter appears in *Global Financial Markets* by Ian H. Giddy (D.C. Heath, 1994).

The theme of the chapter is simply that *there are close interdependencies between national and Eurocurrency interest rates, between interest rates in different currencies, and between the spot and forward exchange markets that link those currencies.*[1] By identifying these linkages we hope to avoid the misunderstandings that arise from viewing the Eurodollar market in isolation rather than in relation to competing domestic and foreign currency credit markets and the foreign exchange markets.

This chapter provides the framework and mechanics of Eurocurrency rate linkages. The chapter is concerned with interest rate relationships of two types:[2]

1. Competition between the domestic and external credit markets in a particular currency

2. Competition between pairs of external markets for credit denominated in different currencies

In dealing with these and related questions, we rely on the **efficient markets** argument: that competition will tend to equalize expected rates of return on similar securities and that effective interest-rate differentials will persist only if the securities possess different risk attributes or if barriers such as capital controls prevent arbitrage between two markets. In the first three sections, therefore, we argue that there is nothing particularly special about the Eurocurrency markets and that, other things being equal, one would expect arbitrage to ensure equality between bank interest rates in the domestic and external markets. We then show why Eurobanks tend to offer more attractive loan and deposit rates than do domestic institutions, and how arbitrage between internal and external markets may be inhibited by controls on international capital flows or other market imperfections.

---

[1] The U.S. dollar and German mark portions of the Eurocurrency markets will be the focus of discussion partly because the bulk of Eurocurrency transactions occur in dollars and marks, but primarily for convenience of exposition. For the most part, however, that which holds for the relationship between, say, the U.S. and Eurodollar markets also holds in principle for the Swiss national market and the EuroSwiss franc market, the British money market and the Eurosterling market, and so forth.

[2] Another factor affecting interest rate linkages is transaction costs. These are accounted for in the appendix, where we derive the "arbitrage tunnel." For the purpose of establishing the basic linkages in the chapter, however, such costs are unimportant. In covered interest arbitrage, for example, the total transactions costs have been estimated to be 0.15 percent or less. See Jacob A. Frenkel and Richard M. Levich, "Covered Interest Arbitrage: Unexploited Profits?" *Journal of Political Economy*, April 1975, pp. 325–338.

Arbitrage between deposits in the same Eurobanking center, but denominated in different currencies, is not subject to capital controls. Hence interest rates differ only because of expected exchange rate changes. If exchange rates were fixed, rates on different Eurocurrencies would be identical. In a later section, we employ this notion to show how Eurocurrency interest rate differentials adjust so as to equal the expected rate of change of the exchange rate, which in turn equals the forward exchange premium or discount. We also show how this relationship is consistent with the interest rate parity theorem, which says that arbitrage ensures equality between interest rate differentials and the forward premium or discount.

These concepts are taken a step farther in a section that describes the relationship between Eurocurrency yield curves and the expected path of future exchange rates. A more formal statement of this relationship may be found in the appendix. This chapter ends with a look at the term structure of Eurocurrency interest rates—rates at different maturities. In the next chapter we show how the Eurocurrency market's range of instruments is effectively broadened through links to the futures markets—both interest rate and currency futures—and other Eurodollar hedging and positioning instruments.

The focus of this section and the next will be the nature of the competition and arbitrage between each national money market (such as the New York market) and the corresponding external market (such as the dollar-denominated portion of the Eurocurrency market).

COMPETING INTERNAL AND EXTERNAL CREDIT MARKETS

Sherlock Holmes always liked to visit the scene of the crime; Nero Wolfe preferred to stay at home and think about it. Our wish is that each one of our readers visit a trading room to see the real thing; but for the orchid-tenders and for those who have seen enough of it, the next best thing is to read the newspaper.

When it comes to international finance, America is a backward country, and as of 1993, its major financial papers still did not print a full range of Eurocurrency interest rates. As may be seen in Figure 3-1, only Euro*dollar* rates can be found in the "Money Rates" section of a financial newspaper. To make the best of it, however, the numbers do provide good evidence of the relationship between interest rates on different instruments in the dollar money market. In particular, observe where Eurodollar rates lie in relation to domestic CD and Treasury bill rates. One may also see a widening of the bid-offer spreads in the longer, more thinly traded, maturities.

Figure 3-2 provides a better picture of the Eurocurrency market as a whole. In papers such as the London *Financial Times* and the *International Herald Tribune* one finds data on Eurorates for deposits in a number of Eurocurrencies. Observe the differences between currencies: in rate levels,

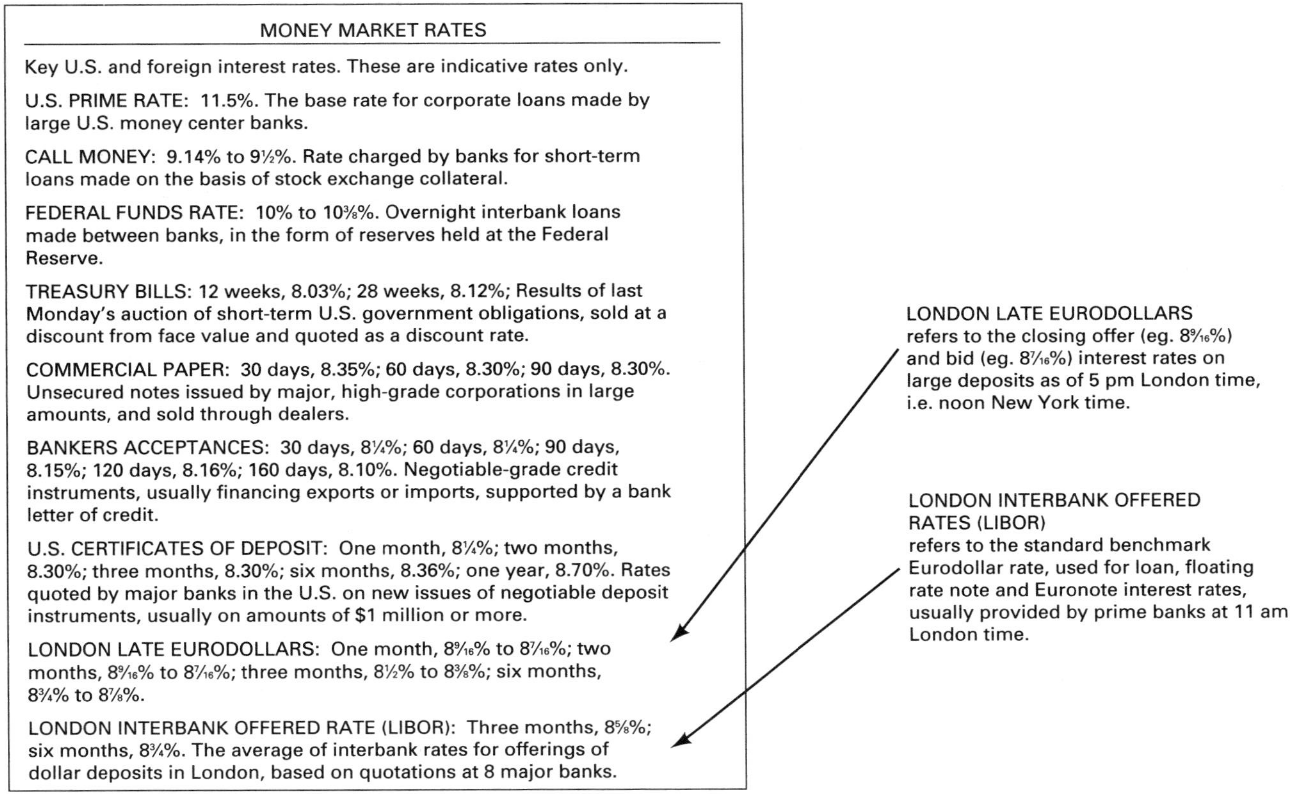

MONEY MARKET RATES

Key U.S. and foreign interest rates. These are indicative rates only.

U.S. PRIME RATE: 11.5%. The base rate for corporate loans made by large U.S. money center banks.

CALL MONEY: 9.14% to $9\frac{1}{2}$%. Rate charged by banks for short-term loans made on the basis of stock exchange collateral.

FEDERAL FUNDS RATE: 10% to $10\frac{3}{8}$%. Overnight interbank loans made between banks, in the form of reserves held at the Federal Reserve.

TREASURY BILLS: 12 weeks, 8.03%; 28 weeks, 8.12%; Results of last Monday's auction of short-term U.S. government obligations, sold at a discount from face value and quoted as a discount rate.

COMMERCIAL PAPER: 30 days, 8.35%; 60 days, 8.30%; 90 days, 8.30%. Unsecured notes issued by major, high-grade corporations in large amounts, and sold through dealers.

BANKERS ACCEPTANCES: 30 days, $8\frac{1}{4}$%; 60 days, $8\frac{1}{4}$%; 90 days, 8.15%; 120 days, 8.16%; 160 days, 8.10%. Negotiable-grade credit instruments, usually financing exports or imports, supported by a bank letter of credit.

U.S. CERTIFICATES OF DEPOSIT: One month, $8\frac{1}{4}$%; two months, 8.30%; three months, 8.30%; six months, 8.36%; one year, 8.70%. Rates quoted by major banks in the U.S. on new issues of negotiable deposit instruments, usually on amounts of $1 million or more.

LONDON LATE EURODOLLARS: One month, $8\frac{9}{16}$% to $8\frac{7}{16}$%; two months, $8\frac{9}{16}$% to $8\frac{7}{16}$%; three months, $8\frac{1}{2}$% to $8\frac{3}{8}$%; six months, $8\frac{3}{4}$% to $8\frac{7}{8}$%.

LONDON INTERBANK OFFERED RATE (LIBOR): Three months, $8\frac{5}{8}$%; six months, $8\frac{3}{4}$%. The average of interbank rates for offerings of dollar deposits in London, based on quotations at 8 major banks.

LONDON LATE EURODOLLARS
refers to the closing offer (eg. 8 9/16%) and bid (eg. 8 7/16%) interest rates on large deposits as of 5 pm London time, i.e. noon New York time.
LONDON INTERBANK OFFERED RATES (LIBOR)
refers to the standard benchmark Eurodollar rate, used for loan, floating rate note and Euronote interest rates, usually provided by prime banks at 11 am London time.

FIGURE 3-1. Eurodollar and U.S. Money Market Rates. Arbitrage ensures a close linkage between the Federal funds rate, the domestic CD rate, and the Eurodollar rate.

Nov 21	Short term	7 Days notice	One Month	Three Months	Six Months	One Year
Sterling	15–$14\frac{7}{8}$	15–$14\frac{7}{8}$	$15\frac{1}{8}$–$15\frac{1}{16}$	$15\frac{3}{16}$–$15\frac{1}{16}$	$15\frac{1}{16}$–15	$14\frac{3}{4}$–$14\frac{5}{8}$
U.S. Dollar	$8\frac{1}{2}$–$8\frac{3}{8}$	$8\frac{1}{2}$–$8\frac{3}{8}$	$8\frac{1}{2}$–$8\frac{3}{8}$	$8\frac{1}{2}$–$8\frac{3}{8}$	$8\frac{8}{16}$–$8\frac{3}{16}$	$8\frac{5}{16}$–$8\frac{3}{16}$
Can. Dollar	12–$11\frac{3}{4}$	$12\frac{1}{8}$–$11\frac{7}{8}$	$12\frac{1}{8}$–$11\frac{7}{8}$	$12\frac{1}{8}$–$11\frac{7}{8}$	12–$11\frac{3}{4}$	$11\frac{13}{16}$–$11\frac{9}{16}$
D. Guilder	$8\frac{3}{16}$–$8\frac{3}{16}$	$8\frac{3}{16}$–$8\frac{3}{16}$	$8\frac{3}{8}$–$8\frac{1}{4}$	$8\frac{7}{16}$–$8\frac{5}{16}$	$8\frac{1}{2}$–$8\frac{3}{8}$	$8\frac{1}{2}$–$8\frac{3}{8}$
Sw. Franc	$6\frac{3}{4}$–$6\frac{1}{2}$	$7\frac{1}{4}$–$6\frac{15}{16}$	$7\frac{7}{16}$–$6\frac{15}{16}$	$7\frac{15}{16}$–$7\frac{13}{16}$	$7\frac{15}{16}$–$7\frac{13}{16}$	$7\frac{7}{8}$–$7\frac{3}{4}$
Deutschmark	$7\frac{9}{16}$–$7\frac{7}{16}$	$7\frac{5}{8}$–$7\frac{1}{2}$	$7\frac{7}{8}$–$7\frac{3}{4}$	$8\frac{1}{4}$–$8\frac{1}{8}$	$8\frac{3}{8}$–$8\frac{1}{4}$	$8\frac{7}{16}$–$8\frac{3}{16}$
Fr. Franc	$10\frac{5}{16}$–$10\frac{3}{16}$	$10\frac{5}{8}$–$10\frac{3}{4}$	$10\frac{7}{4}$–$10\frac{3}{4}$	$10\frac{5}{8}$–$10\frac{1}{2}$	$10\frac{5}{8}$–$10\frac{1}{2}$	$10\frac{9}{16}$–$10\frac{7}{16}$
Italian Lira	12–10	$13\frac{1}{4}$–$12\frac{1}{4}$	$12\frac{7}{8}$–$12\frac{3}{8}$	$12\frac{7}{8}$–$12\frac{3}{8}$	$12\frac{7}{8}$–$12\frac{1}{2}$	13–$12\frac{5}{8}$
B. Fr. (Fin)	$9\frac{9}{16}$–$9\frac{7}{16}$	$9\frac{13}{16}$–$9\frac{11}{16}$	$9\frac{15}{16}$–$9\frac{13}{16}$	$9\frac{15}{16}$–$9\frac{13}{16}$	$9\frac{7}{8}$–$9\frac{3}{4}$	$9\frac{13}{16}$–$9\frac{11}{16}$
B. Fr. (Con)	$9\frac{5}{8}$–$9\frac{1}{4}$	$9\frac{3}{4}$–$9\frac{3}{8}$	$9\frac{7}{8}$–$9\frac{1}{2}$	10–$9\frac{5}{8}$	10–$9\frac{5}{8}$	$9\frac{7}{8}$–$9\frac{1}{2}$
Yen	$6\frac{1}{4}$–$6\frac{1}{8}$	$6\frac{3}{8}$–$6\frac{1}{4}$	$6\frac{7}{16}$–$6\frac{3}{16}$	$6\frac{13}{16}$–$6\frac{11}{16}$	$6\frac{13}{16}$–$6\frac{11}{16}$	$6\frac{13}{16}$–$6\frac{11}{16}$
D. Krone	$11\frac{1}{16}$–11	$12\frac{9}{16}$–$12\frac{3}{16}$	$12\frac{1}{2}$–$12\frac{3}{8}$	$12\frac{3}{8}$–$12\frac{3}{16}$	$11\frac{3}{4}$–$11\frac{9}{16}$	$11\frac{5}{8}$–$11\frac{3}{8}$
Asian $Sing	$8\frac{1}{2}$–$8\frac{3}{8}$	$8\frac{9}{16}$–$8\frac{7}{16}$	$8\frac{9}{16}$–$8\frac{7}{16}$	$8\frac{9}{16}$–$8\frac{7}{16}$	$8\frac{8}{16}$–$8\frac{3}{16}$	$8\frac{1}{4}$–$8\frac{1}{8}$

Long term Eurodollars: two years $8\frac{3}{8}$–$8\frac{1}{4}$ percent; three years $8\frac{1}{2}$–$8\frac{3}{8}$ percent; four years $8\frac{9}{16}$–$8\frac{7}{16}$ percent; five years $8\frac{5}{8}$–$8\frac{1}{2}$ percent nominal. Short term rates are call for U.S. dollars and Japanese yen; others, two days' notice.

FIGURE 3-2. Eurocurrency Interest Rates. In international financial centers such as London, Geneva, and Hong Kong, banks readily quote interest rates on deposits denominated in different currencies.

in bid-offer spreads, and across maturities. Banks in London also offer daily quotations for deposits in "currency baskets," such as the SDR (special drawing right) and ECU (European currency unit).

From Chapter One we have seen that U.S. and Eurodollar banking is similar in most respects. The currency of denomination is the same; the banks doing business are the same; and the terms and conditions of the instruments are almost identical. The *only* thing that differentiates Eurodollar from domestic banking, then, is the fact that they take place in *different locations* with correspondingly different regulations and, perhaps, different risks arising from the jurisdictions in which the units operate.

The answers to issues concerning onshore-offshore rate relationships are consistent with the view of the Eurodollar market expressed in Chapter One—that it can be regarded as simply a segment of the larger market for dollar-denominated deposits and loans. Three questions about relative rates may be raised; the answers lead to a picture of the Eurodollar market like that in Figure 3-3.

1. Which Market Dominates?

Because the total market for short-term assets and liabilities in the United States is large and resilient, rates in any smaller, competing market tend to be dominated by U.S. rates on both the deposit and the loan sides of the market. Thus we have chosen to draw Figure 3-3 under the assumption that

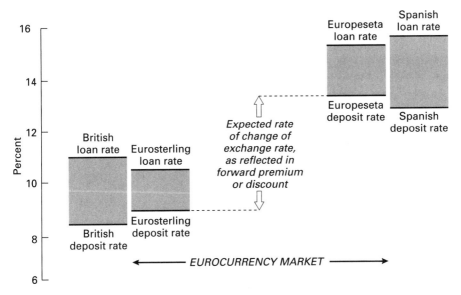

FIGURE 3-3. A Schematic of the Eurodollar Market. This schematic helps visualize the boundaries within which Eurodollar rates normally fluctuate.

Eurodollar rates are constrained by U.S. rates, and not vice versa (although we defer the difficult question of the direction of causality to Chapter Five).

2. What Is the Relationship Between Eurodollar and U.S. Deposit Rates?

Briefly, Eurodollar deposits must normally pay at least as high a rate as in the United States. Otherwise, why would depositors entrust their dollar-denominated time deposit to financial institutions outside the United States instead of a bank in the United States?

Although familiarity, similar business hours, and in special circumstances the desire for political anonymity may occasionally account for such deposits being offered to financial institutions outside the United States, in the vast majority of cases Eurobanks could not offer lower deposit rates than are offered by U.S. banks without losing the deposit. In other words, the supply of deposits to Eurobanks becomes infinitely elastic at the U.S. deposit rate. This is illustrated in Figure 3-3.

3. How Are Eurodollar and U.S. Lending Rates Linked?

Similar considerations apply. Since borrowers consider a loan from a U.S. bank to be as good as, if not better than, a loan from a Eurobank, foreign institutions can compete successfully only if they offer loan rates that are no higher than the effective rates charged by U.S. banks. Factors such as familiarity, business hours, and communications may again play a role. But in a world of sizable transactions (seldom in units of less than $5 million), where the transactors are large banks, public entities, and corporations that have resident operations in many countries, modern communications technology makes the impact of such factors minimal. Figure 3-3 shows how the demand for Eurodollar loans becomes infinitely elastic at the U.S. loan rate, thus serving as an upper boundary for the movement of the Eurodollar loan rate.

These constraints establish rough boundaries for Eurodollar interest rates.

THE BEHAVIOR OF EURODOLLAR INTEREST RATES

Do Eurodollar interest rates in fact differ significantly from domestic rates? And if so, why?

On the lending side, Eurodollar interest rates at one time had to be noticeably below their domestic counterparts, prime rate loans, to attract borrowers away from their domestic banking relationships. As corporations' knowledge of available alternatives grew during the 1970s, however, they began to realize that a dollar is a dollar wherever you get it, so why not take the cheapest loan you can get? Domestic loan practice began to incorporate the Euromarket principles of roll-over, cost-plus pricing—and both markets were influenced by the fact that the best borrowers had the alternative of borrowing directly, by issuing short-term commercial paper.

Hard evidence to back up the previous statement is scanty. As is observed in the accompanying box, effective loan rates are difficult to pin down; loan rates include a premium for the risk specific to a borrower, and bankers are creative people when it comes to disguising the true cost of funds, through various fees and (sometimes) compensating balance requirements. Nevertheless, it is safe to say that today the effective rates on a U.S. loan are seldom much above what the same borrower would pay for a Eurodollar loan. As a practical matter, the cost of commercial paper issued by U.S. corporations, plus the cost of maintaining lines of credit to back up the paper, may be the best proxy for the U.S. lending rate. It has the advantage of being objective, although at times, it may deviate from the loan rates because the commercial paper market becomes very thin in periods when corporate liquidity becomes a major concern of investors. We shall return to Eurodollar loan pricing practices in Chapter Five.

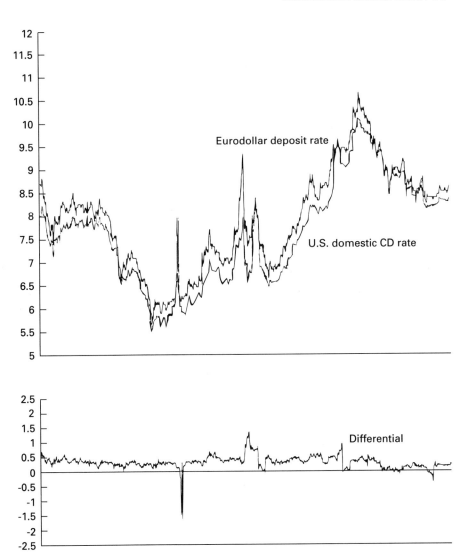

FIGURE 3-4. Plot of Eurodollar and U.S. Bank Deposit Rates, April 1985–1990. Eurodollar rates track domestic rates very closely, but risk and cost factors ensure that a differential remains.

Interest rates on Eurodollar *deposits*, in contrast, do exceed those on domestic bank deposits by a substantial and persistent margin. This is shown vividly in Figure 3-4, which traces 3-month Eurodollar deposit rates and 90-day domestic certificate of deposit (CD) rates over a typical 2-year period.[3] The raw differential is shown at the bottom of the chart; it averages about 1 percent per annum. Why?

A clue to the answer lies in the supply and demand approach taken in Chapter Two and illustrated in a simplified manner in Figure 3-5. According to this framework, the supply and demand curves intersect at the point at which both Eurodollar depositors and Eurobanks are satisfied with the interest rate paid on that particular quantity of deposits. In other words, it is *supply and demand*, both of which are directly competitive with the domestic money market, that determine the size of the Eurodollar market and the premium of Eurodollar deposits. The premium is one that represents both risk and relative cost; it is high enough to induce depositors to willingly hold some of their funds in Eurobanks, and it is low enough to persuade banks to obtain funds in the Euromarket instead of the domestic market.

But look again at Figure 3-4. Isn't the depositors' supply curve much more elastic (flat) than depicted at the point of intersection? Yes, say some. Or, instead, perhaps the Eurobanks' demand curve is much more elastic. Yes, say others. Put differently: What is the dominant influence on the "Eurodollar premium"? Relative risk (to depositors) or relative cost (to banks)?

According to the **market-price-of-risk view**, the Eurodollar deposit rate should lie above the domestic rate at a level given by the risk premium demanded by depositors. Since depositors can readily arbitrage between domestic and offshore assets of equivalent risk, the Eurodollar premium should be determined *only* by relative risks. Because people will not hold a risky instrument if they can purchase a less risky one bearing the same return, the yields on risky assets will be driven up, and the yields on safe assets will be driven down, until there is a well-defined hierarchy of risks and returns. The additional yield required for an additional unit of risk is the market price of risk.[4]

Presumably, depositors would be indifferent between holding domestic deposits at the U.S. deposit rate and holding Eurodeposits at the U.S. rate plus the market risk premium. At this level depositors' supply of funds to

---

[3] It is frequently supposed that the absence of taxes plays a role in depositors' choice of an offshore deposit. This is usually true only for those seeking to *evade* taxes through anonymity. Otherwise, U.S. residents are subject to income tax on both domestic and offshore interest, and nonresidents are not subject to withholding tax on either kind of bank deposit. For more on the tax aspects of Eurodollars, see Chapter Six.

[4] Precisely how the market defines and measures price risk is another issue. Adherents of the market price of risk theory would tend toward the theory that investors have a range of assets and asset combinations to choose from, and that the special risk of Eurodollar deposits is that component of risk that one cannot diversify away by holding Eurodeposits in combination with other assets.

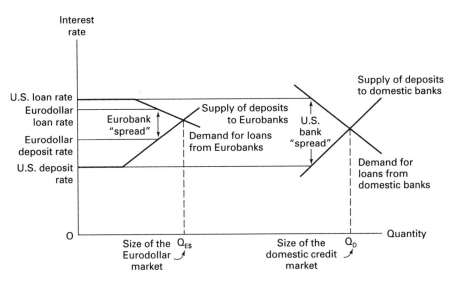

FIGURE 3-5. Eurodollar Supply and Demand. Contrast the market-price-of-risk approach (the Eurodollar rate is higher because depositors perceive additional risk) with the cost-of-regulation approach.

the Eurodollar market would become infinitely elastic. The interpretation of Figure 3-3 would then be that depositors' risk aversion determines the size of the interest differential, and, for a given risk level, a shift in the banks' demand for funds can increase the market's size but not drive rates up.

The other extreme is the **cost-of-regulation view**, which says that the Eurodollar premium is purely and solely determined by the regulatory costs, such as taxes and reserve requirements, of offering domestic rather than offshore deposits. Banks, in this view, are indifferent between obtaining funds in the United States, Nassau, or other Eurobanking centers, except for the regulatory cost differential, which is primarily the cost of holding noninterest-bearing reserve requirements. Banks will shift all their funding offshore if the cost of deposits is lower in the Euromarket than in the domestic market (after adjusting for reserve requirements), and vice versa.

If this cost is X percent and if the U.S. and Eurodollar interest rates are I_{US} and $I_{E\$}$ respectively, then banks would be indifferent between obtaining funds in the Eurodollar market at $I_{E\$}$ and borrowing in the United States at an effective cost of $I_{US} + X$.

The logical implication of this view is that changes in risk perception, familiarity with the market, and other factors will not change the Eurodollar premium. No matter how much, or how little, depositors are prepared to offer at various interest rates, they always get the same rate relative to the U.S. rate. Conclusion? The Eurodollar premium is bank determined, and

LIBOR AND FAMILY

There is no such thing as "the" Eurodollar interest rate. As in any banking market, every transaction involves a newly-made deal, and the agreed-upon rate will depend on the amount lent or deposited, the credit standing of the borrower, the bargaining strength of the parties, and other details of the transaction. By far the most active segment of the Euromarket is the interbank deposit market, centered in London. From this market comes the best-known of Eurodollar rates, the London interbank offer rate (LIBOR). LIBOR has become the fundamental base rate on which actual charges for all but interbank borrowers—the wholesale market—are computed. In the typical corporate loan agreement, this is specified as the arithmetic average of the rates at which six major institutions in London would be willing to deposit dollar funds in or lend to each other at a certain time during the morning. The actual charge to the final borrower would then be fixed at a certain contractually-determined spread above LIBOR. This spread might range anywhere from $1/_4$ of 1 percent to 3 percent and more, depending on the borrower, general market conditions, the maturity, and other factors.

From a borrower's point of view, then, LIBOR plus the appropriate spread represents the effective lending rate, after special conditions of the loan agreement have been factored in, although Eurodollar loans generally tend to be rather straightforward. LIBOR's sister, LIBID, is the corresponding borrowing or bid rate quoted by major banks in London. It is the rate at which they stand ready to accept deposits in large amounts at standard maturities.

During normal times these siblings, the Eurodollar interbank bid and offer rates, seldom separate by more than about $1/_8$ of 1 percent. It is often supposed that this bid-offer spread represents the "transactions cost" of Eurodollar dealing. That this is not so is evident from the fact that any pair of banks that actually engage in a transaction must agree on a rate—which could be the prevailing bid, or the offer (or another rate altogether), but not both! The spread indicates the difference between rates at which banks are willing to "make a market," but nobody actually pays that spread unless he is foolish enough to deposit in Bank X at Bank X's bid rate and simultaneously borrow from the same bank at its offer rate.

LIBOR's American cousins, the most notorious of which is the U.S. prime rate, are equally elusive. In fact, prime's days are numbered—hardly any midsize or large corporation borrows at prime today; many loans are priced at a rate linked to some money market yield, such as the (reserve adjusted) CD rate, the Federal funds rate, or the commercial paper index.

(for a given cost differential) the Eurodollar market's size is depositor determined.

While the market-price-of-risk approach is more solidly grounded in modern asset-pricing theory, the cost-of-regulation view has the support of many observers of the market. Arbitrage seems to be undertaken much more rapidly and in much larger amounts by banks than by individuals, governments, or even corporate depositors. Eurocurrency traders act on the presumption that the Eurodeposit rate differs from the domestic rate almost entirely because of the cost of reserve requirements.

A simple empirical test of these models suggests itself. If the cost-of-regulation theory were correct, then changes in the U.S.-Eurodollar interest rate gap should be a function *only* of changes in the relative costs of borrowing onshore and offshore. Among the various additional costs of funding through domestic deposits are:

1. Reserve requirements
2. Federal Deposit Insurance Corporation fees
3. State and local taxes

Of these, reserve requirements are by far the most important. They are also the most varied, since the effective cost of holding interest-free reserves changes with the opportunity cost of the funds, while FDIC fees and taxes are relatively stable.

Figure 3-6 plots the differential between the Eurodollar and domestic CD bid rates, adjusted for the estimated cost of reserve requirements and Federal Deposit Insurance Corporation fees. As an example of the calculation, say that a U.S. bank receives $100 in domestic deposits and the reserve requirement is 5 percent. The *effective funds received* amount to only $95. But the bank must pay an interest rate of, for example, 15 percent on the full $100 plus estimated FDIC fees and additional taxes. Ignoring difficult-to-measure state and local taxes, the *effective cost of funds* to the bank is therefore as follows:

$$\text{Effective cost of domestic deposit} = \frac{\text{Interest rate} + \text{FDIC fees}}{1 - \text{Reserve requirement}}$$
$$= \frac{15\% + 1/12\%}{1 - 0.05}$$
$$= 15.88\%$$

Thus the additional cost of the reserve requirements is 88 basis points— and this is the extra amount the bank can afford to pay on Eurodollar deposits to achieve the same cost of funds.

If the cost of regulation theory were absolutely correct, and our measurements were free of error, then the adjusted differential would be zero.

In fact, in Figure 3-6, the differential wiggles closely around the zero line for much of the time, suggesting that the Eurodollar premium is dominated, at least in normal times, by the relative costs of regulation. On the other hand, the same chart manifests significant deviations from zero during certain periods. What explains them? In the past, capital controls have inhibited arbitrage. The U.S. capital controls of 1963–1973 produced a positive adjusted gap in 1972 and 1974. The adjusted Euro/domestic differential rose above zero again in 1974–1975, but for a different reason: the perceived risk of Eurodollars rose following the failure of Germany's Herstatt Bank and other international banking problems during that period. Similar concerns were present in the years 1979 to 1983, following the global recession and collapse of commodity prices, and again in the late 1980s as the country debt burden took its toll. In the early 1990s, egregious circumvention of laws and regulations by BCCI, a bank with its headquarters in Luxembourg, shook the financial community.

These examples verify the fact that bank regulatory costs alone are insufficient to explain fully the Eurodollar premium. Although relative costs of regulation dominate the Euro/domestic differential, there are times when the risk premium demanded by depositors rises above the cost differential.

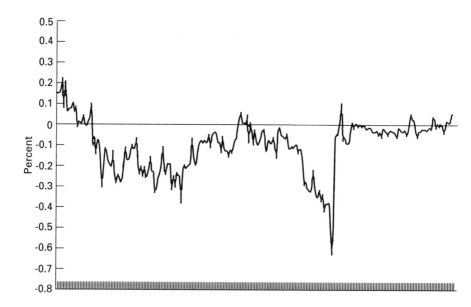

FIGURE 3-6. Eurodollar and Adjusted Domestic CD Rates, April 1989–1990. The effective cost of domestic funds is found by adjusting for regulatory costs: cost = (CD rate + FDIC fees)/(1 - Reserve requirement).

Another way to look at this issue is to consider the difference between the overnight Eurodollar deposit rate and the overnight Federal funds rate. Banks in America regard these two sources of very-short-term funds as virtually interchangeable, since Federal funds are interbank loans and as such not subject to reserve requirements or deposit insurance assessments. (The reasoning is that these regulatory costs were incurred by the first bank that obtained deposits from the public and should not be reimposed when the funds are re-lent in the interbank market.) The bank placing the funds will, of course, do so only at a rate sufficient to recoup the reserve requirement and other costs; hence the Fed funds rate already reflects these regulatory costs. Thus the cost-of-regulation theory would predict that the raw difference between the overnight Eurorates and the Fed funds rate would be approximately zero.

Hence under normal market conditions, both domestic interbank placements and Eurodeposits are exempted from reserve requirements and therefore bear interest rates that exceed the domestic nonbank deposit rate by an amount equal to the relative costs of regulation.

Figure 3-6 bears out this prediction—on average. Once again we find deviations, some of which persist as is shown by the dotted line tracing the 6-month moving average of the rate differential. The persistent deviations above the zero line are attributable to the same factors as in the 3-month market: capital controls in 1972–1973 and international banking risk in the 1974–1975 period. The striking feature of the latter period, however, is not the average so much as the angry volatility of the rate gap and the subsequent pacification of fluctuations. The reason for this probably lies in the penalties imposed by the U.S. government on the use of "managed liabilities" during the high inflation days of 1979–1980 and the inhibitions this created to arbitrage between the two markets.

To sum up, Figure 3-6 confirms the theory that the relative costs of regulation dominate arbitrage between the domestic and offshore markets, except when unusual risks or exchange controls inhibit such arbitrage. We shall return to onshore-offshore arbitrage links in the appendix; meanwhile let us continue to explore the basic framework of how Eurocurrency interest rates are linked—and how, sometimes, they can be uncoupled from their domestic engines.

Three factors producing such uncoupling—capital controls, risk differences, and market imperfections—are discussed in the next section.

CAPITAL CONTROLS AND DIVIDED CREDIT MARKETS

The essence of the Eurodollar market is external financial intermediation: financial institutions (Eurobanks) outside the U.S. banking system compete for dollar-denominated deposits and dollar-denominated loans.

For depositors and borrowers who reside outside the United States, the choice between the domestic U.S. market and the external dollar market involves a choice of jurisdiction governing the transaction and its attendant obligations. Even when foreigners contract with Eurobanks within their own jurisdiction—for example, a Swiss corporation obtaining a Eurodollar loan from a Swiss bank—an international financial transaction occurs: the borrower receives the loan proceeds in New York because only the U.S. banking system offers dollars as means of payments. Thus all such transactions are, legally, international transactions, as they involve either the extension of credit or the effecting of a payment in a foreign jurisdiction.[5] Similarly, for a U.S. resident, every Eurodollar transaction involves an international credit transaction.

Legal restrictions on international transactions come in many different forms, shapes, and sizes.[6] But they all have the same effect on the relationship between internal (domestic) and external (Euro-) markets: they cut the external market off from its internal base. Such controls, to the extent that they are effective, insulate a particular Eurocurrency market from the influence of domestic credit conditions, making exchange rate expectations in conjunction with foreign credit conditions the essential determinants of the currency's Eurorates.

Let us take a closer look at this relationship. We have seen that in the absence of tight controls on international financial transactions, there will be arbitrage between the external and internal segments of the market for dollar credit. This keeps Eurodollar lending and deposit rates within a margin determined by effective domestic lending rates (the upper limit) and domestic deposit rates (the lower limit). History provides illustrations of the impact of controls on this relationship in the case of U.S. domestic rates and Eurodollar rates as well as other markets.

Beginning in 1965 the United States imposed a series of restrictions

---

[5] From the perspective of economic analysis, however, not all Eurodollar transactions involve international capital flows. To illustrate, funds deposited in a Eurobank by a U.S. resident may simply be loaned to another U.S. resident. This round trip of funds through external intermediaries instead of domestic institutions does not involve any of the effects that are germane to international capital flows, such as changes in the monetary base, domestic liquidity, and credit conditions.

[6] For details, see Michael R. Rosenberg, "Foreign Exchange Controls: An International Comparison," in Abraham George and Ian Giddy, eds., *International Finance Handbook*, Volume 1 (New York: John Wiley & Sons, 1983); David T. Llewellyn, "How to Control Capital Flows?" *The Banker*, July 1973, pp. 764–768; Rodney H. Mills, Jr., "Regulations on Short-Term Capital Movements: Recent Techniques in Selected Industrial Countries," *Federal Reserve Board Discussion Paper* (Washington, D.C., November 6, 1972); and Organization for Economic Cooperation and Development, *Regulations Affecting International Banking Operations* (Paris: OECD, 1981).

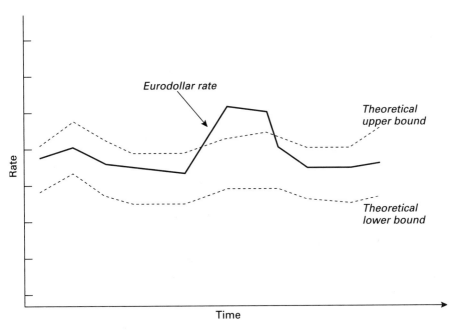

FIGURE 3-7. Breaking the Bounds. U.S. capital outflow controls allowed Eurodollar lending rates to move above the theoretical limit set by the U.S. lending rate.

intended to protect and restrict capital outflows.[7] In combination, these measures effectively narrowed the most important channels of arbitrage between the external and internal markets, although the effectiveness of the controls varied as loopholes were discovered—through transactions involving Canadian entities, private noncorporate deposits, and transactions between quarterly reporting periods—and as a consequence of numerous modifications in the programs and their administration.

Figure 3-7 shows that even Eurodollar lending rates could, and actually did, move above the theoretical limit set by the effective U.S. lending rate.

---

[7] The Foreign Direct Investment Regulations, made mandatory in 1965 and abolished in later January 1974, in effect compelled U.S.-based multinational corporations to finance additional overseas operations with funds raised outside the United States. Partial repatriation of earnings achieved in certain developed countries and strict limitations on working capital positions held abroad complemented these provisions. At the same time, banks and financial institutions in the United States were prevented by the Voluntary Foreign Credit Restraint Program from increasing the level of loans to foreign entities. Finally, the Interest Equalization Tax effectively discouraged most foreign borrowers from raising funds in the United States through the issue of securities.

And when the regulations were abolished, the rates moved promptly within the expected range. Indeed, as our data suggest, this happened several months prior to the actual removal of the controls at the end of January 1974, reflecting the market's correct anticipation of the controls' removal.

In a similar fashion, controls limiting depositor arbitrage may cause rates in the external market to fall below corresponding domestic deposit rates, when effective capital controls prevent an inflow of funds. Germany and Switzerland are cases in point. Both countries at various times during the 1970s imposed controls on the inflow of foreign funds, promptly causing the external deposit rate to fall below the equivalent domestic deposit rate, which would otherwise represent an effective "floor" for the EuroSwiss franc or EuroGerman mark rate. The German example (Figure 3-8) provides a particularly good illustration because the program, while varying in intensity, was at times very effective, and the extent of controls shows up clearly in the difference between internal and external rates. Indeed, substantial differences between domestic and external interest rates can usually be taken as a measure of the effectiveness of capital controls whenever borrowers or lenders wish to move funds into or out of a country, but are prevented from doing so.[8]

Perhaps the most dramatic instance of divided credit markets is that of the EuroFrench franc market in the early 1980s, following the accession to power of a socialist government in the spring of 1981. The external payments situation in France had been under pressure for many years, even prior to the franc's entry into a polygamous liaison with the German mark and other currencies under the European Monetary System (EMS), instituted in 1979. A paramount aim of the French authorities had accordingly become to restrict the scope for speculation against the French franc by both residents and nonresidents. Banks' net foreign currency positions were strictly limited, and residents were prohibited from holding liquid external foreign currency assets. The latter were required to repatriate and dispose of any foreign currency receipts within a very short period of time, and advance payment for imports and forward exchange cover were also severely restricted. To limit nonresident sales of French francs in exchange for foreign currencies, bank and nonbank French franc loans abroad other than in connection with export finance were forbidden.

Banks were even prohibited from entering into forward foreign exchange contracts with foreign banks where the latter would be selling francs forward. In effect, therefore, the Eurofranc market was cut off from virtually all domestic supplies of funds. The limited pool of EuroFrench francs available to nonresidents and the awkward restrictions on forward cover com-

---

[8] Note that the effectiveness of controls can be measured by internal-external rate differentials only to the extent that such differentials are not attributable to differences in jurisdictional risk. For major developed countries, however, the effect of jurisdictional risk differences tends to be minor compared to that of capital controls.

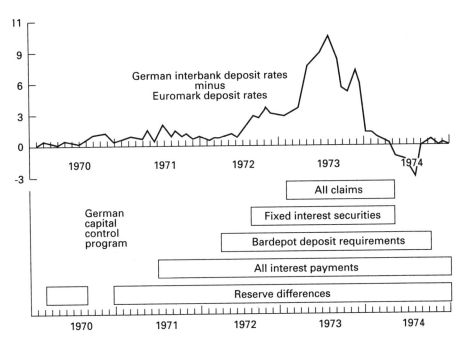

FIGURE 3-8. EuroDeutsche Mark and Domestic German Rates. During the 1970s, German capital inflow controls allowed external DM deposit rates to fall below domestic rates.

bined to make the EuroFrench franc market a shallow, illiquid one, unable to absorb large borrowings or lendings easily without the rates moving substantially. In effect French exchange controls created two separate credit markets, with two separate interest rate structures—and two separate forward exchange markets, with different forward rates being quoted on the internal franc forward market and the external one.[9] Since the primary influence on EuroFrench franc rates could not be the domestic market, external franc deposit rates were much more closely linked to the Eurodollar market and the forward exchange market. EuroFrench franc rates equaled Eurodollar rates adjusted for the cost of cover in the forward market for francs. The forward rate in turn was dominated by currency expectations. When, as happened time and again, nonresidents sought to borrow French francs (or sell francs forward) in anticipation of a devaluation, they would

---

[9] According to dealers in the Eurocurrency market, there were days when the external French franc forward rate was at a discount, while the internal forward rate was at a premium against the U.S. dollar. This could be observed by rates quoted on a Reuters monitor by a domestic French bank such as Credit Agricole and by a similar bank in London or New York. See Julian Walmsley, "Euromarket Dealing," in Abraham George and Ian Giddy, eds., *International Finance Handbook*, Volume 1 (New York: John Wiley & Sons, 1983).

willingly pay interest rates (or forward rates) far in excess of those prevailing (but unobtainable!) in the domestic market. The giddiness of this market reached new heights when, in March 1983, EuroFrench franc interest rates of up to 5,000 percent per annum were paid reportedly on overnight deposits. Speculators and hedgers seemed willing to pay almost anything to borrow French francs and invest them in a strong currency. Figure 3-9, based on 3-month deposit rates in the domestic French and the EuroFrench franc market, provides a truncated picture of strange days in the life of Euromarket dealers. Table 3-1 lists the overnight rates

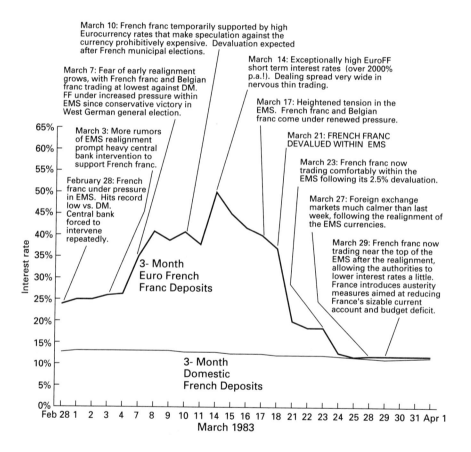

FIGURE 3-9. Strange Days in Euroland. Anticipating a French franc devaluation, EuroFrench franc borrowers drive rates to unheard-of heights, possible because exchange controls prevented domestic funds from flowing out.

Table 3-1. Overnight EuroFrench Franc
Rates on Days Preceding
Realignment of the Franc on
March 21, 1983

	Bid	Offer
Feb. 28	12.75	13.25
Mar. 1	13	14
Mar. 2	13	14
Mar. 3	12.75	13.5
Mar. 4	13	14
Mar. 7	100	200
Mar. 8	150	250
Mar. 9	30	100
Mar. 10	50	125
Mar. 11	25	125
Mar. 14	500	900
Mar. 15	300	800
Mar. 16	25	175
Mar. 17	20	100
Mar. 18	25	100
Mar. 21	25	75
Mar. 22	25	75
Mar. 23	25	75
Mar. 24	12.5	12.875

quoted in the London *Financial Times* on the days preceding the devaluation of the franc. In addition to the huge premium of Euro over domestic rates that appeared, one can see the thinness and trading risks at the time reflected in extraordinarily wide Euromarket bid-offer spreads.

RISK DIFFERENCES BETWEEN DOMESTIC AND EXTERNAL MONEY MARKETS

We have seen that the relationship between domestic and external rates cannot be fully explained by reference to regulatory costs. Perceived risk, apparently, plays a role in the decisions of many banks as well as nonbanks that are potential arbitragers between the two markets. Let us concentrate on the dollar segment to see what these risks might be. In what follows we assume that risk perceptions cannot be "irrational" in the sense of not being based on the best available information: those who persistently make decisions on erroneous and biased grounds will be driven out of the market by their rational competitors.

Risk in credit markets lies in the nonzero probability that an obligation to repay funds at a certain interest rate (in the case of a deposit agreement) or to lend funds on certain terms (in the case of a loan facility) will not be honored. In the international financial markets this risk is closely associated with the presence or absence of government regulations and control. Since, from a regulatory point of view, all Eurodollar transactions are international transactions, this means that each and every such transaction is subject to the potential intervention of not one but two (or more) sovereigns.

A U.S. depositor in the Eurodollar market, for example, holds a claim in one jurisdiction (say, London) but receives payment in another (the United States). He could be deprived of his funds at maturity by an action of either the British government or the U.S. government. In the case of a domestic deposit, only actions by the U.S. authorities matter.[10] For a depositor residing in the United Kingdom, the situation is quite similar. She may own a dollar-denominated time deposit in (1) a U.S. bank, directly, (2) a Eurobank operating in Luxembourg, or (3) a London-based Eurobank. In all three cases, the safety of her funds depends ultimately on the expectation that the United States will not restrict the disposition and transfer of foreign-held dollar funds (i.e., that the United States will continue to observe "nonresident convertibility"). In comparison to the situation of our U.S. investor, the U.K. investor will face a greater risk, to the extent that the U.S. government may restrict nonresident convertibility more readily than it interrupts domestic bank transfers.[11]

What of risk from the point of view of the borrower of Eurodollars? U.S. borrowers may perceive Eurodollar loan commitments as slightly less reliable because of the possibility that a transaction may be foiled by the authorities of the country in which the external financial intermediary operates or by the U.S. government (which could restrict the transfer of funds from a nonresident to a resident). Borrowers outside the United States, too, risk interference from one additional government in the honoring of a loan commitment by a Eurobank compared to a commitment by a U.S. bank. In either case, the foreign borrower's government may restrict the transaction or the U.S. government may intervene in the transfer of funds by nonresidents, depriving the borrower of the use of the loan proceeds. But only in

---

[10] Of course, in countries where new capital outflow controls on residents are feared, external deposits may well be considered less risky by residents who wish to purchase foreign goods.

[11] Residents of offshore banking centers constitute a special case. In the situation represented by example (3), the depositor may well perceive more risk than in either the first or second case, because she is subject to the direct control of her own country regarding foreign currency holdings.

The other special case is that of depositors from countries which are confronted by the risk of selective (political) interference with their assets in particular countries. The concrete example in the 1970s was that of dollar deposits owned by the government of Iran: these may be somewhat less subject to risk of government seizure when held in Swiss banks rather than in banks in the United States. Iranian investors may, therefore, be willing to accept a lower return on dollar-denominated time deposits in banks outside the United States. But these are minor exceptions relative to the bulk of investors whose transactions maintain Eurodollar deposit rates in excess of domestic rates.

the case of a Euroloan can a third government (that of the Eurobanking center) interfere. On the other hand, to the extent that the U.S. government may place quantitative restrictions on U.S. banks' lending to foreigners or some other class of borrowers, these borrowers may feel safer borrowing from the unregulated Eurodollar market. Thus the fear of capital controls, as well as the controls themselves, could allow Eurodollar lending rates to rise above those in the domestic market.

In summary, the risk on external dollar deposits and loans is somewhat greater than on deposits in, and loans from, U.S. domestic banks. The major risks in Eurodollar transactions stem from (1) the removal of nonresident convertibility by the United States, (2) the seizing of assets and liabilities of the Eurobanks by the authorities where they operate, and (3) the possibility that central banks may not function as "lenders of last resort" in the case of Eurobanks. Although the probability of these events occurring is low, they are of sufficient importance to warrant close examination by international depositors. We shall return to some aspects of Eurocurrency deposit risk in Chapter Six.

Differences between U.S. rates and Eurodollar rates may also be affected by differences in the liquidity and the institutional structure of the markets. On the deposit side, the U.S. market has long had the reputation of possessing greater liquidity than the Euromarket. Liquidity is the ability to purchase or dispose of securities at a price close to the present value of future cash flows emanating from it. Liquidity is related to the number of dealers willing to make a market, and to size; on both counts the Eurodollar market is now comparable to the domestic market. Similarly, barriers to arbitrage arising from inadequate information have diminished substantially, as theoretical, practical, and quantitative knowledge about the Eurodollar market has spread to all who take an interest in the major money markets. A large number of corporations and governments now believe they can switch borrowing or depositing into or out of the Eurodollar market with impunity: the learning curve has approached its plateau.

Both these trends have almost certainly led to a secular decline in the interest rate incentive required to attract depositors and borrowers from the domestic into the external market. Still, especially on the loan side, it has been found that U.S. rates appear not to react in a rapid and unbiased fashion to changes in credit conditions and abnormally high or low margins seem not to adjust very rapidly to market conditions.[12] These imperfections

[12] Ian Giddy, Gunter Dufey, and Sangkee Min, "Interest Rates in the U.S. and Eurodollar Markets," *Weltwirtschaftliches Archiv*, Vol. 115, No. 1 (1979), pp. 51–67; also Suresh E. Krishnan, "International Integration of Dollar-Denominated Money Market Instruments," Ph.D. dissertation, The University of Michigan, 1983.

arise from (1) regulatory restraints, such as interest rate ceilings; (2) institutional and perceptual factors, such as the tradition of adjusting the quantity rather than the price of loans when credit conditions change, partly because of the political visibility of the prime rate; and (3) oligopolistic market conditions that result from barriers to entry in the U.S. banking system. Interest rates in the Eurodollar market, on the other hand, are free of governmental or competitive restraints and therefore react with alacrity to changes in credit conditions. As a result, during "tight" credit conditions in the United States, lending-rate differentials become smaller while those on the deposit side widen.

COMPETING EUROCURRENCY MARKETS: INTEREST RATE ARBITRAGE AND CURRENCY EXPECTATIONS

The last two sections described the relationship between Eurorates and corresponding domestic rates. Although the discussion focused on the U.S. and Eurodollar markets, the same set of relationships applies to the internal and external markets for credit in each major currency. Just as Eurodollar loan and deposit rates are constrained by U.S. rates, so are interest rates on Eurosterling, EuroSwiss francs, EuroDeutsche marks (Euromarks), and Euroguilders bounded by corresponding domestic rates *except* when capital controls inhibit arbitrage, as for example in the case of EuroFrench francs. The next question, therefore, is: What is the relationship between rates in different segments of the Eurocurrency market? For example, how do Euromark rates influence Eurosterling rates, and vice versa?

Each Eurorate influences, and is influenced by, the level of interest rates in other Eurocurrency markets and hence by the level of rates in the corresponding domestic credit markets. Other things being equal, a rise in German interest rates, for example, will immediately result in a parallel rise in the Euromark interest rate, which in turn, will tend to raise interest rates in other currencies, such as EuroDutch guilders.

But it is *forward exchange rates* that keep interest rates between Eurocurrency markets different and that temper the influence of a change in one currency's rates on those in other currencies. Forward rates, in turn, are strongly influenced by exchange rate expectations. For example, other things being equal, a shift in the market's expected rate of change in the pound/French franc exchange rate will produce an interest rate change in the Eurosterling market, or in the EuroFrench franc market, or (as is more likely) both. The mutual influences of Eurocurrency interest rates, currency expectations, and forward exchange rates may be summarized as follows:

1. Through the process of **covered interest arbitrage**, interest rate differentials tend to equal the forward premium or discount.
2. Through **speculation**, the forward premium or discount tends to equal the expected rate of change of the exchange rate.
3. Also through speculation, the expected rate of change of the exchange rate tends to equal the Eurocurrency interest rate differential.

These relationships are not only compatible but are, as we shall see, simply different aspects of the same phenomenon. How these processes work is the subject of this and the next section. We shall study the relationship between Eurocurrency interest rates and the foreign exchange markets by looking at the behavior of borrowers and lenders who are considering the use of alternative Eurocurrency markets and bankers who are willing at any time to move funds from one market to another in order to make profits. As exchange rates, interest rates, and currency expectations change, profit opportunities appear and banks and companies are quick to take advantage.

INTEREST RATE PARITY

The most fundamental relationship between interest rates and spot and forward exchange rates is the well-known interest rate parity theorem that results from arbitrage between the spot and forward markets and the Eurocurrency deposit markets. (See box on p. 114 for a definition of spot and forward exchange rates.) **Covered interest arbitrage**,[13] undertaken by large international banks, involves the rapid movement of funds between securities denominated in different currencies in order to profit from different *effective* rates of interest in different currencies after taking hedging costs into account:

Effective interest rate on
a foreign currency deposit = Nominal interest rate + cost of forward cover
                     = Interest rate + forward premium (positive)
                        or discount (negative)

This **interest rate parity theorem** says that covered interest arbitrage equalizes effective interest rates in different currencies. For example, the interest rate on a dollar deposit must equal the interest rate on a German mark deposit covered in the forward market. More specifically,

---

[13] For a review of empirical work on the interest-rate-parity theorem, the reader is referred to Lawrence H. Officer and Thomas D. Willett, "The Covered-Arbitrage Schedule: A Critical Survey of Recent Developments," *Journal of Money, Credit and Banking*, March 1970, pp. 247–257.

Value at $t + n$ of $1 earning
dollar interest rate $I_{E\$}$ = Value at $t + n$ of $1 converted into foreign currency
and earning foreign currency interest rate I_{EDM}, until
$t + n$, when it is converted back into dollars at the
prearranged forward rate

$$\$1\,(1 + I_{E\$}) = \$1 \left[\frac{(1 + I_{EDM})}{S_t}\right] F_t^n$$

where S_t is the spot exchange rate (dollars per German mark) and F_t^n is the
forward rate.

$$\frac{\left(1 + I_{E\$}\right)}{\left(1 + I_{EDM}\right)} = \frac{F_t^n}{S_t}$$

Subtracting 1 from each side gives the **interest rate parity relationship**:

$$\frac{\left(I_{E\$} - I_{EDM}\right)}{\left(1 + I_{EDM}\right)} = \frac{\left(F_t^n - S_t\right)}{S_t}$$

For a period of n days, the right-hand side must be converted to an annualized percentage:

$$\frac{\left(I_{E\$} - I_{EDM}\right)}{\left(1 + I_{EDM}\right)} = \left[\frac{\left(F_t^n - S_t\right)}{S_t}\right]\left(\frac{365}{n}\right)$$

= Forward premium or discount

and if I_{EDM} is small, then, to a close approximation,

$$I_{E\$} - I_{EDM} = \left[\frac{F_t^n - S_t}{S_t}\right]\left(\frac{365}{n}\right)100$$

That is, interest rate differential = forward premium or discount.

Since banks take advantage of such covered interest arbitrage opportunities as soon as they arise, they seldom last very long. In the example given next, Euromark deposit rates would be driven down, $/DM spot rates bid up, and $/DM forward rates bid down to the point at which the arbitrage opportunity no longer exists once the (small) bid-offer spreads and transactions costs were taken into account. In other words, interest rate parity would soon prevail. That is,

Eurodollar interest rate = Euromark interest rate + premium or discount

or

$$\text{Interest rate differential} = \frac{\text{Forward premium or discount in the dollar/}}{\text{Mark foreign exchange market}}$$

Interest rate parity also results from the fact that Eurobanks stand ready to offer loans or deposits in any Eurocurrency but are usually unwilling to have a net exposed position in loans or deposits. If, for example, a Eurobank offers both Eurodollar and Euromark deposits and loans and funds itself with an imbalance of loans and deposits in each currency, it will cover this net imbalance through use of the forward market. Figure 3-10 illustrates this point. The purpose of covering the net exposed dollar assets in this illustration is, of course, to protect the bank from being adversely affected should the dollar have weakened relative to the German mark by the time the

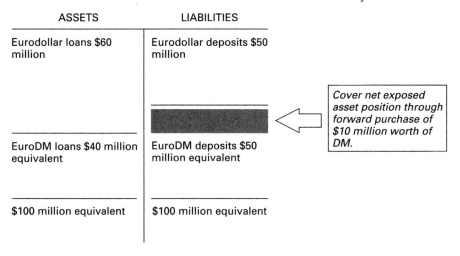

ASSETS	LIABILITIES
Eurodollar loans $60 million	Eurodollar deposits $50 million
	Cover net exposed asset position through forward purchase of $10 million worth of DM.
EuroDM loans $40 million equivalent	EuroDM deposits $50 million equivalent
$100 million equivalent	$100 million equivalent

FIGURE 3-10. A Eurobank Covers Its Currency Exposure. If a bank has a net imbalance of, say, German mark assets and liabilities, it will offset this by means of forward contracts.

Spot and Forward Exchange Markets

The foreign exchange markets for each pair of currencies consists of two parts, **the spot market**, where payment (delivery) is made right away (in practice this means usually the second business day), and **the forward market**. The rate in the forward market is a price for foreign currency set at the time the transaction is agreed to but with the actual exchange, or delivery, taking place at a specified time in the future. We should emphasize this: while the amount of the transaction, the value date, the payments procedure, and the exchange rate are all determined in advance, *no exchange of money takes place until the actual settlement date*. This commitment to exchange currencies at a previously agreed exchange rate is usually referred to as a forward contract.

The **forward premium or discount** is the annualized percentage difference between the spot and forward exchange rates. It is calculated as:

$$\frac{n\text{-day forward rate } - \text{ spot rate}}{\text{Spot rate}} \times \frac{365}{n} \times 100$$

where the exchange rate is defined as domestic currency units per unit of foreign currency, such as $1.50 per pound sterling.

The forward exchange rate is used by both banks and companies to cover or hedge their future cash flows in foreign currencies. The forward contract guarantees an exchange rate at which currencies will be sold or bought, and so eliminates the chance of exchange rate losses for any particular transaction. The forward rate that the parties agree upon depends on the parties' expectations regarding the future behavior of the exchange rate. Under normal circumstances the forward rate tends to equal the market participants' best guess as to the future spot exchange rate. If this were not the case, and if, for example, many believed that future spot rate would be below the prevailing forward rate, they would tend to offer more for forward delivery and drive the forward rate down toward the expected future rate.

A **foreign exchange swap** is a transaction in which a spot transaction and an opposite forward transaction are both agreed upon simultaneously. Swaps of this kind are commonly employed by banks to offset outright forward exchange deals done with corporations. A bank trader, for example, having agreed to deliver Swiss francs to a customer at the end of May, could in principle enter a forward exchange contract to Swiss francs from some other bank. However, the interbank market for such "outright" forwards is less well developed

SPOT AND FORWARD EXCHANGE MARKETS (*CONTINUED*)

than those for swap deals, and for Eurodeposits. Hence the trader will normally buy the Swiss francs for spot delivery; then, since he will not actually need the francs until May 31, he can (and will) enter a spot-sale-and-future-repurchase arrangement with another bank—in other words, he will do a swap.

Alternatively, having bought the Swiss francs spot with, say, borrowed Eurodollars, the trader could choose to put them into a bank deposit—a EuroSwiss franc deposit, in fact—maturing on May 31. He would then have the Swiss francs ready to deliver to his customer on that day. Such a transaction is termed a **money market hedge**. This suggests that the Eurodeposit market is a counterpart to the foreign exchange swap market. Indeed swaps are rooted in deposits and neither Eurodeposits nor foreign exchange swaps can be properly understood without a knowledge of the other.

Note: For greater detail, see Thomas M. Campfield and John G. O'Brien, "Foreign Exchange Trading Practices: The Interbank Market," in Abraham George and Ian Giddy, eds., *International Finance Handbook*, Volume 1 (New York: John Wiley & Sons, 1983), or Julian Walmsley, *The Foreign Exchange Handbook* (New York: John Wiley & Sons, 1983).

deposits and loans mature. But if the dollar is expected to weaken, the bank will face a premium for the forward purchase of German marks. Hence the bank will only be willing to convert Euromark deposits into dollar loans if the Euromark deposit rate plus the $/DM forward premium is equal to or lower than the cost of dollar deposits. Similarly, banks hedging a net exposed asset position in German marks will be willing to convert Eurodollar deposits into mark loans only if the Eurodollar deposits rate minus the $/DM forward discount is equal to or lower than the cost of mark deposits. In equilibrium, then, the forward premium or discount will tend to settle at a rate exactly equal to the interest rate differential between two Eurocurrencies.

The second relationship is that between the forward and spot exchange rates and exchange rate expectations.

The forward premium or discount reflects not only covered interest arbitrage but also exchange rate expectations, because commercial and financial transactors who expect to receive future revenues in currencies other than that which they wish to hold will tend to agree to forward exchange transactions only at an exchange rate close to that which they expect to prevail in the future. Since, in general, the forward exchange rate tends to equal the market's expected future exchange rate, as people's currency expectations change as the result of new information, the forward premium or discount will adjust to roughly equal the expected rate of change of the exchange rate (expressed as an annualized percentage). Hence

Forward premium or discount = Expected annual rate of change
of the exchange rate

That is,

$$P_{\$/DM} = E(R_{\$/DM})$$

where $P_{\$/DM}$ is the dollar/German mark forward premium or discount as before and $E(R_{\$/DM})$ is the annual rate at which the market expects the dollar/German mark exchange rate to change. The relationship between the forward rate and the exchange rate expectations may be termed the "unbiased forward rate theorem."

Let us stop for a moment and compare the two relationships identified so far. The first said that the interest rate differential equals the forward premium or discount; the second, that the forward premium or discount equals the expected rate of change of the exchange rate. Clearly, the two are compatible if and only if interest rate differentials between Eurocurrencies equal the expected rate of change of the exchange rate. *This is indeed the case;* an example will show why.

The assistant treasurer of a large corporation described the process as follows. One of her tasks is to borrow and place funds for short periods in the Eurocurrency market on behalf of the firm's European affiliates. Assume the German unit generates revenues in marks. If, say, the 3-month Eurodollar interest rate is 6 percent per annum and the Euromark rate 4 percent per annum, she will prefer to hold her funds in Eurodollar deposits unless the lower Euromark rate is offset by an expected appreciation of the dollar versus the mark at an annual rate of 2 percent (that is, by 0.05 percent over the 3-month period—neglecting compound effects) or more. Similarly, as a borrower of 3-month funds she will prefer to borrow German marks unless the mark is expected to appreciate at a rate of 2 percent per annum or more. Assuming our treasurer expects the German mark to rise at a 1 percent rate over 1 year, her actions and those of many other companies will tend to bid the Euromark rate up (as depositors move funds out of Euromarks into Eurodollars and borrowers borrow more Euromarks and fewer dollars). At the same time, the sale of marks to obtain dollars by both sets of transactors will bid the dollar/mark spot exchange rate down. If, for convenience, transactions costs are ignored, the incentive for this choice of depositing and borrowing currencies will disappear only when the Euromark rate has been bid up and the dollar/mark exchange rate bid down to the point at which the Euromark rate plus the expected rate of appreciation of the mark approximates the Eurodollar rate; that is,

$$I_{E\$} = I_{EDM} + E(R_{\$/DM})$$

where $I_{E\$}$ and I_{EDM} are the dollar and mark Eurorates and $E(R_{\$/DM})$ is expected rate of change of the exchange rate on an annual basis.

EXAMPLE OF COVERED INTEREST ARBITRAGE

A foreign exchange dealer, in the course of constantly monitoring interest rates and exchange rates quoted by different banks around the world, notices that the following combination rates are available:

90-day interest rates (percent per annum):

Euromark = 4.75 (bid), 5.00 (offer)
Eurodollar = 6.625 (bid), 6.75 (offer)

Exchange rates (dollars per German mark):

Spot = 0.3801 (bid), 0.3802 (ask)
90-day forward = 0.3821 (bid), 0.3823 (ask)

Realizing that when she borrows funds or buys a currency she will have to pay the higher (offer or ask) of the two rates, and realizing that when she deposits funds or sells a currency she will receive the lower of the two rates, the trader makes the following calculation:

Cost of borrowing Eurodollars = 6.75 percent per annum

Return from buying marks in the spot market, depositing them in a Euromark deposit, and simultaneously selling them in the forward market = Euromark rate + forward premium

$$= 4.75 + \frac{0.3821 + 0.3802}{0.3802} \times \frac{365}{90} \times 100$$

$$= 4.75 + 2.03$$

$$= 6.78\% \text{ per annum}$$

Hence by borrowing Eurodollars and depositing them in the Euromark market while covering them forward, the bank can earn 0.03 percent per annum, which, for a $10 million transaction, is $750.

Since any pair of Eurocurrencies will quickly adjust to borrowing and depositing pressures of the kind just described, one would expect that the following relationship would normally hold to a close approximation:

Interest rate in one Eurocurrency market – interest rate in other Eurocurrency market =
Expected annual rate of change of exchange rate

That is, interest-rate differential equals expected annual rate of change of exchange rate. If both Eurocurrency markets are closely linked to their

Forward Rates as Predictors of Future Spot Rates

Is the forward exchange rate truly the market's forecast of the future spot exchange rate? There appear to be *three major views*.

The first, held by many who deal in the market, is that exchange rate expectations have no bearing on the forward exchange rate because the dominant influence on forward rates is the interest differential. Dealers know that the *basis for calculation of all forward rates is the swap rate which comes from the Eurocurrency interest differential* between two currencies for a given period. Clearly (says the dealer), to set a forward rate on any basis other than the spot rate adjusted for relative interest rates would be silly, for it would create a covered interest arbitrage incentive. He will therefore always set his quoted forward rates to equal the interest parity rate. He will ridicule as "academic" any claim the forward rate equals the market's currency expectations, for he personally can calculate the equilibrium forward rate without any reference to expectations.

The dealer's view is both right and wrong. He is absolutely right in saying that the forward exchange rate equals the spot rate adjusted for relative interest rates: as long as covered interest arbitrage is possible, it cannot long be otherwise. At the same time, the dealer is mistaken in arguing that the forward rate does not reflect currency expectations. The reason is simple: as every dealer knows, relative interest rates on Eurocurrency deposits are strongly influenced by the expected strength or weakness of the currencies. For reasons discussed in the text, the interest rate differential reflects the market's forecast of the rate of change of the exchange rate, and because (from interest rate parity) the interest differential equals the forward premium or discount, it follows that both the forward rate and the relative interest rates reflect the market's currency expectations.

Thus the second view is that—either directly or through relative interest rates—the forward rate, because it equals the market's forecast for the currency, is an *unbiased predictor* of the future spot rate. Speculative positions in deposits or in forward contracts will always bid the forward rate up or down until it equals the expected spot rate. (This is not to say the forward rate is an *accurate* predictor—no forecast can make that claim—but only that *on average* upside mistakes will cancel out downside mistakes.)

The third view is a variant of the unbiased forward rate view: it claims that investors will act on speculative profit opportunities only if the expected profits are sufficient to compensate them for bearing

FORWARD RATES AS PREDICTORS OF FUTURE SPOT RATES (*CONTINUED*)

risk. The existence of *a premium for risk would make the forward rate a biased predictor of the spot rate.* According to financial theory, the size of the risk premium would be a function of the covariance of returns from forward speculation with returns on some market portfolio of assets. In other words, the supply of speculative funds may not be perfectly elastic because of investors' risk aversion.

In theory, the risk premium may be positive, negative, or zero. Thus the forward rate could underestimate or overestimate the expected spot rate. Since we cannot directly measure market expectations, we will never know for sure whether such a risk premium exists. Years of research on the subject, however, has produced no well-accepted evidence that the risk premium is either very large or consistently positive or negative. The performance of models that incorporate a risk premium has not proved consistently superior to those that assume the risk premium is zero.

respective domestic markets, domestic as well as Eurocurrency interest rates are linked to one another through the spot and forward exchange rates, and adjustments that occur in Eurocurrency rates must also occur in domestic credit markets. This relationship, which is sometimes termed the **international Fisher effect**, shows how the two notions of how the forward premium or discount is determined (*covered-interest arbitrage* and *forward rate equals expected future spot rate* theories) are consistent, compatible, and indeed two sides of the same coin.

The three theorems that have been described may now be brought together and summarized in a *single statement* of the normal relationship between Eurocurrency rates, spot and forward exchange rates, and exchange-rate expectations: *The borrowing, lending and hedging actions of banks and corporations tend to ensure that the interest-rate differential between two Eurocurrency markets equals the forward premium or discount and also equals the expected exchange-rate change expressed as an annual rate.*

In the absence of capital controls, or other barriers, all credit markets are linked to one another through arbitrage and currency expectations. The final situation will resemble that illustrated in Figure 3-11.

EUROCURRENCY INTEREST RATES, EXCHANGE RATE EXPECTATIONS, AND THE UNBIASED FORWARD RATE QUESTION

One insight that follows from the last section is that the question of how Eurocurrency interest rates relate to the expected rate of change in the

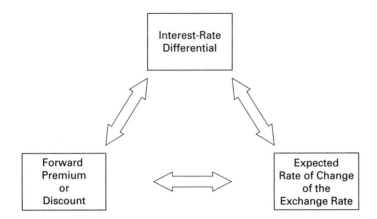

FIGURE 3-11. Money and Foreign Exchange Market Linkages. The interest rate differential equals the forward premium or discount which tends also to equal the expected exchange rate change.

exchange rate is the same question as has long been asked about the forward exchange rate, namely, is the forward rate an efficient and unbiased predictor of the future spot exchange rate? This is simply because the latter question can be stated as testing whether

$$F_t^n = E(S_{t+n})$$

where F_t^n represents the forward rate at time t for maturity at $t + n$ and S_{t+n} the actual spot rate at $t + n$.

Put differently,

$$\frac{F_t^n - S_t}{S_t} = \frac{E(S_{t+n}) - S_t}{S_t}$$

Or, from the interest rate parity identity,

$$\frac{1 + I_d}{1 + I_f} = \frac{E(S_{t+n})}{S_t}$$

The left-hand side is the relative interest rate ratio; the right-hand side, the expected exchange rate change expressed as a ratio. Thus testing the unbiased forward rate equation is equivalent to testing whether relative interest rates equal the anticipated rate of change of the exchange rate.

The theory of efficient markets is based on the notion that current prices reflect all available information, including market participants' expectations about future prices and, further, that all new information that is received by the market is analyzed and immediately incorporated into expectations about future prices. From these expectations, decisions to buy and sell are made, and thus the expected prices are converted into current prices.

These considerations apply to all organized asset markets, which include markets for spot and forward foreign exchange. The current spot rate reflects anticipated supply and demand conditions and the forward rate contains information about the future spot rate. This is because as a contractual price, the forward rate offers opportunities for speculative profits for those who correctly assess the future spot price relative to the current forward rate.

Because expectations of future spot rates are formed on the basis of presently available information (historical data) and an interpretation of its implication for the future, they tend to be subject to frequent and rapid revision. As previously noted, the actual future spot rate may therefore deviate markedly from the expectation embodied in the present forward rate for that maturity. These deviations are in the nature of a forecast error which is known only after the fact, that is, when the future has become the present. Formally, the forecast error is expressed as

$$F_t^n - S_{t+n} = e_{t+n}$$

where e_{t+n} is the error. One way of looking at the error term is to regard it as a measure of speculative profits or losses: you buy at the forward price and sell at the realized spot, or vice versa, and so the difference is your gain or loss. Can they be consistently positive or negative? A priori reasoning suggests that this should not be the case. Otherwise, one would have to explain why consistent losers do not quit the market, or why consistent winners are not imitated by others or do not increase their volume of activity, thus causing adjustment of the forward rate in the direction of their expectation. Barring such explanation, one would expect that the forecast error is sometimes positive, sometimes negative, alternating in a random fashion, driven by unexpected events in the economic and political environment. Over sufficiently long periods of time, allowing a large number of decisions, e_{t+n} should average out to zero. This is the statistical basis for the view that the forward rate is an unbiased forecast of the future spot rate, and that the error is random.

Many have sought to test this proposition.[14] Unfortunately, tests of market efficiency on this basis involve testing two propositions jointly: first, they test the underlying model that generates foreign exchange rates; second, they test the proposition that participants indeed set the forward rate equal to the expected future spot rate. Thus conclusive empirical verification of the existence of market efficiency is virtually impossible to achieve. It should be noted, however, that this definition of efficiency leaves out sources of bias that may be known to market participants and may be incorporated, quite rationally, into the forward rate. Thus, there may be "systematic" deviations of the forward rate from the expected future spot rate compatible with market efficiency. The latter concept refers only to the processing of information; yet the relevant information set may well contain factors that cause systematic deviations of forward rates from expected future spot rates. Forecasting errors can therefore be classified as random or systematic, leading to unbiased or biased forecasts. The latter, in turn, may be due to inefficient pricing processes or may be perfectly consistent with an efficient market.

The important thing for the reader to understand is that there may well be economic as well as technical factors that make the forward rate, and relative Eurocurrency interest rates, a biased predictor of the future spot rate. The concept is discussed briefly here, and in more detail in the appendix.

Just as models of exchange rate determination have come to recognize that people hold more than money in their portfolios, so the theory of foreign exchange has evolved towards a *portfolio* view of market efficiency. Decisions to speculate in foreign exchange, the story goes, are made on the basis of *risk* as well as expected *return*. Even if there is money to be made from speculation, people may not act unless the profit is commensurate with the risk of taking an open position in a currency. Instead, the forward rate will differ from the expected future spot rate by a *risk premium*, γ (gamma):

$$F_t = E(S_{t+1}) + \gamma + e_{t+1}$$

This proposition sounds reasonable: even speculators are risk averse and will refrain from exploiting a profit opportunity if the expected return is too low. But now comes the hard part: How big is the risk premium? Is it positive or negative? And what factors determine the risk premium?

Modern portfolio theory offers a logical starting point for the analysis of

---

[14] See, for example, the survey in Richard T. Baillie and Patrick C. McMahon, *The Foreign Exchange Market: Theory and Econometric Evidence* (Cambridge: Cambridge University Press, 1989).

the nature and price of risk in foreign exchange speculation. Portfolio theory says that there is a linear relationship between risk and return—the higher the risk, the higher the expected return—but that investors do not get rewarded for taking risk that is diversifiable. Anyone can diversify, the theory goes, by combining a particular asset (such as foreign exchange) with the "market portfolio" so it would be the degree of covariance with investors' feasible market portfolio that would determine the risk premium in the forward exchange rate. Hence to understand the pricing of any risk premium, we must address the issue of diversifiable versus nondiversifiable risk in the broader context of an international capital asset pricing model. It would, for example, be risky to hold securities denominated in a currency whose value is positively correlated with that of other assets: the securities are afflicted with a risk that cannot be diversified away and a risk premium would be required. But difficult questions arise as to the definition of "other assets" and the relevant investment universe, as well as consumption patterns of international investors.

On the latter subject, any investor in foreign fixed-interest securities faces a purchasing power risk, because of the uncertainty of future inflation. So long as inflation rates are not perfectly (positively) correlated among countries, it would pay to diversify portfolios internationally. In portfolio balance, therefore, it is theoretically possible that real return expectations differ between domestic and foreign securities because of residual purchasing power risk.[15] Put somewhat differently, systematic deviations from the international Fisher relationship are possible when one or the other country has issued an "excessive" amount of government debt[16] relative to its share in the minimum-variance, internationally diversified portfolio.[17] Accordingly, a premium above and beyond the expected depreciation could be explained as compensation for investors to increase their holdings of foreign currency assets, of which "excessive" amounts have been issued.

Further, for a risk premium to exist, the risk of holding a foreign currency asset must be nondiversifiable. With risk-neutral investors, any risk premium will be competed away, since it represents expected excess profits. If there is a systematic risk premium on, say, dollar-denominated securities

---

[15] There should be no residual exchange risk because there is a perfect negative correlation for deviation from purchasing power parity for any two currencies, guaranteeing, in principle, complete diversifiability.

[16] Government rather than private debt is necessary for a risk premium, for with private debt, gains to borrowers will be losses to lenders and the perfect negative correlation of such returns permits the complete elimination of this risk through an appropriate diversification strategy.

[17] See, for instance, Rudiger Dornbusch, "Exchange Rate Economics: Where Do We Stand?" *Brookings Papers on Economic Activity*, Vol. 1 (1980), pp. 143–185.

(perhaps because too many dollar-denominated securities have been issued by the U.S. government), then it might pay, in terms of lower nominal and expected real interest cost, to issue securities in other currencies.

In theory, the risk premium may be positive, negative, or zero. Thus the forward rate could underestimate or overestimate the expected spot rate. Since we cannot directly measure market expectations, we will never know for sure whether such a risk premium exists. Years of research on the subject, however, has produced no well-accepted evidence that the risk premium is either very large or consistently positive or negative. The performance of models that incorporate a risk premium has not proved consistently superior to those that assume the risk premium is zero. Frankel, in a review of research on exchange rate changes, states that:

> the proportion of exchange rate changes that are forecastable in any manner—by the forward discount, interest rate differential, survey data, or models based on macroeconomic fundamentals—appears to be not just low, but almost zero.[18]

What emerges from these considerations is the recognition that deviations of the forward rate from the expected future spot rate can be due to different factors which will, moreover, interact in complex ways. Some possible sources of forward-rate bias are explored in Appendix 3-A. While this subject is frustrating for the analyst, it may prove comforting to know that even international investors do not get excess returns very easily.

INFLUENCES ON EUROCURRENCY RATES: HOW THEY ACTUALLY WORK

Thus far we have identified the major interest rate relationships and influences that normally prevail in the Eurocurrency markets. This section will complement those by examining in more detail how these influences are transmitted to produce the equilibrium relationships among internal credit markets, external credit markets, and foreign exchange markets. The reader familiar with these mechanisms should skip this section. The framework will involve six major variables in the dollar and German mark markets:

Two Internal Interest Rates

1. The domestic U.S. interest rate
2. The domestic German interest rate

---

[18] Jeffery Frankel, "Flexible Exchange Rates: Experience Versus Theory," *Journal of Portfolio Management* (Winter 1989), pp. 45–54.

Two External Interest Rates

1. The Eurodollar interest rate
2. The Euromark interest rate

Two Exchange Rates

1. The spot exchange rate (dollars per mark)
2. The forward exchange rate

All these interact with one another. There are, however, two major sets of independent, or exogenous, variables affecting Eurocurrency rates. These are (1) domestic credit conditions in the United States and Germany, as influenced by national growth rates, monetary policies, and so forth and (2) exchange rate expectations, influenced by inflation rates, trade flows, and government policies, among other things. The remaining variables are generally dependent, or endogenous, variables and change in response to changes in the independent variables. A change in U.S. interest rates, for example, usually produces changes in Eurodollar rates, dollar/mark exchange rates, and mark-denominated interest rates. Not infrequently, however, the reverse may happen—that is, the change in Eurocurrency and foreign exchange rates produced by a domestic interest rate change may, in turn, produce a feedback effect on domestic interest rates.

The following two cases will suggest how changes in these two major independent variables, domestic credit conditions and exchange rate expectations, make themselves felt in the Eurocurrency and foreign exchange markets.

Case 1: The Effect of a Change in Credit Conditions

A change in credit conditions or interest rates in the domestic credit market of one country immediately induces arbitrage until rates in the external market are in line with domestic rates. Next, covered interest arbitrage tends to restore the relationship between Eurocurrency and spot and forward exchange rates. Finally, the impact is felt on (as well as constrained by) other domestic credit markets. Assume, for example, an initial position showing only small differences between internal and external interest rates and foreign exchange rates at interest rate parity with respect to Eurocurrency rates:

> U.S. 90-day rate = 7.5%
> Eurodollar rate = 8% per annum
> German 90-day rate = 3.5%
> Euromark rate = 4% per annum
> Spot exchange rate, dollars per German mark = 0.400
> 90-day forward exchange rate = 0.404

Hence

$$\text{Forward premium} = \frac{0.404 - 0.400}{0.400} \times \frac{360}{90} \times 100$$

$$= 4\% \text{ per annum}$$

$$= \text{interest rate differential}$$

(To make the calculations simpler we have assumed a 360-day year.)

Now suppose that the actions of the U.S. monetary authorities raise the U.S. interest rate to 9.5 percent. Since the U.S. rate is no longer aligned with Eurocurrency and foreign exchange rates, arbitrage and expectational forces described in earlier sections will cause changes in interest and exchange rates that will restore the equilibrium relationships.

First, internal-external equality will be restored; that is, borrowers will switch to the Eurodollar market and depositors to the U.S. money market. Because the U.S. market is larger than the Eurodollar market and is more directly subject to U.S. monetary policy, Eurodollar rather than U.S. rates will adjust. Hence one may expect to see Eurodollar rates move rapidly up to 10 percent. A similar process would occur for any pair of markets in which the internal money market is large relative to foreign money markets. Relatively small domestic money markets, such as the Swiss one, are much more subject to external influences, such as changes in foreign credit conditions or currency expectations.

Next, interest rates and exchange rates in the external markets will adjust to conform to the interest rate parity and the unbiased interest rate differential conditions. Any or all of four variables—the Eurodollar rate, the Euromark rate, the spot exchange rate, and the forward exchange rate—may bear the brunt of the adjustment.

1. The *Eurodollar rate* may move down as investors find dollar interest rates more than compensating for the forward premium on the dollar/mark exchange rate and banks borrow marks to make dollar loans. However, Eurodollar rates are largely constrained by U.S. rates and are likely to move little because of the size of the dollar credit market relative to that of other Eurocurrency and domestic credit markets (the U.S. money stock constitutes almost 40 percent of the total of the 10 major industrial countries). In general, the Eurocurrency interest rate will adjust to arbitrage only to the extent that (a) the domestic monetary authorities are unwilling or unable to fix corresponding internal rates or (b) capital controls widen the

effective limits within which Eurorates can move relative to domestic rates.

2. *Euromark interest rates* will tend to rise, as arbitrage and speculative transactions become attractive and this moves funds out of Euromarks and into Eurodollars, even after the forward premium and expected rate of change of the exchange rate are taken into account. Again, Eurorates will be constrained by domestic rates; Euromark rates will move to the upper limit provided by domestic German rates, which themselves may be pulled up because of the relatively small size of the German money market.

3. The *spot exchange rate* (i.e., the price of German marks) will be bid down as investors and arbitragers sell marks in order to buy dollars and invest them in Eurodollar deposits. The spot rate often will bear much of the brunt of an interest rate change, except when the authorities are willing and able to fix the exchange rate by buying all the marks offered at a fixed dollar price.

4. The *forward dollar/mark* exchange rate may be bid up as more and more investors enter contracts to purchase marks forward to hedge their dollar investments. The forward rate also usually absorbs much of the impact of an interest rate change because this forward market is seldom influenced directly by government intervention. Because of the unbiased forward rate theorem, however, the forward rate is constrained to equal the market's expected value for the future spot exchange rate; hence when investors' exchange rate expectations are unaltered by the interest rate change, the forward premium will adjust through changes in the spot rate rather than changes in the forward rate.[19]

To sum up, when the interest-rate differential widens as a result of changed credit conditions, arbitrage and speculation will tend to narrow the interest-rate differential and widen the differential between forward and spot exchange rates in order to restore interest-rate and expectations parity. In the example above, the following adjustments might have followed the 2 percent rise in U.S. rates:

Eurodollar rate	From 8 to 10 percent
Euromark rate	From 4 to 4.5 percent
German rate	From 3.5 to 3.95 percent
Spot exchange rate	From 0.400 $/DM to 0.399 $/DM
Forward exchange rate	From 0.404 $/DM to 0.4045 $/DM

---

[19] On the other hand, if the rise in U.S. interest rates reflects higher expected inflation in the United States, exchange rate expectations will change and the forward rate will do some or all of the adjusting.

Hence

$$\text{New forward premium} = \frac{0.4045 - 0.399}{0.399} \times \frac{360}{90} \times 100$$

$$= 5.5\% \text{ per annum}$$

$$= \text{Eurocurrency interest rate differential}$$

Case 2: The Effect of a Change in Currency Expectations

A change in the international financial community's exchange rate expectations will widen or narrow the forward premium (or discount), a change that will be matched by changes in relative interest rates, in such a way as to maintain interest rate parity and the domestic-external rate structure. As before, the impact of a change in currency expectations may be examined by assuming an initial set of interest and exchange rates at interest rate parity in the dollar and German mark markets. The conditions we ended up with after the first adjustments were

> U.S. 90-day rate = 9.5%
> Eurodollar rate = 10% per annum
> German 90-day rate = 3.95%
> Euromark rate = 4.5% per annum
> Spot exchange rate = 0.399 $/DM
> 90-day forward rate = 0.4045 $/DM

As was shown in the previous section, the forward premium of 5.5 percent equals the Eurocurrency interest rate differential. Now suppose that statistics indicating a sudden jump in the inflation rate are released in Germany; as a result, investors expect a deterioration in the German trade balance and a lower demand for German marks. The consensus now is that the mark will rise over the next 3 months to only 0.402 instead of the present expected 0.4045 $/DM. The markets are now in disequilibrium and will undergo adjustments of the following nature.

1. The *forward exchange rate* will tend to adjust to match the new expectation: that is, the forward rate will drop from 0.4045 to 0.402. This will result from the actions of speculators, who will be willing to sell German marks forward at 0.4045, hoping to profit in 3 months' time by purchasing marks in the spot market at 0.402 and selling them at the contract rate of 0.4045. In addition, investors will be less willing to hold uncovered mark deposits and so will seek to hedge them by selling marks forward. These actions will

continue until the forward rate equals the expected future spot rate, 0.402 $/DM.

2. The *Euromark interest rate* will tend to rise. With a lower forward rate, the forward premium on the mark will have dropped (from 5.5 percent to 3 percent) and will not be sufficient to compensate for the lower Euromark interest rate. Arbitragers will therefore move funds out of Euromarks and into dollars, thus bidding the Euromark interest rate up to the extent that it is not constrained by German domestic interest rates. The Euromark rate may even pull internal interest rates up with it to a minor degree.

3. The *domestic German interest rate* will be pulled up, as depositors switch from domestic to offshore deposits, and as German banks fund their Euromark loans in the cheaper domestic market.

4. *Eurodollar rates* will tend to drop. By buying spot dollars, depositing them in the Eurodollar market, and selling them forward at 0.402 for marks, investors can earn 10% − 3% = 7%, much higher than the 4.5 percent available on Euromark deposits. As more funds are deposited in the Eurodollar market, rates will drop unless they are completely constrained by the U.S. domestic credit market.

5. The *spot exchange rate* will tend to drop. As investors seek to liquidate Euromark deposits and purchase dollar deposits, they will sell marks for dollars on the spot market and bid the price of marks down. Normally, the spot rate will undertake most of the adjustment necessary to restore interest rate parity once expectations have altered the forward rate. If the government intervenes to fix the exchange rate, however, the spot rate can adjust very little, and interest rate parity must be restored through interest rate changes.

In this situation, opportunities for profits will rapidly disappear as the forward rate moves down followed by a rise in the Euromark rate and a drop in the Eurodollar and dollar/mark exchange rate. If interest rates change much, the spot rate will adjust less, and the altered interest rates may affect currency expectations and thus feed back to the forward rate. If it is assumed, however, that in the absence of capital controls the monetary policies of national authorities prevent interest rates from moving much, if at all, the change in currency expectations just described may result in the following changes to restore parity:

Forward exchange rate	From 0.4045 $/DM to 0.402 $/DM
Euromark rate	From 4.5 to 5%
German rate	From 3.95 to 4.45%
Eurodollar rate	Unchanged at 10%
U.S. rate	Unchanged at 9.5%
Spot exchange rate	From 0.399 to 0.397

Hence,

$$\text{New forward premium} = \frac{0.402 - 0.397}{0.397} \times \frac{360}{90} \times 100$$

$$= 5\% \text{ per annum}$$

$$= \text{Eurocurrency interest rate differential}$$

In the past, when capital controls were in effect and the Bretton Woods system kept spot rates fixed, much of the adjustment took place in Eurorates, particularly in those of the smaller Eurocurrency markets. The result could even be negative interest rates, as actually occurred in the Euromark market during the summer of 1972.

It is easy to see that under a system of fixed exchange rates, interest rate changes or currency expectations can have significant effects on domestic credit markets and thus reduce the independence of national monetary policies. Fixed rates in conjunction with covered interest arbitrage facilitate the international transmission of interest rates and monetary policies. While this transmission has been described as occurring most naturally and conveniently through the Eurocurrency markets, it can, of course, take place directly between national credit markets.

INTEREST RATES, EXCHANGE RATES, AND INFLATION

One of the puzzles of international finance is the question of the *interrelationships between inflation, interest rates, and exchange rates.* Consider:

- Does a high Eurodollar interest rate (relative to other currencies) mean the dollar will be strong?
- Does a high Eurodollar interest rate (relative to other currencies) mean the dollar will be weak?

The answer to both questions is yes, or perhaps no! In fact, it depends. It depends on whether the high dollar interest rate reflects tight monetary policies, designed to reduce inflation, or whether the high rate merely reflects inflationary expectations. It also depends on whether one is talking about the long run or the short run.

The currency can strengthen when the interest rate rises. This happens when a country, seeing its currency actually or potentially falling, tightens the credit reins, raising interest rates and attracting funds into the currency. When traders see this, they are prepared to take advantage of the higher interest rates because they do not expect the currency to fall to offset the interest rate gain.

On the other hand, there are at least as many instances—often in the same currencies—when a higher interest rate means a *weaker currency*. When interest rates are high because of a high expected rate of inflation, then people also expect the currency to fall. Indeed, according to the *purchasing power parity* theory, the currency might be expected to fall by an amount equal to the inflation rate differential, on average. Thus any gain from the higher interest rate would tend to be offset by the currency depreciation.

It is the countries with higher inflation rates and weaker currencies— the French franc and the Italian lira, for example—that exceed the interest rates on strong currencies with lower inflation rates, such as the Swiss franc and German mark. In general, consistently high rates of inflation lead to higher interest rates and falling currencies—but temporary deviations from the interest rate–inflation rate link can induce capital flows to the country whose rate has risen.

The United States and Argentina are two examples of the contrasting effect of interest rates on exchange rates. In the early 1980s the United States had a high interest rate, which led to a very strong dollar value against other currencies. On the other hand, Argentina had a much higher interest rate (often exceeding 100 percent) and a very weak currency. These extreme examples illustrate the point that to reconcile the two seemingly opposed views of how interest rates and exchange rates are related, one must look behind the interest rate, at (1) changes in interest rates that are *real* versus those that are *nominal* and (2) the timing of inflation's effect on interest rates.

The difference between the United States and Argentina might only be a matter of the magnitude and rapidity with which interest rates respond to inflation expectations. In both countries, the exchange rate reacts positively to an increase in the real interest rate. Put differently, the question is when something—such as an expansion of the money supply—happens to increase a country's inflation rate, how readily do prices, interest rates, and exchange rates react?

- *Prices of goods* (i.e., inflation) tend to react slowly, in part because intertemporal commodity arbitrage, which requires storage, is expensive.
- *Prices and rates in financial markets*, where arbitrage is cheap, change rapidly and information dissemination permits future effects to be fully anticipated—expected future rate changes happen immediately.

The slow adjustment of the price level following a one-shot monetary expansion means that at first interest rates and exchange rates *both fall*; later they *both rise*. But once inflation has fully set in, interest rates will have risen and exchange rates will have fallen enough to offset the inflation. The main point is that the effect of a change in the interest rate on the exchange rate depends on the *source* of the interest rate change. If the interest rate falls because of a monetary policy short-term effect, or because the government is keeping the rate down, it is a *drop in the real interest rate*—inflation has not fallen and the exchange rate falls. But if the interest rate falls because of a monetary contraction, as will eventually happen as inflation expectations fall, the market will recognize that the *real interest rate is unchanged*, and the currency will not fail.

Finally, a real interest rate change can occur as a result of the imposition or removal of interest rate and exchange *controls*. Especially in a country with high inflation and devaluation, when the rate rises to approach market levels, capital and the exchange rate could respond positively (e.g., as in Argentina); conversely, a too-low rate might precipitate a devaluation.

THE TERM STRUCTURE OF EUROCURRENCY INTEREST RATES

The term structure of interest rates is the relation between interest rates and time to maturity. Typically this relationship, also called the **yield curve**, is a plot of U.S. Treasury yields at a particular point in time, in which the interest rate is plotted on the vertical axis and time to maturity on the horizontal axis. Term structure theory is concerned with why the yield curve has a particular shape at a particular time. While there is some dispute as to the role of institutional constraints and liquidity preference in influencing the yield curve (see box), all agree that expectations of future short-term rates play a dominant role in determining the level of longer-term rates.

For our purposes it suffices to observe that whatever explanation of the term structure holds for the domestic market should also hold for the external or Euromarket. In the absence of capital controls, arbitrage would ensure the virtual equality of internal and external rates at each maturity, and whatever holds for the domestic market would also hold for Eurorates. In other words, there is normally no independent Eurodollar term structure of interest rates.

If capital controls were in place and affected all maturities equally, the internal term structure might not be identical to the external one. But since Eurorates would tend to be at the same position relative to the internal rates at each maturity, a nearly identical term structure would hold. If capital controls affected some maturities but not others, the term structure should still be identical as long as expectations of future rates were the same, since the expectations theory, along with arbitrage in one maturity, would bring external rates in other maturities into alignment with internal rates. If, for example, internal-external arbitrage were possible between short-term but not long-term deposits, identical forecasts for future short-term rates in both the internal and external credit markets should result in identical long-term rates in both markets.

What about the relationships between the term structures of interest

THEORIES OF THE TERM STRUCTURE

Interest rates of different maturities tend to move in tandem. As a rule, long-term rates are less volatile than are those on short-term deposits, the reason being that short-term interest rates are very sensitive to the short-term outlook for credit conditions, whereas long-term rates are affected to a greater degree by long-term inflationary expectations.

Why does the yield curve assume a particular structure? Why do long-term rates differ from short-term rates?

The best-known explanation is the **expectations theory** in which expectations of future interest rates constitute the sole determinant of the yield-maturity relationship. Each investor can buy either long-term securities and hold them or buy short-term securities and continually reinvest in shorts at each maturity over his holding period. In equilibrium, therefore, the expected return for each holding period would tend to be the same whatever alternative or combination of alternatives was chosen. As a result, the return on a long-term bond would tend to equal an unbiased average of the current short-term rates expected to prevail during maturity of the long-term bond. Knowing this one may calculate the implicit or expected short-term rate for any future period based on actual rates of interest prevailing in the market at a specific time.

While most theory and evidence attests to the importance of interest rate expectations in the term structure of interest rates, the economist Sir John Hicks and others have argued that long-term rates in fact tend to differ from the average of expected short-term rates because market participants prefer to lend short unless offered a premium sufficient to offset the risk of lending long. Hicks argued that these **liquidity premiums** tend to be greater the longer the maturity of the bond.

A third theory, the **preferred habitat** hypothesis of Modigliani and Sutch, argues that bond markets are segmented by maturity and that the maturity preferences of market participants are so strong that they tend to borrow and lend only in a particular range of maturities. Therefore, there are several different credit markets and interest rates tend to be determined by supply and demand in each and not so much by interest rate expectations.

In a survey on which this note is based, Van Horne concluded that because recent evidence indicates a bias toward upward-sloping term structures, the term structure appears to be best explained by a combined theory of expectations and risk aversion.

Note: See James C. Van Horne, *Financial Market Rates and Flows* (Englewood Cliffs, NJ: Prentice Hall, 1990, especially Chapter 5).

rates in different Eurocurrency markets? Because there can be no capital controls separating the Euromarkets, all that keeps the yield structures different is the expectation of exchange rate changes, and any risk premium. The relationship between the term structures of two Eurocurrency markets, such as the Eurodollar and Euromark term structures, principally reflects the forward premium of discount and currency expectations at each period in the future. In other words, by comparing the term structure of interest rates in two Eurocurrency markets, one may be able to derive the **term structure of exchange rate expectations**.

Of course, if well-developed forward markets exist for all maturities, the term structure of exchange rate expectations may be derived directly from the series of forward exchange rates, to the extent that these equal the expected future spot rates. For most markets, however, longer-term forward markets are nonexistent or too thin to be reliable. In such cases it may be useful to employ the term structure of interest rates in two credit markets to deduce the term structure of exchange rate expectations.

SUMMARY

In this chapter the major determinants of Eurocurrency interest rates were identified as domestic and foreign credit conditions, forward exchange rates and exchange rate expectations, and three sets of factors that might inhibit arbitrage—capital controls, risk factors, and transactions costs.

External or Eurocurrency interest rates, it was argued, are always linked through arbitrage to internal rates, although capital controls can weaken this linkage. In the absence of capital controls, external loan and deposit rates are bounded by loan and deposit rates in the internal credit market. Eurocurrency rates are linked to one another through covered interest arbitrage in such a way that the interest rate differential equals the forward premium or discount between two currencies. In addition, market transactors, through the process of borrowing and lending in different currencies, cause the forward premium or discount, and the interest rate differential, to equal the expected rate of change of the exchange rate. As a result, the path of exchange rate changes that the market expects can be deduced by comparing the term structures of interest rates in two Eurocurrency markets.

The reader will recognize that these relationships do not necessarily hold at all times in exactly the form described here. It is not certain, for example, that the forward rate is always an unbiased predictor of the future spot exchange rate, although the evidence for a systematic, identifiable bias is mixed. But the relationships as presented have enough generality to explain a wide range of phenomena in the international money market. Moreover, they fit in well with two other relationships well known to students of international financial markets: the purchasing power parity theorem and the Fisher effect. The purchasing power parity theorem says that the difference between inflation rates in two currencies equals the rate of change of the exchange rate. But we know that the difference between interest rates in two currencies equals the expected rate of change of the exchange rate; therefore, interest rate differentials must also equal differences in expected inflation rates. Is this the case? Indeed it is, according to the Fisher effect: interest rates in a particular currency must be higher the higher the rate of inflation that is expected, to offset the loss of purchasing power suffered by investors. Thus commodity price expectations, currency expectations, and interest rates are linked to one another in a coherent fashion.

All the relationships between credit and foreign exchange markets described in this chapter result from a continual process of simultaneous interaction. Any deviation from interest rate parity, for example, will set in motion a number of transactions that will change interest rates and exchange rates, and this change will trigger further transactions until interest rate parity between Eurocurrency and foreign exchange is reestablished. The interest rate parity theorem describes an ex post relationship toward which rates will tend to move. However, which part of the total readjustment is actually accomplished by changes in which rate cannot be determined a priori; this depends on the relative sizes of the credit markets involved, on exchange rate expectations, on the degree of institutional flexibility and efficiency in the market, and, of course, on government regulations and intervention.

SELECTED REFERENCES

Adler, Michael and Bruce Lehmann, "Deviations from Purchasing Power Parity in the Long Run," *Journal of Finance*, December 1983, pp. 1471–1488.

Aliber, Robert Z., "The Interest Rate Parity Theorem: A Reinterpretation," *Journal of Political Economy*, November 1973, pp. 1451–1459.

Aliber, Robert Z., "The Integration of the Offshore and Domestic Banking System," *Journal of Monetary Economics*, Vol. 6, 1980, pp. 509–526.

Ashby, D. F. V., "Analyzing the Maturity Structure of the Eurodollar Market," *The Banker*, July 1973, pp. 769–772.

Baillie, Richard T., and Patrick C. McMahon, *The Foreign Exchange Market: Theory and Econometric Evidence*. Cambridge: Cambridge University Press, 1989.

Beenstock, Michael, "Forward Exchange Rates and 'Siegel's Paradox'," *Oxford Economic Papers*, Vol. 37, 1985, pp. 298–303.

Bergstrand, Jeffrey H., "Selected Views of Exchange Rate Determination After a Decade of `Floating'," *New England Economic Review*, Federal Reserve Bank of Boston, May/June 1983, pp. 14–29.

Cornell, Bradford, "Spot Rates, Forward Rates, and Exchange Market Efficiency," *Journal of Financial Economics*, Vol. 5, 1977, pp. 55–65.

Cumby, Robert E., and M. Obstfeld, "A Note on Exchange Rate Expectations and Nominal Interest Rate Differentials: A Test of the Fisher Hypothesis," *Journal of Finance*, Vol. 36, 1981, pp. 697–703

Deardorff, Alan V. "One-Way Arbitrage and Its Implications for the Foreign Exchange Markets," *Journal of Political Economy*, Vol. 87, 1979, pp. 351–364.

Dooley, Michael P., and Peter Isard, "Capital Controls, Political Risk and Deviations from Interest Parity," *Journal of Political Economy*, Vol. 88, No. 2, March/April 1980, pp. 370–384.

Dooley, Michael P., and J. R. Shafer, "Analysis of Short-Run Exchange Rate Behavior: March 1973 to November 1981," in D. Bigman and T. Taya, eds., *Exchange Rate and Trade Instability*. Cambridge, MA: Ballinger, 1983.

Dornbusch, Rudiger, "Expectations and Exchange Rate Dynamics," *Journal of Political Economy*, Vol. 84, December 1976, pp. 1161–1176.

Dornbusch, Rudiger, "Exchange Rate Economics: Where Do We Stand?" *Brookings Papers on Economic Activity*, Vol. 1, 1980, pp. 143–185.

Dufey, Gunter, and Ian Giddy, "Eurocurrency Deposit Risk," *Journal of Banking and Finance*, Fall 1984.

Fama, Eugene, "Forward and Spot Exchange Rates," *Journal of Monetary Economics*, November 1984.

Finnerty, Joseph, and Thomas Schneeweis, "Time Series Analysis of International Dollar Denominated Interest Rates," *Journal of International Business Studies*, Spring/Summer 1979, pp. 39–52.

Fisher, Irving, *The Theory of Interest*. New York: Macmillan, 1980.

Frankel, Jeffrey A., "A Test of the Existence of the Risk Premium in the Foreign Exchange Market vs. the Hypothesis of Perfect Substitutability," Federal Reserve System, International Finance Discussion Papers, No. 149 (Washington, D.C.), August 1979.

Frankel, Jeffery A., "On the Mark: A Theory of Floating Exchange Rates Based on Real Interest Differentials," *American Economic Review*, September 1979, pp. 610–622.

Frankel, Jeffery, "Flexible Exchange Rates: Experience Versus Theory," *Journal of Portfolio Management*, Winter 1989, pp. 45–54.

Frankel, Jeffery, and Menzie Chinn, "Exchange Rate Expectations and the Risk Premium: Tests for a Cross-Section of 17 Currencies," National Bureau of Economic Research (Cambridge, MA), Working Paper No. 3806, August 1991.

Frankel, Jeffery, "Quantifying International Capital Mobility in the 1990s," in D. Bernheim and J. Shoven, eds., *National Saving and Economic Performance*, pp. 227–260. Chicago: University of Chicago Press, 1991.

Frankel, Jeffery A., "Measuring International Capital Mobility: A Review," *AEA Papers and Proceedings*, May 1992, pp. 197–202.

Frenkel, Jacob A., "A Monetary Approach to the Exchange Rate: Doctrinal Aspects and Empirical Evidence," *Scandinavian Journal of Economics*, Vol. 78, June 1978, pp. 255–276.

Frenkel, Jacob, A., and Richard M. Levich, "Covered Interest Arbitrage: Unexploited Profits?" *Journal of Political Economy*, April 1975, pp. 325–338.

Frenkel, Jacob A., and Michael L. Mussa, "Asset Markets, Exchange Rates and the Balance of Payments," National Bureau of Economic Research (Cambridge, MA), Working Paper No. 1287, March 1984.

Fukao, Mitsuhiro, "The Risk Premium in the Foreign Exchange Market," unpublished Ph.D. dissertation, University of Michigan, Ann Arbor, 1981.

Giddy, Ian H., "An Integrated Theory of Exchange Rate Equilibrium," *Journal of Financial and Quantitative Analysis*, December 1976, pp. 883–892.

Giddy, Ian, "Why Eurodollars Grow," *Columbia Journal of World Business*, Fall 1979, pp. 54–60.

Giddy, Ian, Gunter Dufey, and Sangkee Min, "Interest Rates in the U.S. and Eurodollar Markets," *Review of World Economics (Weltwirtschaftliches Archiv)*, No. 1, 1979, pp. 51–67.

Hacche, G. and J. C. Townsend, "A Broad Look at Exchange Rate Movements for Eight Currencies, 1972–80," *Bank of England Quarterly Bulletin*, December 1981, pp. 489–509.

Hakkio, Craig S., "Expectations and the Forward Exchange Rate," *International Economic Review*, Vol. 22 1981, pp. 663–678.

Hakkio, Craig S., "Does the Exchange Rate Follow a Random Walk? A Monte Carlo Study of Four Tests for a Random Walk," *Journal of International Money and Finance*, June 1986, pp. 221–229.

Hansen, Lars P. and J. Hodrick, "Forward Exchange Rates as Optimal Predictors of Future Spot Rates: An Econometric Analysis," *Journal of Political Economy*, Vol. 88, 1980, pp. 829–853.

Hartman, David, "The International Financial Market and U.S. Interest Rates," National Bureau of Economic Research, (Cambridge, MA), Working Paper No. 598, December 1980.

Hendershott, Patric. "The Structure of International Interest Rates: The U.S. Treasury Bill Rate and the Eurodollar Deposit Rate," *Journal of Finance*, September 1967, pp. 455–465.

Herring, Richard J. and Richard L. Marston, "The Forward Market and Interest Rate Determination in the Eurocurrency and National Money Markets," in Carl H. Stem et al., eds., *The Eurocurrency Markets and the International Monetary System*, Washington, D.C.: American Enterprise Institute, 1976.

Hewson, John, and Eisuke Sakakibara, *The Eurocurrency Markets and Their Implications*. Lexington, Mass.: D. C. Heath, 1975.

Hodrick, Robert J., and S. Srivatava, "An Investigation of Risk and Return in Forward Foreign Exchange," *Journal of International Money and Finance*, April 1984.

Isard, Peter, "Exchange Rate Determination: A Survey of Popular Views and Recent Models," Studies in International Finance, No. 42. Princeton, N.J.: International Finance Section, Princeton University, May 1978.

Johnston, R. B., "Some Aspects of the Determination of Eurocurrency Interest Rates," *Bank of England Quarterly Bulletin* (March 1979), pp. 35–46.

Kaen, Fred, and George Hachey, "Eurocurrency and National Money Market Interest Rates: An Empirical Investigation of Causality," *Journal of Money, Credit, and Banking*, August 1983, pp. 327–338.

Kern, David, "Interest Rates and the Currency Structure of the Euromarkets," *Euromoney*, May 1973, p. 26.

Klopstock, Fred H., "The Euromarkets Tighten Their Links with New York," *Euromoney*, August 1975, pp. 25–30.

Kobrin, Stephen J. "Political Risk: A Review and Reconsideration," *Journal of International Business Studies*, Vol. 10, No. 1, Spring-Summer 1979, pp. 67–80.

Kohlhagen, Steven W., The Behavior of Foreign Exchange Markets—A Critical Survey of the Empirical Literature, *Monograph Series in Finance and Economics*, Monograph No. 3, New York University, 1978.

Kreicher, Lawrence, "Eurodollar Arbitrage," *Federal Reserve Bank of New York Quarterly Review*, Summer 1982, pp. 10–22.

Krishnan, Suresh E., "International Integration of Dollar Denominated Money Market Instruments," Ph.D. Dissertation, University of Michigan, Ann Arbor, 1983.

Kwack, Sung, "The Structure of International Interest Rates: An Extension of Hendershott's Tests," *Journal of Finance*, September 1971, pp. 897–900.

Levich, Richard M., "On the Efficiency of Markets for Foreign Exchange," in R. Dornbusch and J. Frenkel, eds., *International Economic Policy: An Assessment of Theory and Evidence*. Johns Hopkins University Press, 1979.

Levich, Richard M., "Evaluating the Performance of the Forecasters," in Richard Ensor, ed., *The Management of Foreign Exchange Risk*, 2nd ed. pp. 121–134. London: Euromoney Publications, 1982.

Levich, Richard M., "Empirical Studies of Exchange Rates: Price Behavior, Rate Determination and Market Efficiency," in R. W. Jones and P. B. Kenen, eds., *Handbook of International Economics*. pp. 979–1040. New York: Elsevier Science Publishers, 1985.

Levin, Jay H., "The Eurodollar Market and the International Transmission of Interest Rates," *Canadian Journal of Economics*, May 1974, p. 205.

Little, Jane S., *Euro-Dollars: The Money Market Gypsies*, Chapter 3. New York: Harper & Row, 1975.

Llewellyn, David T., "How to Control Capital Flows?" *The Banker*, July 1973, pp. 764–768.

Longworth, D., "Testing the Efficiency of the Canadian Exchange Market Under the Assumption of No Risk Premium," *Journal of Finance*, Vol. 36 (1981), pp. 43–50.

Lutz, Friedrich A., "The Eurocurrency System," *Banca Nazionale del Lavoro—Quarterly Review*, September 1974, pp. 183–200.

Marston, Richard C., "Interest Arbitrage in the Eurocurrency Markets," *European Economic Review*, Vol. 6, 1976.

"Measuring International Capital Mobility: A Review," *AEA Papers and Proceedings*, May 1992, pp. 197–202.

Meese, Richard A. and Kenneth J. Singleton, "Rational Expectations, Risk Premia, and the Market for Spot and Forward Exchange," Federal Reserve System (Washington, D.C.), International Finance Discussion Papers, No. 165, July 1980.

Mills, Rodney H., Jr., "Regulations on Short-Term Capital Movements: Recent Techniques in Selected Industrial Countries," *Federal Reserve Board Discussion Paper*, Washington, D.C., November 6, 1972.

Mills, Rodney, "Structural Change in the Eurodollar Market: Evidence from a Two-

Equation Model," Board of Governors of the Federal Reserve System (Washington, D.C.), Discussion Paper No. 33, November 1, 1973.

Morgan Guaranty Trust Co., *World Financial Markets,* monthly publication.

Officer, Lawrence H., "The Purchasing-Power-Parity Theorem of Exchange Rates: A Review Article," *IMF Staff Papers,* March 1976, pp. 1–60.

Officer, Lawrence H., *Purchasing Power Parity and Exchange Rates: Theory, Evidence and Relevance.* Greenwich, CT: JAI Press, 1982.

Organization for Economic Cooperation and Development, *Regulations Affecting International Banking Operations,* Paris: OECD, 1981.

Otani, Ichiro and Siddarth Tiwari, "Capital Controls, Interest Rate Parity, and Exchange Rates: A Theoretical Approach," *International Economic Journal,* Vol. 4, Spring 1990, pp. 25–44.

Rosenberg, Michael R., "Foreign Exchange Controls: An International Comparison," in Abraham George and Ian H. Giddy, eds., *International Finance Handbook,* Vol. 1. New York: Wiley, 1983.

Shapiro, Alan C., "What Does Purchasing Power Parity Mean?" *Journal of International Money and Finance,* Summer 1983, pp. 295–318.

Stein, Jerome L., M. Rzepczynski, and R. Selvaggio, "A Theoretical Explanation of the Empirical Studies of Futures Markets in Foreign Exchange and Financial Instruments," *The Financial Review,* Vol. 18, February 1983, pp. 1–32.

Walmsley, Julian, "Euromarket Dealing," in Abraham George and Ian H. Giddy, eds., *International Finance Handbook,* Vol. 1. New York: Wiley, 1983.

APPENDIX 3-A
Causes of Bias in the Forward Rate

This appendix explores some ways in which a possible bias in the forward rate as a predictor of the future spot exchange rate may be explained. We break the analysis into three parts: technical factors, political risk, and a premium for exchange risk.

TECHNICAL FACTORS

One of the sources of systematic differences is a technicality known in the literature as the Siegel paradox, which is based on a mathematical concept called Jensen's inequality. If residents of two countries consume a common basket of goods, the foreign exchange rate will generally lie between the expectation of the future rate defined in terms of one currency and the expectation of the future rate defined in terms of the other currency. However, the practical significance of the Siegel paradox is negligible when the (expected) variance of the exchange rate is not excessive, and it disappears altogether when purchasing power parity (PPP) holds.[1]

Transactions costs incurred by speculators who are buying or selling foreign currency forward are another potential source of bias. If the expected future spot rate is given by $E(S_{t+n})$, the current forward rate for that maturity is F_t^n, and T is the per unit transactions cost (all quoted in foreign currency units per dollar), then a speculator will sell foreign currency forward so long as

$$E\left(S_{t+n}\right) \;<\; F_t^n - T$$

[1] For a thorough analysis of this phenomenon, see Michael Beenstock, "Forward Exchange Rates and 'Siegel's Paradox,' " *Oxford Economic Papers*, Vol. 37, 1985, pp. 298–305.

and speculative profits are eliminated when

$$E\left(S_{t+n}\right) = F_t^n - T$$

Similarly, speculators will buy foreign currency forward as long as

$$F_t^n + T < E\left(S_{t+n}\right)$$

and will cease to speculate when

$$F_t^n + T = E\left(S_{t+n}\right)$$

From these conditions, when the spot exchange rate is rising and is expected to continue doing so, then the forward rate is likely to underestimate the future spot rate and vice versa for a falling spot rate. Unless there is a secular trend in the exchange rate, a sufficiently large number of observations would eliminate any *measurable* bias due to transactions costs.

POLITICAL RISK

While Siegel's paradox and transactions cost may be dismissed as mere technicalities in the context of the foreign exchange markets, or as being at most of minor importance, the incidence of political interference in the market process by government is a different matter altogether. The point may best be made by an example from Great Britain. If Her Majesty's government were prone to interfere with the rights of nonresidents' sterling assets, one might expect that those who purchase sterling for forward delivery will demand a premium, that is, more sterling for every dollar, other things being equal. By the same token, one would expect U.K. interest rates to be systematically higher than warranted on the basis of expected exchange rate changes alone.

Table 3A-1 illustrates this point in terms of interest rates: given a spot rate of $2 per pound, the 12-months forward is $1.92, while the expected future spot rate is assumed to be $1.94 under these conditions. Of course, the latter cannot be observed directly; the only evidence would be an "undershooting" of the forward rate by $0.02 or, in terms of interest rates, an interest differential of 100 basis points per annum on average, provided the political risk premium is constant over time, and provided further that transactors don't make systematic errors in judging the future exchange rate of the pound sterling.

While this example might clarify the effect of political risk on forward rates and interest differentials, it is much more difficult to estimate it ex ante. Even though this may be an intractable task, a modest contribution can

TABLE 3A-1 Bias in Forward Rate in Presence of Political Risk

	United States (no risk of intervention)	United Kingdom (substantial risk of intervention)	United Kingdom (no risk of intervention)
Interest rates per annum	5%	9%	8%
Forward discount % per annum	—	4	3
Expected depreciation % per annum (unobservable)	—	3	3

be made by an attempt to clarify conceptually the elements that comprise that catch-all concept, "political risk."

To begin with, the term "political risk" is not terribly meaningful and cannot readily be made operational. It is both overly confining and confusing. The focus should probably be on current and potential impacts of the political environment upon investors' transactions. More precisely, one should be concerned with the probability that changes in the political environment will reduce returns to the point where investments would no longer be acceptable on the basis of ex ante criteria.[2] Obviously, those exchange controls, that is, quantitative restrictions on international flows of financial assets, that affect existing positions of nonresidents would fall under this category. What is less often recognized is that quantitative restrictions in domestic credit markets have the very same effect: they add an additional constraining element to arbitrage.

Government actions that affect exchange rates or interest rates through market intervention measures, such as open market operations by the central bank, are generally held to contribute to exchange risk, which can be taken fully into account by market participants in setting forward premia and interest rate differentials, respectively. But the differentiation between quantitative restrictions and price fluctuations is not so clear. Obviously, political factors can and will influence central bank monetary policy; for example, such factors may render it especially erratic.

Further, exchange rate fluctuations may themselves give rise to exchange controls if the body politic considers them to be "excessive." In any case, market efficiency presupposes that prices are arrived at by competitive, profit-seeking transactors. If a central bank is not motivated by profitability, and if its actions are so massive that it succeeds in shifting

---

[2] Stephen J. Kobrin, "Political Risk: A Review and Reconsideration," *Journal of International Business Studies*, Vol. 10, No. 1, Spring/Summer 1979, pp. 67–80.

prices from equilibrium points, the forward rate or interest differential will not be an unbiased predictor, nor will the market be efficient.

A further point of distinction is necessary. Risk refers to uncertainty— here, the uncertainty of future capital controls. It is therefore necessary to distinguish between interest differentials or premia in the forward market that are caused by existing controls—which may place a taxlike burden on assets in a certain jurisdiction—and differentials that are due to expected, hence future, capital controls.[3]

Once political risk is put in the proper perspective, it becomes obvious that it is closely related to the unsystematic risk of a portfolio. For one, erratic open market policies or intervention in foreign exchange markets can lead to the exchange risks described in the paragraphs that follow. At the same time, it is quite possible that a causal relationship exists between interest differentials due to political risk based on the prospect of future capital controls, and the gross supply of debt outstanding against different governments, relative to the distribution of world wealth among residents of different political jurisdictions.[4] This point, however, leads directly to a somewhat different category of explanations for the existence of a systematic bias.

EXCHANGE RISK PREMIA

The general "parity" framework often used in this book relies on the forward rate being an unbiased predictor of the future spot exchange rate, and so is inconsistent with the existence of exchange risk premia. One of the simplifying assumptions is that real interest rates are stable, so that an (unexpected) change in monetary policy, for example, will affect only nominal rates. This assumes that prices of goods and services will adjust instantaneously to changes in financial markets. Obviously this is not the case. Prices for goods and services tend to be much more sticky than prices of financial assets because of existence of contractual relationships and, more prominently, the prevalence of market imperfections (unions, large corporations, technological advantages). As a result, there will be transitory changes in real interest rates that may persist for some time when the change in monetary policy is not expected to last.

Another assumption is the perfect substitutability of goods within a country and across borders. This amounts to saying that all goods are homogeneous and that there are no nontradable goods, which implies that both

---

[3] This point has been clearly made in Michael P. Dooley and Peter Isard, "Capital Controls, Political Risk and Deviations from Interest Parity," *Journal of Political Economy*, Vol. 88, No. 2, March/April 1980, pp. 370–384.

[4] Ibid., p. 371. These authors also present empirical data that are consistent with this hypothesis.

the law of one price and purchasing power parity hold. However, since PPP refers to the average price (i.e., price levels), it is possible—when arbitrage in goods' markets is imperfect—that purchasing power parity holds but the exchange rate changes. This would be the consequence of relative price changes in each country and the resultant impact on the commodity composition of trade. Conversely, it is possible for the exchange rate to remain unchanged while price-level changes differ at home and abroad.[5]

A further assumption implicit in the equilibrium framework is perfect substitutability between domestic and foreign financial assets. If domestic and foreign bonds are perfect substitutes, they must have the same expected real return; hence, differences in nominal interest rates can only mirror the expected exchange rate change. In other words, simple monetary models of the kind sketched in this chapter assume that real, inflation-adjusted, interest differentials cannot persist. Many now believe that they can, because after all, people do arbitrage between nominal, not real, interest rates. This has been shown in a simple but ingenious fashion by Jeffery Frankel.[6] He decomposes the real interest differential into a *country premium* and a *currency premium* as follows. Begin by defining the real interest differential as

$$r_R - r_R^* = \left(r_N - E[I]\right) - \left(r_N^* - E[I^*]\right)$$

where r_R and r_N are real and nominal interest rates, respectively, and $E[I]$ is the expected inflation rate. Real interest rates are nominal rates minus the expected inflation rate. Now decompose the right-hand side into three parts:

$$r_R - r_R^* = \left(r_N - r_N^* - FD\right) + \left(FD - E[s]\right) + \left(E[s] - E[I] - E[I^*]\right)$$

where FD is the forward discount on the domestic currency and $E[s]$ is the expected depreciation of the domestic currency.

The first term $(r_N - r_N^* - FD)$ is the covered interest differential. It can be called the *country premium* because it captures barriers to arbitrage attributable to national boundaries: transactions costs, information costs, present and expected capital controls, taxes, and default risk. The second term $(FD - E[s])$ is the deviation from the international Fisher effect, or the *exchange risk premium*. The third term $(E[s] - E[I] - E[I]^*)$ is the expected real depreciation. Frankel calls the last two together the *currency premium* because they pertain

---

[5] The conditions for law of one price (LOP) are therefore more stringent than those for purchasing power parity. The latter are after (mistakenly) interpreted that changes in price levels lead to changes in exchange rates, while the former implies that causation proceeds in the opposite direction. However, both LOP and PPP variables are simultaneously determined.

[6] "Measuring International Capital Mobility: A Review," *AEA Papers and Proceedings*, May 1992, pp. 197–202.

to differences in assets attributable to currency of denomination rather than country of jurisdiction. Only if one believes that all these are zero, or that they coincidentally offset one another, would one expect that real interest rates are equal between countries.

Hence it is important to repeat that the results of the equilibrium framework must be viewed as approximate, long-run tendencies only, for purchasing power parity may not hold for extended periods of time, the substitutability of assets may not be perfect, and the market for financial assets and real goods may not clear instantaneously.

When other than monetary assets are allowed for, then any investor in fixed-interest securities faces a purchasing power risk, because of the uncertainty of future inflation. So long as inflation rates are not perfectly (positively) correlated among countries, it would pay to diversify portfolios internationally. In portfolio balance, therefore, it is theoretically possible that real return expectations differ between domestic and foreign securities because of residual purchasing power risk.[7] Put somewhat differently, systematic deviations from the international Fisher relationship are possible when one or the other country has issued an "excessive" amount of government liabilities[8] relative to its share in the minimum-variance, internationally diversified portfolio.[9] Accordingly, a premium above and beyond the expected depreciation could be explained as compensation for investors to increase their holdings of foreign currency assets, of which "excessive" amounts have been issued.[10]

The foregoing considerations abstract from the issue of diversifiable versus nondiversifiable risk in the broader context of an international capital asset pricing model. It would, for example, be risky to hold securities denominated in a currency whose value is positively correlated with that of other assets: the securities are afflicted with a risk that cannot be diversified away, and a risk premium would be required. But difficult questions arise

[7] There should be no residual exchange risk because there is a perfect negative correlation for deviation from purchasing power parity for any two currencies, guaranteeing, in principle, complete diversifiability.

[8] Government rather than private debt is necessary for a risk premium, for with private debt gains to borrowers will be losses to lenders, and the perfect negative correlation of such returns permits the complete elimination of this risk through an appropriate diversification strategy.

[9] See, for instance, Rudiger Dornbusch, "Exchange Rate Economics: Where Do We Stand?" *Brookings Papers on Economic Activity*, Vol. 1, 1980, pp. 143–185.

[10] An interesting empirical exercise would be to analyze the so-called "dollar overhang" in this context: if there is a dollar overhang relative to, say, the mark, it should be true that

$$FP = i_{US} - i_{DM} = d + \text{(relative excess demand for DM securities)}$$

where FP = forward premium on the mark, i = nominal interest rates, d = expected appreciation of the mark (depreciation of the $), and (...) measures the risk premium for holding dollars.

as to the definition of "other assets" and the relevant consumption patterns of international investors. As noted in the chapter, for a risk premium to exist, the risk of holding a foreign currency asset must be nondiversifiable. With risk-neutral investors, any risk premium will be competed away, since it represents expected excess profits. If there is a systematic risk premium on, say, dollar-denominated securities, because too many dollar-denominated securities have been issued by the U.S. government, then it might pay, in terms of lower nominal and expected real interest cost, to issue securities in currencies that are relatively "underrepresented."

It remains true that deviations of the forward rate from the expected future spot rate can be due to different factors that will, moreover, interact in complex ways. The empirical evidence on the existence of a risk premium is ambiguous. In some of the early studies, Cornell[11] and Frankel,[12] using rather different methodologies, came to the conclusion that, with respect to the currencies and sample periods used in their studies, a risk premium cannot be confirmed. On the other hand, Meese and Singleton[13] found evidence of a time-variant risk premium for the Canadian dollar and the German mark, but not for the Swiss franc, during 1976–1979. More recently, Frankel and Chinn, using survey data from a panel of 17 countries, found that the exchange risk premium was important but highly variable in all but a few of the countries.[14] Given the difference in models, statistical techniques, currencies, and sample periods, not to mention the fact that exchange rate expectations are not directly observable, this inconclusive state of affairs is not surprising.[15] In con-

---

[11] Bradford Cornell, "Spot Rates, Forward Rates, and Exchange Market Efficiency," *Journal of Financial Economics*, Vol. 5, 1977, pp. 55–65.

[12] Jeffery A. Frankel, "A Test of the Existence of the Risk Premium in the Foreign Exchange Market vs. the Hypothesis of Perfect Substitutability," Federal Reserve System (Washington, D.C.), International Finance Discussion Papers, No. 149, August 1979.

[13] Richard A. Meese and Kenneth J. Singleton, "Rational Expectations, Risk Premia, and the Market for Spot and Forward Exchange," Federal Reserve System (Washington, D.C.), International Finance Discussion Papers, No. 165, July 1980.

[14] Jeffery Frankel and Menzie Chinn, "Exchange Rate Expectations and the Risk Premium: Tests for a Cross-section of 17 Currencies," National Bureau of Economic Research (Cambridge, MA), Working Paper No. 3806, August 1991. See also the survey in Jeffery Frankel, "Quantifying International Capital Mobility in the 1990s," in D. Bernheim and J. Shoven, eds., *National Saving and Economic Performance* (Chicago: University of Chicago Press, 1991), pp. 227–260.

[15] For a comprehensive review of exchange rate behavior during the 1970s, see G. Hacche and J. C. Townsend, "A Broad Look at Exchange Rate Movements for Eight Currencies, 1972–80," *Bank of England Quarterly Bulletin*, December 1981, pp. 489–509. For a review of the literature and the theory on exchange risk premium, see also Jerome L. Stein, M. Rzepczynski, and R. Selvaggio, "A Theoretical Explanation of the Empirical Studies of Futures Markets in Foreign Exchange and Financial Instruments," *The Financial Review*, Vol. 18, February 1983, pp. 1–32.

clusion, the consensus of research seems to be that there is evidence of a risk premium, but that it is unstable.[16]

---

[16] E. Fama, "Forward and Spot Exchange Rates," *Journal of Monetary Economics*, November 1984, and R. J. Hodrick and S. Srivatava, "An Investigation of Risk and Return in Forward Foreign Exchange," *Journal of International Money and Finance*, April 1984. Various empirical results are summarized in R. T. Baillie and P. C. McMahon, *The Foreign Exchange Market: Theory and Econometric Evidence* (Cambridge: Cambridge University Press, 1989).

Chapter Four

EURODOLLAR FORWARDS, SWAPS, FUTURES, AND OPTIONS

EURODOLLAR INTEREST RATE RISK HEDGING TECHNIQUES

Interest rate risk management has now become a fundamental aspect of practical finance, be it the investment of funds, the trading of a position, or the financing of a corporation. Just as the Eurocurrency market allows the separation of currency of denomination from the country of jurisdiction, so the tools described in this chapter permit the separation of the investment or financing vehicle from its interest rate characteristics. These tools give the financial manager enormous flexibility in tailoring the firm's interest rate exposure to its needs or views.

A typical application of interest rate risk management is one where a financial institution faces an anticipated short-term future funding requirement, or an anticipated temporary cash surplus. Both expose the funds manager to the risk of interest rate changes from the present until the time when the borrowing or lending occurs. There are five ways in which such interest rate risks can be hedged:

- By mismatched maturities
- Through a forward interest rate contract
- By entering into an interest rate swap
- By taking a position in interest rate futures
- By buying fixed interest options

Locking in a future interest rate through maturity mismatching is simple although somewhat cumbersome. Consider a corporate treasurer who anticipates in June that she will have temporary funds on hand for some future period, say, during July and August. To eliminate the interest rate risk, she will borrow the same amount at a fixed rate now for a period ending on July 1. The borrowed funds are then placed in a fixed rate deposit maturing two months later, at the end of August. The funds that she obtains on July 1 will be used to repay the loan, while she still has money invested at a known rate and maturing when she needs it, at the end of August. Equally, if she instead anticipates needing money for a future period, she could borrow fixed-rate money now for repayment at the end of August and place the funds in a fixed interest deposit maturing on July 1. This will effectively lock in her future borrowing cost.

Some banks, knowing that they can do the mismatching themselves (and more efficiently) and lock in their own future cost of funds, are willing to guarantee their borrowers a set-in-advance, future fixed borrowing rate. Depositors can similarly be offered a guaranteed rate. This is a forward interest rate contract, commonly known as a future rate agreement, or FRA for short. Variations of it come with other names: forward forward, forward rate contract, and forward rate agreement.

While FRAs are designed to hedge interest rate risk for a single future period, for longer maturities when annual or periodic coupon payments must be made, the appropriate hedging technique is the interest rate swap. This entails an agreement to exchange fixed for floating interest payments or to exchange floating payments linked to two different market benchmarks.

The best developed market for hedging interest rate risk at present is the interest rate futures market. In principle, interest rate futures are similar to an FRA in that they are contracts for delivery of a certain fixed interest instrument, such as a bank certificate of deposit, at some future date and at a known rate. In practice, they differ from forward contracts in important ways, which we shall describe shortly.

Fixed income options are like futures in that they are exchange-traded contracts for future delivery of fixed income instruments. Options, however, offer greater flexibility in that they provide the right, but not the obligation, to go through with the deal. They can be particularly useful to firms that face contingent interest rate risk—a future funding need or commitment that might, after all, not materialize if interest rates rise or fall beyond a certain level. Later we shall introduce a technique for using these options to hedge contingent Eurodollar interest rate risk.

FUTURE RATE AGREEMENTS

An FRA is an agreement between two parties to lock in a certain interest rate for a fixed period beginning at a fixed date in the future. This technique originated from one used in the Eurodollar interbank market in the 1970s. For some obscure reason, the original practice was known as a "forward forward."

A forward forward is a commitment on the part of one bank to deposit funds at an agreed interest rate at some date in the future in another bank, which also agrees to pay that rate. Thus the first bank commits itself to accepting not only the deposit rate but also the credit risk of the second bank, whatever the latter's condition at the future date. The second bank has locked in not only the rate but also the availability of funds.

Because a forward forward constitutes a 100 percent credit risk as well as a rate commitment, the market has not developed well and has rarely been available to nonbank borrowers wishing to lock in a cost of funds.

A major step forward was taken in the mid-1980s with the development of the Future Rate Agreement, one which works through cash compensation for interest rate changes rather than through actual borrowing or lending of funds. This feature allows much—but not all—of the credit risk to be eliminated.

An FRA may be defined as a contract between two parties to fix a future interest rate at a specified level for a specified future period. One party fixes its lending rate, while the other fixes its borrowing rate. If, at the start of the specified period, the market rate turns out to be different from the fixed-in-advance rate, the "losing" party compensates the "winning" party.

Consider a simple example of an FRA. Bank Bumiputra Malaysia wants to lock in its cost of 6-month borrowing starting 9 months from now. Bumiputra telephones Standard Bank in London.

STAN: So you want to lock in the LIBOR interest rate in nine for six? Ten pounds?

BUMI: Months you mean. Millions you mean. Yes. What rate can you quote me? I see that today's sterling LIBOR is 8%.

STAN: Righto, but the yield curve is upward sloping. We can quote you $9^1/_8 - 9^5/_{16}$. That means we'll lock in your *borrowing* LIBOR cost at $9^5/_{16}$ or your *depositing* LIBOR at $9^1/_8$.

BUMI: Okay, I'll take the $9^5/_{16}$ borrowing rate. But how does the deal work?

STAN: Well, we don't exactly guarantee *your own* borrowing cost. We simply assure you that LIBOR will be $9^5/_{16}$. If, nine months from now, LIBOR is actually above $9^5/_{16}$, we'll pay you the difference. For example, if LIBOR is 11 percent, we'll pay 11 percent minus $9^5/_{16}$ percent, that is, $1^{11}/_{16}$ percent. So if you borrow at LIBOR, your net cost will still be $9^5/_{16}$ percent.

BUMI: I see. What if LIBOR falls to, say, 7 percent?

STAN: Then you pay us $2^5/_{16}$ percent, semiannual. Of course, if LIBOR turns out to be exactly $9^5/_{16}$ percent, then neither of us pays the other.

How did Stan come up with his quotes of $9^1/_8 - 9^5/_{16}$? An FRA is purely and simply a forward contract and can be priced by means of the "implicit forward interest rate" calculation. This calculation is based on the assumption that any forward rate commitment can be hedged by simultaneous borrowing and lending for different maturities.

For example,

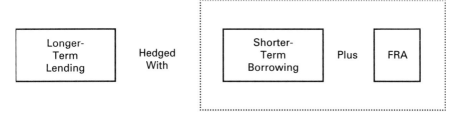

Since each side of a hedge position must be equal, we can deduce that, given the longer-term rate and the shorter-term rate, one can figure out the implicit FRA rate.

The quick-and-dirty formula[1] is:

$$
\begin{aligned}
\text{FRA rate} &= \text{Implicit "forward" interest rate from yield curve} \\
&= \frac{\left[\text{Longer - term rate} \times \text{longer maturity}\right] - \left[\text{shorter - term rate} \times \text{shorter maturity}\right]}{\text{Maturity differential}}
\end{aligned}
$$

Although a future rate agreement is typically used to hedge a borrowing or lending rate, the agreement does not entail actually making or receiving a loan during the specified period. Instead, the rate is locked in by the method of cash compensation for the gain or loss suffered by each party to the contract.

Many banks that are reluctant to make a lending commitment are nevertheless perfectly willing to make a future rate commitment because this is

---

[1] The precise formula is

$$
\text{FRA rate} = \frac{\left(1 + i_n\right)^n}{\left(1 + i_m\right)^{n-m}}
$$

where i = interest rate, n = longer maturity, and m = shorter maturity.

something they can easily hedge by mismatched borrowing and lending, or in the FRA market itself.

One party (the borrower or "buyer" of an FRA) will receive a payment from the other if the actual interest rate rises above the fixed rate, or the other party (the lender or "seller" of an FRA[2]) will be compensated by the first party if the actual rate falls below the fixed rate. The amount of compensation will be the difference between some actual market rate (typically LIBOR) at the beginning of the specified period and the agreed-upon fixed rate. That difference is adjusted for the length of the specified period (e.g., 3 months) and multiplied by the dollar principal amount of the agreement (say, $10 million).

For example, if the agreed-upon rate is 10 percent and 3-month LIBOR turns out to be 12 percent at the beginning of the 90-day period, the "seller" must pay the "buyer" the 2 percent differential. That differential in dollar terms would be

$$(12\% - 10\%)(\frac{90}{360})(\$10 \text{ million})$$

except that we must also discount this amount for 3 months, at the market rate of 12 percent because it is paid at the beginning of the period instead of at the end, when interest is normally paid. So the calculation becomes

$$\text{Cash payment} = \frac{(12\% - 10\%)\ (90/360) \times \$10 \text{ million}}{(1 + \dfrac{12\%}{4})}$$

$$= \frac{0.05 \times 10}{1.03} \quad \text{(in millions of dollars)}$$

$$= \$48,543.60$$

Since the actual LIBOR exceeds the contractual LIBOR, this is the amount the "lender" must pay the "borrower."

More generally, the formula for the start-of-period cash compensation by "lender" to "borrower" in an FRA is, for a LIBOR-based contract,

$$\text{Cash compensation} = \frac{\{[(\text{LIBOR} - \text{fixed rate}) \times \text{length in days}]/360\} \times \text{principal}}{1 + [(\text{LIBOR} \times \text{length in days})/360]}$$

---

[2] A word on FRA terminology: the term "buyer" of an FRA for the party receiving compensation if rates rise above the set rate is used because banks "sell" FRAs to borrower clients to protect them against higher costs on floating-rate loans.

As with any forward contract, where one party has to deliver something to another party at some time in the future, there is a risk of default. Clearly, if the actual rate moves away from the fixed rate, the borrower will owe the lender some cash, or vice versa. The payment will not be made until the start of the contractual period, which may be many months away, even if LIBOR has already moved substantially in one party's favor.

Therefore, in an FRA, each contracting party faces a potential credit exposure. When the market rate moves, the amount of the exposure equals the market rate minus the fixed rate times the principal adjusted as shown. The amount of potential exposure is determined quite simply by the maximum amount that the market rate could move away from the fixed rate during the remaining time of the contract.

EURODOLLAR INTEREST RATE SWAPS

A future rate agreement is simply a forward contract where two parties agree to exchange a fixed rate for a floating rate—usually LIBOR—during some future period. But an FRA locks in only one period's borrowing or lending rate. When the parties agree to exchange fixed for floating rates over a number of future successive interest contract periods (typically 3-month or 6-month periods), the contract is called an interest rate swap. Interest rate swaps are used to convert variable-rate debt or assets into fixed rate, or vice versa. Indeed such an interest rate swap can be viewed as a string of FRAs with increasingly longer maturities:

$$n - \text{Period SWAP} = \text{FRA}_{1,2} + \text{FRA}_{2,3} + \cdots + \text{FRA}_{n\text{-}1,n}$$

the FRAs covering successive periods in the future.

An **interest rate swap** is a contract between two parties where they agree to exchange interest payments of two different kinds at fixed dates in the future. (Another term for interest rate swaps is *coupon swaps*.) In the Eurodollar market, one of these payments is usually the 3- or 6-month LIBOR rate. In some such swaps both sides are floating, for example, 6-month LIBOR against an index of Eurocommercial paper rates. A swap in which both sides are floating is called a "floating floating" or a "basis" swap.

Typically, Party A will agree to pay LIBOR every 6 months to Party B, who in turn will agree to pay a fixed interest rate to A every 6 months for the duration of the contract. Thus, if A had a fixed rate liability, he can now use the fixed interest receipts to service that debt and the LIBOR receipts become the new base for A's debt servicing. B might have had LIBOR-based debt in the first place, but by paying a fixed rate to A he receives the variable-rate component, LIBOR, which he passes on to his creditors each 6 months, thus fixing his cost of debt.

We may illustrate this technique by means of a simple example. We begin with Alpha who has 5-year fixed rate debt on which he is paying 1 percent above today's 5-year Treasury note (which it wants to convert into floating) and Beta who has floating rate debt on which he is paying 6-month LIBOR plus 0.25 percent—or 25 "basis points" to use the jargon (the cost of which he wants to fix). Schematically, the deal looks as follows:

Before the Swap

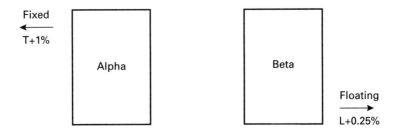

Alpha's Situation: Paying 5-year Treasury + 1%
Alternative cost: LIBOR flat, floating

Beta's Situation: Paying LIBOR + 0.25%
Alternative cost: T + 1.75%, fixed

Now Alpha and Beta meet, probably with the help of a match-maker. They exchange vows: Alpha promises to pay LIBOR – 0.25% to Beta every 6 months. Beta vows to pay today's Treasury note rate, plus 1% per annum to Alpha every 6 months.

After the Swap

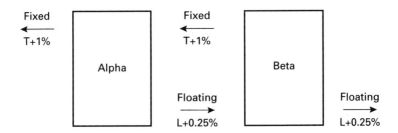

Alpha's New Situation

Debt: ≈ Paying 5-year Treasury + 1%
Swap: ≈ Paying LIBOR – 0.25%

Receiving 5-year Treasury + 1%
Net cost: LIBOR − 0.25%, floating

Beta's New Situation

Debt: ≈ Paying LIBOR + 0.25%
Swap: ≈ Paying 5-year Treasury + 1%
Receiving LIBOR − 0.25%
Net cost: T + 1.50%, fixed

The union is a success! Alpha ends up paying a floating rate that will drop if interest rates fall. His net cost is 1/4 percent below the Eurodollar offer rate, 25 basis points cheaper than he otherwise would have been able to get directly. Beta ends up paying a fixed rate at only 1.5 percent per annum above the U.S. Treasury rate, lower by 1/4 percent than he estimates the all-in cost of raising fixed rate money in, say, the Eurobond market.

From each according to his ability, and to each according to his need—that's the principle of swapping. Just as forward exchange contracts can convert the currency of denomination of a Eurodeposit, so interest rate swaps can convert the interest rate base of an instrument or liability.

Swaps are widely used not only to lower borrowers' costs but also to manage interest rate exposure in a flexible fashion. For example, 6 months

---

SWAP VALUATION

A swap entails a contractual *fixed rate* on one side and a contractual *floating (short-term) rate* on the other. Hence the value of the swap is like the value of a fixed-rate bond financed with a short-term instrument.

As a result, the fixed-rate side of a swap rises and falls in value just as fixed-interest corporate obligations do when interest rates fluctuate. In the example, had interest rates fallen, Alpha would have gained and so would have to be compensated for giving up the swap. At any interest reset date, the value of the gain—the change in the value of Alpha's swap position—is approximately equal to the change in the price of a corporate bond that had 5 years to mature on the date of initiation of the swap. Between interest reset dates, the value of the swap depends on the change in the value of the fixed-rate side (a function of longer-term rates) *and* on the change in the value of the short-term side (a function of money market rates).

This also means that Alpha would incur an equivalent loss if Beta defaults on the swap at this point. More generally, each party to a swap faces mutual potential credit risk (or "counterparty risk") arising from the possibility of default after interest rates have moved.

after the swap just described took place, rates may have fallen. Alpha now decides to fix his cost of funds again, human nature being what it is. Happily, he does not have to break his vows but can instead phone a swaps trader who will either enter into a second, offsetting swap with Alpha or, less likely, assume the remaining swap with Beta. In effect the swap has been "reversed" (or traded), producing a gain or loss on the remaining payment obligations. For a discussion of how this gain or loss is evaluated, see the accompanying box "Swap Valuation."

EURODOLLAR FUTURES

Eurodollar futures, like their domestic counterparts, are contracts for delivery of a certain amount of bank deposits at some future date. The deposits to be delivered may be Eurodollar time deposits or Eurodollar CDs, depending on the particular contract and may be settled either by cash compensation or by delivery of the CD of a major bank. The futures price agreed upon the day the contract is bought or sold determines the locked-in Eurodollar interest rate and, as with forward contracts, no money changes hands at the time the contract is entered into. In both markets, gains or losses are incurred as a result of subsequent interest rate fluctuations.

The total gain or loss will equal the difference between the futures price (or forward rate) and the spot interest rate on the date of maturity of the contract, multiplied by the amount of the contract.

The difference between the forward and futures markets is that in the forward market, a profit (or loss) is realized on the maturity date, while in the futures market all profits and losses must be settled on a daily basis. This procedure, called "marking to the market," requires that funds change hands each day. The funds are added to or subtracted from a mandatory margin account that traders are required to maintain. In contrast, in the forward market no money changes hands until delivery occurs at maturity.

This means that futures provide a means of managing interest rate risk with negligible credit risk, unlike the FRA and swap techniques.

If (as a result of an interest rate drop) the value of a Eurodollar CD futures contract increases during the course of a day, the holder receives cash; if it falls, the holder must pay the loss. This happens every day for every change in price up to the final day of the contract. A 1-basis-point change in the Eurodollar rate produces a $25 gain or loss. This is because each contract covers a $1 million 3-month deposit, and $1,000,000 \times 0.01\% \times 0.25\% = 25. On the maturity date, the futures price must equal the cash (spot) price of the EuroCD. Hence, the payment required on the maturity date to buy the underlying CD is simply its spot price at that time.

Figure 4-1 illustrates how changes in the actual 3-month Eurodollar rate are tracked by changes in the Eurodollar futures contract yield (not perfectly, of course, because the futures yield represents the implicit forward interest rate) and how, as the contract approaches its last trading date (September 18, in this case), the futures yield must converge to the cash yield. Note how the "basis," the cash-futures differential, approaches zero as the contract matures (bottom of Figure 4-1). Figure 4-2, the bar graph, is derived from Figure 4-1. It shows your daily gains or losses, credited or debited to your margin account, assuming you held a short position in one Eurodollar futures contract. (A short position would be used, for example, to hedge a borrowing cost—the equivalent of "buying" an FRA.)

The other chief feature of the futures market is that futures are traded through organized exchanges with clearing houses, such as the International Monetary Market (IMM) in Chicago. (The specifications of the IMM contract are provided in Appendix 4-A.) Trading in standardized interest rate contracts is conducted by open auction on the floor of the exchange. The trading

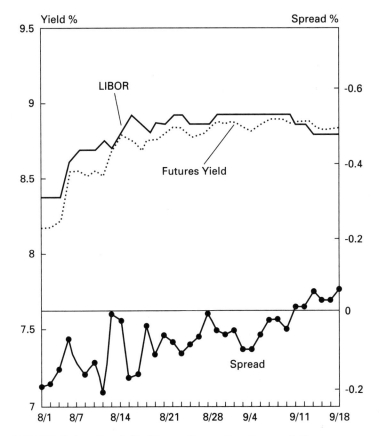

FIGURE 4-1. Eurodollar Future (September Contract): Futures Yield Versus (Spot) LIBOR, August 1 to September 18.

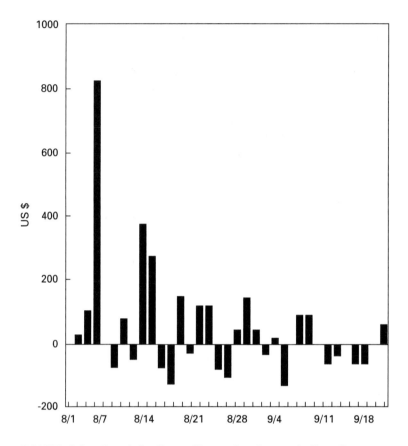

FIGURE 4-2.   Eurodollar Future (September Contract): Short Position
(Daily Gain/Loss), August 1 to September 18.

matches individual buyers and sellers to set prices; however in executing each sale and purchase the clearing house of the exchange takes the opposite side of each position. The fact that losses are realized and settled every trading day limits the risk of default to the clearing house.

Eurodollar futures can be particularly useful for banks, borrowers, or investors that wish to lock in a future interest rate in the Eurodollar market. For example, a money manager who anticipates having funds to invest in the short-term fixed-income markets at a known time in the future can hedge against the risk that interest rates might drop by the time of actual investing. Such an investor can hedge this risk by buying a futures contract immediately at a specified rate for delivery at a specified future time. If interest rates fall by the delivery date, the contract will appreciate in value. The appreciation in value on the futures contract can offset the investor's "opportunity loss" from the actual decline in interest rates. Thus, for investors anticipating funds to be available for investment in the future, the appropriate futures market hedge is the purchase of a futures contract—a "long hedge."

Borrowers in the money markets can also use interest rate futures to protect themselves against increases in interest rates by selling an interest rate contract for future delivery. If interest rates rise by the delivery date, the value of the futures contract will drop. The financial manager can buy back the contract for a lower price, thus making a gain. The gain from the futures contract can offset the increase in the cash borrowing costs. Thus, for borrowers anticipating actual borrowing in the future, the appropriate futures market hedge is a "short hedge."

As is illustrated in Figure 4-3, the holder of a long Eurodollar futures contract gains or loses in a symmetrical fashion as the "forward" rate rises or falls, thus locking in that rate. Thus the basic techniques for hedging Eurodollar interest rate risks are as follows:

- An investor wishing to hedge against a future fall in the Eurodollar interest rate would buy Eurodollar futures contracts (a long hedge).
- A borrower wishing to hedge against a future rise in the Eurodollar interest rate would sell Eurodollar futures contracts (a short hedge).

Examples of each are given in the boxes on the following pages. The rates

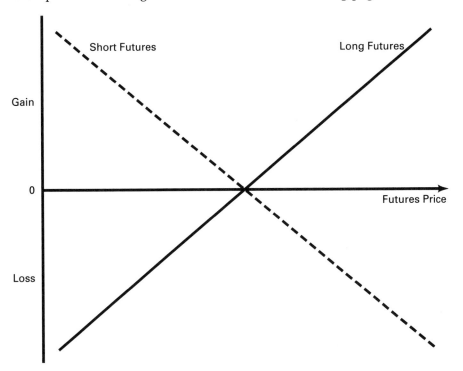

FIGURE 4-3. Eurodollar Futures "Profit Profile."

used are actual ones although the names and dates have been disguised to protect the innocent. As might be expected, the hedge is not a perfect one, since the Eurodollar contract is unlikely to match precisely the characteristics of the instrument being hedged. This lack of perfect offset is known to practitioners as **basis risk**; students of portfolio theory would call it **covariance**, that is, the degree to which the value of one position is negatively correlated with the value of the other position.

The second example is a particularly interesting one, for those who have the patience to work through the numbers, because it shows how short-term futures can be used to hedge longer-term instruments (in this case, 3-month futures are used to hedge a 6-month loan).

The second example also demonstrates that near-term futures (such as the December 1991 contract) can be used to hedge more distant interest rate risk (June 1992 in the example), as long as the hedge is rolled over—that is, successive short-term hedges can substitute for (nonexistent) distant futures contracts. The hedge will not be perfect: you face a risk whenever the *slope* of the yield curve changes. However, the roll-over hedge technique does protect against a movement in the *level* of interest rates.

In summary, the two techniques noted are

- To hedge a longer-term instrument than the instrument of the futures contract, take out multiple interest rate contracts, for the successive periods within the longer-term instrument's time span. This is called a **strip**. (For example, to fix your cost of Euromarket funding for the 9-month period starting in December, sell a December, a March, and a June contract.)

- To hedge a more distant period than is available in the futures market, one may hedge with a less distant futures contract as long as it has sufficient liquidity and replace this with other contracts, closer to the desired period, as they gain in liquidity. This is called a **stack**. (For example, to fix the return on a Eurodeposit 2 years hence, buy the 12-month contract, hold it for 3 months, roll into a new 12-month contract, and so on until the desired maturity is achieved.)

It is not unusual for these two situations to be combined. For example, a bank might wish to lock in the cost of 3-year money funds, funded in the 91-day Eurodollar CD market. This involves a longer maturity than the 3-month Eurodollar contract and extends beyond the horizon of the most distant currently available contract. We would then have to hedge out as far as possible (say, $1^1/_2$ years) with a set of contracts of different delivery dates and hedge the remaining periods with successive "roll-overs" of distant futures contracts as they become available. At each point you would hold a number of futures contracts equal to the amount in millions times the number of interest contract periods being hedged.

USING EURODOLLAR FUTURES TO HEDGE INTEREST RATE RISKS

Case 1. On Wednesday, August 3, 1989, the cash manager for CBS Corporation, Jinni Featherstone-Witty, received a telex saying that CBS would receive a dividend payment of $21 million from its Australian affiliate. The payment would be made on November 17, 1989. JFW decided that she would arrange for the funds to be deposited in a Eurodollar deposit in Singapore pending repatriation to the United States in mid-February 1990. To hedge the interest received on the 3-month deposit from November 17 to February 16, she chose to buy Eurodollar futures contracts. These contracts are linked to 3-month Euro time deposits of major banks. The closest delivery date was the December contract: December 15, to be precise. She would have to buy 21 contracts of $1 million each. The sequence was as follows:

CASH MARKET	FUTURES MARKET
August 3, 1989 -Do nothing 3-month Eurodollar rate: 10.50%	Buy 21 $1 million December Eurodollar; price: 88.88, yield: 11.12%
November 17, 1989 Deposit $21 million in Singapore at the 3-month Eurodollar rate: 9.875%	Sell the 21 December Eurodollar; price: 89.90, yield: 10.10%
	Gain: +102 basis points, or $2,550 per contract, since each basis point is worth $25 (see Figure 4-4). Total futures gain = 102 × $25 × 21 = $53,550

Net effective interest rate received (assuming the futures gain can also be invested at 9.875%):

$$= \left\{ \frac{\left[\$21,000,000 \times (0.09875 / 4)\right] + \left[\$53,550 \times (1 + 0.09875 / 4)\right]}{21,000,000} \right\} \times \frac{12}{3} \times 100$$

$$= 10.92\%$$

This illustrates the fact that JFW, by hedging in the futures market, was able to assure CBS of a return of approximately 11.12 percent, the December Eurodollar futures rate as of August 3. The actual rate she obtained was 10.92 percent. The effect of such less than perfect hedging as noted earlier is called basis risk.

Using Eurodollar Futures to Hedge Interest Rate Risks (Continued)

Case 2. Edgar "Egg" Hatcher, chief offshore funding manager for Barclays Bank in New York, received a call from a Barclays loan officer on February 28, 1990. The loan officer had a customer who wished to borrow $13 million for 6 months starting on June 1, 1992. The customer was apparently willing to pay a premium to obtain a locked-in rate, but needed to get a quote very quickly. Could Egg Hatcher cook up something that would enable Barclays to offer such an FRA? Looking at his Reuters screen, Egg observed the following futures rates:

3-Month Eurodollar Deposit Contracts

Maturity	Price	Yield	Open Interest
March '90	94.84	5.16%	6,263
June '90	95.12	4.88	13,344
September '91	94.97	5.03	8,733
December '91	94.90	5.10	3,486
March '92	94.72	5.28	8

Egg brooded on these facts for a while: this was not quite what he wanted. The contracts did not go far out enough, and in any case he was reluctant to deal in a contract date with only eight contracts outstanding, such as the March '92 contract. Also, the contracts were for 3-month, not 6-month maturities. He then hatched the following plan to hedge his borrowing cost during the 6-month period starting June 1, 1992. He would hedge the first three of those 6 months by selling 13 December '91 contracts now, and rolling those over (replacing them) with March '92 and finally June '92 contracts as volume built up in these. He would hedge his funding cost for the second 3-month leg, beginning on September 1, 1992, in a similar manner; by selling 13 December '91 contracts and subsequently replacing these with, in turn, March '92, June '92, and September '92 contracts. This "roll-over" hedge technique, admittedly imperfect, would protect him against shifts in the overall level of interest rates.

The December '91 contract, he saw, had a yield of 5.10 percent. He called the loan officer and (to be on the safe side) quoted him a base funding rate of 6 percent; the lending officer could add an appropriate spread onto the rate. His use of futures to hedge his cost is shown on the following page.

Thus Egg Hatcher was able, in mid-1992, to fund the 6-month loan at an effective cost very close to the 5.10 percent futures rate prevailing back in February 1990 when he had promised a fixed forward rate to the customer.

USING EURODOLLAR FUTURES TO HEDGE INTEREST RATE RISKS (CONTINUED)

CASH MARKET

February 28, 1990
3-month Eurodollar rate: 5.375%
Commit "forward" funding rate
of 6%

April 5, 1990
3-month Eurodollar rate: 6.70%

September 1, 1990
3-month Eurodollar rate: 8.125%

When today's trades are
completed the hedge is fully in
place and nothing need be done
until the date of the loan.

June 1, 1992
Issue 3-month $13 million
Eurodollar deposit at going rate
of 7.375% per annum
Cost: $239,687.50 ($13 million ×
0.0775/4)

August 1, 1992
Issue 3-month $13 million
Eurodollar deposit at going rate
of 7.75%
Cost: $251,875 ($13 million ×
0.0775/4)

Total interest cost = $491,562.50

FUTURES MARKET

December '91 contract price: 94.90
(yield: 5.10%)
Sell 26 December '91 contracts (2
times 13)

December '91 contract price: 94.00
(yield: 6.00%)
March '92 contract price: 94.30
(yield: 5.70%)
Buy 26 December '91 contracts
Sell 26 March '92 contracts
Gain: $58,500 (90 basis points × $25
× 26)

March '92 contract price: 92.15
(yield: 7.85%)
June '92 contract price: 92.30 (yield:
7.70%)
September '92 contract price: 92.45
(yield: 7.55%)
Buy 26 March '92 contracts
Sell 13 June '92 contracts
Sell 13 September '92 contracts
Gain: $139,750 (215 basis points ×
$25 × 26)

June '92 contract price: 93.05
(yield: 6.95%)
Buy 13 June '92 contracts
Loss: $24,375 (75 basis points × $25
× 13)

September '92 contract price: 92.50
(yield: 7.50%)
Buy 13 September '92 contracts
Loss: $1,625 (5 basis points × $25 ×
13)

Total futures gains/losses =
$172,250

Net effective interest rate paid (ignoring interest on futures gains/losses):

$$\left[\frac{(\$491{,}562.50 - \$172{,}250)}{\$13{,}000{,}000} \right] \times \frac{12}{6} \times 100 = 4.9125\%$$

Thus, to hedge a $1 million, 3-year, variable-rate loan, starting on January 1, 1991, you would:

On January 1, 1991:

Borrow funds in the cash Eurodollar market for the first leg (say, for a period ending December 15, 1991).

Sell one December '91 contract (to hedge 12/92–3/92)
Sell one March '92 contract (to hedge 3/92–6/92)
Sell one June '92 contract (to hedge 6/92–9/92)
Sell one June '92 contract (to hedge 9/92–12/92)
Sell one June '92 contract (to hedge 12/92–3/93)
Sell one June '92 contract (to hedge 3/93–6/93)
Sell one June '92 contract (to hedge 6/93–9/93)
Sell one June '92 contract (to hedge 9/93–12/93)

(In fact you would sell a total of eight contracts corresponding to the eight interest-contract periods to be hedged, including six June '92 contracts because no more distant ones are yet available.)

On March 15, 1991

Buy five June '92 contracts
Sell five September '92 contracts

On June 15, 1991

Buy four September '92 contracts
Sell four December '92 contracts

On September 15, 1991

Buy three December '92 contracts
Sell three March '93 contracts

On December 15, 1991

Buy two March '93 contracts
Sell two June '93 contracts
(Also: Buy one December '91 contract, issue 3-month EuroCD, repay debt)

On March 15, 1992

Buy one June '93 contract
Sell one September '93 contract
(Also: Buy one March '92 contract, issue 3-month EuroCD, repay previous one)

And so on. At this point you have a full array of short futures contracts corresponding to the borrowing periods remaining, and all future 3-month borrowing periods are hedged. Using futures alone, you have replicated the hedging purpose of an interest rate swap—with less precision, admittedly, but with greater liquidity and much diminished counterparty exposure.

HOW TO READ THE NEWSPAPER

Figure 4-4 contains an annotated replica of Eurodollar futures quotations as they appear daily in the financial pages of newspapers such as *The Wall Street Journal* or the *Financial Times*.

FINANCIAL FUTURES

Close or "settlement" price, normally the last trade, used for marking to market, that is, daily adjustment of margin accounts. Calculated as Price = (100 – yield).

Past year's highest and lowest prices.

Contracts traded at the International Monetary Market in Chicago (Eurodollar futures are also traded at LIFFE in London, SIMEX in Singapore, and elsewhere)

The face value of the contract is $1 million. That means that each basis point (0.01%) change in the 3-month contract price is worth $25. ($1,000,000 × 0.0001 × 1/4)

The Eurodollar futures yield is an "add-on" yield, not a discount rate, and as in the Eurodollar market is calculated on a 360-day basis.

Change from previous day's closing price.

3-MONTH EURODOLLAR DEPOSITS (IMM)
$1 MILLION; PTS OF 100%; ADD-ON YIELD

SEASON			DAY				OPEN
HIGH	LOW		HIGH	LOW	CLOSE	CHG.	INTEREST
92.36	88.84	DEC	91.67	91.58	91.66	+0.03	182,908
92.46	88.90	MAR	92.20	92.07	92.18	+0.03	195,424
92.35	88.82	JUN	92.30	92.19	92.28	+0.05	81,368
92.21	88.74	SEP	92.18	92.05	92.16	+0.07	45,947
91.99	89.85	DEC	91.89	91.79	91.88	+0.06	33,134
91.90	89.96	MAR	91.83	91.73	91.82	+0.05	30,005
91.85	89.91	JUN	91.71	91.60	91.71	+0.05	26,812
91.83	90.04	SEP	91.64	91.53	91.64	+0.06	22,100

EST. SALES 140,561 (MON. SALES 57,726)

Expiration months of actively traded contracts. On the actual expiration date, the third Wednesday of the expiration month, the futures yield converges to the cash market yield, that is, to LIBOR.

Number of contracts sold on that day (equals number of contracts bought!)

Number of contracts open as of previous trading day. (Each unit represents a long and a short contract.)

FIGURE 4-4. Eurodollar Futures Quotations. Eurodollar futures can be used to hedge as much as seven years out. To find locked-in yield, subtract price from 100.

Eurodollar futures on the IMM are contracts for delivery of a $1 million time deposit in one of several major banks in London at some specified future date. The Eurodollar futures price is actually an index that is calculated as 100 minus the yield (in annual percentage terms). The yield for Eurodollar time deposits is calculated as an add-on yield (i.e., as a percentage of the initial value—$1 million—rather than as a percentage of the maturity value of the instrument. The latter is a discount yield and is used for T-bill yield calculations.). Comparing the "price settle" and "yield settle" columns, one can see that the add-on yield is simply 100 minus the settlement price, the closing price at the end of the trading day.

THE HEDGE RATIO APPROACH

The discussion and examples so far show that Eurodollar futures contracts can be used to hedge the interest rate risk inherent in a floating-rate Eurodollar instrument, such as an adjustable-rate loan, a floating-rate certificate of deposit (FRCD), or a floating-rate note (FRN). Nevertheless, it was evident that one can seldom find a set of Eurodollar futures whose maturity dates and underlying instruments precisely match those of the interest rate setting periods of the Euroinstrument. Some risk remains because of "basis risk"—the futures contracts may change in the right direction, but by an amount greater than or less than the rise or fall of interest rates paid or received on the variable-rate instrument.

The hedge ratio approach faces this issue head on: it says that one should explicitly take into account the correlation between changes in the instrument hedged and changes in the value of particular futures contracts. Another term for this is the price sensitivity of the futures with respect to the instrument being hedged. If you know this relationship, you determine the ratio of futures contracts that best hedges one unit of the underlying instrument.[3] For example, if you want to hedge a Eurodollar CD whose value, you have found, goes down 2 percent for each 1 percent rise in short-term interest rates, and the near-term Eurodollar futures contract's value falls only 1/4 percent for a 1 percent rise in the Eurodollar rate, then you would sell eight Eurodollar futures contracts to hedge a $1 million CD.

A key element in this approach is a measure of how much futures prices and cash prices will change for a given change in interest rates. A versatile measure is the duration of the instrument. Calculated from the weighted present value of future cash flows, the duration of an instrument tells you

---

[3] For information on hedge ratio or price sensitivity approaches, see Robert Kolb, *Interest Rate Futures* (Richmond, VA: Robert F. Dame, 1982), Chapter 5, or Robert Kolb and R. Chiang, "Improving Hedging Performance Using Interest Rate Futures," *Financial Management*, Vol. 10, No. 4, 1981, pp. 72–79.

how much, in percentage terms, a bond or futures contract will fall in value for a 1 percent rise in interest rates. The next section provides a brief review of the concept.

Since this method is designed to hedge against changes in the value of a security, it is of particular interest to portfolio managers who wish to avoid any loss that might result from interest rate fluctuations on bonds that they hold and anticipate selling or on bonds that they anticipate buying.

DURATION

The duration of a bond—or any other fixed income instrument, including futures, FRAs, and swaps—is a measure of its interest rate sensitivity. A bond with a duration of 2 will suffer a fall in value of (approximately) 2 percent if bond yields rise by one percentage point. As a rule, bonds with longer maturity are more vulnerable to interest rate changes; however, duration measures this vulnerability more precisely because it takes into account the size and timing of coupon payments.

Duration can also be calculated for a portfolio of fixed income securities, simply by figuring the weighted average of the durations of each security. One can also measure the duration—change in value for a given interest rate change—of interest rate contracts, such as Eurodollar futures, future rate agreements, and interest rate swaps.

Measurement

Duration is measured as a weighted-average term to maturity in which the weights are the present value of cash flows from the bond.

$$\text{Duration} = \frac{\left\{\sum_{t=1}^{n}\left[CF_t t / (1+r)^t\right]\right\} / \left\{\sum_{t=1}^{n}\left[CF_t / (1+r)^t\right]\right\}}{m}$$

where

CF_t = interest and/or principal payment in period t
t = number of periods to the interest and/or principal payment
n = number of periods to final maturity
r = yield to maturity
m = number of interest payments per year

Use

To control interest rate risk, because the price sensitivity of a bond to changes in interest rates is related to a measure called modified duration:

$$\text{Modified duration} = \frac{\text{Duration}}{1 - (\text{market yield} / m)}$$

where m is the number of coupon interest payments per year. The modified duration measures the percentage change in the price of an instrument for a 1 percent change in the yield. So to obtain the percentage change in an instrument's price, multiply its modified duration by the market yield. Knowing the duration of each of two instruments allows one to determine the number of the first intrument needed to hedge the second. In other words, relative duration provides the hedge ratio. In financial institutions, a strategy of setting the average duration of assets equal to the average duration of liabilities will immunize a portfolio from the effects of a change in interest rates.

Limitations

The Macaulay measure of duration, just shown, assumes a flat yield curve and parallel shifts in the curve. Also, a bond's duration changes slightly as the market yield changes. For practical purposes, these effects are small as long as rates have not changed a great deal. When yields change substantially, however, one should take into account the bond's convexity. Convexity measures how much duration changes for a given change in yield. Most fixed-income instruments have positive convexity, meaning that as yields rise, the price sensitivity (duration) falls, and as yields fall, the duration increases. From the point of view of a portfolio manager, positive convexity is a desirable characteristic.

A EURODOLLAR FUTURES PLUS TWO FORWARD EXCHANGE CONTRACTS EQUALS A EUROPULA FUTURES

Back to the futures. German marks, Swiss francs, and even pounds sterling have feelings too, so why all this talk about Eurodollar interest rate futures and swaps? The answer, of course, is that everything we've said about dollar contracts applies to those worthies too. Active Eurocurrency futures contracts now exist for Euroyen and several of the major European currencies. In some others, however, swap and futures contracts are less developed if they exist at all. Such is the case with the Pula, a purely hypothetical currency.

So now we're going to show you how to create a fake EuroPula—or Eurocurrency—interest rate futures contract. The trick is to use the interest rate parity relationship to combine a Eurodollar futures contract with one long and one short Pula currency forward or futures contract. Let's look at it intuitively. The EuroPula interest rate (on, say, a 3-month deposit in Zurich) equals the Eurodollar interest rate plus the Pula/dollar interest rate differential. This holds true from here to eternity. Also, foreign exchange dealers' arbitrage ensures that the Euromarket dollar/Pula interest rate differential equals the forward exchange premium or discount ("forward premium" for short). We assume this too will hold true for the foreseeable future.

Knowing this we can

Create a simulated EuroPula interest rate futures contract (i.e. lock in a future Pula interest rate)	by	Locking in the future Eurodollar interest rate (by means of a Eurodollar futures contract)	and	Locking in the forward premium (by means of a simultaneous futures purchase and futures sale of Pulas for different dates)

To illustrate—using another currency—assume a Eurobanker wants to guarantee to a customer the price of a 3-month Europeseta loan to be provided in mid-March and repaid in mid-June. He will

1. Sell a March Eurodollar futures contract (to lock in the cost of borrowing Eurodollars);
2. Buy pesetas forward for delivery in mid-March (to lock in the cost of exchanging the borrowed dollars into pesetas); and
3. Sell pesetas forward for delivery in mid-June (to lock in the cost of exchanging the pesetas back into dollars to repay the dollar debt).

We have illustrated the technique using foreign exchange forward contracts to hedge the interest differential. Currency futures contracts might just as well have been used, although major banks and corporations would normally find forwards more convenient: They can be executed for odd amounts, odd maturities and settlement is at maturity only, as a rule. In addition, a Eurodollar interest rate swap may be used instead of a Eurodollar futures contract to hedge the dollar interest rate, thus converting a Eurodollar interest rate swap into, say, a EuroFrench franc interest rate swap. This technique would not, however, normally be used for short-term interest rate hedging of the kind illustrated in the example.

All in all, the cross-currency interest rate hedging technique is a versatile device that can be employed in a number of ways. Let's see some examples.

A U.S. bank has easy access to dollar funds but wants to commit itself to lending at a fixed-in-advance rate in a foreign currency. As described in the example earlier, the bank would short a Eurodollar interest rate futures at the same time buying the foreign currency forward at the earlier date and selling it forward at the later date.

A Japanese multinational firm wishes to lock in the future cost of borrowing Korean won. Again, the technique is to lock in the dollar rate and simultaneously lock in the interest differential by means of a "forward swap." The firm would sell a Eurodollar futures contract for delivery near to the starting date of the loan, buy won forward with dollars for the same delivery date, and sell won forward futures for delivery on a date close to the loan repayment date. In general, no matter where the borrower is located, he can lock in the cost of borrowing his own or any foreign currency using Eurodollar futures as long as there exists a forward exchange market that will allow him to lock in the future interest rate differential between dollars and that currency.

An Austrian pension fund manager finds a newly issued Eurodollar bond priced to yield a rather attractive return but wishes to hedge its value in Austrian schillings for 6 months. Also, he does not have the funds now to buy it—he will do so in a month's time. Can he lock in the rate of return? Certainly; nothing fancy about it. We don't have to worry about coupons since Eurobond interest is paid annually. All we need is two sets of hedges: one to lock in the price at which the bond will be bought and another set to lock in the price at which the bond will be sold. Hedging the dollar price of a bond for some future date entails using the hedge ratio approach described earlier. Given the hedging futures contract—Eurobond futures if available, otherwise Eurodollar futures—and the price sensitivity of this contract with respect to the bond being hedged, we can (imperfectly) lock in the buying price (by buying Eurodollar futures) and the selling price (by selling futures) in dollars. Call these P_{BUY} and P_{SELL}, respectively. To lock in the Austrian schilling buying price, we buy $\$P_{BUY}$ Austrian schillings forward for delivery in 1 month (the buying date) and sell $\$P_{SELL}$ Austrian schillings for delivery in 7 months (the selling date). This locks in the total market cost and revenue, that is, the return in Austrian schillings.

As a final example, put yourself in the place of a British foreign exchange dealer who believes that the interest rate differential between Germany and Switzerland is abnormally wide. You think that it will narrow within the next 3 months. Since the interest differential in the Eurocurrency market equals the forward premium between the two currencies, you can bet on a change in the interest differential by taking a position in a forward swap. If the EuroGerman mark rate falls relative to the Eurodollar rate, the forward premium will narrow; thus the DM/SF cross rate (the value of the mark in terms of Swiss francs) for near delivery will rise relative to the cross rate for more distance delivery. To position yourself to gain from this, buy francs with marks for, say, 3-month delivery, and sell francs for marks for 6-month delivery. If the interest gap falls within the next 3 months, the position will have produced a profit. But don't believe us—try it out for yourself with an example.

This last application is a good place to end this section because it illustrates the fundamental feature of cross interest rate hedging: that the forward swap—one long and another short forward exchange—is purely a device to take a position on an interest rate differential. When it's coupled with a position on a dollar interest rate, as a Eurodollar futures contract provides, then it produces a position on another interest rate. The latter can be used to speculate on a change in the foreign interest rate, or, when done together with an existing, opposite position, to hedge against such a change.

THE CURRENCY SWAP

We have pointed out that long-term interest rate swaps are, in effect, forward contracts and are thus substitutes for futures contracts. Whatever can be done with futures can also be done in principle with swaps, and vice versa. The currency swap (more accurately called a cross-currency interest rate swap) is a technique that does for the medium- and longer-term financial market what the cross-currency interest rate futures hedge achieves in the short-term market. A currency swap is a technique that takes floating-rate debt servicing in one currency (coupon and principal repayments) and hedges the cost in terms of another currency. It is thus a combination of an interest rate hedge and a currency hedge. The currency swap can be used for a corporate or other borrower that wishes to:

1. Change a floating-interest-rate debt (or investment) denominated in one currency into a fixed-interest-rate debt (or investment) denominated in another currency, or

2. Change a fixed-interest-rate debt (or investment) denominated in one currency into a floating-interest-rate debt (or investment) denominated in another currency.

In other words,

Just as the forward and futures markets create hedges across currencies and maturities in the international money market, so currency swaps and interest rate swaps link various segments of the international capital markets. The roles of different kinds of swaps are shown schematically in Figure 4-5.

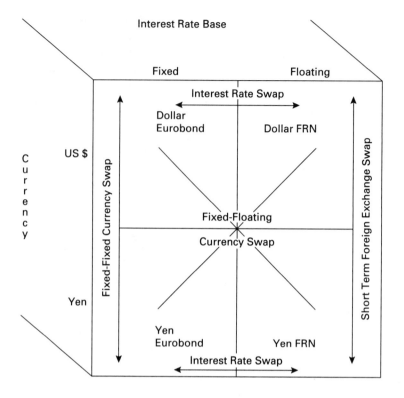

FIGURE 4-5. How Swaps Link the International Capital Markets.

EURODOLLAR OPTIONS

Futures, forwards, and swaps are all contracts in which two parties oblige themselves to exchange something in the future. They are thus useful to hedge or convert known currency or interest rate exposures. An option, in contrast, gives one party the right but not the obligation to buy or sell an asset under specified conditions while the other party assumes an obligation to sell or buy that asset if that option is exercised.

Since 1982, options on various fixed income instruments, such as Treasury bills and bonds, have been traded on organized exchanges. In addition, options are widely sold and traded over the counter. The exchange contracts take two forms: (1) options on so-called physicals, that is, actual securities, and (2) options on futures. Eurodollar options have been traded since 1985. The most active contract in Eurodollar options are options on Eurodollar futures, requiring delivery of the underlying futures contract. Options on cash instruments may be purchased over the counter, but for many purposes options on futures suffice. Let us see how these work and how they are related to Eurodollar futures. (Specifications of the most popular contracts traded on U.S. exchanges are provided in Appendix 4-B.)

As with all options, there are two kinds of Eurodollar options: puts and calls. A **call option** gives the holder (or "buyer" since he must pay for his rights) the right to purchase a Eurodollar time deposit on a certain date, one bearing a certain interest rate, say, 12 percent. If, at expiration, the market interest rate turns out to be higher than the rate specified in the option contract, say, 13 percent, it will make sense for the option holder to let the option expire. But if the market rate is 9 percent, below the contractual rate, the holder of the Eurodollar call option will exercise his right to receive an instrument at the higher rate. A **put option** is, conversely, the right to sell a Eurodollar time deposit at a contractual rate to the writer (or original seller) of the option. [4]

The buyer of any option will, of course, have to pay cash for the rights he receives. This up-front option price is called the premium. The greater the likelihood of the option being exercised profitably, the higher is the premium.

Eurodollar options are useful for anyone who requires a gain if interest rates go one way, but wants protection against loss if rates go the other way. The most the holder of an option can lose is the premium he paid for it. Naturally, the option writer faces the mirror image of the holder's picture: if you sell (or "write") an option (call or put), the most you can get is the premium if the option dies for lack of exercise. The writer of a call option can face a substantial loss if the option is exercised, that is, he is forced to deliver a Eurodollar deposit at an above-market interest rate (below-market price). If he wrote a put option and the put is exercised, then he is obliged to buy the Eurodollar at a below-market interest rate (above market price).

Unlike futures, forwards, and swap-type hedges, therefore, Eurodollar options represent an "asymmetrical" risk profile. This lopsidedness works to the advantage of the holder and the disadvantage of the writer—but that, after all, is what the holder is paying for. When two parties enter into a symmetrical contract, like a forward, both can gain or lose equally and neither party feels obliged to charge the other for the privilege. Forwards, futures, and swaps are mutual obligations; options are one sided. As may be seen in Figure 4-6, the holder of a call has a downside risk limited to the premium paid up front; beyond that he gains one-for-one with the price of the underlying security.

From the asymmetrical risk profile of options it follows that they are ideally suited to offsetting Eurodollar interest rate risks that are themselves asymmetrical. The risk of a forward rate agreement is symmetrical: hence, matching it with a Eurodollar option will not be a perfect hedge—doing so would leave you with an open, or speculative, position. For symmetrical

[4] A note on options terminology: we refer to the *original seller* as the writer of an option, since only the writer remains obligated throughout the life of the contract (unless he himself buys it back). The purchaser of that option can sell it in the secondary market, but of course in doing so assumes no obligation to the new buyer.

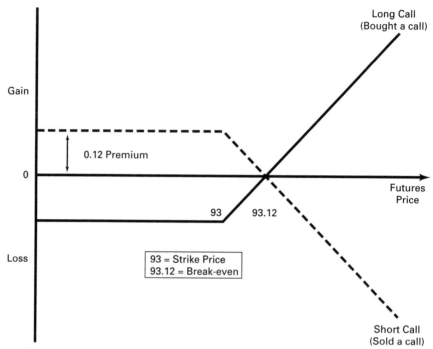

FIGURE 4-6. Eurodollar Options "Profit Profile."

risks, Eurodollar futures, FRAs, and interest rate swaps are suitable hedges. Eurodollar options are suitable hedges for institutions whose interest rate risk is already lopsided, and for those who choose to speculate on the direction and volatility of rates. The following are examples of possible uses of Eurodollar options. We leave it to the reader to decide which are speculative and which are the hedges.

Hedging Floating-Rate Securities

Investors in floating-rate securities are exposed to falling rates. If rates decline, the coupon on the floater will reset at a lower level. Call options on Eurodollars can be purchased to effect a floor rate. The strike price of the option will determine the effective minimum coupon. If rates decline below the strike price, profits from the call option position will compensate the investor for the lower coupon on the floater. These options are particularly suitable in situations where the resets on the floater are based on the 3-month LIBOR rate. Call options also offer the investor the flexibility to alter the degree of desired protection.

Bank and Thrift Liability Management

A bank or thrift institution whose outlook is for short-term interest rates to rise can hedge the issuance of certificates of deposit with put options on

Eurodollars. A put option purchase will allow the bank to realize a lower cost of funds in the event of a rate decline but protect the bank if rates rise. Alternatively, if futures had been used as a hedge vehicle, the bank or thrift would have "locked in" the funding cost.

Hedging "Cap-Rate" Loans

A lender incorporating a "rate cap," as is typical in adjustable rate mortgages, has interest rate risk if rates should rise above the cap rate. To protect against this exposure, the lender could purchase puts on the Eurodollar futures contract at a strike price which closely matches the cap rate. If rates rise above the cap, the profit from the put position will compensate the lender and offset the interest rate on the loan which is capped at below-market rates.

Hedging Contract Bids

A contractor making a bid to provide goods or services that will have to be financed at an uncertain cost if the bid is won may want to have the assurance but not the obligation of a known borrowing cost. The contractor buys a Eurodollar put option and incorporates the option cost into his bid. If the bid is accepted, his option will give him a gain if rates rise, offsetting his higher cost. If the bid is not accepted, he can let the option expire or sell it, perhaps even at a profit.

Hedging Debt That Has a Minimum Rate

Issuers of floating-rate notes linked to LIBOR frequently guarantee that the rate will never fall below some "floor" rate, such as $5^{1}/_{4}$ percent. If LIBOR does drop below $5^{1}/_{4}$ percent, these borrowers, who are often banks, will find themselves paying an above-market rate. Buying Eurodollar call options can protect them against such a risk.

How do these Eurodollar options work in practice? As mentioned, there are two kinds of options—options on futures and options on cash—whose distinguishing characteristics we will outline shortly. However, all exchange-traded options have the following features in common. As with Eurodollar futures, they are standardized contracts with a face value of $1 million and four expiration dates: March, June, September, and December (the same as for the Eurodollar futures). Both the strike price and the price of the underlying security are quoted as an index, defined as 100 minus the Eurodollar interest rate. For example, if the Eurodollar cash (or futures) yield is 11.75 percent, the index is 88.25. A call option gains value, and a put loses value, as this index rises (i.e., as the Eurodollar rate falls). Conversely, if the index falls (when rates rise), a Eurodollar call option loses value while a put gains.

No Eurodollar options contract entails delivery of a genuine Eurodollar time deposit. All involve a form of **cash settlement**, where the option seller has to pay the holder an amount equal to the option's **intrinsic value**—the difference between the strike price and the price of the "deliverable security" (actually the index mentioned earlier), which in turn is linked to LIBOR. Actual delivery of a Eurodollar would be difficult because time deposits are nonnegotiable and because of uncertainties about which bank's liability would be delivered—a problem that plagued the moribund domestic CD futures market.

In exchange-traded options contracts the **margin requirements** differ from futures contracts in that the option holder is never required to deposit money in a margin account, because he has no obligation to perform after paying the premium. Since the writer must perform if the option is exercised, he is required to deposit margin when a position is opened. As in the futures market, the margin account will be marked to market daily to reflect changes in the option's value. The price or premium of Eurodollar options is quoted in percent; for example, an option price of 1.50 means 1.50 percent of $1,000,000, that is, $3,750. Each basis point, or 0.01 percent, is 0.0001 × $1,000,000 for 3 months or $25. Thus, if you bought a call option priced at 1.50 and the reference index rose by 0.20 percent (because the Eurodollar rate fell by 0.20 percent), then you would have gained 20 × $25 or $500. The minimum price move is 0.01, or $25.

Finally, there is no limit on how much the price can move during any given trading day.

OPTIONS ON CASH VERSUS OPTIONS ON EURODOLLAR FUTURES

The two kinds of Eurodollar options—options on the instrument itself and over-the-counter options on Eurodollar futures contracts—serve essentially the same purpose, which is to give a one-way hedge against movements of LIBOR. Both contracts are linked to LIBOR, because the cash option and the futures contract are both settled by cash compensation linked to LIBOR at the maturity date. On that maturity date, when the futures contract has zero days to run, the Eurodollar futures yield has converged to LIBOR. The Eurodollar futures option expires on the last trading day of the underlying futures contract, so the futures option converges to the cash price too.

In other markets, the choice between a cash option and a futures option rests on convenience of delivery: individual Treasury bonds, for example, may be costly and time consuming to deliver. The design of Eurodollar options contracts effectively circumvents such problems. Another aspect is the ease with which the option can be hedged and arbitraged with the underlying security. The option on futures has an advantage, for Eurodollar futures are an active and liquid instrument. Since both the Eurodollar options and futures are traded on the same floor and processed through the same clearing system, exercise of the option can be easily accomplished by book entry. Exercise of a Eurodollar futures option contract results in a long futures position for a call buyer or a put writer and a short futures position for a put buyer or a call writer. This may be an inconvenience in those rare instances of early exercise, for the options trader may prefer cash settlement to ending up with a futures position.

The IMM Eurodollar option is an **American option** with privilege of early exercise. **European options**, in contrast, allow users to write options with confidence that they will not be involuntarily liquidated prior to expiration. This feature facilitates certain trading strategies, such as spreads and straddles and arbitrage between options and forwards or futures by assuring the trader that the position will not be broken prematurely.

A final point: since American options offer an additional right—the privilege of exercise on any date up to the expiration date—it gives the buyer greater flexibility and the writer greater risk. American options will therefore tend to be priced slightly higher than European options.

HOW TO READ THE NEWSPAPER AGAIN

Figure 4-7 displays the newspaper quotations of Eurodollar futures options prices in Chicago. From these quotations you may see which options are actively traded and perhaps find one that meets your needs. Say, for example, you expect to invest $5 million in March and are prepared to pay to be sure of getting at least 8 percent on your money. This implies that you want to buy a Eurodollar deposit at a reference price (100 – yield) of 92. What you want, in other words, is five March Eurodollar call options with a strike price of 92. According to the quotations, this would cost you 0.39, or $975.

Remember that Eurodollar futures are quoted such that the value of each "basis point" (0.01) in the contract is worth $25. This represents the value of a 0.01 percent change in the rate on a 3-month $1 million deposit. By convention, option premiums are quoted in a similar fashion. Thus the quote of 0.39 for the September 1993 call represents a $975 premium (39 × $25 per 0.01).

Say you bought five March '92 calls. You are now "long" five calls. If I sold them to you, I am "short" five March '92 calls. The upward-sloping line in Figure 4-6 illustrates what happens to you at expiration. The downward-sloping line is me. The call gives you the right to buy at 92. Obviously, if the market price is less than 92 (the Eurodollar rate is above 8 percent), exercising is pointless so you might as well let your option expire; go to the gym, if exercise is what you want. The option is "out of the money." Your net loss is the 0.39 premium you paid. (The 39 basis points are also my net gain: as the one with the obligation, I'm relieved you didn't exercise.) If the Eurodollar rate turns out to be below 8 percent, say, 7.95 percent, the contract price will

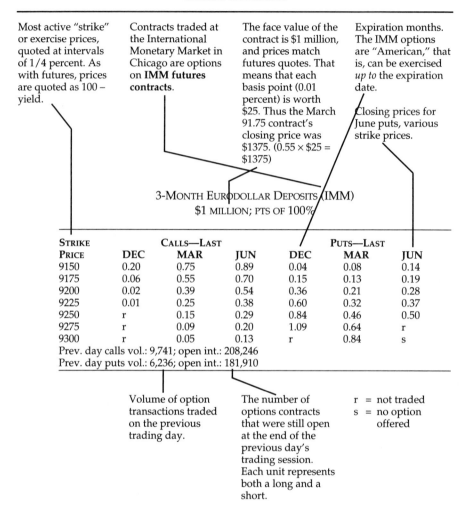

Options on Futures

| Most active "strike" or exercise prices, quoted at intervals of 1/4 percent. As with futures, prices are quoted as 100 − yield. | Contracts traded at the International Monetary Market in Chicago are options on **IMM futures** contracts. | The face value of the contract is $1 million, and prices match futures quotes. That means that each basis point (0.01 percent) is worth $25. Thus the March 91.75 contract's closing price was $1375. (0.55 × $25 = $1375) | Expiration months. The IMM options are "American," that is, can be exercised *up to* the expiration date.

Closing prices for June puts, various strike prices. |

3-Month Eurodollar Deposits (IMM)
$1 million; pts of 100%

Strike Price	Calls—Last			Puts—Last		
	DEC	MAR	JUN	DEC	MAR	JUN
9150	0.20	0.75	0.89	0.04	0.08	0.14
9175	0.06	0.55	0.70	0.15	0.13	0.19
9200	0.02	0.39	0.54	0.36	0.21	0.28
9225	0.01	0.25	0.38	0.60	0.32	0.37
9250	r	0.15	0.29	0.84	0.46	0.50
9275	r	0.09	0.20	1.09	0.64	r
9300	r	0.05	0.13	r	0.84	s

Prev. day calls vol.: 9,741; open int.: 208,246
Prev. day puts vol.: 6,236; open int.: 181,910

Volume of option transactions traded on the previous trading day.

The number of options contracts that were still open at the end of the previous day's trading session. Each unit represents both a long and a short.

r = not traded
s = no option offered

FIGURE 4-7. Eurodollar Options Quotations. Using Eurodollar options on futures, investors can lock in minimum yields (buy calls) and borrowers can lock in maximum costs (buy puts) for anticipated needs.

be 92.05 and you will exercise at 92, gaining 0.05, which offsets part of the premium you paid bringing your net loss to 0.34. A price of 92.39 is the break-even point—beyond that the option has made you money, and you gain on a point-for-point basis the higher the price, and the call writer loses the same amount. So if the Eurodollar rate finishes at 7.1 percent, you make $2,250 (90 basis points × $25) and I lose—that's the risk of being a writer.

Let's refer back to the newspaper where we originally found out that on Tuesday (today) you had to pay 0.39, that is, $975, for the March '92 call option. A day passes. On Wednesday morning you read the paper again and discover that the price of that same option has fallen to 0.36. That means that if you had sold the option the day after you bought it you would have lost $0.03 \times \$25 = \$75$. Even if you didn't sell it, you should kick yourself because you could have bought it $75 cheaper a day later. (Don't be too unhappy because we know that in the end you're going to wind up ahead.) As for me, the starving writer, I made $75—which benefits me only if I buy back the option I sold, except that the lower premium means that I don't have to keep quite as much in my margin account.

One last question: Why did the value of the Eurodollar call option fall? There could have been a number of reasons having to do with volatility and the like (see the section on pricing options), but in fact the reason was simpler: the Eurodollar futures price went down, as Wednesday's newspaper would surely tell you. But why did the Eurodollar futures price fall? Again, simple: because Eurodollar interest rates themselves rose—which would also be reported in the newspaper. But enough questions. Enough newspaper.

CAPS, FLOORS, COLLARS, AND CAP FLOATERS

We observed earlier that while an FRA or a futures is a one-shot hedge, able to lock in an interest rate for one period only, the interest rate swap provides a multiperiod hedge. Analogously, a *cap* or *floor* can do for a series of interest rate periods what put or call options can do for one period.

Bronx Bank, for example, has made a 5-year term loan to Times Square Properties (TSP). The interest rate is 3-month LIBOR + 1.25 percent. The client, however, wants protection against rising rates for the first 2 years of the loan. So Bronx will sell TSP a cap that will ensure that TSP's cost of funds will never exceed, say, 13 percent. Had Bronx's client been an investor, wanting protection against rates falling *below* a certain level, the bank would have sold a *floor* to the client.

Caps and floors, which limit the rise or fall of a specified floating interest rate to a certain level, are in effect a "strip" of put or call options, respectively.

A **cap** is an agreement by the seller of the cap to compensate the buyer, usually a borrower, whenever the hedged reference rate (usually LIBOR) exceeds a specified "ceiling rate." For this protection against rising rates, the borrower pays a premium, usually up front. For example, assume Company Ecks, borrowing money for 3 years at 6-month LIBOR, wishes to prevent its semiannual borrowing cost from ever exceeding 9 percent. LIBOR is now 7 percent. Bank Wuy sells a "cap" to Ecks for a front-end price of 4 percent of the principal amount being hedged. Then for the next 3 years, if LIBOR exceeds 9 percent at any of the five subsequent semiannual rate fixing dates, Wuy will pay Ecks the difference between LIBOR and 9 percent. If LIBOR turned out to be 10 percent, for example, then Wuy would pay Ecks 10 percent – 9 percent on a semiannual basis, that is, 1/2 percent of the amount being hedged. If LIBOR then fell to 8 percent at the next 6-month period, no payment would be made because LIBOR is below the ceiling rate.

The previous discussion showed how a Eurodollar put option effectively provides a hedge against LIBOR rising above a certain interest rate for a given 3-month period. A cap does exactly the same—except that it hedges against LIBOR (or some other reference rate) rising above a certain interest rate for a series of sequential periods. It follows that a cap is simply the equivalent of a series, or strip, of put options, each starting where the last one ended. The fee the hedger pays up front is the sum of the premia he would pay for all of the put options he is buying. Indeed a corporation can simulate a cap by a strip of exchange-traded put options, although most caps sold by banks would be tailored to suit the particular customers' needs in a way not possible with standardized Eurodollar options.

For example, based on Figure 4-7, a borrower could simulate a 9-month cap at 8 1/2 percent by purchasing the December, March, and June puts with a strike price of 91.50. For each $1 million hedged, this would cost the sum of the three puts, that is, (4 + 8 + 14) × $25, or $650.

Figure 4-8 illustrates the workings of a simple 2-year cap, and Figure 4-9 provides a realistic set of prices for caps and floors, for a given set of yields, maturities, and (implicit) volatility expectations.

A **floor** is merely the downside equivalent of a cap. It is an agreement by the seller to pay the buyer any amount by which LIBOR, or another reference rate, falls below the preset "floor" during a series of future interest-fixing periods. If LIBOR is 7 percent and the floor or minimum rate is set at 5 percent, for example, the seller would pay the buyer 5 percent less LIBOR whenever LIBOR falls below 5 percent on any future interest fixing date (such as every quarter) for, say, the next 7 years. Since the floor agreement hedges against rates falling below a fixed (strike) rate for a sequence of future periods, it is the equivalent of a strip of Eurodollar call options.

A **collar** is the simultaneous purchase of a cap and sale of a floor. The net cost is the value of the cap less the value of the floor. Borrowers often prefer to purchase a collar rather than a cap because the out-of-pocket cost is lower. The effect of purchasing a collar, of course, is that while the borrower's periodic interest cost cannot exceed a certain maximum rate, neither can his cost fall below a (different) minimum level. Take Company Ecks who earlier bought a cap from Bank Wuy for 4 percent. Say Ecks bought a collar instead, one that incorporated a ceiling (as before) of 9 per-

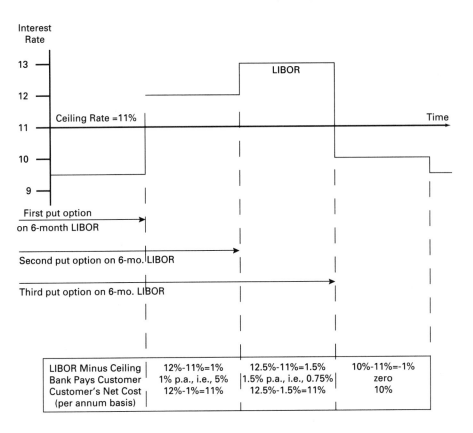

FIGURE 4-8. An Interest Rate Cap. This two-year interest rate cap is equivalent to three put options.

cent but also a floor of 5 percent. Then if LIBOR exceeds 9 percent, Wuy pays Ecks, but if LIBOR goes below 5 percent, Ecks pays Wuy. If the floor that Ecks provides to Wuy is worth, say, 3 percent, then the net cost to Ecks of the collar is only 1 percent. As illustrated, Ecks's reference borrowing rate can only fluctuate between the ceiling rate of 9 percent and the floor rate of 5 percent.

Caps, floors, and collars are, we have seen, the equivalent of combinations of put and call options. They may (in principle) therefore be traded and hedged like other fixed income options—by taking offsetting positions in the options or futures markets. Sometimes, however, a bank may be able to offset a cap sold to the customer by purchasing (at a lower price!) an identical cap from another customer. This is known as the "counterparty" rate hedge business, as opposed to the "warehouse" business.

Sample Cap and Floor Quotation Sheet

Caps	9.0%	9.5%	10.0%	10.5%	11.0%	11.5%	12.0 %	12.5%
1 YR	0.27	0.21	0.16	0.13	0.11	0.09	0.08	0.07
2 YR	1.16	0.88	0.69	0.54	0.43	0.34	0.26	0.20
3 YR	2.56	2.10	1.71	1.40	1.14	0.92	0.76	0.62
4 YR	4.08	3.43	2.89	2.43	2.04	1.71	1.44	1.21
5 YR	5.67	4.86	4.15	3.55	3.03	2.59	2.23	1.91
7 YR	9.29	8.15	7.16	6.29	5.52	4.85	4.27	3.78
10 YR	13.81	12.34	11.03	9.87	8.84	7.93	7.12	6.41
FLOORS	**6.50%**	**6.75%**	**7.00%**	**7.25%**	**7.50%**	**7.75%**	**8.00%**	**8.25%**
1 YR			0.01	0.06	0.10	0.18	0.26	0.37
2 YR	0.01	0.06	0.14	0.24	0.37	0.52	0.68	0.88
3 YR	0.07	0.16	0.26	0.40	0.59	0.08	1.02	1.30
4 YR	0.13	0.26	0.42	0.62	0.83	1.09	1.41	1.76
5 YR	0.24	0.42	0.65	0.91	1.19	1.54	1.90	2.33
7 YR	0.55	0.79	1.10	1.46	1.86	2.29	2.79	3.34
10 YR	1.34	1.73	2.17	2.66	3.21	3.81	4.47	5.19

FIGURE 4-9. Cap and Floor Prices. The numbers in the table are the prices a bank's customers would face for a cap or floor on 3-month LIBOR. The upper panel, **caps**, are the percentages a customer would pay for various ceilings and maturities. The lower panel, **floors**, are the percentages a customer would receive for selling a floor to the bank, again for various floor rates and maturities. For example, the bank would sell a $100 million, 11 percent cap for 5 years at $3.03 million. Or the bank would purchase a $100 million, 7.5 percent floor for $1.19 million. Together these constitute a 7.5 percent – 11 percent **collar** that would cost a customer $1.84 million. (Such a table would be used for indicative purposes only; to obtain up-to-the-minute quotations, and would have to ask the bank's interest rate products group for "live" prices.)

Natural sellers of caps are investors who are willing, in return for a lump-sum fee, to limit the return they receive on variable-rate investments, or institutions whose borrowing cost is limited to a maximum level but whose asset return is not. Typical of the latter is a bank making LIBOR-based loans while funding itself by issuance of a "cap floater."

A **cap floater** is a floating-rate note with a periodic interest rate tied to LIBOR, but where the rate will not exceed a certain "cap" rate. Some FRN investors are willing to accept the ceiling on their investment return for the sake of the 25 to 50 basis points higher coupon rates that these cap floaters provide over conventional, uncapped, FRNs. The issuer is in effect paying an additional, say, 0.30 percent per annum for the cap. He may be able to sell the cap to a bank for more than that—for, say, 0.40 percent per annum—and so reduce his annual borrowing cost by 10 basis points. A **collared floating-rate note** has both a cap and a floor, offering the investor a minimum interest rate (perhaps even above today's short-term rate) in exchange for a limit on the height to which the rate can go. These are created by "stripping" the cap and the floor off the FRN from the issuer's point of view. The issuer sells the cap to, and buys the floor from, a bank, reaping a net gain that reduces his effective cost of funds below what he would normally pay.

This concludes our brief review of option-based hedging methods. We have hardly scratched the surface of the weird and wonderful option-linked instruments and option financing techniques that are being dreamed up by creative bankers. But once the principles behind Eurodollar and other fixed income options have been grasped, it is not difficult for inventive minds to come up with a few innovations.

EURODOLLAR OPTION PRICING

Option pricing is a hairy topic. In what follows we will give an intuitive view of why some options are priced very cheaply and others are more expensive—in other words, what determines option prices. We will do so with minimal reference to formal option pricing models. While our discussion refers to call options, most of what is said applies *pari passu* to put options. Moreover, once one knows the price of a call, one can use the "put-call parity" equation to figure the price of a put. This relationship, and the method for creating a "synthetic put" is given in Appendix 4-C.

To a large extent Eurodollar options are priced like other kinds of options—stock options, commodity options, foreign exchange options, and index options. All options provide downside protection with upside opportunity, and it is the value of this combination that gives the option its value.

Put differently, *the value of any option depends crucially on the probability of the option being exercised*. A glance back at Figure 4-7 will remind us that some of the quoted option contracts are quite likely to be exercised, and others are quite unlikely. A deep out-of-the-money option, such as the June '94 call, is rather unlikely to be exercised, since there is a pretty trivial probability that the Eurodollar futures price will rise to 94 by the June 17 exercise date. (From Figure 4-7 we see that the June Eurodollar settlement price was 92.55 on June 5, so Eurodollar interest rates would have to fall by about 145 basis points in 12 days for the June '94 call to be worth exercising.) One shouldn't bet much on that horse; neither, apparently, will the market. For the rate hedger, great downside protection, but no upside opportunity. One can get such opportunities by staying home watching TV. Figure 4-10, a diagram of how theoretical Eurodollar option prices change with different Eurodollar reference prices (i.e., different forward interest rates) shows why this is so. The deep out-of-the-money option, where the strike price far exceeds the Eurodollar index, is worth next to nothing.

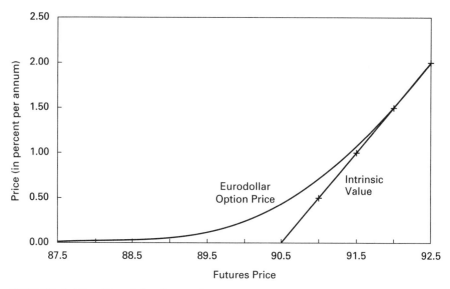

FIGURE 4-10.   Eurodollar Option Pricing.

Of course, for out-of-the-money options where the market price is quite close to the strike price, the upside potential becomes significant and the option becomes more valuable.

Returning now to Figure 4-7, the table of option prices, one can easily identify an option whose exercise is a near certainty. Take the June 91.50 call. Almost sure to win, this option has a price that reflects that fact. Indeed, you could exercise it now and lock in the exercise price 91.50 and sell the futures to receive $92.55. Because it's such a sure thing, it's almost like a futures or forward contract which is the ultimate sure thing. But nobody in his right mind pays an up-front premium for a futures contract; any rational person will come to the conclusion not to pay much more for the option than its intrinsic value—the gain that could be locked in by exercising it now. That gain is $92.55 – $91.50 = $1.05. The traded price of the call was 1.05. Thus the market paid only $0 (0 basis points × $25) for the negligible downside protection that is the only thing that differentiates a deep in-the-money option from a futures contract.

Now that we've taken a look at two rather extreme options—a "nothing" option and a "nothing but a futures" option—we can move toward the middle ground, towards those options whose downside protection and upside potential are significant. As you can guess, those are "at-the-money" options—ones whose strike price is equal or close to the going market price. Those are the options worth paying for, and their price reflects that fact. To recap, all option prices consist of two parts:

| Price | equals | Money you could lock in now | plus | Value from downside protection plus upside potential |

In options market parlance:

| Price | equals | Intrinsic value | plus | Time value |

The relative importance of the intrinsic value and time value components are summarized in the table below.

KIND OF OPTION (MARKET PRICE RELATIVE TO STRIKE PRICE)	INTRINSIC VALUE	TIME VALUE
Deep out-of-the-money option	Zero	Negligible, because of trivial upside potential
Slightly out-of-the-money option	Zero	Considerable, because of downside protection plus substantial upside potential
At-the-money option	Zero	Maximum, because of greatest downside protection *and* greatest upside potential
Slightly in-the-money option	Equals difference between strike and futures price	Considerable, because of upside potential plus substantial downside protection
Deep in-the-money option	Equals difference between strike and futures price; constitutes bulk of option's value	Negligible, because of trivial downside protection relative to futures contract

If you're with us so far you've learned quite a bit about how Eurodollar options prices change as rates change, something very important for anyone trading Eurodollar options. To complete our intuitive survey of option pricing, we must turn to the two other important determinants of Eurodollar options prices—interest rate volatility and time left to expiration of the option, and the risk-free interest rate. Together these determine, for a given level of "inness" or "outness" of the money (i.e., for a given point on the X-axis in Figure 4-10), what the "time value" of the option should be. The time value depends on the value of both downside protection and upside potential. For a given strike and market price, this depends purely on the probability of the market moving above (or below) the strike between now and the expiration date. That probability depends principally on how much time is left and how volatile Eurodollar rates are. Volatility is defined as the annualized standard deviation of daily price, or interest rate, changes.

Putting the market relative to the strike price, the risk-free interest rate, the time to expiration, and the expected volatility together to figure out the theoretical option price requires a model, such as modifications of the famous Black-Scholes model. While the mathematics of these can be complex, modern option pricing theory is derived from building blocks of relatively simple arbitrage strategies—arbitrage between options and the underlying instrument—that provide the trader with only the risk-free rate of return. Perhaps the most significant feature of these models is that while expectations of *volatility* of prices is a factor, they do not rely on expectations

---

THE DELTA AND THE GAMMA

The sensitivity of a given options price to the futures price is called the **delta**. Delta is the mathematical symbol used as shorthand for the so-called **hedge ratio**. It tells the trader how many futures contracts to use to offset the price behavior of one options contract. For example, if an option has a delta of 0.4, then 100 options will gain or fall in value like 40 futures contracts. So a bank might write $100 million Eurodollar call options for a customer and "delta hedge" itself by buying 40 Eurodollar futures contracts. Unfortunately, deltas themselves change often; so a delta hedge approach involves calculating daily or even more frequently the proportion of the underlying Eurodollar futures contract which should be held long (or short, to hedge a put). Only continual adjustments of this proportion will allow the option writer to hedge his market risks. The technique requires an options pricing model and depends crucially on the trader's guess of future interest rate volatility.

The rapidity with which the delta changes for a given change in the futures price is called the **gamma**. The gamma is represented in the option price diagram by the *curvature* of the line. (The delta is the first derivative of the option price; the gamma is the second derivative.) To avoid being whipsawed by changes in the delta, an option writer can hedge his short option position more precisely by using something that behaves like the instrument he sold—something that has a similar delta *and* a similar gamma. This is called gamma hedging. The obvious way to hedge an option, therefore, is with another option. Of course, relative to using futures, options are costly. In sum, when options traders want to sleep well (but not eat well!), they buy options to hedge the options they have written.

regarding the *level* of future prices or rates to determine the correct price of an option.

The *risk-free interest rate* plays a discounting role in the option pricing formula, relating the range of possible future gains to the premium paid up front. The major drawback of the Black-Scholes model in pricing options on Eurodollars or Eurodollar futures is that constant short-term interest rates are assumed. This constraint is not crucial when options on common stocks, bonds, or bond futures are priced, because these securities tend to exhibit price behaviors that are—to a certain degree—independent of movements in short-term interest rates. However, when options on Eurodollars or other money market securities are priced, the model's efficacy suffers. This is due to the high degree of correlation that exists between movements in various money market rates and the risk-free rate input used in the options pricing model. Therefore, models have been developed that take account of this problem.

Obviously the greater the *time to expiration* the greater the probability of significant price or rate movement and the higher the time value. Other things being equal, the time value drops off sharply as an option approaches maturity particularly in the last month or so.

Time, intrinsic value, and the market interest rate can all be measured quite easily. The hardest thing is *volatility* itself, because what matters is not past but future volatility of rates. Clearly the greater the volatility, the higher is the value of the option, so two traders with a different view of rate volatility will place a different value on the same option. Expected volatility, in short, is the key variable in pricing options. As noted earlier, options prices are not affected by changes in expectations about the level of Eurodollar rates—only their variability.

This concludes our discussion of option pricing. Appropriately, we have ended up reinforcing a point made earlier—that Eurodollar options are not the best vehicles for betting on the level of interest rates. Anyone with a view on rates is better off employing futures, forwards, or an interest rate mismatch position. Options are for those who understand volatility and who have a view of volatility of rates that differs from the market's view as embodied in market option prices — or for those who require an option's asymmetric risk character to hedge their naturally asymmetric risks, such as a bank issuing a Eurodollar floating-rate note with a minimum rate, an "embedded" option.

SUMMARY

This chapter has provided a framework for understanding hedging and positioning instruments derived from plain vanilla Eurodollar deposits. Just as the Eurocurrency market allows the separation of currency of denomination from the country of jurisdiction, so the tools described in this chapter permit the separation of the investment or financing vehicle from its interest rate characteristics. Contracts such as futures, forwards, options, and swaps are collectively called derivative securities. Our task has been to show how they can be used in the hedging of Eurodollar and Eurocurrency interest rate risk.

We have also sought to demonstrate that all these hedging instruments are related to one another, and to the underlying Eurodollar market itself, through a set of arbitrage conditions. Eurodollar forwards, futures, and swaps are all, to a degree, substitutes for one another. Foreign currency futures or forwards can be used with these instruments to simulate, or arbitrage against, equivalent hedges in other currencies. Eurodollar options, which provide asymmetrical interest rate hedges, can be combined to replicate interest rate caps, floors, and collars. And to wrap it all up, the pricing of Eurodollar options is based on the principle of one's being able to replicate an option with a position in cash or futures, and vice versa. In Euroland, everyone is kin to everyone else even when they don't look alike.

SELECTED REFERENCES

Beidleman, C. R., ed., *Cross Currency Swaps*. Homewood, IL: Business One-Irwin, 1992.

Bierwag, G. O., et al., "Duration: Its Development and Use in Bond Portfolio Management," *Financial Analysts Journal*, July–August 1983, pp. 15–35.

Dufey, Gunter and Ian H. Giddy, "The Evolution of Instruments and Techniques in International Financial Markets," Société Universitaire Européene de Recherches Financieres, Series 35A, 1981.

Kolb, Robert, *Interest Rate Futures*. Richmond, VA: Robert F. Dame, 1982.

Kolb, Robert, and R. Ghiang, "Improving Hedging Performance Using Interest Rate Futures," *Financial Management*, Vol. 10, No. 4, 1981, pp. 72–79.

Marshall, John F. and Kenneth R. Kapner, *The Swaps Market*. Miami: Kolb Publishing, 1993.

Reurolana, Eli M., "The Recent Growth of Financial Derivative Markets," *FRBNY Quarterly Review*, Winter 1992–93, pp. 28–43.

Schwartz, Robert and Clifford Smith, eds., *The Handbook of Currency and Interest Rate Risk Management*. New York: New York Institute of Finance, 1990.

Smith, Clifford W., Jr. et al., "The Evolving Market for Swaps," *Midland Corporate Finance Journal*, Vol. 3, No. 4, Winter 1986, pp. 20–32.

Swap Finance. London: Euromoney Publications (3 vols.), updated periodically.

Turnbull, Stuart M., "Swap: A Zero Sum Game?" *Financial Management*, Spring 1987, pp. 15–21.

APPENDIX 4-A
Eurodollar Futures Contract Specifications

SPECIFICATIONS	THREE-MONTH EURODOLLAR TIME DEPOSIT CHICAGO INTERNATIONAL MONETARY MARKET (CME)	
Size	$1,000,000	
Contract delivery and settlement	Cash settlement of the charge in the Eurodollar futures price from previous to last trading day, based on a final settlement price of 3-month LIBOR obtained from 12 reference banks randomly selected during the last 90 minutes of trading.	
Yields	Add-on	
Hours	8:30 A.M. – 2:00 P.M. EST	
Months traded	March, June, September, and December	
Minimum fluctuation in price	0.01 (1 basis point) ($25 pt)	
Limit move	1.00 (100 basis points) ($25 pt) No spot month limit	
Last day of trading	2nd London business day before 3rd Wednesday of expiration month.	
Delivery date	Last day of trading	
Minimum margins	Initial $2,000	Maintenance $1,500
Eurodollar/CD Spread	Initial $500	Maintenance $400
Eurodollar/T-bill spread	Initial $700	Maintenance $600
Spread margins	Initial $400	Maintenance $200
Delivery month margin	Initial $400	Maintenance $1,500
Delivery month spread margins	Initial $400	Maintenance $200

189

APPENDIX 4-B
Eurodollar Options Contract Specifications

SPECIFICATIONS	OPTION ON EURODOLLAR FUTURES(CHICAGO CME)	OPTION ON EURODOLLAR TIME DEPOSITS (PHILADELPHIA PBOT)
Underlying security	One Eurodollar IMM time deposit futures contract of the specified contract month.	Contract represents annualized yield on 3-month time deposit with face value of $100,000 Eurodollar reference price. Calculated as (100 annual yield).
Exercise of contract	"American" option: may be exercised on any day *up to* the expiration date.	"European" option: may only be exercised *on* the expiration date, after trading terminates in the expiring series.
Expiration months	March, June, September, and December (same as Eurodollar futures contract).	Same.
Expiration dates	Second London business day before the third Wednesday of the contract month (same as Eurodollar Futures contract).	Same.
Trading hours	8:30 A.M. TO 3:00 P.M. EST.	Same.
Strike prices	Quoted as an index (points of 100 percent) equal to 100 yield. Strike prices set at intervals of 0.50 (50 basis points).	Quoted as index (points of 100 percent) equal to 100 yield. Strike prices set at intervals of 0.25 (25 basis points).
Option premiums	Premiums quoted in points of 100 percent. Each 0.01 represents $25. An 0.01 is also the maximum price fluctuation.	Same.
Daily price limit	None.	None.

190

SPECIFICTIONS	OPTION ON EURODOLLAR FUTURES (CHICAGO CME)	OPTION ON EURODOLLAR TIME DEPOSITS (PHILADELPHIA PBOT)
Exercise settlement and delivery	Settled by obliging call writer to open *long* IMM Eurodollar futures contract and call holder to open a *short* contract, at the strike. (Put writer and holder do opposite.) The effect is a transfer of funds from the writer's futures account to the holder's account equal to the dollar difference between the strike price and the latest Eurodollar futures settlement price.	Settled in cash based on PBOT Eurodollar option settlement price. Final settlement price from two random samples of 3-month Eurodollar time deposit quotes on last day of trading. From each sample, two highest and two lowest quotes are eliminated. Final settlement price is 100 less average of remaining quotes, rounded to nearest 0.01 percent. Effectively, the difference between the strike price and LIBOR.
Margin requirements	Option buyers must pay the option premium in full.	Option buyers must pay the option premium in full. Option sellers must provide margin equal to the premium plus $720 for in- and at-the-money options or the premium plus $720 less the out-of-the-money amount, with a minimum of the premium plus $300 out-of-the-money options.

APPENDIX 4-C
Put-Call Parity

While options and futures are distinct instruments, their prices are linked by a fundamental arbitrage relationship called put-call parity. This stems from the fact that buying a call and selling a put, both for the expiration date and exercise price E, gives a pattern of gains and losses that duplicates that on a long futures contract with a price of E. Think about a trader who buys a call and sells a put. He will gain dollar-for-dollar on the call by the amount the futures price rises above E, or lose dollar-for-dollar on the put by the amount the futures price falls below E, just as he could have had he bought a Eurodollar futures contract. Of course he has had to pay for the call (and he has received the put premium). So to figure the price at which the trader has effectively purchased currency forward one should take into account the difference between the premium C paid for the call and the premium P received for the put, plus interest (i) on this difference since premiums are paid up front. The total profit picture taking into account the premia, is illustrated by the thin line in Figure 4C-1. It looks just like a futures!

The net cost of this "synthetic futures" is

$$E + (C - P)(1 + i)$$

If the cost of locking in the future Eurodollar interest rate using this strategy is cheaper than locking it in via a plain old futures at the going futures price F, the trader will do an arbitrage called a reversal—couple the long call and short put with a sale of Eurodollar futures, earning a profit:

$$\text{Profit from reversal} = F - E - (C - P)(1 + i)$$

What if the opposite is true? What if buying a futures contract is cheaper than locking in the rate by combining puts and calls? Well, the trader will then perform the mirror image act, one called conversion. Here the trader creates an artificial short futures position by buying a put, selling a call, and investing (or borrowing) the difference between the two premiums at an

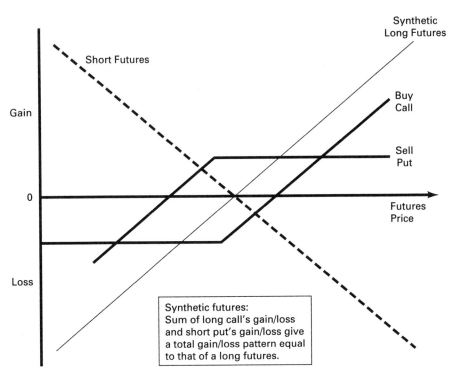

FIGURE 4C-1.   Put-Call Parity: How a Long Call Plus a Short Put Can Replicate a Long Futures.

interest rate i. Coupled with a long futures at F, the conversion produces a profit:

$$\text{Profit from conversion} = E + (C - P)(1 + i) - F$$

Easy, right? Dream on! Lots of traders read this before you did and rushed to take advantage of any price anomalies between futures and options prices. In doing so they drove call and put prices to the point where no profits remained. So by now the right-hand side of both equations equals zero. This implies that in equilibrium the difference between the call and put premiums for an option with strike price E will be equal to the difference between the Eurodollar futures price F and E, discounted to the present at the market interest rate i:

$$C - P = \frac{(F - E)}{(1 + i)}$$

This is the relationship we call put-call parity.

For amusement the reader may wish to go back to the newspaper extracts in the chapter and see if put-call parity holds, and imagine how much money he or she could make. The problem with doing so, of course, is that published prices do not necessarily reflect the prices at which you and I could deal, nor were the reported trades in the put, call, and futures contracts concluded at precisely the same time. In fact one of the problems with doing conversions or reversals, or for that matter any arbitrage, is the difficulty of executing two or more trades simultaneously.

Chapter Five

EUROMARKET FUNDING PRACTICES

PRACTICES IN THE INTERNATIONAL MONEY MARKET

The essential concept of the international money market is the separability of country of jurisdiction from currency of denomination. This is nowhere more important than in the manner in which international banks fund their operations, and, looking at it from the other side, in the decisions of investors as to what kind of deposits—or other money market instruments—in which to place their funds. In this chapter and the next, we examine the institutional structures, procedures, and practices that have evolved in the market. This chapter examines the markets and instruments which bring banks as borrowers and depositors as investors together. The separability of currency from jurisdiction has long provided opportunities and risks that must be understood by both sides. Today, moreover, the separability of market risk features—currency, interest rate, and even credit risks—from the underlying instrument means that funding management consists of not only *how to fund* a bank's assets but also *how to modify that funding* to balance the characteristics of assets and liabilities and off-balance-sheet commitments. Thus we must draw on the hedging and positioning instruments of Chapter Four to show how FRAs, swaps, and futures have now become integral components of the funding manager's toolkit. We also borrow from the next chapter because some international banks' lending instruments, such as floating-rate notes, note issuance facilities, and medium-term notes, are used by others to assure themselves of longer-term availability of funds.

Our aim is not to present an "operations manual" for conducting international banking; rather we focus quite narrowly on the question of how the growth of the external market and the nature of its financial processes have resulted in distinct practices and institutions for the borrowing and lending of funds. This reflects our belief that institutional arrangements do not appear by accident but evolve in response to market incentives in the context of specific regulatory and public policy constraints.

PARTICIPANTS IN THE MARKET

One unique feature of the international money market is the diversity of its participants, the wide range of borrowers and lenders that compete with one another on the same basis. The international money market is simultaneously an interbank market, a lending market where private and public entities raise funds, and a deposit market for corporations and governments. In contrast, most domestic credit markets are segmented and compartmentalized by borrower or lender. For example, in the U.S. market various sectors are dominated by particular institutions: the Federal funds market is virtually the exclusive domain of commercial banks, the market for commercial paper is dominated by large corporations, and a huge segment of the money market is concerned exclusively with government-issued paper. While these segments of the domestic money market are linked, they all retain a high degree of distinction.

By contrast, the international money market is extremely homogeneous in its treatment of borrowers and lenders. On both borrowing and lending sides, few, if any, features discriminate among the participants, apart from classical economic considerations: minimum size and credit risk as perceived by a market guided by profit-maximizing objectives. And the market's "instruments" are always liabilities of financial institutions. No regulations compel investors to differentiate among them, and there is little, if any, pressure on the financial intermediaries to favor one borrower over the other for reasons other than return and risk.[1]

---

[1] The exception, of course, is in the internationally, sometimes officially, coordinated country-rescue efforts on behalf of borrowers such as Mexico—and we regard these as an aberration with little connection with the Euromarket *per se.*

Yet the participants in these markets are as diverse in character as they are geographically widespread. Hundreds of banks and corporations, mostly originating in North America, Western Europe, and Japan, are regular borrowers and depositors in the market. Commercial banks form the institutional core of the market. The banks enter the Eurodollar market both as depositors and as lenders; they purchase as well as issue financial securities. Twenty or so of the world's largest banks, commanding assets of several trillion dollars, play a dominant role in the Eurodollar market—particularly in the interbank deposit market, since these largest banks are sometimes able to attract a disproportionate volume of deposits, which are then re-lent to other Eurobanks. These and other banks also play the role of linking the external with the domestic market, taking funds from and/or placing funds in the market. The size, breadth, and depth of the interbank market enable banks to adjust their liquidity positions with relative ease without approaching the central bank for help. We shall discuss the interbank market at greater length shortly.

Corporations have been huge placers of funds in the Eurodeposit market during the 1980s, but the volume of funds deposited by any individual entity tends to be quite variable and of a short-term character. For example, in the mid-1980s Japanese and Korean firms placed large sums of temporary money generated by export revenues in various Eurocurrencies, as did a number of U.S. and European firms engaged in takeovers and mergers. These replaced the oil and other commodity-based firms that were the great depositors of the late 1970s.

Governments and central banks have also appeared on the deposit side of the market; this factor became evident during the late 1960s, when several European governments sought higher returns on their surplus dollar reserves. Large-scale government depositing reappeared in the mid-1970s, as oil-exporting nations turned to the large international banks for safe, high-yield investments of their dollar surpluses. In the 1980s the major OECD central banks, having overcome their erstwhile reluctance to encourage the growth of the Eurodollar market, placed an increasing volume of reserves that were used for foreign exchange intervention, in the offshore market. In doing so they often used the Bank for International Settlements (BIS) as an agent. Then and now, sovereign entities are sensitive to the political dimension of national boundaries—as depositors they are attracted not only by the relatively high yield, flexibility, and liquidity of the market but also by the anonymity and choice of jurisdiction that the market offers. The market allows them to hold foreign currency–denominated liquid assets outside the country where the respective currency serves as means of payment.

Private individuals are in relative terms only minor participants in the international money market, (although wealthy private investors have always been important in the Eurobond market). In recent years, as the range and flexibility of the deposit instruments available have increased, so has the willingness of individuals to make investments in Euronotes, Eurocommercial paper, and London dollar CDs, which are available in denominations as small as $10,000.

Finally no description of the market's participants would be complete without mention of the money market brokers—the ill-dressed, cockney-speaking characters whose business of matching supply and demand in the global money market is conducted in noisy, boilerhouse rooms. Here they help harness and reallocate billions of dollars of interbank deposits and other instruments in London, Singapore, and elsewhere, never owning a cent of the money themselves. Without them, the market would be neither so efficient nor so colorful.

EUROMARKET FUNDING

Bankers conventionally divide the means by which the bank's assets are financed into three parts: deposits, borrowings, and capital.

Deposits are considered special because they include noninterest-bearing payment ("checking" or "current") accounts, because they are relatively stable and because they often bear a privileged position, such as being insured, in the banking system. But these special features are creatures of regulation, inertia, and a degree of nonprice competition, little of which is found in the Euromarket. For our purposes, therefore, we treat deposits and **borrowings** as one—they all consist of "bought money," paying a market rate in a free, uninsured money market. As for **capital**, it too is largely a figment of the regulator's imagination, for it consists not only of equity but also of those liabilities considered sufficiently long term and subordinate to provide a cushion against loss for depositors and the regulators themselves (see Chapter Six). Some of the longer-term sources of funds considered in the final section of this chapter qualify as primary or secondary capital. For the most part, however, this chapter is concerned with Eurocurrency deposits and other forms of competitive funding in the international money market.

Deposits (special status)
Borrowings (bought money)
Capital (regulatory requirement)

Any bank, domestic or international, must consider the cost, availability, maturity, and interest risk of borrowed funds employed to finance its earning assets. A well-managed bank will seek to balance its assets and liabilities simultaneously in a way that (1) maximizes the spread between borrowing and lending rates while minimizing the riskiness of its assets; (2) maximizes the volume of loans extended, given its capitalization and the available rates on deposits and loans; and (3) maximizes the liquidity of the bank while minimizing the amount of cash and low-return assets held.

Liability management in itself aims to (1) assure the continued availability of funds at a reasonable cost (i.e., at close to prevailing market rates), (2) maintain a stable deposit base, (3) minimize the cost of funds, and (4) minimize the "mismatch" between the interest rate risk of assets and that of liabilities. In addition, some banks seek to profit from such money market techniques as arbitrage (taking advantage of differences in yields between similar money market instruments) and "riding the yield curve" (borrowing at short maturities and depositing at longer maturities, or vice versa, to profit from differences between the bank's forecast of future interest rates and those implied by the prevailing yield curve).

These aspects of liability management are little altered when we consider Eurobanks rather than domestic banks. Eurobanks wish to minimize the cost of loanable funds and manage the maturity structure of their deposit liabilities in such a way as to take advantage of expected increases or decreases in interest rates. There is, however, one fundamental distinction between funding the domestic bank and funding an overseas branch. Since domestic branches operate within a single country's borders, they may be funded in a consolidated fashion by the bank's or bank holding company's funding unit, and (with some exceptions) the funds may be pooled.[2] In contrast, all foreign branches, Euro and otherwise, are located in a different jurisdiction and so must fund themselves independently to a greater or lesser degree. Branches operating within countries with exchange controls, in particular, must of necessity fund their local currency loan portfolios to a large degree without relying on the head office's pool of funds.[3] Eurocurrency branches fall somewhere in between, because the relatively free transferability of most Eurocurrencies allows a pooling of funds among branches and between the parent bank and the offshore branches.

Several branches of the same bank operating in several different "open" jurisdictions may well be funded as a group, for example, Bank X may fund all its Caribbean branches together, lending funds freely between one unit and another according to need. But for tax, capital control, and other "sovereign dimension" reasons, funding is more often segregated than not. As a general rule, the more funds transfers are (or could be) constrained, the more likely international banks will operate each Eurobranch as a separate funding unit.

There are other differences, principally ones of emphasis, arising partly from the fact that the Eurodollar market is largely a wholesale banking sys-

---

[2] The exceptions lie in the legal restrictions that countries sometimes impose on the transfer of funds between different banking corporations owned by the same holding company, as in the U.S. Bank Holding Company Act, or on the transfer of funds between the principal bank and certain special-purpose units, such as international banking facilities.

[3] Marcia Stigum and Rene Branch, *Managing Bank Assets and Liabilities* (Homewood, IL: Dow Jones-Irwin, 1983) address this topic.

tem. A substantial proportion of day-to-day Eurobanking activities consists of the active "trading" of Eurocurrency deposits—that is, borrowing short-term funds from other banks and redepositing these funds in the interbank market. This means that the liability management of a Eurobank is closely tied in with the management of cash and liquid assets. In this respect, a Eurobank is most closely comparable with the money market departments of large money market center banks in the United States.

Domestic banks usually hold cash and liquid assets for three reasons: to meet reserve requirements, to maintain precautionary, liquid assets against unexpected future loans needs or deposit withdrawals, and to maintain a safe, fixed income investment as part of the bank's portfolio. This last reason is related to the bank's capital adequacy: the smaller the proportion of equity on the balance sheet, the greater the proportion of Treasury bills and other relatively liquid securities that a prudent bank will tend to have.

Eurobanks are not subject to reserve requirements imposed by monetary authorities. If they hold noninterest-bearing deposits, they do so purely for precautionary and transactions purposes. The optimal level of precautionary balances that such a bank should maintain is a function only of (1) the additional return available on earning assets, (2) the probability that net disbursements (cash outflows) will exceed the precautionary balances, and (3) the cost of running out of precautionary balances and having to obtain funds from other banks or nonbanks or from the shareholders. Since the precautionary balances of Eurobanks are noninterest-bearing demand deposits held, say, in New York banks, there is a strong incentive to keep as little as possible in this form. In addition, Eurobanks have no demand deposit or checking account liabilities—only time deposits of one form or another. *This means that a Eurobank, unlike a typical domestic bank, always has some forewarning of pending withdrawals.*[4]

To explore this point a little further, it may be useful to refer to the hypothetical balance sheet of a Eurobank shown in Table 5-1. The various categories of funding sources are shown, including short-term borrowings from other Eurobanks, nonbank time deposits, and negotiable London dollar certificates of deposit. These are the major sources of funds. Others that are used include floating-rate loan rates, Eurobonds, loans from other branches, and domestic funds from the parent bank.

Yet there is one important financial commitment not shown on the conventional financial statements of a Eurobank—the loan commitments and

---

[4] This applies even to "call" deposits. With few exceptions, Eurodollar deposits and withdrawals take place on the "2-day-delivery" basis. That is, funds deposited or withdrawn on a particular day are not actually delivered to the receiver of funds until 2 days later, excluding holidays (i.e., not until the third clear business day). For example, if Eurobank A arranges on May 26, a Friday, to deposit $5 million in Eurobank B, the actual deposit will not occur until 2 business days later (i.e., Tuesday, May 30). In this respect settlement practices in the Eurocurrency market imitate those of the foreign exchange market.

TABLE 5-1.   Balance Sheet of a Eurobank

ASSETS	LIABILITIES
1. Reserve balances in "nostro" accounts for clearing purposes	1. Interbank deposits
2. Interbank deposits or ("placements")	2. Nonbank time deposits ("placements")
3. Other money market investments, such as Euronotes	3. London dollar CDs
4. Medium- to long-term securities, such as floating-rate notes	4. Notes and bonds
5. Medium- to long-term nontraded instruments, such as syndicated loans	5. Loans from other branches
	6. Loans from parent bank
	7. Share capital held by parent bank

lines of credit held with that bank by other banks and by nonbank institutions. These lines can involve a substantial financial liability at a time of tight credit. Conversely, the asset side of the balance sheet does not show the lines of credit that the Eurobank has with other Eurobanks and with domestic banks. In addition, Eurobanks maintain an extensive network of informal interbank credit facilities.

These lines and facilities, together with the forewarning of withdrawals of time deposits, allow Eurobanks to retain negligible amounts in demand deposits. Indeed, in the case of Eurodollars, the primary functions of those deposits that are retained in New York banks are the clearing of transactions plus an amount held to compensate the New York bank for providing checking account facilities. In other words, the interbank network permits both a high degree of efficiency in putting deposited funds to work and the maintenance of a close-to-zero proportion of precautionary balances.

The absence of demand deposit facilities and the geographically diverse nature of the market's participants mean that, in contrast to most domestic banks, Eurobanks have no captive deposit base.[5] Hence they have to compete aggressively on the open market for all deposits. And even if one or more banks should obtain a geographical or industrial advantage, that monopolistic advantage would soon be eroded as a result of the ease of entry to the market and the fact that banks from many different countries are less likely to respect cartels than is a homogeneous group of banks.

The mark of good, conservative Eurobank liability management, then, is the ability to attract and retain funds whenever needed at as low a cost as possible and, of course, to earn as high as possible a return on liquid assets, including reserve balances. First, the Eurobank must offer deposit liabilities that have a sufficiently attractive combination of yield, liquidity, and safety to attract funds from competing financial institutions and markets. Second,

---

[5] Bankers frequently use the term "natural" deposit base, a euphemism for having a privileged position in a local market protected by regulatory barriers to entry and ceilings on interest rates.

the bank must build deposit trading relationships and create a market presence by being a two-way trader of funds and, ultimately, by maintaining interbank lines and facilities that provide backup availability of funds. "Liquidity management" or ensuring access to cash whenever required is as much a part of the funding manager's skills as is earning a profitable spread between liabilities' costs and assets' return.

Because Eurobanks lack the natural deposit base in which deposits are rolled over semi-automatically, the funding manager has to pay closer attention to matching the interest rate period, the commitment period, and, of course, the currency of the deposits he obtains, with the assets being funded. The shape of his assets is customer driven; funding must adjust. Flexibility in choosing the form of deposit to issue becomes very important. Even so, a perfect match may often not be possible, except at a penurious price—so the funding department must manage mismatches between the assets funded and the instruments issued. Going further, he will seek to profit from deliberately mismatching from time to time. This will be discussed in the paragraphs that follow.

Throughout this book we have emphasized the link between Eurodeposit business and foreign exchange trading. This link reappears in the funding function: banks frequently borrow in the Eurocurrency market to obtain funds, say, yen, required for delivery in a foreign exchange transaction, and in turn deposit the funds obtained in exchange, say, dollars. More on transactions of this type, and on swaps, follows.

To summarize, the Eurocurrency deposit market is employed as a funding source by banks in several ways:

- To take customer deposits and pay them a rate superior to almost any other money market alternative;
- To match-fund the bank's loans and its investments in other assets such as Euronotes and floating-rate notes;
- To obtain funds of one kind (e.g., maturity) to mismatch them against assets of a slightly different kind (e.g., longer maturity);
- To provide flexible access for large banks to a huge international pool of funds;
- To provide relatively inexpensive access to funds by smaller or less known banks, who might have difficulty in attracting dollar deposits from nonbank depositors;
- To provide lines, facilities, commitments, and relationships that give banks greater assurance of "availability" of funds under changing market conditions.

The funding manager of today looks at the Eurodollar market as only one of several means of funding a loan or asset book: after all, he could perhaps borrow in the domestic U.S. market at a rate which, when adjusted for reserve requirements, FDIC fees, and taxes, will be very similar in cost to the Eurodollar rate. He may be able to issue nondeposit liabilities, such as commercial paper on Euronotes, and he can often borrow in a different Eurocurrency and cover the currency risk in the forward exchange market.

As a practical matter, our funding manager in a London or Singapore Eurobank will normally turn to the vast, flexible *interbank market* as the obvious repository for, or source of, funds. Let us now see how this is done.

THE INTERBANK MARKET

The interviews that we have conducted with Eurocurrency traders and others suggest that the interbank liabilities of Eurobanks seldom fall below 40 percent, while a number of Eurobanks rely *entirely* on the interbank market as a source of funds. The average Eurobank has 80 to 90 percent of its deposit liabilities owed to other banks although aggregate data provided in the quarterly reports from the Bank of International Settlements show a declining trend as capital adequacy constraints and credit concerns have come into prominence in the early 1990s.

What explains this phenomenon? Is not the function of money markets in general and of the Eurocurrency market in particular to borrow funds from savers and provide credit to borrowers? Of course it is. Yet savers and borrowers are separated from one another—not only by geographical distance but also by preferences for certain maturities, degrees of liquidity, amounts, terms and conditions, and financial institutions. In some cases these different preferences are reconciled by the same bank: a Swiss bank may take deposits, for example, from Middle Eastern investors and lend them to borrowers such as Japanese firms and European governments. More commonly, however, Eurobanks will rely on the interbank market, which will readily take or lend large amounts of funds at competitive rates rather than search out borrowers and lenders for every individual transaction. Indeed, there are often several layers of interbank transactions before funds deposited in the market find their way to an ultimate borrower or to a national money market.

Thus the interbank markets for domestic and external bank deposits serve the crucial role of ensuring the allocational efficiency and flexibility of the international money market. In the Eurocurrency market, in fact, the majority of transactions occur between two or more Eurobanks rather than between Eurobanks and third parties. And the balance sheets of typical Eurobanks reveal the interesting feature that the majority of deposits are obtained from Eurobanks, while the majority of the assets are deposits in other (or the same) Eurobanks. Interbank trading of deposits dominates the action in the Eurocurrency market.

The principle of the Eurocurrency interbank market is quite simple: one bank takes a deposit from the public and places (deposits) the funds with another bank, who in turn on-lends the money. Let us now trace a typical transaction.

The Assistant Eurocurrency Trader of the Nassau (Bahamas) branch of First Interstate Bank is sitting at her desk in the bank's Los Angeles headquarters when she receives a telephone call late in the afternoon from the Assistant Treasurer of the international division of John Deere Company. The Nassau branch is likely to be staffed and run entirely in the bank's U.S. offices; the bank's physical presence in Nassau may be no more than a nameplate on an office building and a file drawer in a lawyer's office. (Of course, Eurocurrency operations are run out of fully fledged branches as well as nominal ones.)

In response to an inquiry from the Deere official the Eurocurrency trader provides the bank's rate on 30-day deposits in Nassau.

INTERSTATE TRADER: "9 1/4, good for 5 or 10."
DEERE A.T.:　　　 "Give me a rate on 2."
INTERSTATE TRADER: "9 1/8, 2's a little hard to lay off this late in the day."

Piddly little amounts like $2 million often carry an inferior interest rate, because, as the trader pointed out, it may be hard to "lay off" (redeposit) an odd amount of funds readily in the interbank market, particularly when New York and London are closed.

DEERE A.T.: "Okay, that's still better than I've heard."

So they agree on the rate of 9.125 percent per annum. Apparently the Deere A.T. has checked rates at other banks, and perhaps also looked at quotations shown on his Reuters screen, but one should not forget that screen quotations are indicative only and that trader quotations are not necessarily comparable if taken sequentially, because the whole market may be moving up.

After hanging up, the trader will write the details on a "ticket," by hand or computer, which, after being checked and processed by the bank's operations department, will result in a confirmation slip or computer communication being sent to John Deere Co. (A confirmation may also be sent to the Bahamas, if a set of books is maintained in Nassau.) The ticket will specify the date Deere will transfer the funds to First Interstate Bahamas (normally 2 business days later, the so-called "spot" date) and the date of repayment with interest (32 business days later). The interest would be calculated, by convention, on a 360-day-year basis:[6]

$$9.125\% \times (30/360) \times \$2,000,000 = \$15,208.20$$

---

[6] In the case of sterling deposits, a 365-day year is used.

Two business days later the funds will be wire transferred to First Interstate. Deere will do this by instructing Harris Bank in Chicago, where Deere maintains a checking account, to make a CHIPS payment to First Interstate, for account of Interstate's Nassau branch.[7]

At this point (i.e., 2 days later) Interstate will have "Clearing House Funds," which is a sort of computerized play money that international banks use to keep track of who's paid what to whom during the day. At the end of the New York day, the *net* amount owed by each bank to each other bank is determined and paid in good money, Fed funds, that is, reserve accounts maintained at the Federal Reserve Bank. Even though the money has been deposited offshore in the Bahamas, the underlying transfer of funds is always effected by means of debits and credits to "nostro" accounts maintained in New York banks, chiefly because it is most convenient to have all clearing done through a single system.

Back to our First Interstate Nassau trader in Los Angeles. By the act of accepting a 1-month deposit from Deere, her branch is long (or "overborrowed") 1-month money. Wishing to lay off the money immediately on a matched basis, but fearing the illiquidity of the West Coast market at this hour of the day, she has been on the telephone to the Singapore branch of Interstate arranging to place the $2 million; the Singapore overnight trader agrees to take the deposit onto his own books at $\frac{1}{32}$ of 1 percent over the deposit rate paid by the Nassau branch; hence a second deposit transaction is concluded, this time between two branches of the same bank. Singapore willingly takes on the funds because they have experienced a demand for funds in the region in the past few days and because interest rates seem to be firming.

For a few hours, while the rest of Asia is rubbing the sleep out of its eyes, the Singapore Eurodollar trader has a "position": he has agreed to take on 1-month funds at $9\frac{5}{32}$ without yet having found a home for them. Rather than unload them in a thin market, he is betting on his intuition that rates will rise a bit. Eventually, First Interstate's Chief Eurocurrency Trader in Singapore gets into the office and takes over the position. Rates have hardly moved, but hearing the morning's chatter he feels they may be a bit wobbly, so it's time to lay off the position: to reinvest the money. He may lend the funds either to other banks or, more profitably, to a corporate or governmental borrower. If we assume that none of the latter are seeking funds under a previously concluded loan agreement from Interstate's Singapore branch at that particular moment, he will seek to re-lend the $2 million in

---

[7] CHIPS stands for Clearing House Interbank Payments System, the computer-based clearing arrangement that is used for virtually all international dollar payments between banks. It is located in New York.

the Eurodollar interbank market at as high a rate as possible. Other Eurobanks, with less ready access to nonbank deposits than First Interstate, are willing to pay slightly more for the funds than the prime banks' cost of funds. Such banks can still lend at a profit to nonbank borrowers or perhaps to other banks.

Glancing at his Telerate screen, at a "page" similar to the one shown in Figure 5-1, the chief Eurocurrency trader notices that the yield curve has an upward-sloping shape, that is, that longer-term rates exceed shorter-term rates; so he chooses to place the $2 million, along with another $8 million that the overnight trader has accumulated, into a 3-month interbank deposit. He is "taking a view" on interest rates—a view that rates will not rise more than the "break-even" or "forward forward" rate (see Chapter Four).

But how to find out which bank is willing to pay the best rate for Interstate's deposit? Such traders have "direct-wired" telephone linkages to other dealing rooms in Singapore, Hong Kong, Tokyo, and elsewhere, and so he could call several other banks directly, perhaps after checking their indicative rates on Telerate. Since contacting each of a number of banks directly can be both expensive and time consuming and therefore increase the risk of an interest rate change before a transaction can be consummated, most Eurobanks now rely heavily on **money brokers**. This is in fact what the Interstate trader does: he calls his favorite Eurocurrency broker firm, say, Murray Jones, which is expected to provide him immediately with the bid and offer rates quoted by various Eurobanks. The bank could request quotes for call, 7-day, 30-day, 3-month, 6-month, or 1-year deposits, denominated in U.S. dollars, German marks, Swiss francs, French francs, Japanese yen, or Canadian dollars, and a lot more.[8] Right now he's interested in placing 3-month money, so he asks: "How are your 3 months?"

BROKER: "Three-quarters, seven-eighths, major Japanese, Hong Kong branch."
TRADER: "Okay at the bid, $10 million, what name?"
BROKER: "Name is Fuji."
TRADER: "Okay, done."

---

[8] At the short end of the maturity spectrum, the effective dates of Eurodeposits are as follows, assuming today is day 0 and ignoring holidays:

Days (start and end)	Maturity of deposit	Trader's Jargon
0 to 1	1 day	Overnight (O/N)
1 to 2	1 day	Tom/next (T/N)
2 to 3	1 day	Spot/next (S/N)
2 to 9	7 days	Spot/week (S/W)
2 to 16	14 days	Spot/fortnight (S/F)

08:32 EST	WORLD EUROCURRENCY MARKET			PAGE 271
	EURODOLLAR	EURO STERLING	EURO GERMAN MARK	EURO ECU
1 Month	$8\frac{1}{8}-\frac{1}{4}$	$15\frac{1}{8}$	$8\frac{1}{4}-\frac{3}{8}$	$10\frac{15}{16}-11\frac{1}{16}$
2 Months	$8\frac{1}{8}-\frac{1}{4}$	$15\frac{1}{8}$	$8\frac{7}{16}-9\frac{9}{16}$	$11\frac{1}{8}-\frac{1}{4}$
3 Months	$8\frac{3}{16}-\frac{5}{16}$	$15\frac{1}{8}-\frac{3}{16}$	$8\frac{5}{8}-\frac{3}{4}$	$11\frac{5}{16}-\frac{7}{16}$
6 Months	$8\frac{1}{4}-\frac{3}{8}$	$15\frac{1}{8}-\frac{1}{4}$	$8\frac{7}{8}$	$11\frac{1}{2}-\frac{5}{8}$
9 Months	$8\frac{5}{16}-\frac{7}{16}$	$15\frac{1}{8}-\frac{1}{4}$	$9\frac{1}{8}$	$11\frac{1}{2}-\frac{5}{8}$
12 Months	$8\frac{7}{16}-\frac{9}{16}$	$15\frac{1}{8}-\frac{1}{4}$	$9\frac{1}{8}-\frac{1}{4}$	$11\frac{1}{2}-\frac{5}{8}$

FIGURE 5-1. Telerate Screen Showing Eurocurrency Interest Rates.

Thus the broker, in touch through direct lines with many other banks and securities firms, serves the role of finding the best possible price for deposits. The broker also preserves the anonymity of the counterparty bank, providing only certain clues about the kind of credit quality, nationality, and location of the other bank. The broker may also chat briefly about the depth of, and the pressures in, the market. The rates brokers quote are "two-way prices"—a bid and an offer. They do not take positions themselves. In this case, with the "big figure" (9 percent) being understood as being the base, the broker showed Fuji's two-way price as 9 3/4 percent, the rate Fuji was willing to pay on deposited funds, and 9 7/8 percent, the rate at which Fuji was willing to place funds. By dint of quoting a two-way price, the Eurodeposit trader becomes a *market-maker*—he's in the fray, hitting and being hit, testing the market, a player to whom others can normally come to do a deal.

A market-maker never knows, in quoting rates, whether his bid will be "hit" or his offer "lifted"—but he will "trim" the quotes in such a way as to influence the outcome. For example, if other banks in Hong Kong are quoting 9 11/16– 9 13/16, Fuji may have quoted 9 3/4– 9 7/8 so as to be more likely to receive funds than to lend because the Fuji trader was seeking to offset an "overlent" position. This technique sometimes backfires. For example, if another bank, finding itself short of funds and sensing an upward trend in rates hits Fuji's offer, the poor Fuji deposit trader would end up with a doubly overlent position and would have to scramble to fund it in a rising market.

The reader will have noticed that the First Interstate dealer did not say "Done" until he was sure with whom he would be entrusting the bank's money for 3 months. Most banks establish limits on how much they will place with any other given bank, nationality, and location, and the trader is bound by these limits. Not only must the credit risk of the bank be evaluated, but also the bank's *nationality* and the central bank backing that it implies. In addition, Eurodeposit rates can be affected by sovereign risk associated with the country of location (and therefore jurisdiction) of the deposits and by transfer risk—the possibility that the authorities of the underlying currency might freeze transfers in that currency. We return to these concepts later in this chapter.

Given their limits, the traders will try to obtain the best market price irrespective of the character of the counterparty. An empirical study[9] of deposit rate quotations showed that neither country-specific nor bank-specific characteristics seemed to have any bearing on deposit rates quoted. Confronted with this result, Eurocurrency dealers themselves express the view that rate differences almost never reflect risk, and that these differences are a result of particular banks' temporary funding requirements.

In part, this phenomenon may be attributed to the high tempo and competitiveness of the international banking markets. Following domestic practices, Eurobanks at one time conducted international money market dealing only with a limited range of "first-class" banks. As more banks entered the market, the definition of first class became looser; by the mid-1970s, some 200 banks were active takers of large interbank Eurodeposits, and by the early 1990s, at least 1,000 banks were dealing at interbank rates. With volatile interest rate and currency conditions, the dealing-room people found that they lacked both the time and the data to make continual creditworthiness judgments about all these banks. Inevitably, other senior bank officers have come to make credit judgments for the dealers who are then free to make interest rate judgments. With the credit decision separated from the market's hour-to-hour price-setting process, credit officers have great difficulty in undertaking price discrimination among borrowing banks. Experience has taught bank management that the dealer must be free to bid for and place funds at going market rates, and not be subject to some externally imposed tiering. Instead, risks are limited by credit rationing, by internally imposed limits on the extension of credit, rather than by discriminatory pricing of interbank deposits. Banks bid more when they have a "need for funds," less when they have a "surplus." Dealers assert that they are "too busy watching rates to consider the status of a bank and to try to squeeze an extra few basis points on deposits," even when placing funds with a less than prime bank.

Occasionally, the rate paid by a particular bank will rise to reflect the bank's declining creditworthiness. A decline in a Eurobank's reputation will result in a cutback in the funds available to it from a number of other banks. It will be forced, perhaps temporarily, to bid slightly higher than the market to fund its normal needs. Alert dealers who observe a bank persistently bidding above market will draw this to the attention of credit officers who in turn will seek out the reason for the taking bank's unusually prolonged demand for funds. Until that reason is found, dealers may be asked to "cool it" on lending to that particular bank.

---

[9] Ian H. Giddy, "Risk and Return in the Eurocurrency Interbank Market," *Greek Economic Review*, 1982.

Figure 5-2 shows a fictional sample limit sheet. Such documents are for internal use only, although they may be shown to bank supervisors and even hungry-eyed researchers. Recipient banks are not told of their limits, but banks that are active Eurodealers quickly come to discover the limits other banks have set for them, simply by borrowing until they run up against those limits. Limits are periodically reviewed, and on occasion, the reaching of a limit will trigger a reevaluation of the informal line by the lending bank; if all is well, the line will be expanded.[10] Less frequently, the standing of a bank or group of banks will deteriorate and limits will be contracted. For example, this happened to Polish and Argentinean banks in 1980.

Back in Singapore our Eurocurrency deposit broker, upon learning of Interstate's decision, quickly contacts the Eurocurrency desk at Fuji Hong Kong and concludes the transaction between the two banks, earning a fee of perhaps 1/32 of 1 percent. Confirmation of the deal is mailed, and the funds are wired for delivery 2 business days later. All dollar payments are cleared in the United States—as usual, therefore, the parties would debit or credit entries on the books of banks in the United States.

Let us briefly look at the other side of the coin. A few days earlier, Fuji Bank's Tokyo office received a request for a short-term, $40 million loan from a Japanese trading company located in Minato-Ku. The trading company obtained the loan on a 3-month roll-over basis at 1/4 percentage point over LIBOR, the standard London interbank offer rate. The night before the trading company had indicated an immediate need for dollar funds; the Eurodollar dealer in Tokyo quickly telexed his counterparts in the New York and London offices of Fuji Bank with a request for funding. Fuji's Hong Kong branch was, through various brokers, able to obtain the funds at an average cost of 1/16 below LIBOR; $10 million of these came from First Interstate in Singapore. The funds were then transferred by the Hong Kong branch of Fuji Bank for credit to the New York account of the trading firm for same-day delivery. (This is a special, expedited transaction.) At the conclusion of this routing of funds from Moline to Minato-Ku, each of several banks or branches has earned a narrow gross spread, out of which must come the cost of communications, paperwork, salaries, rents, and so forth—and a profit.

This example should shed some light on the essential nature of the Eurocurrency interbank market. It serves as a worldwide clearing house to

---

[10] For a more detailed discussion of the granting of interbank lines, see Steven I. Davis, *The Eurobank* (New York: John Wiley & Sons, 1976), Chapter 4; Rudi Weisweiller, ed., *Managing a Foreign Exchange Department* (Cambridge: Woodhead-Faulkner, 1985), Chapters 5 and 6; and Heinz Riehl and Rita Rodriguez, *Money and Foreign Exchange Dealing*.

Sample Limit Sheet
Internal Lines for Money Market Transactions
(US$ millions)

International Bank Facility Available for HQ and All Branches in Europe, United States, Bahamas, and Caymans	Foreign Exchange Limit		Money Market Limits							Total Exposure Excluding FX
			Overnight Euros and Fed Funds		Term Euros and Fed Funds		Maximum Exposure		Other Existing Commitments	
	Old	New	Old	New	Old	New	Old	New		
Banque de Seine S.A. (Paris)	110	130	12	15	25	25	37	40	—	40
Banco do Seine (Brazil)										
São Paolo (subsidiary)*	10	10	—	—	5	5	5	5	—	5
Total for Seine	120	140	12	15	30	30	33	45	0	45
Banco Banco S.A. (Venezuela)	0	10	—	—	0	15	0	15	3	18

*Backup letter from Paris.

FIGURE 5-2. Sample Limit Sheet.

provide information about, and bring together, borrowers and lenders, buyers and sellers of credit of diverse needs and locations. It does so at a very low cost, unburdened as it is by restraints on competition, regulations, and central bank reserve requirements. First Interstate has earned a return for knowing about Fuji Bank (otherwise, Deere could have deposited directly in Fuji Bank). Fuji Bank had an advantage in knowing more than Interstate about a potential borrower at that particular time. The broker's role is obvious.

Yet it is difficult to explain the huge volume of interbank transactions purely on the basis of matching ultimate borrowers' and lenders' needs. A substantial proportion of interbank deposit trading appears to take place simply for the sake of continuing to appear as active participants in the market. Several of the bankers interviewed by the authors indicated a willingness to borrow and re-lend at a negligible margin or even without a profit, to keep the bank's name in the market, to expand its balance sheet to promote the appearance of size, or to respond to mutterings on the part of certain net lenders that some banks always appear as borrowers and are therefore not making a "contribution" to the market. More than one individual asserted that certain banks "would not lend to you unless you also lent to them!" Many Eurobanks' balance sheets are swollen with deposits in banks, which in turn hold deposits in the first bank.

On the surface, this appears to be an unnecessary recycling or churning of interbank deposits with cosmetic rather than economic value. And perhaps it is. Some Eurobankers explain that this practice provides a form of insurance, that depositing with many banks assures reciprocity should the bank experience a liquidity squeeze. But this suggests a market sharing practice that is not easy to reconcile with the high degree of competitiveness among Eurobanks. Nor does it explain why large, sound banks with ready and continual access to noninterbank deposits insist on being both lenders and borrowers of interbank funds at all times. We believe that neither a cosmetic nor an insurance function is necessary to explain the phenomenon. Instead, we would argue that interbank trading on both sides of the market serves a pure information function. It provides traders with information both about the ebb and flow of market demand and supply, and it allows traders to stay in close touch with the market's "feel" for the ability and soundness of individual traders and banks. Recalling how difficult it is to evaluate Eurobanks in an objective fashion, it becomes clear that trading deposits may in a sense be an efficient way of trading information about individual banks and their techniques. Since interbank margins are low or nonexistent, this form of information transfer occurs at little cost to the public.[11]

[11] For another systematic framework for the economic functions of the Eurocurrency market, see Richard J. Herring and Richard C. Marston, "The Forward Market and Interest Rates in the Eurocurrency and National Money Markets," in H. Stein, J. Makin, and D. Logue, eds., *Eurocurrencies and the International Monetary System*, American Enterprise Institute, Washington, 1976.

DEPOSITORY INSTRUMENTS: TIME DEPOSITS AND CDs

The depositor in the Eurocurrency market can choose between two major instruments, fixed time deposits (TDs) and certificates of deposit. The bulk of the deposits is in the form of time deposits. The maturities of these deposits range from 1 day to several years, with the majority being in the range of 7 days to 6 months. Rates are usually negotiated competitively between the depositor and the bank, with a minimum of documentation; a confirming telex by the bank is typically all the physical evidence needed by the depositor. Time deposits are for fixed periods, of course. Nevertheless, Eurobanks can be flexible if the depositor wishes to withdraw funds early. When this is done, the rate is reset at a level appropriate to that for shorter maturities which prevailed when the deposit was originally made. However, because of their fear of damaging their reputation for financial acumen, depositors rarely "break" deposits but rather go out and borrow, using the deposit as collateral if necessary.

Following their successful introduction in the United States a few years earlier, negotiable certificates of deposit (NCDs, or simply CDs) appeared in the London Eurodollar market in 1967. At that time only a few Eurobanks offered them; now, almost all major Eurobanks issue London dollar CDs. As in New York, negotiable CDs were issued in London to provide a more liquid and therefore appealing investment instrument. The intention was, in part, to attract a greater proportion of corporate and other nonbank deposits into the market. Eurobanks tend to prefer deposits obtained from outside the interbank market: they are often slightly cheaper, since they avoid the "turn" taken by each Eurobank as it borrows and/or lends interbank funds. And nonbank deposits are usually more stable and available for longer maturities than are interbank funds. In sum, they serve to diversify the bank's deposit base.

EuroCDs are offered by certain banks in centers other than London and in currencies other than U.S. dollars. In principle, the operation of these markets is similar to the London dollar CD market. As with any such market, however, its development is contingent upon the establishment of a secondary market. This is all but nonexistent in nondollar Eurocurrencies and in other centers such as the Bahamas and Singapore.

The Eurodollar CD has placed the Eurodollar market in more direct competition with the New York money market, by offering depositors the safety and liquidity that are assured by a large and active secondary market. The instruments are available in a variety of denominations, ranging from $10,000 to several million and in maturities from "call" and "overnight" to 5 years or more.[12] A number of banks and other financial institutions, such as

---

[12] The volume of outstanding deposits, CDs as well as time deposits, is very heavily concentrated in the short maturities.

affiliates of U.S. investment banks, as well as U.K. merchant banks and discount houses, assure the continuation of the secondary market by acting as "market-makers"—being willing to buy or sell the CDs at given prices at any time.

In most respects London dollar CDs are identical to their domestic counterparts. They are issued on frequent occasions by all major Eurobanks, although the secondary market has focused on the issues of the top American, Canadian, British, and Japanese banks. Evidence of ownership is provided by a certificate showing the amount, interest rate, and date of maturity and is payable to bearer (see Figure 5-3). The additional liquidity of the deposits usually enables banks to offer interest rates slightly (about 1/8 percent) below those offered on regular time deposits. The certificates

---

Negotiable U.S. Dollar Certificate of Deposit

SUSHI BANK
Singapore Branch
Asia House, Shenton Way, Republic of Singapore

Certificate No. 02365
U.S.$1,000,000

Date of Issue: September 29, 1990
Maturity Date: September 29, 1991
Interest Rate: 8.75 per cent per annum

THIS CERTIFIES that there has been deposited with SHUSHI BANK (SINGAPORE BRANCH) (the "Bank") at the above address the sum of ONE MILLION U.S. DOLLARS repayable to the bearer on the Maturity Date as stated above, upon surrender of this certificate, through the medium of an Authorized Depository in the Republic of Singapore, to the Bank at the above address, by draft drawn or telegraphic transfer through a bank in New York City.

Interest on the deposit will accrue from the Date of Issue to the Maturity Date at the rate stated above. The interest shall be payable semi-annually upon presentation of this certificate, through the medium of an Authorized Depository in the Republic of Singapore, to the Bank at the above address, by draft drawn on or telegraphic transfer through a bank in New York City, on each Interest Payment Date as provided on the reverse hereof. A record of an interest payment endorsed hereon and initialled by an authorized officer of the Bank shall be conclusive evidence of the discharge of the obligations of the Bank in respect of the interest payment in question. All payments shall be made without any deduction of any present or future taxes, duties or other imposts levied by or on behalf of the Republic of Singapore unless the Bank is required by law to make such a deduction. If any such deduction is required, the Bank will pay such additional amount as will result in receipt by the bearer hereof of such amount as would have been received had no such deduction been required.

All rights and obligations herein shall be determined by the laws of the Republic of Singapore.

Authorized Signature

FIGURE 5-3. Example of Negotiable Eurodollar CD. While all dollar payments are made through the U.S. payments system, this deposit is the liability of the branch and subject to the laws of Singapore.

are issued by, say, the London banking office against the payment of the dollar amount into its "nostro" accounts in its head offices, branches, or correspondent banks in New York. The London branch usually waits until word is received from the New York office that payment has been received before issuing the certificate to a bank nominated by the depositor. In some cases issuance may take place prior to such notification. Maturing certificates are repaid with interest at the New York office or correspondent of the issuing bank upon the surrender of the certificates by the depositor to the London bank. If the holder is an individual or corporate depositor, payment is made to a designated U.S. bank. Dealings in the market are, as in the time deposit market, by telephone, fax, telex, or cable and are generally for settlement 2 business days following the transaction.

The usual form of issuance of Eurodollar CDs is as tap CDs. Tap CDs are issued in single amounts, say, $1 million or $5 million, whenever a bank requires funds in a particular amount for a particular maturity. The usual purpose would be to fund a Eurodollar loan. The issuing bank "taps" the market at very short notice by setting a rate and informing brokers of the conditions of the issue. The rates differ from bank to bank, and a prospective depositor with liquid funds can easily "shop around" for the best terms, since many banks are willing to quote a rate every day. Despite its original intention, the tap CD remains very much an interbank instrument. In another attempt to broaden the market to nonbank depositors, Eurobanks have introduced a new variation with greater distinction. This is the tranche CD.

Tranche CDs take their name from the French word meaning "slice." Their distinctive feature is that they are "sliced" into several portions with greater appeal to those investors who prefer an instrument with a smaller denomination than those of conventional tap CDs. Unlike tap CDs, tranche CDs are "managed" issues, offered for sale to the public in a fashion analogous to a securities issue. Both the average maturities (3 to 5 years) and total amounts ($15 million to $100 million) are greater than those of tap CDs. They are placed in advance of issue with large underwriting and selling groups, generally the same houses that underwrite and distribute Eurobonds. Indeed, they have been termed a hybrid between a money market instrument and a short-term Eurobond. Tranche CD issues are usually denominated in increments of $10,000, and each slice has the same interest rate, issue date, interest payment dates, and maturity structure. Because a large portion of these issues are acquired by banks, brokers, and investment managers on behalf of fiduciary clients, market quotations for tranche issues are readily available in newspapers and on ticker services. This contrasts with a quotation for a specific tap CD, which must be sought from a particular bank or dealer. These features obviously contribute to the resilience of a secondary market.

The secondary market for London dollar certificates of deposit is reasonably well developed. Dealers, banks, and brokers stand ready to buy and sell many banks' CDs at a spread between bid and offer rates of about 1/4 of 1 percent. As yet, however, this market is not normally as deep or resilient as that in New York. This is largely because fewer dealers have been attracted to make markets at all times. A number of discount houses, for whom dollar CDs is a sideline, will simply dispose of their inventory in periods of falling interest rates and become mere brokers instead of market makers. Thus large purchases and sales often have an impact on rates. Depositors are faced with the following dilemma: to obtain the best rate for a particular maturity, at least $1 million must usually be invested. But a sale prior to maturity of a CD of a size approaching $5 million may well drive the price of that CD down slightly. This would be unlikely to happen in the larger New York market, and may account for some of the difference between U.S. and Eurodollar CD rates.

An improvement that has increased the size and depth of the secondary market is the computerized clearing center for London dollar CD transactions organized by a major Chicago bank. This bank guarantees completions and final payment on transactions handled through the clearing system, thus preventing the recurrence of a Herstatt-type default, in which a delivery is made but the purchaser goes out of business before providing payment because of international time differences. This is a further refinement of an established practice in the market, where most large investors and dealers will keep all their CDs in a custody account maintained by one of their banks. This facilitates trading in the secondary market as all dealers know where the CDs of a given customer are to be delivered or to whom to look for delivery. The concentration of all these negotiable securities with a single, trustworthy institution further facilitates control and auditing procedures. A few depositors, of course, prefer to keep their bearer certificates elsewhere, away from the prying eyes of the authorities.

London dollar CDs are subject to very few regulations or constraints, although of course all banks in London are supervised by the Bank of England.[13] No taxes are charged or deducted by the issuing bank, nor are the CDs subject to any U.S. taxes unless the depositor is a U.S. resident or citizen. As with all Eurodollar deposits, they are not subject to FDIC (Federal Deposit Insurance Corporation) or Federal Reserve requirements, nor is there any U.K. stamp duty imposed upon the transfer of the certificates for purchase or repayment. The issuing banks are, however, subject to Britain's Inland Revenue Law, which does not permit interest to be paid on CDs of maturities greater than 5 years. Thus a bank located in Britain is effectively precluded from issuing a CD for, say, 8 years. This restriction has been circumvented by the development of forward forwards, described in Chapter

---

[13] Some self-regulation, primarily in the secondary market, is provided by the International CD Market Association.

Four, which allow depositors and banks to agree in effect upon an extension of a deposit's maturity.

In conclusion, the development of the Eurodollar negotiable certificate of deposit provides an attractive complement to the range of sophisticated institutions and instruments that comprise the international money market. The market for dollar-denominated CDs, however, has not developed a volume sufficient to match its domestic counterpart, and negotiable Eurocurrency CDs denominated in other currencies remain rare. Banks and money managers apparently neither value nor exploit the negotiable feature of CDs highly, probably because they can achieve a high degree of liquidity by holding very short-term time deposits to maturity without a sacrifice of yield. They simply borrow overnight or similar short-term money in the event of an unanticipated cash shortfall. CDs probably do not make up more than 5 percent of total Eurocurrency deposits.

THE CREDIT RISKS OF EURODEPOSITS

Considerations of the creditworthiness of particular banks play a role in the Eurocurrency market similar to that of domestic money markets. The more sophisticated depositors in the market—money managers in large banks and corporations—undertake a careful evaluation of the quality and diversity of Eurobanks' loan and money market portfolios; of the earnings performance, cost control, size and reputation of the parent bank; of the sophistication of the banks' Eurocurrency traders; and so forth. As was noted earlier, much of this information is gathered in the course of daily interbank borrowing and lending activities.

The unique feature of the Euromarket is that the participants' varied nationalities, practices, and degree of financial disclosure induce a much greater reliance on informal channels of information than is the case, for example, in the U.S. money market. For the same reason depositors who do not have access to such information tend to place funds with the largest and best-known banks rather than incur the expense and time involved in checking the credit standing of the smaller and medium-sized Eurobanks, despite the slightly higher deposit rates offered by the latter. In addition, nonbank depositors and central banks generally prefer to do business with the large international banks, on which they can rely for other services such as funds transfer and the provision of loans.

Some bankers in Eurodeposit centers such as London profess to be concerned about the "capital adequacy" of Eurobank branches. We believe that any number purporting to measure the capital adequacy of the Eurobank branch or affiliate of a larger bank matters only to the extent that authorities such as the Bank of England believe them to be important and conduct their regulatory policy accordingly. In themselves, figures measuring a branch or affiliate's leverage are meaningless since the obligations of the branch are essentially the obligations of the parent bank and must be seen in the context of the financial resources of the parent. The concept of capital adequacy is a difficult one even in the domestic context. When applied to an offshore branch or even a wholly owned subsidiary, it is next to useless.

In addition to the creditworthiness of the bank in its own right, many interbank players place equal, or greater, emphasis on the bank's nationality. The market attaches considerable importance to the likelihood that the parent bank, and hence its branches, will be supported by a strong central bank in the event of a crisis. How big is the bank in its home country? How important is that bank's solvency to its home country's authorities? American banks may be able to obtain Eurocurrency deposits more cheaply than other institutions because the U.S. Federal Reserve Board stands behind them. State-owned banks such as the Development Bank of Singapore find it easier to attract funds, *ceteris paribus*, than private banks. In addition, banks of the country in whose currency the deposits are denominated are regarded as having better access to the domestic money market as well as central bank lending in that currency and therefore are less likely to face difficulties in repaying such deposits.

Thus credit risk and country risk are intertwined. In the next section, however, we are concerned not with governmental support but rather with governmental interference with the repayment of Eurocurrency deposits.

THE COUNTRY RISKS OF EURODEPOSITS[14]

The Eurocurrency market is, like so much of finance, a creature of regulation. Eurocurrency banking is always carried out in jurisdictions that provide Eurobanks with a systematic competitive advantage over those banks that pursue financial intermediation in a national market. The authorities of these "offshore centers" allow banks a great deal of freedom with respect to those credit activities that are denominated in foreign currencies, especially when the counterparts in the transactions are nonresidents, because such transactions do not affect domestic credit conditions. The unique feature of Eurobanking is that it allows banks to choose among jurisdictions. Since the banking authorities of offshore centers are thus in effect forced to compete with one another, the regulations that evolve tend to be those that favor banks and their depositors.

But every silver lining has a cloud. In choosing a separate, more favorable jurisdiction, the bank and depositor are subject to potential adverse actions by the authorities of the host country. Such adverse actions are rare

---

[14] The authors have explored these issues in much greater detail in "Eurocurrency Deposit Risk," *Journal of Banking and Finance*, Vol. 8, 1984, pp. 567–589.

but not unheard of, and all depositors should factor that possibility into their decision to deposit funds within a particular jurisdiction.

Because an offshore branch remains a part of the same corporate entity, even though it is located in a separate country, the depositor who puts his money in Midland Bank's Paris branch is still putting his money in Midland Bank P.L.C., the whole bank. Should the branch run short of funds or make bad loans and hence be unable or unwilling to repay a deposit, the depositor may turn to the bank's head office and still expect repayment. In U.S. law, this principle has a long history of judicial support, dating from a 1917 incident in which Sokoloff, a Russian citizen, successfully sued a U.S. bank for repayment at the New York home office of his ruble deposit at the Petrograd branch.[15] The U.S. courts held that the Petrograd branch, in anticipation of nationalization by the Bolsheviks, had effectively ceased to operate without giving depositors a chance to withdraw their funds. The court decision in that case stated explicitly that the property and assets of branches belong to the parent bank and that ultimate liability for the debt of a branch rests upon the parent bank.

More recently, a U.S. appeals court reaffirmed the principle of corporate liability by deciding that Chase Manhattan Bank in New York was responsible for piaster deposits in the Saigon branch when the branch closed in 1975, several days before the official takeover proclamation by the invading North Vietnamese revolutionary forces.[16] In the court's view, a bank is obliged to "inform its depositors of the date when its branch will close and give them the opportunity to withdraw their deposits, or, if conditions prevent such steps, enable them to obtain payment at an alternative location." The court went on to say that if such measures fail, fairness dictates that the parent bank be liable for deposits which it was unable to return.

Regardless of the merits of the latter decision, the lesson is clear: *where an action by the bank itself inhibits repayment of a deposit in a foreign branch, the parent bank remains liable. But where repayment is prevented by an action of the foreign government, U.S. and other courts have generally held that a bank's liability will be measured by the law of the jurisdiction where the foreign branch is located.*[17] This is made clear to those who buy Eurodollar CDs by the statement on the front of the certificate, "Governed by and subject to the laws of the United Kingdom" or words to that effect, as in Figure 5-3.

---

[15] *Sokoloff* v. *National City Bank*, 250 N.Y. 69, 80, 164 N.E. 745, 749 (1928).

[16] *Vishipco Line* v. *Chase Manhattan Bank, N.A.*, 660 F. 2d 854 (2d Cir. 1981), reh. denied, no. 81-7052 (2d Cir. Nov. 30, 1981).

[17] A major tenet of jurisprudence, domestic and international, is that a court should not subject anyone, even a bank, to double liability in cases where laws conflict or overlap. Most courts are extremely reluctant to take jurisdiction over the case if there is another jurisdiction which also could claim the right to decide the case.

The country risk (or "sovereign risk") of Eurocurrency deposits arises from the general rule that if the foreign branch is relieved from liability, then the head office is also relieved from liability. Essentially, the determination of liability results from the application of the doctrine of sovereignty and the recognition of foreign governments. This notion gains its strongest force in the **act of state doctrine**, described by one judge as follows:

> Every sovereign State is bound to respect the independence of every other sovereign State, and the courts of one country will not sit in judgment on the acts of the government of another, done within its own territory.[18]

This doctrine was brought to bear on a court conflict in which repayment of certain interbank deposits in the Manila branch of Citibank were suspended following a debt moratorium imposed by the government of the Philippines in 1983, and earlier when Mexico froze dollar deposits in banks located in Mexico.[19] More generally, the following acts of a recognized government can relieve the home office of liability for the failure of its foreign branch to repay deposits at maturity:

1. Imposition of exchange controls, unless such controls violate a treaty signed by that government, or the deposit is outside the state imposing the controls;
2. Moratoria or bank holidays;
3. Disturbed conditions (civil war, etc.). This case is not clear, but may temporarily relieve the bank from settling its liabilities; and
4. Seizure of assets (nationalization) with disposition of liabilities.

This means that if a country grabs some or all of a branch's assets, it (and not the parent bank) is held to be liable for that proportion of the branch's deposit liabilities.

The list demonstrates what nonsense it is to say that Eurodollars are "unregulated." To the contrary, as a result of venturing far from home, they can incur a plurality of country risks. Not only does the country of *location* of the branch give rise to country risk, but also a government whose *currency* is used for offshore deposits may interfere with transfer of funds made by the offshore depositor, since payments are invariably cleared in the country of the currency. Finally, the *authorities of the parent*

---

[18] *Underhill* v. *Hernandez*, 168 U.S. 250 (1897).

[19] The Mexican authorities deprived holders of dollar deposits in Mexican banks—both residents and nonresidents—of their right to obtain funds in U.S. dollars: instead they were permitted to make withdrawals only in Mexican pesos at the official rate of 69.5 pesos per U.S. dollar at a period when the rate for pesos outside of Mexico and in the black market fluctuated between 90 and 130 pesos per U.S. dollar.

bank may have control or influence over the disposition of offshore deposits.[20]

But common sense will clear up some of this bleak assessment. Any good Eurobanker can steer wary depositors toward a more favorable configuration of country risk. To minimize the leverage which various sovereigns might have over him, the depositor himself should neither be present nor have any economic interests within the jurisdiction of the host country, the country of the currency, and the bank's home country. In addition, the depositor can reduce his vulnerability to the sovereignty of the situs of the deposit by ensuring that the recipient bank is able and willing to transfer the situs of the deposit at a moment's notice—which in turn means that the offshore branch should have little or no economic interest in remaining in the host country. In the ideal offshore deposit, a nonresident depositor would place hard currency, freely transferable funds in a major, third-country bank branch located in a country with a favorable regulatory climate but an insignificant local economy.

COMMERCIAL PAPER AND EUROCOMMERCIAL PAPER

Large, reasonably well-known banks can use **commercial paper** as a substitute for bank deposits as a source of short-term funding. Commercial paper is unsecured short-term debt typically sold by a corporation to money market investors. The maturity of such paper can be as short as 1 day and as long as 270 days. In the United States, where the market is extremely well developed, the dominant buyers are institutional investors whose investment guidelines require the purchase only of rated paper. To obtain a rating from Moody's or Standard & Poor's, the issuer of commercial paper must support it with a "backup line" of credit access from a commercial bank. This line may in some cases be informal, but typically must be a written commitment. Although it does not have the force of a guarantee of the paper, the backup line does provide the issuer with assured liquidity (access to funds) with which to repay the paper upon maturity.

U.S. banks do not issue commercial paper directly—only through their holding companies—because the Federal Reserve deems bank-issued commercial paper to be deposits and so subjects them to reserve requirements and FDIC fees. The same applies to proceeds of commercial paper issued by a bank holding company and channeled to its banking subsidiary. The result is that the U.S. commercial paper market is not used to fund *directly* banks' Eurodollar assets.

---

[20] The U.S. freeze of Iranian deposits in 1979 was extended to dollar deposits in foreign branches of U.S. banks. Whether the freeze order would ultimately have survived the legal challenges brought in the courts of the United Kingdom, France, and Switzerland is quite uncertain. The issue was rendered moot in January 1981 by the political settlement of the hostage crisis.

Eurocommercial paper, also called Euronotes, are similar short-term unsecured notes but are issued outside the jurisdiction of the United States. ECP, as the instrument is termed, is used by a number of international banks for short-term funding purposes. The paper is in bearer form and normally unrated—hence not necessarily supported by a backup line. The big advantage is that it is among the cheapest form of short-term paper available. High-quality borrowers can issue Eurocommercial paper at around LIBID, that is, at about 1/8 below LIBOR. The best-known of these can issue at yields 1/16 or 1/8 below LIBID, which is approximately the same rate as is paid on Eurodollar CDs, which are instruments of comparable liquidity. Eurocommercial paper is traded, albeit not very actively, on a secondary market centered in London.

CROSS-CURRENCY FUNDING AND FX SWAPS

Unlike domestic banks, Eurobanks can offer deposits denominated in any of several different currencies, or even in a combination of currencies such as the European currency unit (ECU). The interest rates on deposits in different currencies can easily be compared by adjusting the nominal rate by the forward premium or discount on that currency. Since the currency of denomination of any deposit can readily be converted into another currency by hedging in the forward market, the effective interest cost tends to be equalized across currencies. This relationship, the interest rate parity theorem, was discussed in detail in Chapter Three.

Consider a Eurodeposit dealer in the Luxembourg subsidiary of Deutsche Bank. Seeking to fund a purchase of 3-month Euronotes, he finds that the Euro DM desk has just taken a $5 million Deutsche mark deposit from a company in Hamburg at $5\frac{1}{2}$ percent, an attractive rate. Rather than waste this opportunity, he'll use the DM deposit to fund the dollar investment. To make this work and to avoid currency risk, he must exchange the DM for dollars *spot* (delivery in 2 days) and also sell the dollars to be received upon maturity of the Euronote *forward* (for delivery in 3 months). The technique is illustrated in the following diagram:

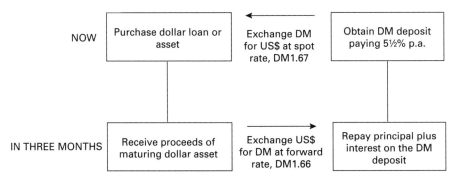

A simultaneous spot purchase and forward sale of a currency is called a *foreign exchange swap*. Swaps such as these are traded in money market dealing rooms everywhere. As we explained in Chapter Three, FX swap rates are quoted as the difference between the spot and the forward rate. The Deutsche mark is typically at a premium in the forward market, meaning that it is worth more for future delivery than it is in the spot market. For example, if the spot quotation for dollars in terms of marks is DM1.67, and the 3-month swap quotation is 0.01, then the forward rate is DM1.66. A dollar buys fewer DM in the forward market than in the spot market.

From our Eurodeposit dealer's viewpoint, this means that he incurs a *loss* of DM0.01 for every dollar obtained in this fashion. This is because he must purchase dollars at DM1.67 but sell them in 2 months at DM1.66. On an annualized basis, this "cost of hedging" amounts to 2.4 percent:

$$\left[\frac{DM0.01}{DM1.67}\right] \times \frac{12}{4}$$

Added to the German interest cost of $5\frac{1}{2}$ percent p.a., the total cost amounts to 7.9 percent p.a., or 7.94 percent p.a. if computed precisely.[21] The German mark deposit in conjunction with a foreign exchange swap has created the equivalent of a dollar deposit to fund the dollar liability. As long as the all-in cost of funding in this fashion is cheaper, the dealer will employ it in preference to straight dollar funding. Normally, of course, *interest rate parity* ensures that the two methods cost the same—because the swap rate, as an annualized percentage, equals the Eurocurrency interest rate differential in equilibrium.

In effect, the Eurodeposit dealer has transformed a German mark liability into a dollar liability by means of a forward exchange contract. More generally, forward contracts enable one to transform any fixed income asset or liability into another currency, as is indicated in the accompanying box.

---

[21] The precise calculation of the cost of cross-currency funding is:

$$\left[\left(1 + \frac{R_n}{12/n}\right)\frac{S}{F} - 1\right]\frac{12}{n} \times 100$$

where

R = foreign currency interest rate
S = spot exchange rate, foreign units per U.S. dollar
F = forward exchange rate, foreign units per U.S. dollar
n = number of months' maturity

HOW TO CHANGE THE CURRENCY DENOMINATION
OF AN ASSET OR A LIABILITY

1. A foreign currency asset
   + a forward sale* of the foreign currency
   = dollar asset.
2. A dollar asset
   + a forward sale of the foreign currency
   = foreign-currency asset.
3. A foreign currency liability (debt)
   + a forward purchase of the foreign currency
   = dollar liability (debt).
4. A dollar liability (debt)
   + a forward sale of foreign currency
   = foreign currency liability (debt).

* Purchase and sale transactions are versus dollars.

ASSET-LIABILITY MANAGEMENT

By now it should be clear that for all practical purposes those engaged in Eurobank *funding* are necessarily drawn into the business of Eurodeposit *trading*—performing the balancing act of matching or selectively mismatching the risk characteristics of money market assets and liabilities. Managing these risks is what some call "international treasury management." Asset-liability management is the subset that deals with **market risks**, such as interest rate risk and currency risk, with an emphasis on *interest rate risks* and *availability* or liquidity risks. The other kinds of risks to be managed, of course, are credit risks and country risks.

The section that follows deals with the management of interest rate risk in a financial institution that funds itself and invests in the international money market. After that, we look at the use of derivative instruments—FRAs, futures, and swaps—in asset-liability management. Finally, we survey the use of longer-term instruments such as floating-rate notes, note issuance facilities, and medium-term notes to assure the availability of funds.

INTEREST RATE RISK, GAPPING, AND "DURATION MATCHING"

Taking interest rate risk is at the very heart of banking. People put their money into a bank in part because they require the flexibility that short-term deposits provide, while companies borrow from banks because they want the peace of mind that longer-term loans offer. So banks borrow short and lend long, at least so they used to do. The escalating interest rates of the late 1970s and early 1980s changed all that. Asset-liability management is now the watchword.[22]

Borrowing short term and lending long term is fine as long as two conditions are fulfilled. First, the yield curve should conform to its "traditional" shape: upward sloping. If 6-month rates are higher than 3-month rates, then a bank borrowing for 3 months and lending at the 6-month rate is earning a **positive spread**. Banks can and have conducted their business on the basis of this profit for long periods—as long as interest rates do not rise sufficiently to wipe out the spread earnings. So the second condition is that short-term interest rates remain below the **break-even rate**—the rate at which you neither make nor lose money from mismatched banking. This break-even rate is the same as the implied forward rate discussed in Chapter Three. In the example, it is the 3-month rate that would have to prevail in 3 months' time to make the compounded cost of funding equal to the 6-month rate.

Bankers in the Eurodollar market had long ago learned to price their loans on a floating-rate basis, as a spread over 6-month LIBOR, so that they could fund loans with 6-month money and be assured of a positive spread over their cost of funds without interest rate risk. But spreads became narrower and narrower, and the pressure to fund a little cheaper increased, so many banks were tempted to shorten up their funding to "ride the yield curve," at least selectively.

By the mid-1980s banks around the world learned from experience the riskiness of borrowing short and lending long. Not only had short-term rates repeatedly risen above the forward rates implied in the yield curve, but the curve itself was *inverted* on several occasions. Management of the **gap** between the pricing period of assets and that of liabilities assumed added importance.

There are two ways to look at the risk of interest rate mismatching in the funding decision. The traditional banker's method is called **gapping**, because it focuses on a "ladder" of gaps between the repricing dates of assets and those of liabilities. A money desk may have 3-month assets funded with 1-month liabilities, producing a positive gap, vulnerable to rising interest rates. But then the desk's 6-month assets may be financed with 9-month deposits—a negative gap, that would benefit from a rate rise. The cumulative gap may be positive, negative or zero, depending on the ebb and flow of business at any particular point in time and on the money traders' views.

A ladder of gaps for the Hong Kong branch of a hypothetical bank is illustrated in Figure 5-4. Eurodollar assets and liabilities on the branch's bal-

---

[22] For more on this subject, see Marcia Stigum and Rene Branch, *Managing Bank Assets and Liabilities* (Homewood, IL: Dow Jones-Irwin, 1983).

INTEREST MISMATCH LADDER—HONG KONG BRANCH

	ASSETS	LIABILITIES	NET
0–7 days and variable rates	8,124	20,554	–12,430
7 days–3 months	76,400	98,098	–21,698
3–6 months	84,876	46,543	38,333
6–12 months	18,998	16,329	2,669
1–2 years	8,768	9,353	–585
2–5 years	4,786	3,985	801
Above 5 years (includes capital)	6,035	13,125	–7,090
Total	207,987	207,987	0

FIGURE 5-4. "Ladder" for the Management of Interest Rate Risk. In this schedule of categories, each containing the value of assets and of liabilities that mature or are subject to a rate adjustment within that time interval (the "gap"). For each interval the net gap provides an indication of the direction and magnitude of the effect on earnings of a change in interest rates. Amounts in this illustration are in thousand U.S. dollars.

ance sheet are divided up into *repricing intervals*—in this case, 0 to 1 month, 1 to 3 months, and so forth. Each rung on the ladder contains the value of assets and of liabilities that mature or are subject to a rate adjustment within that time interval (the "gap"). For each interval the net gap provides an indication of the direction and magnitude of the effect on earnings of a change in interest rates. The annualized earnings sensitivity for each interval approximately equals 1 percent of the average gap times the length of the interval in years. The overall effect on the branch's earnings of a change in rates evidently depends not only on the direction of rates but also on any change in the shape of the yield curve. More precise estimates of the effect of given configurations of interest rate changes can be derived from bank earnings simulation models, which are no more than giant computerized versions of a gap ladder spreadsheet.[23]

The usefulness of a gap schedule is that it allows management to identify quickly which categories are most sensitive to rate rises and falls, so that assets or liabilities can be lengthened or shortened to accord more closely with the bank's view on interest rates and with its tolerance for risky mismatches. Its chief shortcoming is that the information it provides is fragmented and relates only to current earnings, not to the effect on the institution's net worth.

[23] Some such bank models were surveyed in K. J. Cohen, S. F. Maier, and J. H. Vander Weide, "Recent Developments in Management Science in Banking," *Management Science*, Vol. 27, No. 10, October 1981, pp. 1097–1119.

Enter **net worth duration**. Duration, the reader may recall from Chapter Four, measures the percentage change in the market value of an asset or liability for a one-percentage-point change in interest rates. The duration of a short-term funding instrument such as a Eurodollar time deposit is equal to its maturity. For example, a 3-month TD will fall in value by approximately $1/4$ percent if 3-month yields rise from 5 percent to 6 percent. On the asset side, the duration of a floating-rate loan is measured by the time to the next repricing date, not by the maturity of the facility. By toting up all assets' durations, weighted by the value of the assets, one can estimate the total asset duration of a bank or bank unit. Subtracting liabilities' duration from assets' duration gives the *net worth duration* of the bank. Net worth duration is approximately the percentage change in the net worth of the balance sheet resulting from a one-percentage-point change in rates.

Knowing net worth duration permits management to position the bank for any anticipated changes in rates. To insulate the bank from rate changes, net duration must be set to zero. This is done, of course, by adding or subtracting assets or liabilities until the duration of assets matches the duration of liabilities. Only when the asset-liability managers of the institution feel that interest rates are likely to move in a particular direction more than is implied by the term structure of interest rates should net duration be allowed to become significantly positive (when rates are expected to fall) or negative (when rates are expected to rise). And when management has such a strong view, the net *dollar duration*[24] should never exceed the tolerable loss, given the bank's capital.

Yet assets and liabilities themselves do not tell the whole story of the interest rate risk faced by the institution, for swaps, forward contracts, and standby letters of credit entail interest rate risk too. Moreover assets and liabilities themselves are clumsy instruments, often too illiquid to be used to fine-tune a bank's interest rate exposure. For precision work, international bankers use Eurodollar futures, FRAs, and swaps.

INTEREST RATE FUTURES, FRAS, AND SWAPS IN FUNDING MANAGEMENT

All but the most hide-bound of banks operating in the Euromarkets today make active use of futures and swaps to manage their interest rate risk position; future rate agreements (FRAs) and, for some, Eurodollar options are also frequently used. Derivative securities such as these are used in lieu of buying, selling, or issuing deposit-type assets or liabilities to adapt to changing interest rate views or fears. Whether the bank or branch uses a gap lad-

[24] "Dollar duration" is the duration of an asset (or of a balance sheet) multiplied by its dollar value. Dollar duration thus measures how much, in dollar terms, can be gained or lost if rates move 1 percent in a favorable or unfavorable direction.

der or duration to measure interest rate exposure, it can use futures or swaps to narrow the gap or deliberately take a position.

For example, the Hong Kong branch whose Eurodollar book was depicted in Figure 5-5 is exposed to rising interest rates. This vulnerability can be reduced by selling fixed-rate assets or by replacing overnight funds and other maturing liabilities with longer-term deposits or borrowings. However, if the existing set of assets and fundings has been obtained on favorable terms, it makes no sense for the bank to dispose of them simply because they bear the wrong interest rate risk configuration. Derivative instruments should be used to alter the branch's interest rate exposure instead. The $38 million gap between the bank's 3- to 6-month assets and liabilities, for example, can be partially closed by selling an equivalent amount of Eurodollar futures. The hedge will be very crude but can be put in place in a matter of minutes and reversed as easily.

The techniques for using futures, FRAs, swaps, and options in interest rate risk management were described in Chapter Four, and it would be redundant to repeat them here. Table 5-2 summarizes the features of the four categories of instruments, and the four examples that follow on p. 229 illustrate their use.

Again, these four techniques of managing the Eurobank's interest rate risk profile without buying or selling assets are contrasted in Table 5-2. To recap, futures are appropriate for those who wish to avoid counterparty risk problems and who require the ease and liquidity that Eurodollar futures possess. When a single period's interest risk needs to be hedged, or when the period to be hedged differs from those covered by futures FRAs can provide a hedge with less basis risk—but also with less liquidity if the hedge may have to be reversed. Swaps provide similar tailored hedges with much less basis risk than futures, and cover the multiple hedging periods that characterize bonds or multiperiod funding plans. Finally, options cost money up front, so they are only for those occasions when the bank has a view both on the direction and the volatility of rates—views that differ from those implied in market rates, including options premia.

The fact that banks now use these derivative instruments in active asset-liability management is consistent with the *separability* theme of this book: banks can specialize in taking funds and making loans of the kind that best exploits their competitive advantage, without being constrained by any objectives of interest rate risk management; the latter can be achieved as a separate function through the use of futures, FRAs, swaps, and options.

AVAILABILITY RISK AND LONGER-TERM FUNDING INSTRUMENTS

We have sought throughout this chapter to separate the issues of the *interest rate period* of funding techniques from the *availability period*. Two banks participate in a 4-year, floating-rate loan. One funds the loan by issuing a 4-year

TABLE 5-2. The Use of Derivative Instruments to Hedge an Interest Rate Mismatch

	EURODOLLAR FUTURES	FUTURE RATE AGREEMENTS (FRAs)	INTEREST RATE SWAPS	EURODOLLAR OPTIONS
Technique—hedging a positive gap	Sell futures	Buy FRA	Receive floating, pay fixed	Buy puts; benefit if rates fall
Technique—hedging a negative gap	Buy futures	Sell FRA	Receive fixed, pay floating	Buy calls; benefit if rates rise
Available how far out?	2–7 years	Up to 10 years	Up to 15 years	1–1½ years
Interest period hedged	3 months	Very flexible; 1 month to several years	Typically 3- or 6-month periods in sequence	3 months
Liquidity	Very good except in further-out maturities	Easily available; more cumbersome to unwind	Plentiful availability; more cumbersome to unwind	Quite good except in further-out maturities
Basis risk	Standardized instruments and maturities can give rise to high basis risk	Low; can be tailored to suit hedger's needs	Low; can be tailored to suit hedger's needs	Same as futures
Credit risk	Very low because of daily marking to market	Significant because counterparty must pay at start of single hedged period	Highest because counterparty must pay at end of multiple hedged periods	Very low

Summary: For flexibility and no counterparty risk, use futures; for a tailored one-shot hedge, use an FRA; for a tailored multiperiod hedge, use swaps; and to benefit from a view while obtaining insurance against volatility, buy puts or calls.

	ASSETS	LIABILITIES
Bank A has funded a 6-month asset with 3-month Eurodollar deposits. To avoid mutual credit risk evaluation and for ease and flexibility, it hedges the mismatch, on a duration-weighted basis, using futures.	Maturity: 6 months Interest period: 6 months	3-month deposit Short Eurodollar futures

	ASSETS	LIABILITIES
Bank B has funded an 8-month fixed-rate asset with 3-month money. To hedge the remaining 5-months with precision and low counterparty risk, it enters into an FRA agreement with a major bank. The FRA has less liquidity than futures.	Maturity: 8 months Interest period: 8 months	3-month deposit Buy FRA: "in 3 for 5"

	ASSETS	LIABILITIES
Bank C has funded a floating-rate loan with a 3-year, fixed-rate note. To hedge a multiperiod mismatch like this, the bank enters into an interest rate swap to convert the fixed rate liability into a floating rate liability. The swap has counterparty risk and is a lot less liquid than futures.	Maturity: 3 years Interest reset period: every 3 months	Maturity: 3 years Interest period: 3 year fixed Interest rate swap: Receive fixed, pay floating

	ASSETS	LIABILITIES
Bank D has funded a 5-month fixed-rate asset with 2-month money. To be able to take advantage of anticipated lower rates without risking a possible sharp rise in the cost of funds, the bank buys a *put option*. If LIBOR rises, the option gains value—this gain offsets Bank D's higher cost of funds. The option premium is worth paying because the bank combines a view on the direction of rates with a fear of volatility.	Maturity: 5 months Interest period: 5 months	2-month deposit Buy Eurodollar put option

floating-rate note; the other, by borrowing 3-month money in the interbank market. In both instances the interest rate period of the funding is 3 months, but the first bank's availability period is 4 years while that of the second bank is 3 months. The latter has a funding or availability period mismatch, which is risky for two related reasons:

1. The bank that has to roll over short-term funding may later face a higher cost of funds relative to the market, so that even though its funding matches interest reset periods, its earned spread may narrow or become negative.

2. The bank's perceived credit risk may deteriorate to the point where it is simply unable to roll over its funding at any price.

The degree to which availability risk should be of concern is a function not only of a potential deterioration of the issuer's credit standing, but also of the depth, maturity, and stability of the markets for bank liabilities. For example, the Eurodeposit market has grown to the point of providing an extremely reliable source of funds to solid institutions, but the same cannot be said of the Eurodollar floating rate note market, which at certain points in recent years has almost completely dried up as a source of funds.

In this section we identify several means by which banks manage their availability risk. Some of the techniques involve the extension of credit or access to credit by other banks, so that they reappear in more detail in Chapter Six.

There are two fundamental ways of locking in the availability of funds for a period long enough to match a loan commitment period: by issuing debt of the desired maturity or by obtaining a commitment of availability from another bank or group of banks. The latter tends to be cheaper, but it is also riskier, since there is always the chance that the committing bank may default on, or weasel out of, its commitment just when it is most needed. Long-term debt gives you money in hand, and that's the safest.

Let us deal with commitments first. Eurocommercial paper or Euronotes, mentioned earlier, can be cheap and extremely flexible, but a bank's ability to roll over this source is by no means assured. That's why there's an alternative to ECP programs in the form of **note issuance facilities** (**NIFs**). In a NIF, a Euronote issuance paper program is accompanied by an *underwriting commitment*, a commitment to the "availablity" of funds, issued by a group of banks. Note issuance facilities, also called revolving underwriting facilities, have become a major source of Euromarket financing since they developed in the early 1970s. NIFs are medium-term arrangements—usually 3 to 10 years—between a borrower and a group of banks, under which the borrower can issue Euronotes in its own name. Under this arrangement, underwriting banks are committed either to purchase any notes which the borrower cannot sell or to provide standby credit, in either case at a predetermined spread relative to some reference rate such as LIBOR. Underwriting fees are paid on the full amount of the line of credit, regardless of the amount currently drawn. The fee may be 5 basis points for top borrowers and range up to 15 basis points for less creditworthy borrowers. When funds are needed, the leading bank will arrange to market the Euronotes at the most favorable rate available to the issuer, usually making them first available to a prearranged group of banks called the "Tender Panel." These banks may keep the notes for themselves or seek to resell them to other investors. More on this technique appears in the next chapter.

Of the funding sources that entail actual issuance of longer-term claims, the **term CD** is surely the oldest. This is simply a bank deposit with a maturity of anywhere from 1 to 10 years, and major banks today continue to quote bid-side rates for Eurodollar deposits of this kind. When such deposits are issued within the United States, the holder is a depositor like any other and benefits from deposit insurance, while the issuer pays the cost to the FDIC. No insurance cover is, of course, provided in the Euromarket, but long-term Eurodollar CDs still carry the protection of deposit seniority over equivalent bonds. Term CDs can be issued with either fixed or floating rates.

The big disadvantage of the CD market, Euro as well as domestic, is its illiquidity. For this reason alone many investors prefer **Eurobonds**, with a well-developed clearing and secondary trading mechanism. Banks are today among the biggest issuers of straight Eurobonds. Most fixed-interest Eurobonds issued by banks are combined with an interest rate swap or currency swap to create the equivalent of a dollar-denominated floating rate liability, as in the third example in the previous section. A number of such issues carry *index features*—for example, many bank-issued Eurobonds in the early 1990s had the value of their principal linked to the Japanese or some other stock market index. Of course, the issuing bank had no intention of taking on the index risk; instead the embedded option or forward contract was sold to a third party, as part of a deal struck by the arranging institution. The issuer's sole intention was to cream off a little of the benefit provided by selling the embedded forward or option to reduce its cost of funds.

For the most part, when a bank wants longer-term money, it wants floating-rate money to match the interest reset character of its loans and other assets. Hence Eurobonds with floating rates, called **floating-rate notes**, constitute the ideal medium- to long-term funding vehicles. Unlike straight or hybrid Eurobonds, however, FRNs have no natural investor base beyond other banks themselves. Moreover the market suffers from less liquidity even than straights. (Liquidity is hindered by the fact that banks tend to hold onto them for longer-term, spread-earning purposes, rather than seeking to trade them for a profit.) Finally, the FRN market has never wholly recovered from the "perp" debacle of the late 1980s (discussed in the paragraphs that follow).

The market taketh, and the market giveth. One of the most important developments in longer-term funding in the 1980s and 1990s has been the **medium-term note** (**MTN**) market and its offshoot, the **deposit note** market.[25] While some banks fund themselves with MTNs, particularly the bank holding company or with their offshore vehicles, the majority of MTN issuers are nonbanks, so we will defer discussion of MTNs until Chapter Six. For banks, however, a similar technique has been developed which is variously known as certificate of deposit notes, continuously offered deposit notes, medium-term deposit notes, medium-term bank notes, or 3(a)(2) notes. For ease of explanation we shall use the term "deposit notes."[26]

As we shall see, the continuously offered medium-term note market is an extension of the CP market; in much the same way, the deposit note market helped extend the maturities in the CD market where traditionally the greatest activity was in maturities of less than a year. To understand bank issues, one has to look at the regulatory framework. U.S. banks can raise funds at the level of the bank in the form of deposits which includes various CDs. Commercial paper, however, can be effectively issued only at the bank holding company level and the proceeds can only be used for nonbank activities. This is typically accomplished by "downstreaming" the proceeds from the bank holding company into the nonbank affiliates, for example, leasing companies, mortgage companies, and other vehicles. If a bank holding company makes available commercial paper proceeds to the commercial bank, the Federal Reserve will impose reserve requirements, negating any cost advantages.

For the investor, of course, it is significant whether paper is issued at the bank holding company or whether the liability is an obligation of the bank. The Continental Illinois story in 1984 clearly documented that the U.S. authorities were willing to bail out all depositors but not bank holding company creditors. Thus deposit notes constitute unconditional, direct, and general obligations of the issuing bank. They rank in line with the bank's other unsecured and unsubordinated indebtedness, *including its other deposit liabilities* (except specially secured deposits). For domestically issued deposit notes, it is important that they are considered as securities issued or guaranteed by U.S. banks or by U.S. branches or agencies of foreign banks and are thus *exempt from SEC registration* under Section 3(a)(2) of the Securities Act of 1933. Such securities are also exempt from the due diligence requirements imposed under Section 12(c) of the act because of the regulated nature of the

---

[25] Deposit notes are issued by commercial banks and have the status of deposits; medium-term notes are issued by corporations, including bank holding companies, and are treated like corporate bonds from a legal point of view. In the United States, bank deposit notes are exempt from SEC registration, as are all MTNs placed privately.

[26] Suresh E. Krishnan, "Deposit Notes/Bank Notes," *New Financial Instruments and Techniques* (Merrill Lynch), July 1988.

issuer. This exemption from SEC regulations, of course, goes only for issues by the bank, not bank holding companies.

Deposit notes are typically issued in the 18-month to 7-year maturity range, although they can be issued virtually for the same maturities as bonds. It is noteworthy that deposit notes in the domestic market with maturities of less than 18 months are subject to reserve requirements under Regulation D of the Federal Reserve Board. They are typically in $100,000 or $250,000 sizes and may be issued either on a fixed- or floating-rate basis. On fixed-rate issues, interest is calculated on the bond-equivalent basis, that is, with a 30-day month, 360-day year. This is slightly different from the CD-equivalent basis, which is calculated on the actual number of days divided by a 360-day year. The basis for floaters can be set in relation to ubiquitous LIBOR and in the domestic market by the commercial paper composite index, the CD composite, the Federal funds rate, and the prime rate or as a spread over the Treasury bill rate and is therefore calculated on the money market–equivalent yield basis. On a bank's balance sheet, deposit notes are characterized as deposits. They can also be classified as "other borrowed money" on the issuing bank's balance sheet, in which case they are currently not subject to FDIC assessments. However, for purposes of ranking claims upon insolvency, it is not relevant whether the claims are classified as deposits or "other borrowed money." While deposit notes are generally not rated, high-quality banks can sometimes achieve small savings by issuing them in preference to other short-term obligations. While investors differentiate in the intermediate- and longer-term maturities, this is not true for shorter maturities. Thus, a highly rated bank may have a relative cost advantage over a lesser rated bank in issuing longer-term debt.

Deposit notes may be issued in either an underwritten or continuously offered market using one or more dealers. It is interesting to know that with a continuously offered program, interest payment dates are usually established at the program's inception for all fixed-rate notes of a particular bank, regardless of the issue date of maturity. For example, a bank may establish a $500 million deposit note program from which tranches of anywhere from 5 to 50 million notes are issued in various maturities throughout the year. However, all the notes will have the same semiannual interest payment dates. The important feature is that both continuously offered as well as underwritten deposit notes provide banks with a flexibility to take advantage of financing opportunities that might momentarily present themselves. This makes deposit notes a particularly effective asset-liability management tool. They are ideal for bank treasury departments that need to match funds' specific maturities. Issuers can lock in profitable spreads between their return on assets and cost of funds. In the secondary market, continuously offered and underwritten notes of the same issuer are reported to trade similarly because they are fungible. In the offshore market, banks issue in locations that do not impose withholding taxes on deposit notes. Interestingly, since U.S. deposit notes are deposits for tax purposes too, U.S. withholding taxes do not apply regardless of the provisions that modified U.S. withholding taxes on corporate and government bonds.

At this point we've discussed a number of different ways in which an international bank can reduce its availability or liquidity risk by extending its funding. We have not, however, solved one of the biggest funding problems facing banks these days—*capital*. Financial institutions, experience has shown, can get themselves mired in some nasty swamps, and they usually do so en masse. So regulatory requirements for capital have stiffened (see Chapter Seven), and banks cannot grow unless they find ways to raise so-called **regulatory capital**. In defining capital requirements the authorities are trying to create a buffer between bank losses and depositors. So they insist that banks have an adequate proportion of funding that does not have to be paid back any time soon (to avert temporary funding crises) and which in addition would be subordinate to depositors if the bank found itself without the wherewithal to service all its claims. At the top of the list, naturally, is **equity**, but raising equity is expensive, it dilutes ownership and control, and from time to time is very difficult to raise in sufficient amounts.

So banks are always looking for ways to issue debtlike securities that satisfy the regulators' requirements for primary capital. These include mandatory convertible securities, preferred stock, and perpetual debt. We conclude this section with a brief discussion of the latter.

The **perpetual floating rate note** was an invention of the 1980s, designed to satisfy bank capital requirements. Conventional Eurodollar FRNs were familiar instruments; many banks in Europe and Asia held large portfolios of them as substitutes for bank loans. Some were long-term notes; banks did not mind too much, for if they tired of them they could always sell them in the secondary market. So why not extend the maturity a bit, to forever? "Like dated FRNs," the sales pitch went, "they will trade at or close to par at each interest reset date." Perps, as they were affectionately called, were issued in the billions. Almost all were issued by banks, merchant as well as commercial, and almost all were bought by commercial banks. Capital-thirsty banks loved to issue them because they satisfied capital requirements. Spread-hungry banks loved to buy them because they paid a teeny bit more, as a spread over LIBOR, than dated FRNs. There was one little catch. To ensure the perps qualified as capital, the fine print specified that the perps were subordinate to all conventional debt. Coupons could be deferred, if necessary, or skipped altogether, without triggering an event of default. Pretty soon it dawned on the regulators that their wards had a lot of preferred stocklike securities in their portfolios and that these were being treated no differently from regular FRNs. "Hold it," said the Bank of England, "if you're going to hold quasi-equity among your assets, then you should allocate 100 percent capital against them." Other authorities soon followed suit. The game was over.

The market went into a tizzy as Japanese and European banks sought to unload billions worth of the paper. Even the conventional FRN market was dragged down and has suffered illiquidity ever since.[27] Years later, some of the paper reappeared as "Phoenix" bonds, packaged together with zero-coupon bonds to create dated securities, and the repackaged perpetual came into fashion in a minor way as a tax-advantaged funding technique, but most of the remaining perps still trade at a severe discount from par value—and probably will do so forever!

SUMMARY

International banks have enormous resources for funding themselves in the international money market. This chapter has told a story of fast, flexible, and cost-efficient markets with few barriers to entry. In the course of describing the banks' funding sources and the manner in which they use them, we have sought to emphasize the common theme of "separability." The Eurocurrency market itself separates the decision of "in what currency to fund" from "in what jurisdiction to fund." Multioption facilities now give banks and their customers alike access to domestic and Euromarkets as they choose. This epitomizes the character of the international money market— sufficiently integrated to provide dual access, but sufficiently segmented by residual regulations and practices to provide special advantages to some under certain conditions. Banks and bank branches in the Euromarket do not have "natural" pools of transactions deposits; rather they are able to fund themselves in the interbank or nonbank Euro time deposit market, in the Eurodollar CD market, or by issuing Eurocommercial paper. Each bank, finding money in the market in which it has a comparative advantage, can then use forward exchange contracts and/or interest rate hedging instruments to transform the nature of the funding into the required currency and with the desired rate risk profile. Similarly, liquidity or availability risk can be minimized or actively managed by the selective use of longer-term funding instruments such as note issuance facilities, Eurodollar floating-rate notes, and deposit notes. In the next chapter we look at the ways in which banks operating in the international money market can put their funds to use. We discover that certain of the instruments used by some banks for funding can be investment vehicles for others.

SELECTED REFERENCES

Bank for International Settlements, *Recent Innovations in International Banking*. Basle: BIS, April 1986.

---

[27] A contributing but not decisive factor was the introduction of floating-rate CMOs (collateralized mortgage obligations) offering assets (at least in terms of credit risk) at a better spread.

Cohen, K. J., S. F. Maier, and J. H. Vander Weide, "Recent Developments in Management Science in Banking," *Management Science*, Vol. 27, No. 10, October 1981, pp. 1097–1119.

Davis, Steven I., *The Eurobank.* New York: John Wiley & Sons, 1976.

Dufey, Gunter and Ian H. Giddy, "Eurocurrency Deposit Risk," *Journal of Banking and Finance*, Vol. 8, 1984, pp. 567–589.

Krishnan, Suresh E., "Deposit Notes/Bank Notes," *New Financial Instruments and Techniques*, Merrill Lynch, July 1988.

Riefler, Donald B., and Lazaros P. Mavrides, "Funding Sources for Banks of Various Sizes." In *The Bankers Handbook*, 3rd ed. (New York: John Wiley & Sons, 1988).

Riehl, Heinz, and Rita Rodriguez, *Money and Foreign Exchange Dealing.*

Stigum, Marcia, *The Money Market*, 3rd ed. (Homewood, IL: Dow Jones-Irwin, 1990).

Stigum, Marcia, and Rene Branch, *Managing Bank Assets and Liabilities.* (Homewood, IL: Dow Jones-Irwin, 1983).

Weisweiller, Rudi (ed.), *Managing a Foreign Exchange Department.* Cambridge: Woodhead-Faulkner, 1985.

Chapter Six

LENDING TECHNIQUES IN THE INTERNATIONAL MONEY MARKET

Contents: *Theme: Unbundling the Features of a Loan   Features of Eurocurrency Loans Special Eurocurrency Clauses   A Paper Chase: Clauses in Loans to Countries Syndication and Securitization of Lending Instruments   The Techniques of Syndication Securitization and Transferability of Loans   Trading Loans   Trading LDC Debt Intermediated Versus Direct Credit   RUFs to ECP: From Intermediation to Direct Securities Markets   Eurocommercial Paper as a Lending Device   Medium-Term Note Programs   A Footnote: True Securitization of Loans   Summary   Selected References   Appendix 6-A: Clauses in Typical Eurodollar Loan Agreements*

THEME: UNBUNDLING THE FEATURES OF A LOAN

What is so special about lending in the offshore market? After all, banking is banking, wherever it is done. It involves handing out other people's money to entrepreneurs, governments and their entities and then trying to get it back with interest—or at least get the interest. At a very fundamental level, that goes for banking worldwide. However, a seemingly simple loan embodies a large number of different features and aspects of risk, and over time bankers have learned to isolate or "unbundle" these features in order to be able to distribute and to hedge the inherent risks—and it is in this respect that the offshore markets have made essential contributions to refinements in lending techniques.

The essence of the contribution of the offshore markets to the evolution of modern lending technology is already inherent in the nature of the market itself; as pointed out previously, the Eurocurrency market is the result of a fundamental innovation: the separation of the currency of denomination from the respective jurisdiction.

This basic theme of financial innovation as the separation, or "unbundling," of financial claims has permeated this book on the international money market. We encounter it again as a central theorem explaining the market for "derivative" instruments in Chapter Four: swaps, options, and futures involve the separation of interest and exchange rates from the underlying assets.

What has been true for the Eurocurrency market in general and rate risk management products specifically is also the guiding paradigm for this chapter on lending techniques: *financial claims can be unbundled and repackaged to serve client's needs more efficiently.* Thus we shall explore both the mechanics as well as the economics of separating the provision of funds from the assumption of credit risk, liquidity (or "availability") risk, and other features that are involved in a loan.

Going beyond the narrow confines of traditional lending, the analysis will be expanded further in two directions. First, while financial intermediation is an essential aspect of the Eurocurrency market, from a functional perspective savers and borrowers look at the traditional intermediation job of banks only as one service offering that they may be willing to use. There is, however, always the alternative of circumventing the intermediating bank and its cost by moving funds directly between savers and borrowers. This can be accomplished by using financial institutions only as brokers, as providers of secondary market services, or as counterparties to hedge partial risks only. Indeed, the separation of an asset's liquidity from the ability to unload market risk associated with an asset represents an important aspect of financial market technology that has emanated from the offshore markets and will be analyzed in this chapter. Central to this theme is, of course, the issue of **asset securitization** involving complex trade-offs of value creating liquidity enhancement versus the loss in the value of the agency relationship that an intelligent banker brings to an ongoing relationship with his clients.

Second, we shall emphasize the fact that banks specialize in the assumption of *credit risk*—so we conclude the chapter with a look at both the direct and the indirect means by which they provide credit risk related services.[1]

FEATURES OF EUROCURRENCY LOANS

The previous chapter emphasized the close link between interbank market and final depositing and lending. The major function of the interbank mar-

---

[1] In the final chapter we shall address a further crucial dimension to the lending business in international markets. Just as there is a functional competitive dimension to the choice between the intermediated and the direct channel of transferring funds from savers to borrowers, there is an institutional aspect to the battle for profit opportunities in the Euromarkets: which institutions will be successful at providing the various services that are demanded by clients? And how can resources be assembled and managed to succeed in the competitive Euromarkets? In short, we will look at the *strategic dimension* in international banking markets.

ket is to make the market liquid and flexible to efficiently match up final depositors and lenders. Our focus now shifts to the special lending practices that have become evident in the Euromarket. What follows is not a manual of international lending but an attempt to relate practices that can be observed in the external markets and which differ from those found in national markets to the unique features that distinguish the international money markets from their national counterparts. Specifically, we will show how different lending practices are influenced by differences in competition and the pattern of regulation.

By way of introduction, we find little that is special about the purposes for which funds are borrowed; nor are the types of borrowers different per se, given the nature of the Eurobanks as affiliates of large money center banks. When one observes groups of borrowers making disproportionate use of the external markets (as opposed to the national markets for foreign borrowers), the reason is usually that these borrowers' access to national markets has been restricted.

What of banks' lending practices? A reader of comments on the international banking scene is struck by the persistent allegation of loose lending practices in the market. Yet despite the country lending debacle we have no reason to believe that loan losses in the external market will systematically exceed those in national markets. After all, both the borrowers and lenders are the very same as those that are active in national markets. (The accompanying box identifies some lending goals that agreements in both segments seek to achieve.) Why should the same bank make a loan to perhaps the same customer under less stringent conditions just because the funding of the loan is done in a different segment of the money market?

Although some of these comments about frivolous lending must be discounted as statesmanlike exhortations by banking leaders to their fellow bankers not to compete quite so aggressively, it was certainly once true that loan agreements in the Euromarket tended to be shorter and simpler than domestic ones. While some differences still remain, for the most part the legal profession has managed to persuade their banking clients to make Euroloan agreements almost as cumbersome and clause intensive as domestic U.S. agreements. On the other hand, one may find a number of clauses in certain Euroloan agreements that are not common domestically.[2] What are they, and what special aspects of the Eurocurrency market

---

[2] There is sometimes more to a Eurodollar loan agreement than meets the eye. Loans in the Euromarket are not necessarily made in isolation; they are part of a total relationship between a bank and its customer, spanning two or more markets. Thus, while it appears that the Euroloan to a company's foreign affiliate is really a loan to the same customer, there are significant differences. One is that there often exist guarantees, sometimes only implied, but frequently in the form of a written undertaking. These may range from the simple "comfort letter"—stating that the affiliate is wholly owned and managed by the parent, and that the bank will be notified in case there is any change in these conditions—all the way to a formal ratio maintenance agreement. Without being called a guarantee, the latter is even stronger, in that it

accounts for them? In what follows we deal with maturity or commitment period, pricing and pricing periods, special features of Eurocurrency loans, and clauses in loans to sovereigns. The appendix contains a list of typical features of international loan agreements.

Commitment Period

Bankers in the Eurodollar market have long claimed that their kind have a special preference for short-term loans, perhaps because of the initial uncertainty of the stability of availability of funds in the Eurodollar market. But this overlooks an essential point: a growing and profitable corporate borrower who has achieved an optimal capital structure will never repay bank debt. Instead, debt will be rolled over, or various bits and pieces will be replaced with other sources of (debt) funds. This is, of course, not unknown to intelligent bankers. Why, then, the concern about maturity per se?

Two concepts must be carefully distinguished in this regard: commitment period and pricing period. Pricing may be short term while the commitment is long term. But is a longer-term commitment riskier?

Not necessarily. *The maturity date or commitment period of a loan matters only because it functions as a decision point.* At this date bankers must decide whether they still agree with the borrower's use of funds or whether there are better uses for the funds in terms of return and risk. Whether the loan is designated short-term or long-term affects only the frequency of this review. However, when the renewal of short-term credit lines is such a routine affair that it is no different from the cursory review of quarterly statements submitted by the borrower in case of a term loan, the distinction becomes meaningless. The only remaining difference is that a term loan may protect the borrower from capricious actions by the bank, for example, in the case of collusion between the lending institution and someone interested in the acquisition of the firm. However, appropriate legal remedies and—more important—a reasonably competitive banking structure, will minimize this danger. In any case, whatever the term of a loan, the bank's ability to call is always tempered by the fact that the borrower may go bankrupt and the bank's loss exceeds that of a "workout," where the creditor is permitted to continue operating under the close supervision of the lending institution. Often this involves a reduction of the yield on the loan for the bank in one way or another.

---

assures lenders that the affiliate will always maintain certain liquidity ratios, if necessary with support from the parent. With such an agreement or a formal guarantee, the position of lenders to the subsidiary is even stronger than those that provided funds for the parent. This is because guaranteed lenders can make claims against the subsidiary first, and afterward throw in the unfilled portion on equal terms with the remainder of the creditors against the parent.

GOALS OF A LOAN AGREEMENT

As the market gains maturity and both lenders and borrowers learn through experience, loan agreements tend to converge. Lenders, in particular, learn to distinguish between form and substance. The substance of a good loan agreement is:

1. To protect the lender by ensuring, as far as an agreement can, that the borrower keeps an adequate margin of liquidity, and a proper balance between assets and liabilities, to enable him to absorb any reasonable turn of events without failure.

2. To give rights of action, should the borrower fail to maintain this margin, while there is still some hope of being repaid without enforcing liquidation or while, if forced to liquidate, there are still some assets available for creditors. And above all, to avoid the situation where the bank has no right to press its view, or even to information, until it is invited to put in a receiver.

3. To ensure that the particular loan is in at least as favorable a position as other loans of a comparable nature and ideally as all other loans.

4. To ensure no wasteful or ill-advised usage of funds or unusual disbursement which adversely affect the borrower's viability.

5. To do all the above without hampering the operations of the company or restricting it in a way that may actually work against the lender's interest.

One of the consequences of this ambiguity about the commitment period—which, it must be emphasized, has true meaning only in a given environment with a sophisticated legal structure and well-established standards about acceptable and unacceptable practices—is its strict separation of the pricing period, as we shall see shortly.

Pricing

Euroloan pricing practices reflect the nature of the market as a pure financial intermediary. Loan rates are always fixed for a certain period, usually for 3 or 6 months, reflecting the time span for which the majority of the time deposits is fixed. In contrast, the cost of outstanding loans in some national markets is usually altered whenever the basic bank lending rate (e.g., the prime rate in the United States, the base lending or overdraft rate in other markets) changes.

Since the base lending rate in national markets is frequently subject to outright controls and/or oligopolistic market practices, it tends to fluctuate less frequently but in greater jumps than do Eurocurrency rates. The political nature of the basic lending rate has also caused lending institutions in various countries to adopt a myriad of gimmicks to conceal the true cost of funds. Compensating balance requirements (e.g., United States and Japan), fees for various loan-related services, innovative value dating of credits and debits, and outrageous delays in the transfer of funds all serve to obfuscate the true interest cost and assure the banks the necessary profit in the face of administered lending rates. In the freely competitive international money market there exists neither the need for nor the possibility of using such devices; all-in-the-rate pricing prevails.

The length of the pricing period during which the interest rate of the loan is fixed determines how the risk of an unexpected change in interest rates is apportioned between the lender and the borrower. Inherent in the maturity structure of interest rates is a forecast of future interest rates, and both borrower and lender are faced with the possibility that the actual rate will be above or below the one implicit in the rate prevailing when the loan was fixed. And the shorter the interest rate period, the more frequent is the opportunity to adjust the pricing of the loan in line with current rates in the market.

Both the borrower and the lender can avoid market risk by matching the maturities of assets with those of liabilities. This is much easier for a bank that deals in contractual claims rather than for a corporation whose return on assets may exhibit little positive correlation with the rise and fall of interest rates. To the extent that banks deliberately mismatch maturities, they either engage in speculative interest rate forecasting and/or exploit institutional preferences existing in various nonbank sectors, where transactors are willing to incur a cost for having longer, more secure liabilities and shorter, more liquid assets.[3]

Given the nature of the Eurobanks as pure intermediaries, what has evolved is that lenders are quite liberal as far as the commitment period is concerned but unwilling to carry much of an interest rate risk. Thus a prearranged line of credit is the usual way of borrowing short term. Under such an arrangement a maximum amount is established that can be borrowed within the commitment period, usually one year, but often renewable after a more or less thorough review process. Drawdowns carry interest charges based on the current short-term rate, with adjustments every 1, 3, or 6 months, typically; see Figure 6-1.

---

[3] For evidence on the possibility of a liquidity preference and other aspects of maturity structure of interest rates, see James C. Van Horne, *Financial Market Rates and Flows*, 3rd ed. (Englewood Cliffs, N. J.: Prentice Hall, 1990).

MARGEE TRADING COMPANY INC.
CREDIT FACILITIES TOTALING $300,000,000
SUMMARY OF TERMS

	I. REVOLVING CREDIT FACILITY	II. TERM LOAN
Amount	Up to $200,000,000	$100,000,000
Purpose	To fund the acquisition of Dan Deming Co. and to refinance certain existing indebtedness	Same
Repayment	Reduction of commitment according to attached schedule	Amortization of loan according to attached schedule
Maturity	July 1, 1997	July 1, 1997
Interest rate	1-, 2-, 3-, or 6-month LIBOR as defined in the loan agreement plus 1.25 percent	From closing until maturity, the outstanding principal balance will bear interest at a rate of 11.5 percent payable quarterly in arrears on the first business day of each quarter

FIGURE 6-1. Pricing of Eurodollar Loan Facility: Comparison of features of revolving credit facility (floating rate) versus term loan (fixed rate).

Short-term credits are also extended ad hoc, normally for periods up to 6 months at fixed rates. Medium-term lending is more prevalent and is typically done in the form of a revolving loan facility (or revolver). In this case, the pricing period rarely exceeds 6 months, while commitment periods of up to 15 years and more have been reported, although the majority of loans fall in the 3- to 7-year category. If and when the borrower requires a fixed-rate "term" loan, as illustrated in Figure 6-1, the bank or banks will hedge their risk by entering into an interest rate swap—so the rate on the term loan will reflect current fixed-for-floating swap rates.

The base rate is the London interbank offered rate, LIBOR, which is the interest at which a sample of reference banks in the London Euromarket offer funds for deposit in the interbank market. Loan agreements usually stipulate the banks and the time, typically 11 A.M. London time.[4] The actual interest cost to the borrower is set at a "spread" over the LIBOR rate. This

---

[4] With the growing importance of Caribbean-based Eurobanking, loan agreements now tend to specify 4 P.M. LIBOR rates, which is equivalent to 11 A.M. Nassau time and coincides with U.S. trading hours.

margin reflects (1) general market conditions and (2) the specific circumstances of the borrower (largely how his creditworthiness is judged competitively by the lending institution). Typically, such spreads for both corporate and public borrowers have ranged from $1/4$ percent and even slightly less to 3 percent and above, with the median being somewhere between $1/2$ and $1 1/2$ percent. In special circumstances, the contractual spread increases or decreases in specified ways in future interest periods during the life of the loan. This is to encourage or discourage early repayment of the loan.

In addition to LIBOR-plus pricing, it is a well-established practice in the Euromarket to charge a commitment fee, usually $1/4$ to 1 percent per annum on the unused portion of the loan, payable at the outset. On the other hand, during times when loan demand is weak and the banks are flush with funds, commitment fees fall victim to competitive pressures. However, Euroloan agreements invariably specify a drawdown period of, say, up to 18 months, during which time the funds must be used by the borrower; otherwise, the commitment expires or the borrower is charged the stipulated rate just as if he had taken up the funds.

SPECIAL EUROCURRENCY CLAUSES

In addition to restrictive covenants, or the lack thereof, and the usual clauses referring to pricing, interest payment dates, amortization dates, and specification of how and where funds are payable, Euroloan agreements contain a number of provisions that reflect the structure of the international money market (see Appendix 6-A). There is a central core of clauses which are invariably found in a normal Eurocurrency loan agreement (see Appendix 6-A); other features differ by origin of the lender.

One standard clause rarely found in domestic loan agreements is the **reserve requirement clause**. Originally, banks could not believe that governments would not find a way to apply this time-honored device to the Euromarkets. Therefore, they asked borrowers to indemnify them in case a compulsory deposit at less than market rates of interest would raise the effective cost of funds. Later, these provisions were broadened to comprise all increases in regulatory costs (such as taxes, levies, and so on, except corporate income taxes) suffered by the lender. Sophisticated borrowers, on the other hand, have managed to introduce modifications that delay the imposition of such charges so as to give the borrower an opportunity to prepay.

Because Eurocurrency loans always involve international financial transactions of one sort or another, involving two or more jurisdictions, special provisions to take care of all possible problems are inserted in Eurocurrency loan agreements, usually in favor of the lender. For instance, all payments of principal and interest are to be made *free and clear of taxes* and similar charges, except for withholding taxes and interest, which may be borne by the lending institution provided that it has agreed to do so. In that case, the agreement would specify whether the absorption would be for the life of the loan or on a "best effort" basis. This depends, of course, on the ability of the lender to absorb the withholding tax, or a portion of it in the form of a foreign tax credit against his own corporate income tax. In addition, loan agreements usually indicate whether interest payments would be made net of withholding taxes, or on a "gross" basis, whereby the bank reimburses the borrower for withholding taxes paid upon receiving the tax receipt.

Apart from complex tax effects, the agreements also reflect attempts to stay clear of even remotely possible contingencies in the political arena. For instance, LIBOR can be replaced by a specified New York money market rate should the London market be inoperative on the business day after interest renewal date. Along the same lines, most agreements contain a *Eurocurrency availability clause.* Such clauses limit the drawdown of the loan funds or, at the extreme, permit banks to call for prepayment if funds are not available. These clauses seem to be on the way out as market participants, especially banks, better understand the sources of growth and stability of the international money market, and as fears of restrictions on nonresident convertibility (of the U.S. dollar in particular) are on the wane. Still, standard provisions inserted by many (but not all) banks obliging the borrower to give at least several days, sometimes up to 1 week, notice prior to a drawdown of funds reflect the concern of the banks with potential liquidity problems in the market.

Also directly related to the international nature of the market are special clauses governing in detail *jurisdiction* as well as *judgment currency* necessary for loan agreements that typically touch a number of jurisdictions. The determination of jurisdiction requires careful consideration. Not only must the applicable law and legal practice be sophisticated, but (l) courts must be willing to accept jurisdiction, and (2) it helps when the country is one that has the power to enforce judgments. This does not require the existence of a large expeditionary force (although some lenders undoubtedly wish such a jurisdiction were available) but rather an economy that is of sufficient size that each transactor can ill afford to keep from doing business with it. This, of course, is one factor in favor of U.S. jurisdiction (usually New York, because of the extensive case law on banking matters that has been built up), even in cases where lender and borrower are not residents of that country. Judgment currency clauses are necessary because the courts in many countries, notably the United Kingdom, will only render a judgment in domestic money. In the world of floating currencies, given the usual long delays in the judicial process, particularly between judgment and enforcement, this can cause difficulties when the contract calls for payments in a third currency, such as dollars.

One of the unique clauses that benefit borrowers, increasingly found in agreements governing loans funded in the external market, is a *multicur-*

rency option. According to this clause, the borrower has the choice of drawing funds denominated in one or more stipulated currencies. These are invariably limited to those major convertible currencies for which external deposit markets, or at least active forward markets, exist. On interest renewal dates—after giving at least several days notice as specified in the agreement—the borrower can request a change in the denomination of the loan, or a portion of it, or he can draw additional funds in one of the currencies specified. He will be charged the equivalent of the applicable LIBOR rate for dollars plus or minus an adjustment that is equal to the forward discount or premium on the currency concerned. The amount of the takedown and repayment is governed by the spot exchange rate prevailing 2 days prior to that date, in line with normal foreign exchange delivery practices. Multicurrency clauses are usually written "subject to availability," to allow the lender to cope with unforeseen controls. In that case, the borrower has an option to select another currency, or not to use the facility. The size of the total facility is usually expressed in dollars. Thus, should the borrower have utilized it fully in terms of, say, Swiss francs, and the Swiss franc rises in value relative to the dollar, the borrower is expected to repay the excess in Swiss francs to bring the total within the specified dollar amount, given the new exchange rate.

As bankers and their customers have learned to understand the interaction between external and national money markets better, there has been an increasing trend toward comprehensive facilities that include alternatives of borrowing in specified *national markets* in addition to the segments of the *external market*. For multinational companies, such facilities offer maximum flexibility. For the lenders, it requires either a very extensive network of strong foreign affiliates or, better yet, the formation of an international banking syndicate whose members can make commitments in various national markets as well as the Euromarkets.

A PAPER CHASE: CLAUSES IN LOANS TO COUNTRIES

Questions of jurisdiction take on a special flavor when one deals with loans to sovereign borrowers. So far, we have dealt with factors relevant primarily to private borrowers. Most of these also apply directly when loans are made to governments, governmental subunits, or government-owned enterprises. However, there are some fundamental differences between loans to sovereign borrowers and others. It must be noted at the outset of the discussion that loans to governments are made not only in the Eurocurrency market but also in national markets. But while the problems are not different in substance, the drawing up of loan documentation in national markets is less controversial simply because there is a well-established pattern to which all lenders adhere and, equally important, that is accepted by bank examiners.

These authorities tend to discharge their admittedly difficult task of second-guessing profit-seeking (and better paid) banking executives by adopting a set of formalistic rules with which to pass judgment on the quality of loans. The maintenance of ratios by the borrower and certain formal requirements regarding the documentation feature prominently among the criteria used.

As far as restrictive covenants are concerned, maximum debt ratios, minimum reserve limitations, and restrictions on public expenditures are ultimately useless and can be politically damaging. The fact is that information is often unavailable even to the government in question, and in any case the lender lacks the ability to assure compliance. Indeed, such restrictive covenants may give rise to claims by some forces that the country is run to the dictates of foreign bankers, and the body politic is invited to exercise sovereignty by denying them their "ill-gotten gains," meaning interest and principal. Given the lack of enforcement of agreements against sovereign powers, it has been argued that all one needs in a loan agreement with a sovereign government is a one-sentence statement: "I promise to pay, maybe."[5]

Cross-default clauses, waivers of immunity, and provisions regarding jurisdiction and arbitration take on a special flavor when used in agreements to governments and their subunits. For instance, a new regime may repudiate all previous debt without ever knowing what cross-default means. Similarly, clauses in the loan agreement by which a government expressly waives its sovereign immunity may provide the lender(s) little protection if the courts of the country refuse to accept jurisdiction. And this seems to be precisely the case in the United Kingdom and the United States, the most frequently designated jurisdictions. It appears that as far as British courts are concerned, immunity is waived only if it occurs at the time action is brought (i.e., when the sovereign party involved files an unconditional appearance). U.S. courts are governed by similar principles. Arbitration clauses that are used as substitutes do not help either. Arbitration proceedings by their nature tend to end in compromise, but this is of little use in situations that call for the repayment of specific sums of principal, interest, and fees.

In the face of all these frustrations, lenders have attempted to distinguish among governmental subunits. Thus it is believed that central banks are more reliable borrowers than governments and their other agencies, following the principle that "governments come and go, but central banks stay forever." In a marginal situation, this may make a difference, but the test sample to support this thesis is extremely small.

A related theory of international lending to governments postulates that

---

[5] David Levine, "It's Time for Eurobanks to Work Out What They Mean by Market Practice," *Euromoney*, August 1976, p. 38. Much of the following section is based on this oldie-but-goodie.

loans used to fund specific productive uses—as opposed to general budget
and/or balance-of-payments financing—are more likely to be paid back.
There is only very limited analytical support for this. For instance, evidence
exists that courts are more likely to view transactions with state-owned *commercial* entities just like transactions among private parties. New York
courts, in particular, may apply this "restrictive concept" of sovereign
immunity.

Court decisions in the United States have validated waivers of sovereign immunity in U.S. courts, both for suit and for execution purposes. Still,
as always, there remains the tricky question of seizing the assets of the foreign sovereign. First, there may be no such assets within the court's jurisdiction, and even if there are, you can claim only those assets that are owned by
the borrowing entity itself, not any others of the government of which it
may be a part (in the case of a parastatal). Moreover, the foreign government
may retaliate—not only against U.S. government assets within its jurisdiction, but also those of private U.S. citizens. And, finally, there are global foreign policy considerations which may further diminish the U.S. government's eagerness to help enforce lenders' claims. The situation in other
major countries is analogous.

Apart from the somewhat more clear-cut jurisdictional situation when
dealing with government-owned commercial borrowers, there is also the
special case in which such enterprises sell their output abroad. In that case
the position of the lender is stronger, although even that situation should be
put in its proper perspective. To chase loads of commodities all over the
world attempting to obtain court orders tends to be frustrating and finan-
cially unrewarding.

While the foregoing discussion supports to some degree the case for
lending to certain governmental subunits, there are other factors that offset
the advantages. For instance there is still the age-old problem of double risk
in international commercial lending. A loan can default because the borrower is unable to pay and/or the country of the borrower will not permit
the transfer of funds. To the extent that a government will not support a
governmental subunit or state-owned enterprise, the lender faces a commercial risk in addition to the usual sovereign risk.

All things considered, loan agreements with sovereign borrowers serve
only one purpose: to establish default *clearly* and for all to see. Lenders to
governments do not rely on their *ability* to repay, but on their *willingness*,
although economic conditions may affect the latter. Ultimately, however,
safety for the lender to a country is its perceived and recognized need for
additional funds.[6] And to establish a situation of undisputed default may

[6] See Robert Z. Aliber, *The International Money Game*, 5th ed. (New York: Basic Books, 1987),
Chapter 20, "Optimal Bankrupts: Deadbeats on an International Treadmill."

minimize a sovereign borrower's expectation of obtaining additional funds from other lenders. Its international creditworthiness may be among the most valuable assets a government possesses.

SYNDICATION AND SECURITIZATION OF LENDING INSTRUMENTS

Once upon a time, we recall, banks made loans to borrowers: they built a relationship, got to know the company and its business, and extended the customer a line of credit. When funds were needed, banks loaned those funds, monitored the borrower, tried to work things out through pressure and persuasion when earnings went awry, and expected to get repaid when the loan matured. Nowadays all these functions can be done separately, and some new ones have been borrowed from the securities market. Two of the latter have transformed the character of large-scale, medium-term financing; these are the underwriting and distribution of syndicated credits, and the subsequent trading of certain of these credits among banks and other financial and even nonfinancial institutions. As we shall see, however, underwriting, distribution and trading have adapted themselves to meet the peculiar requirements of the international bank lending business.

We begin this section with a discussion of the loan syndication technique, which is the bankers' hybrid of new issue security distribution and one-on-one bank lending. It is only a short and perhaps logical step from wide primary distribution of small and uniform loan participations to later resale, that is, trading, of these loan units. And if you go that far, why not call a spade a spade, originate loans to be divisible and tradable, and encourage the development of market-makers who sell to all and sundry? Well, we argue, this certainly adds liquidity of a kind, but the value of this must be sufficient to offset the loss of ongoing surveillance and intervention functions provided by the traditional bank lending techniques.

THE TECHNIQUES OF SYNDICATION

In syndication, like bond underwriting, a small group of knowledgeable and well-capitalized banks agrees to provide the entire loan; these banks then sell portions of their share of the credits to a much wider range of smaller or less knowledgeable banks.[7] Syndication of a large loan at origination serves much the same purpose as syndication of a security such as a bond issue. In the Eurocurrency market, an issuer may come from one country with its own regulations and accounting norms, while lenders are from a

---

[7] Rarely, one encounters with partially underwritten syndicated credits and *best-efforts* syndicated credits.

dozen or more other nations. Thus much of their risk reduction is performed not by credit analysis and monitoring and control but by taking a smaller amount of more diversified assets and by relying on the monitoring role of the lead bank or banks.

One of the ways in which international lenders can manage what are essentially incalculable risks is through diversification. Diversification of a bank's assets tends to reduce the risk of loan loss by spreading it over a number of institutions. On the other hand, this increases the cost of making any given loan because it increases drastically the number of relationships between lenders and borrowers. Again, while the problem per se is not unique to the external money markets, the solution found—syndication— reflects the flexibility and innovation that a competitive, unrestricted market offers. Syndication is indeed the most prevalent way of lending in the external markets, whenever the amounts involved are large and the commitment period exceeds 12 months. Publically available sources issued by the OECD and the BIS provide an indication of the composition of publicly announced, syndicated Eurocurrency credits.

A syndicate is a highly structured group of financial institutions, formed by a manager or a group of comanagers that lends funds on common conditions to a borrower. To see what distinguishes syndication in the external markets from loan participation and other forms of joint bank lending which are long-standing practices in national markets, we shall look at syndication from the perspective of the borrower and the participating banks, including the lead manager, the comanagers, and the agent bank.

Although members of a direct syndicate have several, rather than joint, agreements with the borrower, it is usual for the members to appoint a "manager" or an "agent" to act as a conduit between the syndicate and the borrower. This construct allows the dispersion of ownership while retaining some of the benefits of a principal-agent relationship—in particular, the surveillance and negotiation responsibilities of the agent. In practice, the agent may follow a quite different pattern of behavior when legal and fiduciary obligations are guiding it rather than the fear of losing one's own money, which tends to concentrate one's mind wonderfully.

An international loan syndication agreement can take one of two forms (or a combination thereof): a **direct loan syndicate** or a **participation syndicate**.[8] A direct loan syndicate is a multilateral loan agreement in which participant banks, having signed a common loan document, advance funds to the borrower—the obligations of the participant banks are several, rather than joint. A participation syndicate, on the other hand, is similar to a principal-agent relationship. A "lead" bank or banks usually executes a loan

---

[8] See Wood (1980), Semkow (1984), Nirenberg (1984), MacCullum (1987), and Bradlow (1984).

agreement with the borrower and then forms the syndicate by entering into a participation agreement with other banks. The important distinction is that subparticipants are not "co-lenders" unlike in the direct syndication case.

Joint lending by a group of banks is not exactly unknown in national markets. In part this is because almost all countries have laws and regulations limiting the amount that can be loaned by any one bank to any one customer. The reasons are twofold: (1) to protect the customer from undue influence of any one single lender and (2) to protect the bank from being excessively exposed to the credit of any single customer. This forces diversification, something that would in any case be called for by the precepts of prudent financial management. Yet even if domestic banks by law or by choice each provide only part of the funds needed by particular borrowers, there is no obvious reason for lending to be coordinated by the banks themselves.

One way to understand the rationale for syndication is to ask why the borrower cannot approach a number of banks directly and obtain from each a portion of the total funds needed.[9] Compared to separate little loans, the syndication method allows lenders to have much better information about (1) the aggregate amount of lending to any one borrower (especially a country) and (2) the terms and conditions of other segments of the loan and of other lending to the same borrower. Hence they will lend a more appropriate amount and at a lower required rate of return than if these features were uncertain. The risk premium charged by any one lender is related to the ratio of total loans to one borrower in relation to his capital base. Also individual lenders face a rising marginal cost of capital. For both reasons banks will charge a higher spread for a loan from a single bank than the same loan spread over a number of banks.

Another reason for both syndication *and* securitization in the international lending market is the fact the control is minimal and monitoring of less value when the borrower is a sovereign. Lenders cannot easily persuade a country such as Argentina to improve its cash flow prospects by layoffs the way they might be able to do with, say, an automobile parts manufacturer. Moreover the lender does not have recourse to the same legal remedies as with a private borrower.

---

[9] Indeed, this is the usual practice in domestic lending in some countries (including, until recently, the United States) where it is the task of a corporate treasury department to negotiate with various banks; often the result is a common, or at least a coordinated loan agreement. To put the difference succinctly, in domestic lending, the relationships that count are between the borrower and each individual bank. A managing bank may not be necessary, and it may be rare to find a bank participating in the loan on a "casual," one-shot, basis without direct contact with the borrower. In a syndication, on the other hand, the relationship between the lead manager and the participating banks is what matters.

For sovereign borrowers, therefore, syndication and securitization provides lenders with the ability to diversify. A key aspect of syndicated loans to developing countries, as well as to other borrowers, is that in addition to the diversification feature, syndication agreements go far beyond one-on-one relationships between member lenders and the borrower. They provide for explicit cooperation and have risk-equalizing agreements such as cross-default and sharing clauses.

But another factor helps explain why syndication first flourished in the Euromarket, and why, in particular, borrowers are willing to pay the fees for syndication. While some exceptions can always be found, the basic reason is that with the multitudes of potential borrowers and financial institutions in the Euromarket, banking relationships rely only to a limited extent on traditionally established links. To illustrate, a corporate borrower whose banking relationships in the national market had grown gradually, beginning with the local bank that first funded the founder's venture, with additional institutions being added as the loan demand grew, is suddenly confronted by a vast choice of lending institutions as it approaches the external markets. Likewise, for the banks, the number of potential customers suddenly multiplies as they begin to operate in the external markets. With the mass of potential customers, familiarity with any individual borrower decreases, too. The result is the lending of relatively small amounts (international lending is risky) to many different customers: smaller and medium-sized banks of necessity rely on the services of a relatively few large banks, who have long international experience and have shown their confidence in the credit of the borrower by taking a portion of the loan into their own portfolio.

Thus the crucial rationale for syndication is that in the relative anonymity and complexity of the international money market, the managing bank can obtain funds for the borrower faster, in greater amounts and/or at a lower cost, because this form of lending speeds up the process of negotiation with lenders and—most important—it reduces the perceived risk of the institutions that ultimately provide the bulk of the funds.

Of course the problem of bringing together borrowers and lenders in a fragmented market is nothing new; it is the essence of investment banking where the leading underwriter correctly guesses which securities will appeal to investors and, by adding its prestige to that of the issuer (borrower), successfully places the paper. In many national markets, such as Japan, the United States, and the United Kingdom, investment banking and commercial banking have been strictly separated by law. In the unregulated Euromarket, however, nothing prevents commercial banks from borrowing investment banking concepts and techniques and applying them with great success to the problem of large-scale lending. Many of the formalities of syndicated credits can best be understood by looking at securities underwriting in national or international markets.

The relationship between a borrower and the syndicate manager is very similar to that between a corporation and its investment banking house. This relationship is usually one of long standing, because it requires an intimate knowledge of the borrower's requirements, strengths, and weaknesses, as well as of its preferences. Normally, a syndicated loan in the external market is the end result of a decision process in which various alternatives, in terms of markets, instruments, and maturities are considered.

Indeed, it was the traditional U.S. investment banking houses and U.K. merchant banks that first featured prominently as lead managers of syndicated loans in the external markets. However, as the markets gain maturity, these early pioneers are being more and more displaced by large commercial banks, or rather their merchant banking affiliates. Most of the institutional changes observed in the external money market can be attributed to the special conditions in that market. The ultimate competitive advantage of a syndicate manager is to obtain the amount of funds required by a borrower at the best conditions currently obtainable in the market. And while syndication is usually made on a "best-efforts" basis (i.e., technically the syndicate manager obtains a mandate from the borrower to go out and attempt to get the funds via a syndicate), for all practical purposes the borrower expects a commitment, almost equivalent to a firm underwriting. No prospective lead manager can afford to come back to the client and say, "Sorry, we thought we could do it but. . . ." And in this respect the major commercial banks have an advantage that cannot easily be duplicated by the traditional investment and merchant bankers: it is the commercial banks that have the funds. This permits them to speak with much more assurance to a borrower, because even though every lead manager intends to place a very large proportion of the total loan with other banks, as a last resort a commercial bank can always increase its own share should other banks prove less eager to participate than it was anticipated originally.

There is also a second advantage that must not be underestimated: other financial institutions will be much more willing to take on a share of a credit if they know that the syndicate manager is confident enough to take more than just a token proportion into its own loan portfolio. And this fact will significantly contribute to the success of the syndicate by increasing the "sell-out rate," the proportion of the total loan placed with other participants.

It is for such services that borrowers are willing to pay somewhere between $1/4$ and 2 percent "front-end" syndication fees, in addition to expenses. (For an example of the fee structure in a syndicated loan, see Figure 6-2.) An edge in distribution or placement power resulting from direct access to deposits has given the investment banking affiliates of large commercial banks the muscle to partially displace the traditional investment banking houses. Other skills, which are usually germane to investment banking, such as a view of total corporate finance (as compared to nar-

MARGEE TRADING COMPANY INC.
$300 MILLION FACILITY—FEE STRUCTURE

Closing fees to initial lenders	1.76 percent of commitment amount payable at closing
Closing fees to assignees	Over $50 million 1.25 percent Up to $50 million 1.00 percent Up to $25 million 0.75 percent The closing fee will be based on the assignee's aggregate allocated commitment, payable upon execution of the assignment.
Commitment fees	$1/_2$ percent per annum on the unused portion of the revolving credit facility.
Prepayment fees, revolving credit facility	A prepayment fee for payments made other than at the end of a Euroloan period will be calculated in accordance with a formula set out in the credit agreement.
Prepayment fees, term loan	Payments made other than as shown in the repayment schedule will be subject to a prepayment fee in accordance with a formula set out in the credit agreement.
Agent's fee	Payable to agent, First Manhattan Trust, for agency functions in the amount of $100,000 at the closing date and $50,000 per year thereafter unless all facilities are paid in full before these dates.

FIGURE 6-2. Sample Fee Structure for a Syndicated Eurodollar Loan.

row credit evaluation), in-depth knowledge of worldwide financial markets, the ability to structure a loan or a security into a package that is attractive to the providers of funds while appropriate to the borrower's situation—all these technical skills can be bought or duplicated by the commercial banks. These skills are usually housed either in wholly owned London-based merchant banking affiliates or in consortium banks, which are owned by several commercial banks. Most of these organizations are somewhere on the spectrum between pure, fee-earning financial service organizations and asset-building organizations whose income comes from the spreads between deposit rates and lending rates.

Whatever the precise institutional background of the syndicate manager, his ability to persuade other banks to participate in a loan is crucial. The formation of a syndicate is a complex and intricate affair of competition and cooperation. Only a few points can be highlighted here. First, most syndicates are ex post; that is, the syndicate is formed *after* potential lead managers have competed for the mandate from the borrower (and the fees involved), and losing competitors will often join the syndicate as a participating bank. Second, both reciprocity considerations and correspondence relationship with the lead manager are important factors determining who will participate. Third, while relationships with the lead manager are important, the borrower will also press for a role of one sort or another for financial institutions that it wants to reward, or with which it wishes to do business in the future. (And vice versa, many banks have found that a useful way to establish a link with a prospective customer is to participate in the target customer's syndicated credit.)

As a further encouragement to prospective participants, lead managers are invariably expected to share their fees with those that commit funds. While the structure of such "give-ups" varies with competitive conditions, the following ranges are representative:

Lead manager:		1 to $\frac{5}{8}$ percent of total credit
Comanagers:		$\frac{7}{8}$ to $\frac{1}{2}$ percent of manager's proportion of loan
Participants:	$1 million	$\frac{1}{4}$ to $\frac{1}{8}$ percent of manager's proportion of loan
	$3 million	$\frac{3}{8}$ to $\frac{1}{4}$ percent of manager's proportion of loan
	$5 million	$\frac{1}{2}$ to $\frac{3}{8}$ percent of manager's proportion of loan

Usually, the role of lead manager and participants is quite clearly defined. However, comanagers' functions can range all the way from the equivalent of underwriters who guarantee the placement of a specified portion of the syndicated credit to little more than participants who get a larger share of the fees because of a special relationship with the borrower or because they pick up a disproportionately large portion of the credit.

Participants will look to the lead manager not only for fees but also for assurance that the mechanics of the loan are correctly executed. More important, while no participant bank will admit that it does not analyze each and every credit carefully, there is no doubt that there is a certain "comfort factor" involved; otherwise, the loan would be made directly. In this respect some ticklish legal problems arise when things go wrong. To what extent is the lead manager responsible for the information upon which the participating bank made the decision to take a portion of the loan in its portfolio? This information is contained in a "placement memorandum," whose format is similar to a prospectus, which purports to contain all information material to the credit. The information is supplied by the borrower, but the question is to what extent is the lead manager responsible for accuracy and/or omission of material facts. Ultimately, the similarity between loan syndication and securities underwriting raises difficult, and as yet unresolved, legal questions. To what extent are the "participation certificates" that document the participant's claims against the borrower, securities as defined by the U.S. securities laws and/or similar legislation of other countries? And can the participant banks take action against the lead manager for misrepresentation?

Technically, a loan can be syndicated on a *broadcast* basis, whereby the lead manager informs a great many banks by telex about the conditions of the loan and invites offers of participation. This method works best when the credit is well known, the loan uncomplicated, and the market very liquid. Alternatively, participation is negotiated; this is sometimes a lengthy process, especially when the deal is complicated, such as in major project financings. In such cases, called *straight* syndication, the number of banks tends to be smaller because each of the participant banks gets much more involved in negotiations with the borrower. Conceptually, such deals are hardly syndications because the structure of relationships shifts toward traditional forms of joint lending. Figure 6-3 provides a summary of the syndicate structure.

The final party to a syndicated loan is the agent bank. While it may or may not be synonymous with the lead manager, the agent bank has a very distinct function. It acts on behalf of all the banks who provided the funds in supervising and handling the payment of interest and the amortization of

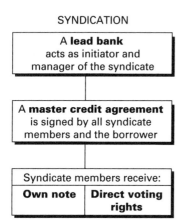

SYNDICATION

A **lead bank**
acts as initiator and
manager of the syndicate

A **master credit agreement**
is signed by all syndicate
members and the borrower

Syndicate members receive:

| **Own note** | **Direct voting rights** |

FIGURE 6-3. Syndication is an arrangement between a group of lenders or **syndicate** and a single borrower evidenced by a master credit agreement.

the loan. The agent bank also administers the collateral and it acts on behalf of the other banks when legal remedies become necessary to collect on time what is due. In default cases the job of the agent bank, normally mundane and clerical, requires a great deal of skill and judgment, especially when the members of the syndicate cannot agree on the appropriate action. "Majority bank clauses" in syndication agreements are designed to guide the agent in such cases. The agent, of course, receives compensation from the borrower, ranging typically from a front-end fee of about $25,000, payable at the completion of the syndication, to $10,000 annually in large syndicated credits.

Again following the pattern of securities underwriting, syndicated credits can be made quietly like private placements, or publicly announced in the form of a "tombstone" advertisement that appears in business journals or weeklies that have substantial international circulation. An example of such an announcement appears in Figure 6-4.

This announcement appears as a matter of example only   August 1992

NORD-OIL
EXPLORATION CORPORATION

US$75,000,000
Multicurrency Term Loan

Arranged by
Scandinavian Bank Group

Lead Manager
Banco Central, S.A.   The Industrial Bank of Japan, Ltd
Kansallis-Osake-Pankki   Scandinavian Bank Group   Swiss Bank Corporation

Managers
Amsterdam-Rotterdam Bank N.V.   BHF Bank   Credit Lyonnais

Funds provided by
Amsterdam-Rotterdam Bank N.V.   Banco Central S.A.   Banco Herrero   Banque du Midi
BHF Bank   Credit Lyonnais   The Industrial Bank of Japan, Ltd   The Irish Poets' Bank
Kansallis-Osake-Pankki   Scandinavian Bank Group   Swiss Bank Corporation

Agent Bank
Scandinavian Bank Group

FIGURE 6-4. Example of a "Tombstone" Announcement of a Syndicated Loan.

To sum up, the prevalence of syndication in the external markets is the result of a lack of restrictions, particularly restrictions that separate investment banking and commercial banking. This permits the application of underwriting techniques to the problem of matching borrowers and lenders without long-established relationships. The facilities available under syndicated credits are the same as those available from individual banks, although very large credits make syndication virtually a necessity. Likewise, loan agreements governing syndicated credits are essentially the same; however, while agreements between borrowers and individual banks can be tailored to the requirements of the respective financial institution, agreements documenting syndicated credits—with many banks from varied national parentages participating—are most representative of the unique lending practices that have evolved in the international money market.

SECURITIZATION AND TRANSFERABILITY OF LOANS

In this section and the next two we'll take a look at the means by which banks have metamorphosed their business from that of intermediary to that of underwriter and distributor—the loan sales business.

Loan agreements or contracts were originally designed to specify the relationship between lender and borrower. As more and more of these contracts are resold to other lenders, however, the agreements have to take account of the nature of the transfer of rights and obligations and to deal with the relationships between the original lender and the new lender—the buyer of the loan. Loan sales typically assume one of two basic forms: "assignments" or "participations." Both approaches are intended to pass the right to interest, principal, and of course the credit risk on to another investor, with no recourse to the original lender.

Figure 6-5 summarizes the differences between the two and highlights the major variations on assignments and participations. In an **assignment**, the original lender gets out of the picture altogether by selling all his rights, interest, and obligations in a credit facility or loan to the loan buyer or assignee. The loan agreement and note (claim) is transferred, with the consent of the borrower, to the assignee. An even stronger divorce and remarriage occurs under **novation**, where the note evidencing the selling bank's claim is canceled and new notes are issued to the purchaser.

More common is the sale of a loan by means of a **participation**, in which the original lender retains a much more centralized role. The lead bank commits to the loan itself and then sells the right to participate in the loan or facility to other banks. Bits of the loan may be resold and resold again, but *the lead bank's relationship with the borrower remains unaltered because the participation is a contract between the buyer and the lead bank, not the borrower.* Thus participants have derivative rights, not direct rights against or obligations to

ASSIGNMENT	PARTICIPATION

| FULL ASSIGNMENT
The sale of *all* of the originating lender's or *assignor's* rights and interest in a credit facility to a purchaser or *assignee*.

In a full assignment:
• The borrower usually acknowledges the assignment.
• The borrower must consent to release of obligation by the assignor.
• The assignee has direct access and enforcement of rights against the borrower.
• The loan agreement and note is transferred to assignee at closing. | PARTICIPATION
An arrangement between a lead bank and one or more lenders or *participants*.

In a participation:
• The lead bank sells the right to participate in a credit facility or loan.
• *Participants have derivative rights, not direct rights against (or obligations to) the borrower.*
• Counterparty risk exists for lead bank, such as lead bank is responsible for funding participants' shares.
• Capital rules affect lead bank. |

| ASSIGNMENT WITH NOVATION
An agreement between the borrower and syndicate that allows the syndicate to add additional (or different) lenders after the initial closing. Novation occurs when (1) the selling bank's note is canceled and (2) new notes are issued to new and original lenders for adjusted amounts.

The added syndicate members:
• Obtain their own notes.
• Enjoy full rights directly with the borrower. | LIMITED VOTING PARTICIPATION
The lead bank retains full rights and is only required to obtain consent for changes to the transaction structure, such as repayment dates or releases of collateral.
FULL VOTING PARTICIPATION
Lead bank has rights to veto any waiver or amendment, but must obtain consent before altering terms of transaction, such as principal or interest.
FULL PASS-THROUGH PARTICIPATION
Lead bank cannot veto a decision by the majority of lenders, and must:
• Obtain consent of participants prior to any waivers or amendments.
• Consult with participants before taking any affirmative action (e.g., accelerate or foreclose on collateral).
• Obtain consent before altering terms of the transaction. |

FIGURE 6-5. Means of Transferring Loans. "Assignment" and "participation" constitute the two basic forms of loan sales.

the borrower. Participation certificates providing evidence of the contract are not negotiable securities and cannot simply be sold; instead, a new contract would have to be drawn up between a buyer and the original lead bank.

The latter arrangement is much less cumbersome than assignment or assignment with novation, but it can lead to some problems. First, the original lender no longer bears the credit risk of the borrower, but if the buyer has assumed a commitment to lend then if the buyer backs out the original lender may have to honor this commitment. Second, the buyer himself has some counterparty risk vis-à-vis the originating bank, for the latter usually continues to administer the collection and distribution of debt service payments. If there is an interruption of payments the new lender may find himself trying to collect undistributed funds from the lead bank as well as unpaid interest and principal from the borrower.

Moreover, "subparticipating" a loan to a wide range of small lenders has some of the disadvantages of pure securitized distribution without the advantage of liquidity (to lenders) or independence (to borrower). The reasons? A plethora of lenders participating in a syndicated Eurocredit can produce conflicts with the borrower and for other lenders in the syndicate if it should become necessary to obtain waivers, consents, or amendments during the life of the loan. Loan agreements have historically been refined to suit the requirements of the borrower-lender relationship; they are complex and (unlike Eurobond issues) typically contain many covenants designed to restrict additional borrowing and to protect against the dissipation of assets or income during the life of the loan. But the very specificity of these covenants means that renegotiation to meet the surprises of reality is not unusual during the life of a medium-term credit. A large number of weak lenders with small participations and without strong relationship ties either directly or indirectly (via ties to lead lenders) can become a nuisance or even a menace to the borrower and its principal lenders should circumstances require changes in the terms of the loan.

Bankers often profess that they prefer assignment and novation to subparticipation. But they go right on selling and purchasing participations, because it is quicker and cheaper and they must get on with the job.

On a more fundamental note, the most desirable position in some respects is that of maximum freedom—the right and means to sell off participations, divide notes, and substitute new lenders of record. This makes marketing easier and reduces price and liquidity risk, *as long as the original lenders place a low value on surveillance and influence rights and on long-term relationship ties with the borrower.* The point is that the economic value of influence rights and of goodwill are lost, not captured by the new owner, if ownership is dissipated. *Hence the value of diversification and of liquidity gained from dispersion of ownership must exceed the value lost from a reduction in agency control.*

TRADING LOANS

We have described the means by which a loan can be sold, but not the rationale for such trading. The answer is **comparative advantage**. Some banks have the resources to originate, service, and monitor loans, but neither the capital nor the cheap deposits to make holding all of them profitable. Other banks lack the teams of relationship officers and originators to bring in and structure the loan business, but have strong capital and plenty of deposits that they want to put to work. They can afford to take thinner spreads because their overhead is lower and perhaps they are getting cheaper money to boot.

A third category is those who buy now to sell later. Typically, these would be large international banks who, in the good old I'll-scratch-your-back-if-you-scratch-mine tradition, have been invited by the originating bank to be part of a syndicate in a Euroloan, but who intend to sell (subparticipate) all or most of the loan to other banks—or, more and more, to non-bank investors such as insurance companies, pension funds, and even cash-rich corporations. For them, a loan is just another instrument to be bought at one price (at origination) and sold at a slightly higher price as quickly as possible.

Most loan sales occur at or soon after the loan or facility is arranged, because that's where the selling banks make their money. Say Paribas joins the syndicate to provide part of the $200 million floating-rate loan facility to Margee Trading Corp. (the example in Figures 6-1 and 6-2). Paribas may commit itself to $30 million; for this it will receive 1 percent up front, $\frac{1}{2}$ percent per annum on the unused portion of the commitment (Figure 6-1), and LIBOR + 1.25 percent per annum on the amount loaned (Figure 6-2). Paribas will now try to sell the full $30 million to its friends and acquaintances, such as smaller French, Asian, and African banks. All three forms of compensation will be negotiated as part of the "price" at which Paribas subpartici-pates the loan. For example, Paribas may offer the loan in $5 million and $10 million lots with a $\frac{1}{4}$ percent up-front fee, $\frac{3}{8}$ percent on the undrawn portion, and LIBOR + 1 percent on any drawdown. If this is acceptable to a buyer, Paribas will have taken a decent cut of the fee structure. If it is not, Paribas will probably be willing to improve the terms, for it will be eager to get the paper off its books as soon as possible so that capital can be freed to underwrite more loans.

There is much less money to be made from the reselling of loans later in their life and the aftermarket is therefore thin and illiquid. Loan "distribution" is perhaps a more descriptive term than is loan "trading." The exception is the market for less-developed country (LDC) debt, where nowadays there is more secondary market trading than new lending. We look at this market in the next section.

Apart from LDC debt, the kinds of loan participations that are traded can be divided into three categories: high-quality loans, defined as loans to borrowers who also have access to the Euro- or U.S. commercial paper market; collateralized loans; and leveraged buy-out (LBO) loans.

Much of the banks' **high-quality loan** business worldwide succumbed, in the late 1980s, to the ability of these borrowers to access the direct markets where they could obtain cheaper financing. The direct markets include Eurocommercial paper and note issuance facilities, domestic commercial paper (at least in the United States and the United Kingdom), medium-term notes, and swapped Eurobonds; of these, the most important is commercial paper in its several guises. Top-name borrowers still borrow from banks, but usually only as a cheaper alternative to commercial paper. Many commercial paper facilities are accompanied by **"backup" lines or facilities**, and some banks provide the borrower with loans cheaper than the rate agreed upon in the backup facility. The borrower will take advantage of this *bid option* money as long as it is competitive with commercial paper. Since commercial paper yields are normally below that which would earn big banks a spread over their cost of funds, the major banks seldom hold onto high-quality loans—they sell them off to other banks or to nonbank investors. The primary and secondary market for such loans is reasonably liquid since the paper is treated as a commodity—participations are sold on a name basis with little or no credit analysis accompanying the investment decision. The banks instead concentrate on earning fees from managing and providing these borrowers' backup facilities (more later). Or if they do provide such financing, it is done as a means to support a relationship with the client so as to generate ancillary business.

Some of the biggest of the "frequent borrowers," such as General Electric and ICI, issue a lot of **asset-backed or collateralized loans** as well as asset-backed commercial paper. This is done through finance subsidiaries that could not borrow in their own right and enables the parent corporations to get both assets and debt off their balance sheets. Pools of short-term assets such as receivables, automobile loans, and the like serve as collateral for loans, domestic and international. Overcollateralization (e.g., $110 of receivables pledged to every $100 of debt) or a repurchase obligation on the issuer's part gives the investor the confidence to buy a participation. Collateralized participations are "story paper," less easy to sell on name alone, but the resulting illiquidity is offset by yields better than those on commercial paper.

More than either high-quality loans or collateralized paper, loans made to finance **leveraged buy-outs** entail difficult credits, complex financing structures, and more involved covenants and other features of the loan documentation. Subparticipation is the usual means of transferring the loans, and the participation certificates are nonnegotiable. A leveraged buy-out is generally financed by means of equity, subordinated, high-yielding debt ("junk bonds"), and senior bank loans. The latter is what is meant by LBO loans. A large proportion of such loans has been issued in the Eurodollar market, and European, Japanese, and Canadian banks have been major providers in addition to U.S. banks; indeed for some of these banks, LBO loans constitute the most active and lucrative part of their loan portfolio: lucrative, because LBO loans often pay generous up-front fees and spreads over LIBOR—usually between 1.5 and 2.5 percent in each case. This leaves quite a lot of room for the originating lender to skim off a part and still resell the loan at a seemingly attractive spread. But repayment often depends on achieving a successful turnaround in the debt-burdened acquisition or on the sale of divisions, so the loans are much riskier than the others described. Hence they can trade at a discount in the secondary market when danger lurks. The lucrative spread is easily overwhelmed by write-offs of bad debt—which is a good point at which to turn to the next subject.

TRADING LDC DEBT

Unlike the incentives for trading commercial and industrial loans, in which diversification, liquidity and genuinely differing perceptions of risk and value motivate trading, trading in LDC debt came out of the developing country debt debacle of the early 1980s that in effect forced a large portion of the loans owned by U.S. and other commercial banks to be unloaded. Other less burdened banks, some financial institutions, and opportunistic investors formed the buyers, of course at severely depressed prices. This meant that at times the prices at which the loans traded bore less relation to their "true" value than to regulation-induced supply conditions.

At one time it was thought that the bulk of depressed loans might be converted into equity (or similar risk-bearing assets) under official debt-to-equity swap programs and debt buy-backs. But those who take risk want actual or potential control over the issuer, and this has proved unacceptable to the majority of countries who have had debt servicing difficulties. Some governments have also worried that the conversion of external debt into newly minted local money might be inflationary, but such considerations have seldom inhibited some others. Instead, the countries have preferred to repurchase the debt themselves whenever they could scrape together enough money to do so.[10] Indeed, as the world's commercial banks have grown increasingly reluctant to dig themselves in even deeper in the Third World, the fact that banks have been willing to exchange loans at big dis-

---

[10] The "Brady plan" for debt burden easing conditional upon economic reform capitalized on the availability of cheap debt by asking the International Monetary Fund and World Bank to help countries repurchase their own debt if they agreed to economic reforms.

counts to face value has offered one of the few ways out of the LDC debt vortex. Of course, using available funds to repurchase debt at far less than face value violates both the spirit and in most cases the letter of the original loan agreement, so most banks recognize the improbability of getting paid back at face value and turn a blind eye. They are happy that at least *someone* is willing to buy the stuff!

One of the few other sources of end-user demand has been provided by Latin American companies restructuring their own finances or taking over enterprises from the debt-burdened public sector. Restructuring companies can win advantageous terms by converting foreign currency government debt, purchased in the market at a discount, into local currency.

Some of the debt is being securitized into fixed or floating-rate Eurobonds with official international credit enhancement; other portions have been packaged into mutual funds.

In some ways this is a market in name only. So-called market-makers do quote indicative prices, (published weekly in the *International Financing Review*—see footnote 11) but the amounts they are willing to buy for their own account is extremely limited. While the market has a nominal annual turnover of $50 to $100 billion, depending on conditions, the average deal size is said to have a *face value* of only $5 million, and trades of this size can move prices unduly.

Trading spreads are sometimes very wide, but typically on the more active debt they are about $1/_4$ point or so. Since fluctuations in price often far exceed this, and since liquidity is so poor, the half-dozen or so market makers must position themselves, looking to buy and hold undervalued debt, to make a profit commensurate with the risk.

Pricing in the interbank secondary market is strongly influenced by the extent to which banks have written down the debt on their books. Indeed any news about how banks reserve for the loans can have more influence on prices than events in the debtor country. Nobody wants to sell the loans at an accounting loss, but banks that have made severe provisions for loss may be quite willing to sell them at an economic loss if they can be sold at above their book value. Recognizing the potential for sales by well-provisioned banks, market makers try to pitch their bid prices just below the level of provisions of potential seller banks. The trouble is that book value may be strongly influenced by recent trading and quoted prices. Book value write-downs can in turn reduce the market-makers' prices in a downward cycle that has at times totally divorced traded prices from economic fundamentals.

The ability of banks to exchange LDC bank loans for "Brady bonds", where banks got the opportunity to exchange the LDC debt for liquid, safe (with respect to principal) bonds, albeit at a below-market yield, furthered the trend toward "securitization" of bank debt—a phenomenon to which we turn in the next section.

INTERMEDIATED VERSUS DIRECT CREDIT

Even a cursory survey of the international markets provides evidence of a bewildering array of lending practices and techniques.[11] Figure 6-6 reflects an attempt to put some order into chaos by ranking a number of lending techniques in terms of the determination of key aspects of a lending in the intermediated market or in the direct market. For example, in a traditional bank loan, *credit risk, funding,* and *yield* would be wholly determined within

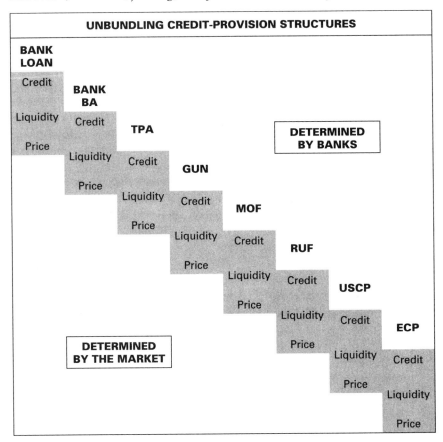

[Key: BA=Bankers Acceptance; TPA=Tender Panel Bankers Acceptance; GUN=Grantor Underwritten Note; MOF=Multiple Option Facility; RUF=Revolving Underwriting Facility; USCP=U.S. Commercial Paper; ECP=Eurocommercial Paper.

FIGURE 6-6. A Spectrum: From intermediated to direct credit.

[11] The most comprehensive survey of current practices in the international money market is provided by the *International Financing Review,* better known as IFR, published weekly in London.

the realm of (competing) financial intermediaries. At the other end of the spectrum, with respect to Eurocommercial paper, an assessment of the credit risk, the liquidity, and the yield would be directly determined in the market, that is, between investors and issuers. Banks as CP dealers only play a broker function. In the case of a banker's acceptance (BA), the rate would be determined by an anonymous market. However, the bank has some influence in terms of the total cost of the loan by pricing the acceptance fee (stamping fee) and the decision to underwrite the credit risk as well as ultimately the funding of the loan.

RUFs TO ECP: FROM INTERMEDIATION TO DIRECT SECURITIES MARKETS

As pointed out previously, the syndicated credit grafted the elements of *underwriting* and *distribution* onto traditional bank lending. This was done largely, as we stated, to distribute risks and create lender solidarity.

As usual, outside pressure on the international banking industry gave rise to further innovation. Regulators as well as suppliers of capital developed concerns about capital adequacy of banks. This in turn militated against the further growth of banks' balance sheets through low-margin assets funded in increasingly competitive money markets. Yet there was a continuing need to reconcile on a global basis the needs of cash-hungry borrowers both from the private and public sectors with the requirements of a variety of savers that needed to employ their burgeoning cash flows. The creation of "facilities" was the banking industry's reply to the divergent needs of the parties involved.[12]

The mechanics of these **revolving underwriting facilities (RUFs)** or **note issuance facilities (NIFs)** are quite straightforward—just as in a syndicated credit, a group of banks underwrites a commitment to the client-borrower; under the facility the borrower can raise funds for a period of anywhere from 3 to 10 years by issuing notes in his own name, typically with a tenor of 1 to 6 months, that the banks will sell at a price to yield not beyond a spread, say, $\frac{1}{8}$, over a reference rate, typically LIBOR. Rarely will the banks put the notes on their books and fund these assets. Indeed to do so would be considered a failure: the whole point of the operation is that the bank(s) will place the notes with investors, such as asset-hungry financial institutions; often smaller banks with captive deposit bases or institutional investors who look for short-term paper.

The facilities derive their economic rationale on the principle of "divide and conquer": the underwriting banks receive a small commitment fee but book no asset. If it works, it does wonders for their return on equity. On the

---

[12] It is often difficult to attribute financial innovations to individuals as they take place within large bureaucratic organizations where it is said that success has many fathers but failure is an orphan. Mr. Philip Colebatch, working for Citibank Hong Kong, deserves the credit for inventing the first revolving underwriting facility.

other hand, cash-rich investors do not have to enter into long-term commitments to part with their funds. They receive paper that yields a market return, and at maturity they can decide whether to acquire another asset or to look for another name if they find better alternatives.

The primary advantage of the facilities over the syndicated loan is clearly the separation of functions that permits each party to perform only that task that it feels comfortable with: it can either sell the available guarantee or it can provide the funds.

Apart from the commitment fee that the underwriting banks receive, they have the opportunity to earn a little "turn" if they have developed effective distribution capabilities that will allow them to ferret out pools of low-cost funds on a global basis.

This distribution capability can be further strengthened by making a credible commitment to investors that the bank will make a secondary market in the instruments and that will enhance the attraction of those notes with more than a very short life. Such secondary market making requires the willingness to position paper—an activity that demands risk capital and hedging capabilities. Thus relatively few banks are really good at this job, and there has been considerable concentration of this RUF/NIF activity in the hands of about 20 large internationally active banks.[13]

For borrowers the facilities provide a great deal of flexibility. Indeed, many never issue any notes and use their facilities strictly as low-cost backup facilities for other short-term borrowing sources, usually commercial paper in the domestic U.S. market. The relevant data show a striking discrepancy between facilities announced and net new issues of Euronotes.[14]

Borrowers obtain not only considerable flexibility in terms of funding— at least as good as with a syndicated credit—they also tend to get them at better rates. Indeed, by the mid-1980s facilities had taken considerable market share from the syndicated loan market. Providing the same flexibility with respect to drawdown and use, with the same committed availability guarantee (slightly but ineffectively limited by a "material adverse conditions" clause) and at a cost relative to LIBOR, which is typically less than a syndicated credit, the facilities grew rapidly.

Competitors who were less successful in originating RUF/NIF mandates, as well as regulators, raised concerns about the risk-reward ratio of the facilities. Weren't they just simply loans off balance sheet? After all, each underwriting bank had to take up the notes from the issuer if they could not be distributed to investors, whenever the investors found the credit spread over LIBOR insufficient for a particular name or because of problems in the offshore market in general. Indeed, a small volume of issues, primarily

---

[13] The annual "league tables" published in *Euromoney* or the *Institutional Investor* (International edition) provide a good picture about the dynamics of this competitive marketplace.

[14] See the Bank for International Settlements, *International Banking and Financial Market Developments* (Basle: BIS, quarterly report).

those for weaker credits, came with a "put option" that allowed the investor to return the paper prior to maturity back to the underwriting bank(s) for principal plus a pro-rata share of the interest. This version of Euronotes clearly involved the very same risk as if the underwriting/distributing bank had booked a loan and everybody agreed that they should be treated as such from a regulatory point of view. Of course, this was the end of Euronote facilities with put options!

However, the proportion of issues with such put features was very small. The overwhelming number and volume of note facilities left the investor with the default risk should such an event occur during the period while the paper was outstanding. In this respect, the banks were in the position of securities houses who pass on all the risks to the investors once they placed securities that they had underwritten. But Euronotes are more tricky; they mature within relatively short time, the bulk having a tenor of 3 to 6 months, as mentioned previously. Thus, if the condition of the issuer deteriorates slowly, but he is not technically in default, the underwriting banks cannot distribute the paper within the spread over LIBOR specified in the commitment; thus they must "eat the paper." In practice then, this becomes very much a matter of how fast the condition of the issuer deteriorates; if he dies slowly the banks find themselves in the same position as if they had extended a loan that went bad. In response to such considerations, the Bank of England began in the early 1980s to subject such facilities to a 20 percent risk weighting for capital adequacy purposes. In practice, that meant a $100 million facility was treated just like a $20 million loan to a given customer. BIS rules on capital adequacy subjected such facilities to 50 percent risk weighting.

Bankers, however, are resourceful, particularly in the international markets, and they were quick to minimize the damage to their business imposed by the new regulations. In response to the new restrictions, they created the MOF, the multiple option facility. To minimize demands on equity capital, an MOF was constructed around a relatively small, **committed revolving credit**, say, $50 million out of a $200 million or $250 million facility. The remainder consisted of several layers of uncommitted facilities such as banker's acceptance facilities in several different markets and commercial paper programs, both onshore and offshore. The client paid a facility fee of, say, 1/16 and was able to use the various facilities if they provided cash at costs competitive with alternative funding sources. While the volume of RUFs/NIFs has decreased substantially, MOFs appear to survive.

EUROCOMMERCIAL PAPER
AS A LENDING DEVICE

At first sight, it may seem odd to use commercial paper, domestic or Euro, to illustrate an offshore market lending technique since this "innovation" has a long and successful history in the U.S. domestic market.

The origins of commercial paper in the United States go back almost a century. The market has grown tremendously, and at the end of the 1980s, it had reached a volume of almost $400 billion paper outstanding. In the United States, corporations and their captive finance companies are the most important issuers. They raise funds efficiently by placing notes with investors, either through a dealer or directly. Many of the investors in turn are cash-rich corporations. However, there are many other buyers, including money market mutual funds and more traditional institutional investors. It is important to note that this investor clientele in the U.S. domestic market tends to be very risk averse. This is because the investment of short-term funds in commercial paper is incidental to the firm's "real" risk-taking activity in the markets for goods and services. Thus it is essential that the paper of an issuer has an acceptable rating by one of the rating agencies such as Moody's or Standard & Poor's. Furthermore, since the market tends to reject the name of an issuer whose credit standing deteriorates, or on rare occasions, when the CP market as a whole is affected by general concerns about credit, availability of funds becomes a problem for the issuer. For that reason, issuers in the U.S. market obtain as a matter of course "committed backup lines" from banks for a small fee. In return, the banks will make funds available when the issuer is shut out from the CP market, albeit usually at a predetermined, stiff price such as the U.S. prime rate or above.

In the 1980s, the USCP market received an additional boost by accepting foreign issuers, or domestic issuers who were considered lesser credits, to sell paper under a letter of credit (L/C) from a reputable financial institution, which effectively transfers the credit risk to the issuer of the L/C. This L/C-backed paper tends to trade at a very small spread of only a few basis points over the paper of the issuer of the L/C since the L/C effectively transfers the credit risk.

The economics of a CP market are founded on the fact that the need for a financial intermediary and the associated cost is eliminated. Of course, this makes sense only if the service provided by the intermediary is not worth its cost. Traditionally, the U.S. market has been characterized by a fragmented banking system that had to bear a number of regulatory costs. At the same time, the nonfinancial sector offered a wider variety of very creditworthy corporate issuers. With the weakening of the money center banks due to the LDC debt crisis in the 1980s, the banking sector has also lost credit standing in relative terms and, accordingly, the CP market has flourished.[15]

Eurocommercial paper, as so often in the offshore market, is a little different. Like its U.S. counterpart, Eurocommercial paper (ECP) is an unse-

---

[15]Robert N. McCauley, and Lauren A. Hargraves, "Eurocommercial Paper and U.S. Commercial Paper: Converging Money Markets?" *Federal Reserve Bank of New York Quarterly Review*, Autumn 1987, pp. 24–35. See also J. S. Alsworth and C. E. V. Borio, "Commercial Paper Markets: A Survey," Bank for International Settlement, Economic Papers, No. 37, April 1993.

cured promissory note, but it is issued and placed outside the jurisdiction of the currency of denomination. ECP was introduced in the early 1970s when the U.S. capital transfer restrictions forced U.S. corporate borrowers to raise funds abroad for international expansion. However, the growth of the ECP market ran into a fundamental problem. The major incentive for avoiding intermediation, that is, evading the regulatory costs, was absent in the Euromarket. Thus bank borrowing and Eurodollar deposits provided for effective competition to the funding via ECP. Disintermediation was unattractive, indeed, until approximately 1982, when the credit standing of major banks began to deteriorate, both onshore as well as offshore. The relative strength of nonbank borrowers, largely well-known multinational corporations and governmental entities, gave them subsequently a significant cost advantage over banks due to the fact that investors were willing to accept lower yields that would enable them to diversify away from perceived bank risks.

A comparison between USCP and ECP illustrates a phenomenon already found in the Eurobond market: various regulations and institutional practices introduce mild barriers to arbitrage, while at the same time investors in each market are driven by somewhat different criteria that lead to (variable) cost differentials between the two markets. Specifically, the market characteristics separating the dollar ECP market from the U.S. domestic CP market are as follows:

- Buyers of ECP, coming from a broad range of countries, draw credit distinctions but do not divide issuers consistently by nationality. U.S. investors in CP systematically require foreign issuers to offer higher yields than like-rated U.S. issuers.

- The average rating of U.S. issuers in the ECP market is of significantly lower quality than U.S. issuers in the USCP market. Foreign issuers in the United States show a distribution of quality significantly better than that of U.S. issuers in the ECP market.

- Central banks, corporations, and banks are the important parts of the investor base for particular segments of the ECP market. The most important USCP holders—money market funds—are not very important abroad.

- The average maturity of ECP remains about twice as long as that of USCP. Thus ECP continues to be actively traded in the secondary market; in contrast, most USCP is held to maturity by the original investors.

- Issuing, clearance, and payment of ECP are more dispersed geographically and more time consuming than they are for USCP.

- Dealing is highly competitive in the ECP market; in contrast, two firms dominate half the dealer-placed USCP.

- To date, all ECP has been placed by third parties. Many USCP issuers place paper directly with investors.

- Credit ratings and committed backup lines associated with them are necessary in the USCP market; in the ECP market, they are common, but paper can be sold without such credit enhancement.
- ECP has been and mostly continues to be priced in relation to bank deposit interest rates. Pricing in the United States is based on absolute rates that vary in relation to rates on Treasury bills and bank certificates of deposit (CDs).

The major difference, then, is again the somewhat different credit assessment in the Euromarket that we have already encountered when discussing the Eurobond market. Interestingly, events during 1989 changed that somewhat. During that year, several issuers of ECP defaulted and investors were hurt. In one or two cases, the markets were simply surprised by the sudden default of the issuer. However, losses in U.S. domestic paper programs were less since the rating agencies in the other cases downgraded the domestic issue and investors reacted in time. More important was the fact that investors were able to react since the maturity of paper issued in the ECP market is several months on average longer than in the domestic market.[16]

In the next section we examine the way in which international banks use medium-term notes (MTNs) as a substitute lending device. Medium-term notes were introduced in Chapter Five as one of the means by which Eurobanks can obtain medium- and long-term funding.

MEDIUM-TERM NOTE PROGRAMS[17]

The MTN is a commercial paper–like instrument that has a maturity rivaling that of a corporate bond. Indeed medium-term notes are issued today with maturities ranging from 9 months to as much as 30 years—a lot longer than is available in the Eurobond market. In contrast to commercial paper, medium-term notes (MTNs) had their origins in the tap CD markets offshore. A medium-term note, the reader may recall, is simply an IOU with a maturity of anywhere from 6 months to 10 years or more, placed at the issuer's risk without the firm underwriting commitment that we find in the bond market. In this respect, the MTN is very similar to CP. Except for the method of underwriting and distribution, however, most of the characteristics of MTNs are similar to those of bonds: they pay coupons, the securities are cleared in the same way, and the same documentation is required.

From the issuer's perspective a company may issue according to its needs for funds and exploit special "windows" of temporary demand for its

---

[16] "EuroCP: A Crisis of Credibility," Euromoney *Corporate Finance*, December 1989, pp. 20–21.

[17] For more detail see Suresh E. Krishnan, "Multi-Tranche Tap Note Programs (MTTNs)," *Currency and Bond Market Trends* (Merrill Lynch), August 24, 1987, pp. 3–4.

paper over certain maturity ranges. The flexibility of the medium-term note structure is what appeals to issuers; like CP, it is a continually offered program with wide-ranging maturity options. Issuing houses appreciate MTNs too; unlike bond underwriting, they do not take an underwriting risk. Investors like MTNs, because the placement house's commitment to make a liquid market is kept alive as long as it is interested in managing the MTN program.

In contrast, with a bond issue, once the bonds are placed, the investment bank quickly loses interest in making a secondary market. The difference in the distribution method also affects the type of customer. Large bond issues tend to favor institutional investors who will relieve the issuing house of its underwriting commitment by snapping up a large chunk of the issue. MTN programs, in contrast, are more flexible and appeal to the upper segment of private investor clientele, who are willing to make yield concessions in return for an acceptable name and a believable promise of liquidity.

The notes are typically unsecured but need not be. They pay interest on a 30/360-day basis, unlike deposits that pay on actual/360 terms. Some have floating rates based on an index such as LIBOR just like FRNs. Unlike corporate bonds, few are callable. Like commercial paper, most domestic MTNs are rated while most Euro-MTNs are unrated.[18] Their most significant distinguishing feature is a subtle one—the fact that their issuance and even maturity is largely *investor determined*, not issuer determined. (This is also true of the Eurocommercial paper market.) Corporate bonds are issued infrequently and often entail relatively heavy issuance costs, so the borrower wants to do the issue in large amounts at a known cost and get it distributed as widely as possible. This means that there must be an underwriting syndicate. Not so with MTNs or deposit notes. Paper is issued through dealers when, in the amount, and for the maturity that the investor wants. MTNs and deposit notes issued by top-name banks have achieved the status of a commodity; very few Eurobonds have.

For example, Siemens, the German industrial concern, as issuer might tell the dealers representing it that Siemens will accept any money in the 1- to 5-year range at a certain spread relative to the benchmark Treasury yields. The dealers would let their customers know from day to day who was offering notes at what rates and the paper would be sold only on a "best-efforts" basis—if and when an investor wanted it. If a Swiss bank trust

---

[18] Like the commercial paper market, the medium-term note market had its origins in the United States. Euro-MTNs are very much like domestic MTNs, with many of the same issuers and the same cast of broker-dealers, although a somewhat different investor base. And, of course, there's no Euro-SEC, so some issuers prefer it from a disclosure point of view. As with the commercial paper market, most MTN programs are now "global": they offer the issuer access to either market, to spread its sources and tap the cheapest.

department calls the broker (say, CSFB) and says "I'll buy $20 million of $3\frac{1}{2}$-year Siemens medium term notes at 45 over," the deal would be struck there and then, and Siemens would only then be contacted to confirm the trade! Much easier than waiting for the right Eurobond to be issued. Cheaper for Siemens too,[19] although perhaps a little less predictable than a $250 million underwritten Eurobond. The bank will still get its quarter billion, albeit in dribs and drabs and at different levels. The MTN market has good, perhaps not outstanding, secondary market liquidity. MTNs by their nature lack the large size of identical bonds issued in a big corporate bond issue, but they have borrowed so many of the successful features of the commercial paper market—such as broker-sponsored programs, continuous offerings of primary paper, and good market-maker support—that they have replaced underwritten Eurobonds and domestic bonds as the preferred source of longer-term funds for many international corporations.

This concludes our discussion of the evolution of particular lending techniques in the international banking market. But the story is not over—new approaches will surely appear before the print is dry. For this reason it is important to gain some perspective on the character of this continual unbundling of the features of lending instruments, a process known to some as "securitization."

A FOOTNOTE: TRUE SECURITIZATION OF LOANS

One hears a great deal about securitization in the banking industry. Yet true securitization of Euromarket or domestic loans is of small dimensions today, and there is reason to believe that it will not come to dominate lending instruments in the future. To see why it is small, consider the three ways in which credit is provided to most borrowers. Traditional bank loans are **intermediated credit**. Bank loans that are syndicated and later sold to investors are done as **private placements**. They are not designed to be traded back and forth; indeed as we have seen most of them take the form of one-on-one contracts and are not negotiable. Commercial paper and bonds, on the other hand, are examples of negotiable, tradable publically issued **securities**. While there is nothing in principle preventing someone from converting a bank loan into a true security, the market has to date found that the private placement method serves the purpose.

---

[19] Siemens may prefer to fund with floating-rate liabilities, so whenever a dealer succeeds in placing some fixed-rate paper, the company will swap it into floating to achieve a sub-LIBOR, perhaps even sub-LIBID, cost of funds.

WHEN LIQUIDITY IS UNNECESSARY

When does it add value? When investors have uncertain cash needs.

What is lost by transferability and securitization? The anonymous transfer of claims breaks down the lender-borrower relationship and sacrifices the monitoring and renegotiating role of the continuous lender.

Why is liquidity less important today?

- Large institutions have long-term liabilities and no frequent need to cash out of the market, and a greater proportion of assets are held by institutions.
- For such institutions, illiquidity is much more tolerable since they can unload market risks via *derivative securities* while retaining ownership of the actual assets.

Thus true securitization of bank loans themselves is rare. The reason is that there is usually substantial value to be had from the relationship between the lender and the borrower—the lender wants to be able to monitor and influence the activities and condition of the borrower, and each may want to alter the terms of the loan if circumstances change. Hence the elaborate provisions in participations and assignments for who will renegotiate if the time comes to do so. With scattered, anonymous investors, the possibility to renegotiate becomes remote. Hence, we believe that illiquidity will prevail and securitization will be exceptional for one major class of the credit market.

While *individual* loans are almost never securitized, there have been attempts to create securities out of *pools of loans*. One way to do this is simply to create a closed-end mutual fund that issues shares and uses the proceeds to purchase a diversified portfolio of loans. Several mutual funds of this kind have been set up to invest in deep-discount loans to developing countries. Investors have a pure equity stake in the servicing and value of the loans (which continue to be administered by the lead manager), and all investors gain or lose equally. The investors in such a fund are obviously pure speculators: earning a miserable spread as in a conventional loan is the farthest thing from their minds.

A different kind of loan securitization takes its cue from the U.S. mortgage-backed securities market. As in collateralized mortgage obligations (known as CMOs), a special-purpose company is set up to purchase a pool of claims—in this case, senior LBO loans. The cash flow from the claims are split up and assigned to different classes of investors in the special-purpose vehicle. In one version, the special purpose vehicle issues floating-rate notes and equity. Holders of the floating-rate notes, issued in the form of a

Eurobond, are promised a set spread over LIBOR and priority on the payment of interest and the repayment of principal. They also get the benefit of diversification.

Because they are safer, the floating-rate notes pay a spread somewhat lower than that on raw LBO loans. The equityholders get the residual. If all goes well and interest and principal are repaid in full, investors in both the floating-rate notes and the equity get a good return; if not, the equity investors bear the first brunt of the losses. The general principle, in both CMOs and repackaged LBO loans, is one of segmenting the cash flow to create new return and risk combinations to tap classes of investors other than the original holders of the claims. If this need is correctly identified and satisfied, the reconstituted pool is worth more than the sum of the individual loans. But if this is done at the cost of a loss of the "monitoring" role of the bank-type investor, the underlying loans become riskier and value may be lost.

We can sum up the value and costs of securitization as follows. *Securitization adds value* when it enables debt to be sold into new markets, giving a wider range of investors a wider choice of assets. If the securities are standardized or at least easily comparable with like securities, they gain liquidity which is important to some (but see the box on the subject of investors for whom liquidity is unnecessary). Loans are worth securitizing when the bank securitizing its assets is able to get a higher price for the package than the sum of the components *is worth to the particular bank.* For example, a pool of diversified loans with sufficient overcollateralization (plus substitutability of assets), and perhaps with letters of credit or surety bonds, may enable the bank to secure a AAA rating on a security backed by otherwise risky debt. If this opens up a new market, it may reduce the cost of capital to the originating financial institution.

Of course investors in such a pool lose all hands-on influence over the borrowers, whose behavior is constrained only by legal remedies and reputation, that is, future recourse to the public market.

So *value is reduced* when the costs of reduced monitoring exceed the gains from diversification, market segmentation, and liquidity. Value is also reduced by the costs of origination and compliance with securities regulations. In addition, the cost of capital to the financial institution may not be reduced and may even rise: (1) the bank has pledged its best assets, and (2) overcollateralization means more assets committed than financing raised (excess has to be financed elsewhere). Both imply that the residual portfolio of the bank is riskier, which should reduce the value of other, uncollateralized debt and of equity of the institution, thus raising its cost of capital by an amount at least equal to the cost savings produced by the securitized loans.[20]

---

[20] Exception: (1) if the debt market or the equity market is not efficient or (2) if the government (FDIC) provides explicit or implicit deposit insurance and does not increase the costs or constraints on the institution following the effective disposal of the less risky assets.

SUMMARY

Euromarket lending differs from domestic lending only insofar as there are few constraints on the fundamental contribution of financial innovation: separation, or "unbundling" of financial claims. The market itself is the result of a fundamental innovation: the separation of the currency of denomination from the respective jurisdiction. In this chapter we have seen how the Euromarket was the forerunner of the now universal practice of syndication, which separates the arranging and servicing of loans from the provision of funds. Just as syndicated Eurocredits provided wider distribution of pieces of a loan or facility, so the techniques of loan transfer allowed banks to resell their pieces in an evolving loan sales market. Large-scale lending has thus assumed many of the attributes of underwriting and distribution in the investment banking world.

Yet it was the Euromarket again that evolved the set of techniques that separate the provision of short-term credit from the provision of "availability" assurance. The note issuance facility allows some banks to buy short-term negotiable paper while others offer longer-term "underwriting" facilities that guarantee issuers' access to the market or to bank credit. This sort of backup facility, and the shepherding of the distribution of related commercial paper and medium-term notes into a much broader investor market, is where the action in Euromarket credit provision is today.

Last but not least, with the Euromarkets as the focal point of international competition for bank loans, it is here where spreads have been driven to their competitive equilibrium, and at occasions below, and that has made bank lending to creditworthy borrowers an activity of marginal profitability for banks even in national markets.

SELECTED REFERENCES

Aliber, Robert Z., *The International Money Game*, 5th ed. New York: Basic Books, 1987.

Bradlow, D., "Outline of Key Legal Issues in International Loan Agreements." In D. Bradlow and W. J. Jourdin, eds., *International Borrowing: Negotiation and Renegotiation*. Washington, D.C.: International Law Institute, 1984.

Davis, Steven I., *The Eurobank*, New York: John Wiley and Sons, 1976.

Einzig, Paul, *The Eurodollar System*, 5th ed. New York: St. Martin's Press, 1973.

Einzig, Paul, *Roll-Over Credits*. New York: St. Martin's Press, 1973 .

"EuroCP: A Crisis of Credibility," *Euromoney Corporate Finance*, December 1989, pp. 20–21.

Gersovitz, M., "Banks' International Lending Decisions: What We Know and Implications for Future Research." In G. Smith and J. Cuddington, eds., *International Debt and the Developing Countries*. Washington D.C.: The World Bank, 1985.

Krishnan, Suresh E., "Multi-Tranche Tap Note Programs (MTTNs)," *Currency and Bond Market Trends*, Merrill Lynch, August 24, 1987, pp. 3–4.

Levine, David, "It's Time for Eurobankers to Work Out What They Mean by Market Practice," *Euromoney*, August 1976, pp. 38–48.

MacCullum, R. K., "Sovereign Debt Restructuring: The Rights and Duties of Commercial Banks Inter Sese," *Columbia Business Law Review*, Vol. 2, 1987, pp. 425–457.

Mathis, F. John, ed., *Offshore Lending by U.S. Commercial Banks*. Washington, D.C.: Robert Morris Associates, 1975.

McCauley, Robert N., and Lauren A. Hargraves, "Eurocommercial Paper and U.S. Commercial Paper: Converging Money Markets?" *Federal Reserve Bank of New York Quarterly Review*, Autumn 1987, pp. 24–35.

McCrary, Dennis, and Jo Ousterhout, "The Development and Future of the Loan Sales Market, "*Continental Bank Journal of Applied Corporate Finance*, (Date), pp. 74–84.

Nirenberg, D. Z., "International Loan Syndications: The Next Security," *Columbia Journal of Transnational Law*, Vol. 23, 1984, pp. 155–175.

Park, Yoon S., *The Eurobond Market*. New York: Praeger, 1974.

Park, Yoon S., "Structure and Function of the Eurocredit Market," *Euromoney*, April 1974, pp. 73–81.

Semkow, B. W., "Syndicating and Rescheduling International Financial Trans-actions: A Survey of Legal Issues Encountered by Commercial Banks," *International Lawyer*, Vol. 18, Fall 1984, pp. 869–892.

Van Horne, James C., *Financial Market Rates and Flows*, 3rd ed. Englewood Cliffs, NJ: Prentice Hall, 1990.

Wood, P. R., *Law and Practice of International Finance*. New York: Clark Boardman, 1980.

Wood, P. R., "Sharing Clauses in Syndicated Loan Agreements." In D. Pierce, ed., *Current Issues in International Financial Law*. Singapore: Butterworth, 1985.

Yassukovich, S. M., "The Duties of a Lead Manager," *Euromoney*, August 1974, pp. 4–6.

APPENDIX 6-A
Clauses in Typical Eurodollar Loan Agreements[1]

1. *Denomination of the loan currency* is, of course, the first step. In a world of floating exchange rates and drastic currency changes, currency risks must be assumed. Availability of funds, on one hand, and purpose and intended use of the proceeds, on the other, are the main determinants for the currency choice. As the currency must have a broad international market and be convertible into other currencies at all times, nearly all loans are denominated in U.S. dollars, followed by Deutschemarks.

2. *Length of the loan* and maturities of repayment are subject to many considerations. Generally, corporate loans do not exceed seven years at the most.

3. *The amount* has no limit, as long as lenders are willing to provide the funds. Corporate borrowers, however, must not overextend themselves. Unsound indebtedness may jeopardize the transaction and the borrower's credit standing.

4. A must in all agreements is a clear stipulation of the *interest rate*. Few loans carry a fixed interest rate; the "variable" or "floating" rate has become generally accepted. It is expressed as a spread or premium in percent per annum above LIBOR, i.e. the London Interbank Offered Rate for six-month Eurodollars. While this procedure is generally acceptable to lender and borrower, the variable subject to competitive negotiation is the size of the premium. A clause that gives lender and borrower the right to cancel the loan at the roll-over date because agreement on the interest rate cannot be reached is becoming more frequent in loan contracts.

---

[1] This material is reprinted with permission from Business International Corporation, *Financing Foreign Operations* (New York: BIC, updated periodically).

5. A clause to cover *general increases in cost* is increasingly demanded by lenders. A special clause now used very frequently is the *reserve requirement clause,* which stipulates that the borrower has to absorb any additional cost the lender incurs when a country requires the lending bank to keep interest-free reserves with the central bank, which in effect increases the cost of money. An example is the reserve which may be required by the United States under Regulation M on any Eurodollar borrowings brought into the country. With this clause, lending banks are also trying to recover any additional cost, even if loosely related to compulsory reserve requirements.

6. Eurodollar availability has usually been taken for granted, and no difficulties have ever arisen in delivery (or repayment) of this currency. However, European banks in particular are concerned about the remote possibility of unavailability of Eurodollars, and a special *availability clause* is creeping into loan contracts. The clause, still hotly disputed, gives the bank the right to call for a prepayment if sufficient dollar funds are not available. The clause would not protect the borrower if invoked.

7. Favoring the borrower is a new, generally acceptable *currency option clause* or "multi-currency option," which permits the borrower to switch currencies and draw down funds in currencies other than the one denominated in the loan agreement. For example, he can draw funds of a Eurodollar loan in Deutschemarks or French francs or any other convertible currency at the current rate of exchange.

   A different type of *currency option* is switching the loan—entirely or in part—into another currency, normally permissible only at roll-over time. Exercising such an option becomes an important choice when a devaluation or revaluation is expected.

8. A *prepayment clause* gives the borrower the right to repay a loan before maturity; banks often do not like this provision, but if a penalty is stipulated difficulties rarely arise.

9. Provisions to deal with possible *default* are essential, and the lender almost invariably insists on a clause covering this risk. Banks often try to go beyond the normal covering and ask for a *cross default clause* that would allow the lender, in case of default of the borrower, to have recourse to any member of the borrowing group. Most borrowers resent this extension of a default provision.

10. A *guarantee clause* will normally be included if the borrower is a subsidiary or his credit standing alone is not acceptable. Government guarantees are frequent.

11. In lieu of, or in addition to, a guarantee, a *negative pledge clause*, stipulating that a firm's assets cannot be used as collateral for additional borrowing, has come into use upon demand by lending banks for more security. Its usefulness is, however, questionable, and even if given by the borrower is often not enforceable.

12. A clause relating to *jurisdiction* is a must in all loan agreements. Borrower and lender must be aware that there are important differences between, for example, U.S. and U.K. law, and in case of court action omission of this clause may raise grave problems.

13. The growth of the Eurocurrency markets geographically (London, Asia, Mid-East, etc.) has encouraged the use of a clause that states that banks can *deliver* the funds from any financial center they choose. Borrowers try to win a similar right of choice from which market to receive the funds. The reason for such clauses is the interest rate differential that may exist between markets.

14. A clause that would stipulate the *use of the loan funds* by the borrower has frequently been included but has lost much meaning. It is unenforceable, but banks always grant a loan based on intended use of the funds.

15. U.S. banks nearly always require *promissory notes* as evidence of the indebtedness, while U.K.-based banks mostly do not. Granting promissory notes can cause problems because of legal differences; if lender and borrower reside in different countries, the legal situation could be quite complicated.

16. A *tax clause* covering the often extremely complex tax situation and its impact on interest rates and cost of the loan has proved to be important. With changing tax laws, banks can pass on higher taxes to the borrower.

17. Funds are frequently *drawn down* by the borrower in stages. It is essential that agreement is reached on a drawdown schedule, stipulating the time periods and amounts. Some agreements provide that borrowers can call in funds over a period of several years, and even the first call has sometimes been postponed until after one year or up to three years (a reverse "grace period"). Large capital projects can be financed this way and the borrower has the guarantee that necessary funds are available when needed. Lenders require a commitment fee for unused funds until they are drawn.

Chapter Seven

PUBLIC POLICY AND THE INTERNATIONAL MONEY MARKET

Contents: *Controlling Money and Banking   The Eurocurrency Market and National Monetary and Exchange-Rate Policy   Case 1: The Eurocurrency Market, Liquidity, and Monetary Control   A Single Currency   Case 2: The Eurocurrency Market, Aggregate Liquidity, and Monetary Control   International Capital Flows   Monetary Policy and the Monetary Base   Monetary Policy and Utilization of the Monetary Base   Measurement and Policy   Currency Substitution   Conclusions on the Macroeconomic Policy Implications of the Euromarkets   The Need for Controls: The Soundness of Financial Institutions   The Need for Controls: Allocation of Credit   Distributional Effects   The Ability of Governments to Control the Euromarkets   Summary and Conclusions   Selected References*

CONTROLLING MONEY AND BANKING

Since its very beginning the Eurocurrency market has been the subject of controversy. Much of the dispute about its origin and its workings has focused on the need to control the market and its institutions. The emphasis of the debate has shifted considerably with the passage of time: in the 1960s the major concern was with the market's alleged destabilizing effects on the exchange parities fixed under the Bretton Woods system. The inexorable trend of accelerating inflation in the 1970s concentrated attention on the market's impact on the conduct of monetary policy. In the second half of that decade, observers were mesmerized by the market's pivotal role in recycling the OPEC surplus into loans to risky countries. Finally, in the wake of the worldwide recessions of the early 1990s, the policy debate shifted to issues of bank safety and prudential control, an issue highlighted

by government bailouts of financial institutions in a number of countries
and the spectacular collapse of the Bank of Credit and Commerce International (BCCI) in 1991. Throughout the decades, a lack of understanding created an aura of mystery about the offshore markets which caused suspicion,
often fueled by policy makers who were averse to free markets to begin with
and were only too happy to find in the international banking market a convenient scapegoat for policies that resulted in too much inflation, or unintended recessions, or both.[1]

Once one abstracts from the concerns and disputes of the day, some
broad areas of agreement about financial market control stand out. First,
economists generally agree that it is a legitimate responsibility of government to control the volume of liquidity in a banking system that is based on
paper currency, where payments are made mostly by transferring the ownership of demand liabilities in commercial banks. This control is necessary if
for no other reason than to keep the growth of the money supply from leading to excessive price inflation. Mandatory reserve requirements on the
deposit liabilities of banks and the open-market purchase and sale of (public
sector) securities are the major traditional means used by monetary authorities to achieve this goal.[2] A related set of policy tools are those that aim at
exchange rates through official intervention—the buying and selling of foreign currencies by the central bank.

A second objective of banking regulation is to ensure the availability of
credit for certain economic activities, groups, and institutions. In effect this
means that the government seeks to allocate credit to groups to whom the
private market will not grant sufficient funds, or to provide favored sectors
with credit at below-market rates.

A third objective of regulating the behavior of banking institutions is to
limit the consequences of a bank failure for depositors and for the financial
system in general. The collapse of a bank, because it holds the means of payment and liquid balances of business firms and households, can have a disproportionately disruptive effect on a community and even on the whole
financial system if failure (or the fear thereof) leads to a banking panic.

[1]Actually, few if any of the problems originated in the offshore markets but were typically the result of recessions in *national* markets. The BCCI case also had little to do with the Euromarkets; losses were incurred through ill-fated treasury activities in London and some of the bank's North American offices got caught taking deposits from drug dealers. The way the bank was liquidated shows clearly a lack of international cooperation: while US regulators were able to obtain several hundred millions in funds for fines, depositors in London and elsewhere got only a fraction of their money.

[2]Other means, such as ceilings on credit volume, restrictions on the payment of interest on deposits, and the maintenance of certain rations among different kinds of assets and/or liabilities, may be considered useful but are not necessary to achieve the basic objective of monetary control. Indeed, such methods generally have a secondary objective associated with the allocation of credit.

All arguments for government intervention in financial markets in general and the banking system in particular fall within one or more of these three basic categories. In what follows we shall examine the case for government intervention in the Euromarkets in these terms. But since the focus of government policy is necessarily on the individual nation state, the relevant question may be phrased as follows: *To what extent is the regulation and control of activities in the external money markets a prerequisite for achieving national objectives of monetary control, safe banking, and improved credit allocation?*

THE EUROCURRENCY MARKET AND NATIONAL MONETARY AND EXCHANGE-RATE POLICY

When a country's monetary system is based on fiat money, the conduct of monetary policy—focusing on the rate of growth of the money supply—becomes an essential function of government economic policy. In all countries, monetary policy tends to be highly politicized because the use of the "printing press" provides power, real or imagined, to affect real output as well as the distribution of income. Moreover, the conduct of monetary policy raises a number of complex technical questions dividing even those who might agree on the general strategy of the central monetary authorities. Such contentious issues range from the question of what is the most appropriate tool all the way to the nature of the mechanism linking a central bank's liabilities to the volume of economic activity.

In times past, the growth of the Eurocurrency markets provided a convenient scapegoat for what is really the failure of the political system to pursue policies that are optimal in the long run. Today most policy makers as well as economists recognize that the offshore market is merely one segment of the broader national money market in a particular currency. Even so it is instructive to consider the functioning and effectiveness of monetary policy in a world where substantial proportions of banking assets are on the books of institutions outside the country where the currency is means of payment. After all, banks operating "offshore" do business in a different regulatory environment than banks "onshore." Does this situation affect the ability of a central bank to conduct monetary policy?

In an appendix to Chapter One the simplistic idea of autonomous multiple credit creation in the Eurocurrency market was laid to rest. However, three issues of interest to those concerned with the monetary implications of the market remain:

1. Does the growth of the Eurocurrency market affect monetary aggregates?

2. Is total liquidity expanded in a systematic way by the growth of an external market?

3. Does the existence and growth of the Eurocurrency market inhibit the pursuit of independent monetary policies by national governments?

As the answer to one of these questions does not necessarily prejudice the answers to the others, we shall address them separately, step by step.

CASE 1: THE EUROCURRENCY MARKET, LIQUIDITY, AND MONETARY CONTROL— A SINGLE CURRENCY

First, we will analyze the situation where financial transactions take place only between a national financial system and its parallel external market. This would, for example, be the case when there are only U.S. borrowers and lenders and they have only two alternatives for borrowing and depositing: the domestic market or the external market based in, say, Nassau (Bahamas). Thus, all financial links between the dollar area (both its external and internal sectors) and the financial markets of other currencies are assumed to be cut off.

As the following example demonstrates, when the Eurodollar market expands because of the transfer of business from a U.S. bank to a Eurobank, *credit extended in the Eurodollar market substitutes for, rather than adds to, domestic credit creation.* However, total credit may be increased as a result of a small amount of bank reserves that are released because Eurobanks are free of legal reserve requirements while domestic deposits are subject to, say, a 5 percent reserve requirement.

EXAMPLE

Consider Figures 7-1 and 7-2. In Figure 7-1, two hypothetical U.S. investors, Able and Kane, each have $200 in time deposits in First

FEDERAL RESERVE BANK OF NEW YORK

T-bills		—	$40	First Manhattan

First Manhattan (U.S.)

Reserves for DD liabilities (20%)	$20	$100	Demand deposits
Loans	80		
Reserves for TD liabilities (5%)	$20	$200	Time deposits due to Able
Loan to Corporation A	190	200	Time deposits due to Kane
Loan to Corporation B	190		

FIGURE 7–1. Time Deposits in the U.S. before a Shift to the Eurodollar Market.

FEDERAL RESERVE BANK OF NEW YORK

T-bills	—	$40	First Manhattan

Second Eurobank Nassau (Bahamas)

Due from First Manhattan	$10	$200	Time deposits due to Able
Loan to Corporation A	90		

First Manhattan (U.S.)

Reserves for DD liabilities (20%)	$22	$100	Demand deposits
Loans	80	10	Due to Second Eurobank
Reserves for TD liabilities (5%)	$10	$200	Time deposits due to Kane
Excess reserves	8		
Loan to Corporation A	190		

FIGURE 7–2. Time Deposits in the Eurodollar Market after Transfer from the U.S.

Manhattan, a large New York bank. These funds, less required reserves of 5 percent, are loaned by First Manhattan to two corporations. The financial system is in equilibrium.

Figure 7–2 depicts a shift of intermediation to the external market and the initial consequences thereof. Able, discovering that Eurobanks are able to offer slightly more attractive interest rates than are domestic banks, withdraws his deposit from First Manhattan and places it with Second Eurobank Nassau—while Kane for reasons of ignorance or risk aversion, makes no such shift. However, the Eurobank is only interested in bidding for these funds when it can lend them at an adequate spread over the deposit rate. Since the bank must pay interest on the Eurodollar deposit, which by definition is an interest-bearing time deposit, it will make a loan almost immediately, usually on the very same day. This process is greatly helped by the fact that First Manhattan finds itself short of funds and considerably less willing to renew the loan to Corporation A, while the external Eurobank is eager to lend. As shown in Figure 7-2, the deposits and loans on First Manhattan's books have shrunk while those of the Eurobank have expanded.

In the example given, no increase in credit extended or aggregate liquidity has occurred, despite the shift of funds to a banking system free of reserve requirements. But the process is not yet complete. While the balance sheet approach of T-accounts can show different static situations, it does not properly depict the dynamic shift to a new equilibrium that occurs as a result of changes in institutions, interest sensitivity, or portfolio preferences.

In particular, three important aspects of the transaction are *not* shown in Figure 7-2.

1. In reality, a number of transfers would occur through the demand deposit accounts in the U.S. Indeed, all Eurodollar transactions are executed through demand deposit accounts in U.S. banks without affecting, *a priori*, the total stock of such deposits.

2. Reserves of offshore banks are minimal. They are wholly or partially loaned out because Eurobanks are not required to retain reserve balances with the Federal Reserve or any other institution; they hold balances only for operating purposes. The $10 of reserves held by Second Eurobank Nassau will be put to work.

3. Excess *domestic* reserves (such as those held by First Manhattan in the example), freed because of the absence of reserve requirements on Eurobanks, may be partially loaned out, so that final credit will increase by a multiple of the freed reserves. The division of this extra credit among demand deposits, domestic and Eurobank time deposits, and currency will depend on interest rates and the portfolio preferences of the public.

EXAMPLE

Figure 7-3 illustrates the possible effects of the last two points. Assume that the $10 that Second Eurobank Nassau had in First Manhattan is fully loaned out (to Corporation C) and after domestic credit has been

FEDERAL RESERVE BANK OF NEW YORK

T-bills		—	$40	First Manhattan

Second Eurobank Nassau (Bahamas)				
Loan to Corporation A	$190		$200	Time deposits due to Able
Loan to Corporation C	10			

First Manhattan (U.S.)				
Reserves for DD liabilities (20%)	$25		$125	Demand deposits
Loans	100			
Reserves for TD liabilities (5%)	$15		$200	Time deposits due to Kane
Loan to Corporation A	190		100	Others' TDs
Other loans	95			

FIGURE 7–3.   Possible Final Credit Expansion after Shift of Deposits to the Eurodollar Market.

expanded on the basis of the $8 of freed reserves, the public holds domestic demand and time deposits in the same proportion as before (1:4).[3] Then, as shown in Figure 7-3, total dollar credit has expanded from $460 to $585 ($200 in Second Eurobank plus $385 in First Manhattan). In other words, for each $1 shift from U.S. banks into Eurobanks, $0.63 of additional dollar credit will be extended. If the new credit had all been placed in time deposits, $1 of credit expansion would have resulted from a $1 shift; if all had been held in demand deposits with 20 percent reserve requirements, only $0.25 of credit expansion would have occurred.

The amount of domestic credit expansion that results from a shift to the Eurodollar market thus depends on the amount shifted (call this x), the reserve ratio on the assets shifted (r), and the domestic credit multiplier (m). Given these, we can determine the expansion as:

$$\text{\textit{Credit expansion resulting from a \$x shift to Eurodollar market}} = xrm$$

The amount of reserves that is freed by the shift is xr. Thus, if the monetary authorities wish to offset the expansionary effect caused by a shift to the external market, they must reduce the banking systems' reserves (high powered money) by xr.

The conclusion so far is quite straightforward:

When depositors shift from deposits in domestic banks to deposits in external banks, the total volume of credit extended rises because domestic deposits are subject to reserve requirements while the same deposits held in Eurobanks are not. In fact, the expansionary effect is precisely the same as it would be if the domestic monetary authorities had reduced reserve requirements to zero on a volume of time deposits equivalent to the growth of the Eurodollar market.[4]

---

[3] In addition, for purposes of exposition, we assume that all new deposits are held in First Manhattan.

[4] The economics of a three stage banking system are documented in greater detail in Manfred Willms, "Money Creation in the Euro-Currency Market," *Weltwirtschaftliches Archiv*, Vol. 112 (1976), pp. 201–30. For a further refinement see Alexander K. Swoboda, "Credit Creation in the Euromarket: Alternative Theories and Implications for Control," Occasional Papers 2, New York: Group of Thirty, 1980, pp. 12–13.

INTEREST ON REQUIRED RESERVES?

Much of the debate about whether the shift of funds to the Eurodollar market deprives the Federal Reserve (the Fed) of monetary control would be moot if the Fed paid a market rate of interest on required reserves. Then banks, domestic and offshore, would not seek out ways to avoid reserve requirements.

This proposal is unlikely to be adopted for two reasons. First, if banks were paid a market rate of interest on their required reserves their incentive to minimize these reserves would naturally be substantially diminished. So they might keep reserves at the minimum (say, 3 percent of deposits) or they might keep a lot more. So the predictability of the relationship between reserves at the Fed and aggregate deposits in banks would be lost. The Fed would therefore not know with any precision what effect an expansion or contraction of "high-powered money" would have on the money supply. The effectiveness of reserve requirements as a tool of monetary policy would vanish.

The second reason is a simpler one. Forcing banks to keep money at the Fed interest free gives the Fed funds which it then invests in Treasury bills and bonds, earning hundreds of millions of dollars a year in interest. This money, which is in effect a tax on banks, goes to pay the salaries and expenses of the Federal Reserve System, and the surplus is turned over to the U.S. Treasury. Neither the Fed nor the Treasury would be eager to forego this hidden tax and replace it with an explicit one.

We would argue that the first reason is a red herring. The Fed hardly ever controls the money supply by altering reserve requirements. It controls money and credit conditions through open market operations, which can be done even if there were no reserve requirements at all. In other words, reserve requirements themselves are quite unnecessary for the conduct of monetary policy, except insofar as they help pay those who do it!

The Portfolio Effect

The analysis presented so far rests essentially on a fixed coefficient multiplier approach. However, this approach has long been subject to criticism because it leaves out changes in asset preferences among banks and the public in response to changes in interest rates, or technological change, or the introduction of new financial instruments with different risk-return attributes.

Specifically, whenever interest-bearing securities become available that can be more easily converted into money without risk of loss on principal—

and liabilities of financial intermediaries are such instruments—households and firms can conduct the same volume of transactions with smaller (average) cash balances. This is because they can now hold some of their wealth in the form of these very liquid financial assets, which are a preferred substitute for (precautionary) cash balances.

This **Tobin-Brainard portfolio effect,** as it is known to financial economists, generally holds whenever there is an improvement in the efficiency of the money markets: new instruments, better organized and transparent secondary markets, and improvements in the management or supervision of the financial institutions who issue liabilities. The traditional explanation focusing on the velocity of money is precisely equivalent: lower average cash balances support the same level of economic activity, or the same cash balances are sufficient for a greater volume of economic transactions.

Another way of looking at the expansionary effect of the growth of an efficient intermediation sector is based on the concept of **net liquidity**.[5] This is a measure derived by assigning weights of moneyness to different assets and liabilities. If a bank issues liabilities (such as short-term negotiable certificates of deposit) that possess greater moneyness than do its investments (such as long-term loans to firms), the bank contributes to net liquidity.

One measure of moneyness is the maturity of a bank's assets or liabilities. The question then is to what extent, if at all, the shift of intermediation from institutions operating domestically to banks in the external market involves an increase in net liquidity if the external institutions engage more in positive maturity transformation (borrowing short, lending long) than do domestic operating banks.

Views on the magnitude of these effects may differ. What is clear, however, is that whether the focus of the analysis is on velocity of money, portfolio shifts, or changes in net liquidity, it is the *incremental* effect caused by the shift from domestic intermediation of credit to the Euromarket that matters. This makes an empirical investigation much more difficult than, for example, simplistically correlating the rate of increase in the price level with the growth rate of the Euromarket.

Has the Offshore Market Expanded Credit?

We would venture the opinion that the expansionary effect of the growth of an efficient money market such as the Euromarket on the United States has been very small indeed, simply because the U.S. already had a very large and efficient money market when the Eurodollar market started to develop. For countries without such a market, the growth of an efficient external money market may well have permitted firms and financial institutions to

---

[5]This is the approach of Jürg Niehans and John Hewson, "The Eurodollar Market and Monetary Theory," *Journal of Money, Credit and Banking*, February 1976, pp. 1–27.

economize on cash balances, and thus have expanded aggregate liquidity, assuming that all else remained unchanged.

But all else does not remain unchanged, particularly if we now consider the third issue: When a substantial proportion of credit is intermediated externally instead of internally, is the ability of the monetary authorities to keep the growth of money within desired limits undermined? Few would dispute that the central bank has the ability to control the monetary base—as long as one abstracts from political pressures that may effectively prevent the central bank from exercising this technical ability as it desires. And changes in the monetary base, in turn, affect the volume of money and credit in the economy. When commercial banks hold their means of payments (reserves) in the form of liquid liabilities of the central bank (high-powered money), and external financial intermediaries, in turn, hold their cash balances in the form of demand deposits in commercial banks, a reduction in central bank money will have a contractionary effect on the aggregate volume of credit, provided that this reduction is not accompanied by an offsetting shift (reduction) in the demand for cash balances by either commercial banks and/or (external) financial intermediaries.[6]

Most of the empirical work on this issue suggests that the demand for cash balances is quite stable over a longer period of time, say a year or longer. This stability is, in fact, *the* basis for aggregate demand policy through changes in the growth rate of the money supply.[7] *Hence, one may conclude that central bank actions influence not only the narrowly defined money supply but also the aggregate supply of credit extended by banks and nonbank financial intermediaries, including Eurobanks.*

This point can be further clarified by drawing parallels to a well-known phenomenon in the domestic market. Since the Eurobanking system is directly analogous to the domestic nonbank intermediary system (both hold their transactions balances in the form of demand deposits in domestic commercial banks), the effect of central bank monetary policy on Eurodollar credit is similar to the effect on credit extended by savings banks, credit unions, and insurance companies. Intervention in the nonbank financial sector is a much less efficient way of controlling aggregate credit expansion than is the more normal method of controlling the reserves of the commercial banks.[8] A central bank can maintain control over *total* credit, whether

---

[6]Note that this would be true even if there were no reserve requirements imposed on commercial banks. In the course of their own liquidity management, such institutions will find it necessary to maintain cash reserves for *operating* purposes in the form of vault cash as well as current account with the central bank.

[7]Central bankers argue, of course, that this degree of stability is insufficient and therefore compulsory reserves are required *in addition* to operating reserves. This is one reason why the Bundesbank has for many years objected to the creation of money market mutual funds in Germany.

[8]See John H. Wood, "Two Notes on the Uniqueness of Commercial Banks," *Journal of Finance*, March 1970, p. 90–1.

extended by commercial banks, savings and loan associations, or Eurobanks. Thus, when the central bank acts to contract the monetary base, the external sector cannot escape its influence on aggregate credit in that currency.

CASE 2: THE EUROCURRENCY MARKET, AGGREGATE LIQUIDITY, AND MONETARY CONTROL—INTERNATIONAL CAPITAL FLOWS

We may now drop our earlier assumption that no international capital flows between markets in different currencies occur. What is the effect on monetary and exchange-rate policy when the Eurocurrency markets act as intermediaries for flows of credit from one national market to another?

Figure 7-4 illustrates three possible patterns of the flow of funds. The first, *Case A*, is the one discussed in the previous section. Money flows from the United States, into the Eurodollar market, and back into the United States. In essence, no international capital flows have occurred: the external market acts simply as a segment of the domestic financial market.

Case B shows an international flow of funds (from the United States to Europe, and vice versa) taking place by way of the Eurodollar market. Here, the Eurodollar market is simply acting as a middleman. The effect of it doing so is discussed in this section.

Case C illustrates a similar international flow of credit, but this time occurring directly between countries instead of by way of the external market, as in Case B. This, of course, represents the traditional form of international capital flows.

A fourth, hypothetical, situation might be one in which credit was "created" in the Eurodollar market and transferred to one country or another. *This possibility does not exist.* Despite the various writings that apparently assume the contrary, a Eurobank cannot make a new dollar loan without attracting dollar funds, and those dollar funds must come from a resident of some country. All Eurodollar loans, therefore, represent either Case A or a version of Case B.

The crucial questions can be formulated as follows: (1) *to what extent (if at all) do the Eurocurrency markets represent a cause of international capital flows, and (2) to what extent and under what conditions do such flows undermine national exchange rate and monetary policy?*

Credit cannot be created autonomously in the Euromarket. Every loan made must be funded with a time deposit. To enable the borrower to spend an amount of x in country A for goods and services, a depositor must have foregone spending at least the same amount in country B (Case B in Figure 7-4), or in country A (Case A in Figure 7-4). Thus Eurobanks act as nonbank financial intermediaries, passing on funds and efficiently transforming risk

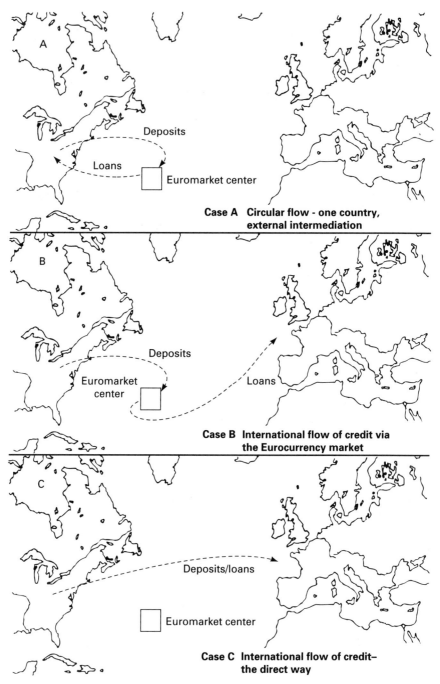

Case A Circular flow - one country,
external intermediation

Case B International flow of credit via
the Eurocurrency market

Case C International flow of credit–
the direct way

FIGURE 7–4. International Credit Flows: Three Cases. The first is simply
domestic financial intermediation via an offshore center. The second
and third show international flows—intermediated and direct.

and maturity aspects of the funds received as deposits and passed on as loans. Consequently, any inflow of funds in one country is exactly offset by outflows in one or more other countries.

Nevertheless, there are some differences between direct capital flows and flows via the Euromarkets. First, the origins and destination of funds flowing through the external market may be more difficult to identify. Second, the growth of the Euromarkets involved the creation of an institutional framework that greatly facilitated the flow of funds between countries. In other words, because of the Eurocurrency markets, the volume of funds that moves from one country to another—*for a given incentive*—may be greater.

To expand on the second point, borrowers can sometimes obtain funds more readily from Eurobanks, which can avoid restrictions such as credit ceilings, lending restrictions, discriminatory administrative regulations, and similar direct constraints imposed by the country whose currency is used to denominate the loan. In other words, without the Euromarkets, most foreign loans would be made by domestic financial institutions, and their behavior is much easier to regulate than that of nonbanks, such as private individuals and business firms. When individuals and corporations deal directly with offshore financial institutions (which are more often than not simply affiliates of the banks they already deal with), it takes more comprehensive means to prevent them from borrowing and depositing than a friendly phone call by the head of the central bank to the chief executives of a handful of large domestic institutions. Thus, the operation of the Eurocurrency market has contributed to the volume of international (short-term) capital flows by opening up an additional, very convenient channel for such flows.

We now turn to the second question at the beginning of this section and see whether and to what extent the potential for an increased volume of international short-term capital flows renders ineffective, or at least reduces, the effectiveness of national monetary policy.

MONETARY POLICY
AND THE MONETARY BASE

Conventional monetary theory assumes that monetary conditions, which determine changes in income, the price level, and interest rates, are affected by either (1) a change in the monetary base directly (central bank high-powered money) or (2) a change in the utilization of a given monetary base.

The classical example of the first effect is the case of the central bank of a country that experiences inflows on the short-term capital account not offset elsewhere in the balance of payments. To prevent the exchange rate from appreciating, the authorities purchase foreign currencies from the banks in return for domestic money; in other words, they intervene in the foreign exchange market. Thus, both central bank assets and liabilities increase.

Now, an increase in central bank liabilities means an increase in reserves held by domestic commercial banks. Such an increase therefore serves as the base for an (unwanted) expansion of the domestic money supply. The authorities can, of course, attempt to offset the increased liquidity by, for example, a change in reserve requirements, open-market operations, and/or quantitative credit controls. In theory, this is easily done; in practice, the result is doubtful. As the authorities try to "sterilize" the excess liquidity by selling government securities, interest rates, which began to drop when domestic liquidity increased, will move up again and regain the level that caused the inflows in the first place. Only if the supply of foreign funds is limited (i.e., if international capital flows have an interest elasticity of considerably less than infinity) will this policy work.[9]

It is here that the Euromarkets come into the act. The very efficiency of the Euromarkets in channeling funds between countries has made funds flows more sensitive to perceived yield differentials (i.e., nominal interest rates adjusted for expected exchange rate changes and political risk). Thus, for all except perhaps the very largest countries such as the United States and Japan, international capital flows may well appear to exhibit unlimited interest responsiveness. If, in addition, the tools of monetary policy are not fully available—when, for example, a suppressed and therefore poorly functioning domestic money market and little outstanding government debt limit open market operations—the authorities may well experience the frustrating feeling of impotence when it comes to conducting effective monetary policy.

One can conclude, then, that under a regime of fixed exchange rates, when the monetary authorities intervene in the foreign exchange markets because they have different exchange rate objectives than private market participants, the authorities are forced to accept one of two alternatives if they insist on pursuing monetary policies which differ from those of other countries. They must either impose exchange controls or abandon their exchange-rate policies. In the past, "natural" barriers to international capital flows may have helped countries to avoid making this choice to a certain degree.

While the increased sensitivity of international capital flows to yield differentials may reduce the domestic effectiveness of monetary policy, this sensitivity correspondingly increases the impact of monetary policy when

---

[9]It has been pointed out that intervention in the foreign exchange market is an alternative to open market policy. For a comprehensive study on central bank intervention in foreign exchange markets see Michael Mussa, "The Role of Official Intervention," Occasional Papers 6, New York: Group of Thirty, 1981. See also "Intervention in Foreign Exchange Markets: A Summary of Ten Staff Studies," *Federal Reserve Bulletin*, November 1983, pp. 830–836.

used for balance-of-payments and exchange rate purposes. With the help of the Euromarkets, it takes only a relatively minor push at the monetary brakes to attract a relatively large volume of external funds, to prevent the exchange rate from depreciating, and to alleviate those (secondary) inflationary pressures that stem from a depreciation of the domestic currency in foreign exchange markets. Indeed, the Euromarkets have more than once been used directly by governments as a source of funds to prop up a weakening currency.

MONETARY POLICY AND UTILIZATION OF THE MONETARY BASE

Can capital flows occurring by way of the Eurocurrency markets affect the utilization of a given monetary base, thus expanding credit? Yes, by making liquid balance management more efficient, as we have seen. First, to the extent that domestic intermediation is subject to reserve requirements, the shift toward external intermediation does, to some degree, involve an escape from such reserve requirements, regardless of the ultimate destination of the credit. This will have expansionary effects, but they are specific, rather well-defined, and limited.

In addition, the Euromarkets permit banks and firms to operate, on average, with fewer idle balances or excess reserves; such funds can readily be deposited in the Euromarkets for any period of time, including on an overnight basis. By the same token, banks know that these markets provide an alternative source of funds if they are willing and able to pay the prevailing rate; domestic markets tend to be much more subject to quantitative credit rationing, either because there are fewer market participants or because of administrative barriers. To a certain extent the easier access holds also for corporations. These features of the market are available not only to those banks and corporations that operate in a country whose currency is used to denominate externally intermediated deposits and loans, but also to entities domiciled in other countries. For example, while there is virtually no deposit-based market for Euroschillings, Austrian banks and firms can invest in the Eurodollar market (e.g., covering their deposits with a forward contract) or borrow Eurodollars and protect themselves from undesired exchange risk with the same technique.

Second, to the extent that the Euromarkets have increased the international mobility of short-term capital, the instances of pools of unused liquidity within each country have diminished. The effect of the Euromarket can be likened in this respect to the market for Federal Funds in the United States, where differences in credit demands on banks in various parts of the country are quickly evened out. Just as with the Federal Funds market, the Euromarket experienced a one-time expansionary effect by allowing better use of a given monetary base. In each case the innovation in financial markets has had only a limited, one-shot effect. Indeed, one can argue that the effectiveness of monetary restraint has been enhanced by reducing the slack in the system.

While the effect of policies that impact on monetary aggregates, via interest rates, such as open-market policy, has been strengthened, other policy measures, particularly credit ceilings, reserve requirements on assets or liabilities, and similar measures will largely lose their effectiveness. Indeed, such restrictions themselves contribute to more credit being routed through the external markets. However, these other policies always have a secondary objective; they are designed not only to limit expansion of credit in general, but to raise revenue (indirectly)[10] or to assure that credit is allocated to specific purposes. The Eurocurrency market tends to make the attainment of such objectives by governments difficult, as we shall see later.

In summary, there is not much to the claim that the Euromarkets render national monetary policy ineffective. The growth of these markets, to the extent that such growth is caused by a shift from domestic to external credit intermediation, has *some* expansionary effects resulting from (1) a freeing of reserves that occurs whenever credit flows go through channels that are unburdened by reserve requirements, and (2) the increased liquidity that appears whenever money markets become more efficient. Both of these effects are static in that they occur only once for each shift in intermediation and can in principle be offset by the central bank through a contraction or lower rate of growth of the monetary base. Central bankers can and should treat the domestic and offshore segments of their currency's money market as an integrated whole, and focus attention on using the domestic monetary base to influence credit conditions in the broad money market.

MEASUREMENT AND POLICY

We have suggested that the effects of Eurocurrency growth need have no impact on aggregate credit expansion because these effects can be counteracted by the authorities in the course of ordinary monetary policy. One must recognize, however, that the changes described above can render the *implementation of* monetary policy more complex, conceptually and in practice, to the extent that monetary policy is executed by attempting to influence an intermediate target, e.g., a monetary aggregate such as M1. Measurement errors regarding this intermediate target can frustrate policy in and by themselves, even if one accepts the fact that (1) the monetary authorities do indeed have a sufficient degree of control over the money supply, and (2)

---

[10]For a thorough review see Marvin Goodfriend and Monica Hargraves, "A Historical Assessment of the Rationales and Functions of Reserve Requirements," *Economic Review,* Federal Reserve Bank of Richmond, March/April 1983, pp. 3–21.

the link between the policy variable and the economy is sufficiently tight. The aggregate, or true, money supply should account for all forms of "moneyness" or liquidity; but all financial assets possess some degree of moneyness and can, in theory, be weighted accordingly in a single measure of liquidity.

In practice, it is necessary to identify one or more proxy measures that best reflect the total amount of money in the economy and which can be influenced by policy. The difficulty of doing so has led to the publication of a range of alternative data series representing different monetary aggregates in various countries. In the United States, for example, four data series, M1, M2, M3, and L, are published regularly in the *Federal Reserve (Weekly) Statistical Release* and the *Federal Reserve Bulletin*. There can be no doubt that the availability of offshore deposits has complicated the measurement and interpretation of monetary aggregates. Together with other structural changes in financial institutions and markets, it has necessitated several revisions in the composition of monetary aggregates.

At present, there is only partial adjustment for Eurodollar deposits. M2, for example, includes overnight Eurodollar deposits by U.S. residents in foreign branches of *U.S.* banks. Obviously, the equivalent amount of deposits in *foreign* banks abroad is omitted. This can cause problems if and when the competitive relationship between foreign branches of U.S. banks and foreign banks in the dollar deposit business of U.S. residents does change. Further, to the extent that U.S. residents hold overnight Eurodollar deposits to support their activities in foreign markets, the M2 series is overstated. However, as the dollar deposits of those foreign residents who do business in the United States in foreign branches of U.S. banks and foreign banks outside the United States are not captured, the M2 series is understated. M3 includes also *term* Eurodeposits of U.S. residents in foreign branches of U.S. banks worldwide, and similar adjustments apply.

Overall, we would venture the opinion that after the revised treatment of Eurodollars introduced in the early 1980s in the U.S. monetary aggregates, this is not a significant problem for monetary policy, unless there are rapid shifts between domestic and offshore assets. The shifts affect not only the link between high-powered money and aggregates (reserves) but also the data (Eurodollar deposits *are* substitutes for some domestic demand deposits and, most definitely, domestic time deposits). The shifts are a function of the relative attractiveness of onshore deposits and loans vs. offshore banking claims. As emphasized in Chapter One, major sources of such differences are cost differences, and they in turn are largely a matter of reserve requirements. The obligation to put a proportion of funds that banks attract as deposits in (noninterest bearing) accounts with the central bank involves an opportunity cost—a cost that is clearly dependent not only on the magnitude of reserve requirements but also on the level of interest rates. When reserve requirements are, say, 5 percent and the interest rate level is 10 percent, the difference in favor of booking deposits offshore is 50 basis points. When the interest rate rises to 15 percent, because of a change in monetary policy for example, the difference becomes 75 basis points—an added incentive to shift deposits and loans in the Euromarket.[11]

Empirical work on the relationship between the growth of the Eurodollar market and U.S. monetary aggregates supports these conclusions. Of the considerable volume of research on this issue, two representative studies shall be mentioned. Covering the years 1973–1979, a period of rapid growth in the Eurodollar market, a study prepared by Federal Reserve Bank of St. Louis economists detects only very minor effects on the U.S. money stock.[12] A study sponsored by the Bank for International Settlements focusing on income velocity arrived at similar conclusions.[13]

CURRENCY SUBSTITUTION

The essence of our discussion with respect to international capital flows has been purely qualitative: yes, the Eurocurrency market makes short-term capital flows more sensitive to changes in relative interest rates or perceived risks. But as long as the central bank in question does not pursue exchange rate policies inconsistent with domestic monetary policy, as in a freely floating exchange rate system, it retains full autonomy over domestic monetary conditions. Relative changes in money supplies will simply be reflected in exchange rate fluctuations. This traditionally accepted notion has come under criticism from those who argue that with the easy availability of (near) money balances internationally, transactors at the margin, such as sophisticated investors and multinational companies, will diversify their cash balances across several currencies.[14] Most importantly, the proponents of the currency substitution phenomenon argue that people respond to changes in the cost of holding one currency in relation to others by changing the composition of their portfolio of diversified cash balances. This switch will alter the demand for money here and in other countries, transmitting

---

[11]For an analysis of this phenomenon in the context of West Germany and Bundesbank policy, see Gunter Dufey and Otmar Issing, "Mindestreservepolitik, Geldmengensteuerung und Euromärkte," in *Geld, Banken und Versicherungen*, Band 1, ed. by Hermann Göppl und Rudolf Henn (Athenäum).

[12]Anatol B. Balbach and David H. Resler, "Eurodollars and the U.S. Money Supply," *Federal Reserve Bank of St. Louis Review*, June/July 1980, Vol. 62, No. 6, pp. 2–12.

[13]Warren D. McClam, "U.S. Monetary Aggregates, Income Velocity and the Euro-dollar Market," Basle: Monetary and Economic Department, Bank for International Settlements, *BIS Economic Papers*, No. 2, April 1980.

[14]Indeed, it has come under criticism from a number of quarters, particularly those that emphasize the role of *fiscal* policy in this matter, but this goes beyond our agenda which focuses on the role of the Euromarkets.

monetary shocks from one country to the other, even in a world of perfectly flexible exchange rates.[15]

The advent of the Eurocurrency markets provided institutional underpinnings to these theories. The growth of efficient markets for external deposits in a number of major currencies, most with a maturity of less than 30 days, with overnight deposits at competitive interest rates readily available, and with international communications being perfected as well as the banks' and corporations' data processing facilities, currency substitution may well have become a phenomenon to be counted on. Suppose, for example, A's central bank increases its domestic money supply relative to the central and banks in major countries elsewhere; then sharp operators expect currency A to depreciate and will, so the theory suggests, reallocate their portfolios to hold less of their balances in currency A and proportionally more in deposits denominated in other currencies. Thus, "currency substitution destabilized the demand for individual national money."[16]

A closer look at the role of Eurocurrency deposits in this scenario will show that, if this holds, it applies only to *domestic demand deposits*. While it is true that offshore overnight deposits can substitute for cash balances to a certain extent, they cannot be used for payments. As pointed out already in Chapter One, at maturity a Eurodeposit is returned to its owner in the form of a demand deposit in the country of the currency in which the offshore deposit was denominated. More important than these technical issues is the consideration that the currency substitution hypothesis is predicated on the change in opportunity cost between cash balances in different currencies. In the offshore market, however, such changes in opportunity cost are quickly reflected in nominal interest rates. Thus interest rates on overnight and other deposits denominated in currency A would instantaneously *rise* relative to those in other currencies offsetting the very incentive to shift! No, the currency substitution argument holds—if at all—only for transaction balances (demand deposits) with zero (or at least below market) returns.

It is not surprising, therefore, that in spite of significant changes in the institutional environment of international banking, currency substitution has been a phenomenon that has eluded empirical verification—probably because it does not happen.[17]

---

[15]The literature on this phenomenon is extensive. See, for example, Marc A. Miles, "Currency Substitution, Flexible Exchange Rates, and Monetary Independence," *American Economic Review*, June 1978, pp. 428–436; and Ronald I. McKinnon, "Currency Substitution and Instability in the World Dollar Standard," *American Economic Review*, June 1982, pp. 320–333.

[16]McKinnon, *op. cit.*, p. 320.

[17]For an empirical study and review of previous work, see Dallas S. Batten and R. W. Hafer, "Currency Substitution: A Test of Its Importance," *Economic Review*, Federal Reserve Bank of St. Louis, August/September 1984, pp. 5–11.

CONCLUSIONS ON THE MACROECONOMIC POLICY IMPLICATIONS OF THE EUROMARKETS

We can summarize the collective insights about the effect of the Euromarkets on macroeconomic policy: Central banks clearly maintain control over aggregate credit; when monetary policy is tightened the effects are felt through quantity effects (liquidity) and price effects (interest rates) in the onshore as well as the offshore segments of a country's money markets.

To the extent that compulsory reserve requirements lead to a subsequent shift of credit flows from channels burdened with reserve requirements to channels where such costs can be avoided, which nowadays include the offshore market as a major component, those with responsibility for monetary policy must simply take these "escape" effects into account. There can be no doubt that this phenomenon causes data problems measuring monetary aggregates, making fine-tuning of monetary policy a bit more difficult. It must also be recognized that monetary policy is a poor instrument for "fine tuning" the economy anyway. Further, the problem can be alleviated greatly by reducing reserve requirements and, perhaps, by broadening their application to all financial intermediaries whose deposit liabilities are used to make payments. Now the public debate about reserve requirements is reduced to the issue of whether they are truly necessary for monetary policy, or merely a means to raise tax revenue from commercial banks.[18] But, in the end, the argument that central banks lose control of aggregate credit without such requirement is on shaky ground.

In the next section, we turn from monetary policy to the prudential regulation of financial institutions. We shall find that while monetary policy has come home, prudential policy has gone international.

THE NEED FOR CONTROLS: THE SOUNDNESS OF FINANCIAL INSTITUTIONS

During the decade of the 1980s and into the 1990s, concern about the impact of the Euromarket on monetary and exchange rate stability has increasingly been replaced by worries about the safety of the financial institutions. Three specific "problems" are usually cited:

---

[18]This was the idea behind the Monetary Control Act of 1980 which reduced reserve requirements to essentially 3 percent but extended these requirements to *all* institutions offering transaction (checking) accounts. For a review of different countries' approaches to minimum reserve requirements, see Richard Mader, "Die Minderreservepolitik im internationalen Vergleich," *Die Bank*, March 1989, 128–133.

1. Unlike in domestic markets, there is no "lender of last resort" in Euroland.
2. Lending practices in the offshore market escape the prudential supervision systems that govern banks' behavior in domestic markets.
3. The existence of a deposit insurance system is being undermined by a competitive market for external deposits.

We shall address each of these issues in turn.

There are two types of banking crises. One is a **liquidity crisis**, best illustrated by the classic "bank panic." The other is financial **disintermediation**, which occurs when funds are suddenly shifted from one set of financial intermediaries to another, or, more correctly, when the flow of funds from savers to borrowers starts to bypass financial intermediaries altogether.

The essence of a classic bank panic is the rapid change in preference by the public in favor of primary money (i.e., notes and coins) instead of banks' liabilities. In terms of monetary theory, the sudden demand for currency relative to demand deposits is equivalent to a drastic increase in reserve requirements. This is because currency in circulation, together with the demand liabilities of the central bank to commercial banks, constitutes the reserve base, or high-powered money.

This sudden contraction of the effective money supply has predictable effects on the nonfinancial sector of the economy: general illiquidity, frantic attempts at liquidating inventories, reduction in the level of output and employment, and economic depression. It is not until price and wage levels have adjusted downward sufficiently that a new equilibrium is reached, or until the central monetary authorities provide additional liquidity sufficient to offset the effect of the shift in asset preference.

Could such events occur in the Euromarkets? First, we should remind ourselves that Eurodeposits are investments, not means of payments. In concrete terms this means that when the holders of Eurodeposits change their preferences, they can obtain payment only in the form of a demand deposit in a bank operating in the country of the currency in which the Eurodeposit was denominated originally.

When the deposits of Eurodollar holders mature, they obtain dollar demand deposits in the United States. From that point on the problem becomes a purely national one, and the Federal Reserve will deal with it as it deals with shifts in the demand for money in general: it can take offsetting action. The point is, if one trusts that the system will cope with liquidity crises originating in the *domestic* market, it is difficult to justify serious concern about the same effects originating in the *external* sector.

Given that Eurobanks are financial intermediaries, the second phenomenon, disintermediation, is more relevant. But what exactly is the basis for concern about disintermediation? When interest rates rise, savings and loan associations and similar special-purpose thrift institutions find themselves unable to compete for funds, either because of regulatory constraints (interest-rate ceilings) or because of the nature of their assets (long-term, fixed-rate mortgages). Depositors withdraw funds at maturity and invest them in direct money market paper such as T-bills, commercial paper, acceptances, and so on. Thus, credit flows are diverted. Apart from the problems that this imposes on the institutions involved, what really makes disintermediation such a political issue is that this shift in credit channels also involves a change in the destination of funds: long-term mortgages for homes are not funded, at least not at rates that people find acceptable, while credit needs of business borrowers for inventories and other short-term purposes are met, although at stiff rates.

In short, concern about a crisis is to some extent concern about credit reallocation. In the Euromarket this is not much of an issue because the outcome of the regulatory process (see box following) is such that this type of credit allocation is simply not sustainable—just as it has become unsustainable in domestic markets, as advances in technology and liberalization of cross border transactions have exposed the sector of special financial institutions to competition for funds from abroad.

All of this does not mean that a general flight from Eurocurrency deposits could not occur; should this happen, however, all funds withdrawn from the external markets would have to be invested, penny for penny, in the corresponding domestic market. The domestic financial institutions will, in all probability, gladly take up the funds offered them, and if necessary the Eurobanks may borrow them back! This process is facilitated by the fact that the bulk of the Eurocurrency business is done by institutions that are affiliates of banks headquartered in a *national* market. To some extent, such shifts do occur quite regularly during periods when market participants become very risk averse. The only significant problem that arises because of such a shift from the external to the domestic market is that deposits previously not subject to reserve requirements would now be subject to them; this would have a contractionary effect, just opposite to the expansionary effect of a shift toward external intermediation previously discussed.

While the preceding analysis referred to the susceptibility for crisis of the *system as a whole*, there still may be a problem when it comes to the soundness of *individual institutions*. Of course, the two are closely related; the first line of defense in shoring up the banking system is to prevent individual financial institutions from failing, especially when they are of major importance. It is at this point that the lender of last resort functions and its implementation problems become closely linked to deposit insurance and prudential supervision.

PRINCIPLES OF BANKING REGULATION

The major concern of a central bank's role as a lender of last resort is to prevent what has become known as a bank panic. Such an event usually begins with the erosion or disappearance of a bank's equity position as a result of sudden and excessive loan losses. Depositors concerned about the safety of their funds in a particular bank will place them in institutions considered safer. Worse, when the failure of one bank casts doubt about the soundness of other institutions, depositors demand *currency*. In monetary theory terms, the sudden demand for currency relative to demand deposits is equivalent to a drastic increase in reserve requirements. The reason for this is that currency in circulation, together with the demand liabilities of the central bank to commercial banks, constitutes the reserve base, or high-powered money. If it is fully loaned up, the individual bank cannot draw on the reserves it must hold with the central bank when it experiences (net) deposit withdrawals. The bank must instead sell marketable securities and call in loans. If this is not sufficient, and often it is not, the bank can go out and borrow funds in the interbank market or the money market (i.e., engage in liability management). If the withdrawal of deposits was caused by concern about the soundness of the bank, such attempts will be unsuccessful and the institution(s) will have to close its doors. It is here that the central bank enters the picture as the lender of last resort. It can make funds available, in the form of either currency or central bank liabilities, and it should have no difficulty in doing this, because it can create domestic money essentially without limit.

In a modern banking system the mere knowledge that the central bank is willing and able to supply additional funds to banks experiencing liquidity problems (a euphemism for the inability to satisfy the requests of depositors for the return of their funds) will in and by itself suffice to prevent sudden shifts out of demand deposits into currency. In many countries there are auxiliary institutions which insure deposits and assure depositors that their funds are available without undue delay, thus preventing runs on banks from occurring in the first place.

The problem inherent in a system of deposit insurance and explicit or implicit promises by the central bank to come to the rescue of *depositors* involves a *moral hazard* that has long been recognized: When depositors become impervious to risk, it is in the interest of shareholders that their agents, i.e., management, undertake investments that yield higher returns but carry more risk!

Principles of Banking Regulation (*Continued*)

One approach to capturing this effect more formally has been developed by Robert Merton who analyzed this situation using option theory.[19] He showed that the insurance in essence permits the operators of a financial institution to "put" the claims of the depositors to the central bank or another government insurance institution whenever the market value of the assets is less than that of the deposit liabilities. Figure 7-5 shows that the value of a depository institution to its operators is greatest when the net worth is zero, i.e., the option is "at the money." Without deposit insurance, the operator of the bank must pay a default risk premium in order to attract funds. If that premium were to be priced fairly, it would approximate over time the difference between the net worth (exercise price) and the value of the option.

The nature of the option also suggests the nature of the assets that the bank will buy. If unconstrained, the higher the risk the more value the bank has for the operators since any upside gain benefits them directly while the downside risk is absorbed by the institution that bails out the

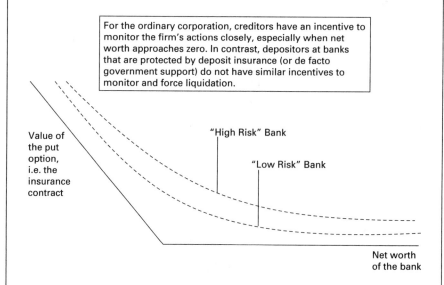

For the ordinary corporation, creditors have an incentive to monitor the firm's actions closely, especially when net worth approaches zero. In contrast, depositors at banks that are protected by deposit insurance (or de facto government support) do not have similar incentives to monitor and force liquidation.

Value of the put option, i.e. the insurance contract

"High Risk" Bank

"Low Risk" Bank

Net worth of the bank

Figure 7–5. The Options Approach to Bank Regulation. Adapted from Kormendi, et al., "The Origins and Resolution of the Thrift Crisis," *Journal of Applied Corporate Finance*, April 1989.

[19]This section borrows in part from Kormendi, et al., "The Origins and Resolution of the Thrift Crisis," *Journal of Applied Corporate Finance*, April 1989. The original idea appeared in Robert C. Merton, "An Analytic Derivation of the Cost of Deposit Insurance and Loan Guarantees: An Application of Modern Option Pricing Theory," *Journal of Banking and Finance*, Vol. 1, No. 1, 1977.

failing bank. Furthermore, when the bank has large negative net worth, the incentive for reckless transactions or even fraud is enhanced. And while these values are not without cost in terms of possible regulatory scrutiny and probability of damaged managerial reputations, the potential for gain is also considerable. In any case, the discipline of creditors (depositors) to monitor the firm's activities very closely under such circumstances is greatly diminished. Thus, the monitoring is all left up to the supervisory authorities. Given the nature of the incentives for managers/shareholders of financial institutions, this puts the spotlight on the relationship between regulators and members of the banking industry.

The modern view of bank regulation espoused by Edward Kane and others[20] is based on a correspondence between theories of market behavior on the one hand and the manifestations of regulatory activity on the other. Financial regulatory services are produced and delivered by governmental entities, because government sponsorship confers a number of marketing advantages on regulatory entities and because regulators have the opportunity to redistribute income, a political process by definition. Financial regulatory services consist of efforts to monitor, discipline, or coordinate the behavior of individual financial service providers for a common good or objective. Regulators also compete for market share; the broader their reach, the better their power, prestige, job satisfaction, perks, and other emoluments.

In exchange for explicit and implicit revenues, producers of regulatory services enhance favorably their regulatory clienteles' customers' confidence. From the point of view of those regulated, costs imposed on them by regulators explicitly and via constraints on operations reduce the value of regulatory services that they perceive. This represents an incentive to "shop" for regulators which involves some transition costs, but also acts as a constraint on regulators. This process will, in turn, dilute regulatory efforts; in "globalizing" markets the effect is heightened by an increase in the availability of regulators.[21] Vice versa, when a regulator and his client-regulatees can keep their constituents, taxpayer/voters, in the dark for a prolonged period to correctly assess the performance of the regulatory system, competition among regulators can lead to inefficiencies in the outcome by permitting short-sighted and self-serving behavior.

---

[20]Edward J. Kane, "How Market Forces Influence the Structure of Financial Regulation," in William S. Haraf and Rose Marie Kushmeider (eds.), *Restructuring Banking and Financial Services in America*, Washington, D.C.: American Enterprise Institute, 1988, p. 343. For a concise survey of the issues involved in bank regulation, see Terence Quinn, "The Economics of Financial Regulation: A Survey," *Central Bank of Ireland Bulletin*, Autumn 1992, pp. 55–70.

[21]Ian H. Giddy, "Domestic Regulation vs. International Competition in Banking," *Kredit und Kapital*, August 1984, pp. 195–209.

When the authorities, or other market participants in the case of a mutual insurance scheme, underwrite a portion of a bank's debt, they will invariably have to constrain the asset allocation decision of the individual financial institution. This is because bank shareholders (and management) can maximize gains by acquiring higher yielding, more risky assets, since the providers of at least a portion of the liabilities (depositors) will be largely indifferent to the increase in risk and will not demand a commensurate risk premium. This is the well-known "moral hazard" problem described in the section entitled "Principles of Bank Regulation." The situation has led to a consistent pattern of regulation, although the institutional arrangements differ from country to country. Virtually everywhere the public regulation of commercial banks includes restrictions on entry into the banking business, restraints that extend both to the establishment of *de novo* institutions and to expansion through branching on the theory that the degree for competition must be limited to prevent it from becoming "ruinous." Further, statutory and administrative limitations are put on existing banks' freedom to conduct business in certain strategic areas (e.g., insurance, commodities trading, underwriting) and on the types of liabilities through which a bank can attract funds.

The above are collectively referred to as **structural regulation**. In contrast, **prudential** regulations focus on the maintenance of an "adequate" capital position, in conjunction with restrictions on the composition of assets: reserves, liquid investments, and loans. Control is exercised specifi-

---

THE PROBLEMS WITH DEPOSIT INSURANCE

Deposit insurance is a controversial issue of public policy in many countries, while the extension of insurance to offshore deposits is a special topic that is known only to the specialists.

In theory, deposit insurance is not necessary to create moral hazards; banks can simply be bailed out by the central bank that controls the money presses. The costs of the bail-out are then distributed throughout the economy via incremental inflation. However, many countries have moved to concentrate the cost of rescue operations on the banks and their customers through special insurance funds which are administered either by banking associations or special official bodies, such as the Federal Deposit Insurance Corporation in the United States. As Figure 7-6 shows, the details of deposit insurance vary all over, particularly with respect to the condition of membership, the method of funding, the cost to the banks, and the extent of protection, but there is a common thread: *de facto* banks have been rescued and depositors have been protected onshore and offshore, without exception.

It must be recognized that Figure 7-6 only provides a snapshot. Deposit insurance is always contentious because of the conflicting principles: the safety of deposits which is equated with the financial system; the moral hazard that is created by uniform insurance contributions; and the difficulties of structuring insurance premiums according to the *ex ante* risk criteria of the assets. Underneath the public debate are pervasive notions of credit allocation to particular sectors, e.g., agriculture, housing, or export transactions.

The debate at the beginning of the 1990s in the United States and the reforms suggested provide an illustration of the key proposals:

- Maintain $100,000 level of coverage; eliminate "too big to fail" doctrine; make uninsured depositors and unsecured creditors suffer some losses of the failed bank, based on weighted average of past FDIC losses. (Proposed by American Bankers Association.)
- Insure all deposits; assess premiums on foreign deposits of U.S. banks. (Proposed by Independent Bankers Association of America.)
- Maintain $100,000 ceiling; reduce premiums for banks with high capital levels and strong "Camel" ratings, provided that the FDIC's reserve is at least 1.25 percent of insured deposits. (Proposed by Conference of State Bank Supervisors.)
- Fully insure $10,000 worth of deposits; insure 90% of remaining deposits; allow one fully insured account per person. (Proposed by Federal Reserve Bank of Minneapolis.)

As far as offshore deposits are concerned, only one proposal, represented by the lobby of small banks who have insignificant activities offshore, suggests assessing premiums on deposits in foreign branches. It is notable that no country has so far felt it possible or necessary to extend deposit insurance fees or *explicit* coverage to offshore deposits. Obviously, a unilateral imposition of such deposits would weaken the role of that country's banks in the international competition for funds and business. The situation is further complicated by the fact that while none of the countries extends insurance protection formally to deposits in offshore branches *de facto*, the extent of the protection has gone far beyond the explicitly stated limitation both in terms of size as well as in terms of location.

cally through the establishment of balance sheet ratios, consisting of maximum and minimum relations between different categories of assets and/or liabilities. In addition, restrictions on the pricing of funds (interest ceilings) and the detailed examination of individual loans are part of the usual regulatory bag of instruments.[22] The link between deposit insurance and these forms of restraint is discussed in the box, "The Problems with Deposit Insurance." Figure 7-6 contains a summary of some deposit insurance systems around the world.

Measures intended to assure the soundness of banks are often more or less anticompetitive and therefore may deprive the public of differentiated and least-cost banking services. This gives rise to the question as to where the government's responsibility for the soundness of financial institutions ends and where the obligation to foster competition begins.

Turning to the offshore market, is there a special problem when loans are made by institutions that operate externally? Any answer must take account of the fact that the bulk of the Eurocurrency business is concentrated on the books of wholly owned affiliates of the banks that are among the largest in their respective national markets. Indeed, are not a bank's Eurocurrency operations simply a part of its total activity from the point of view of banking supervision?

Answering this question necessitates a trip into the murky world of international law, in which definitive laws are nonexistent and where overlapping power relationships further complicate jurisdictional issues. To bring some semblance of orderly analysis to bear on this matter, we find it useful to draw the following distinctions as to the *legal nature of Eurobanks*.

1. Eurocurrency operations can be undertaken at the *head office* of a bank (or a special domestic subsidiary). Clearly, in this case all operations are subject to the supervision of the domestic monetary authorities. And it is up to them to decide whether or not to support the financial institution; but there is no difference in this respect between domestic and foreign business, or the portion of activities denominated in foreign currencies.

   It has been argued that there is a difference in the *ability* of the respective monetary authorities to implement a policy of support. While they have ample domestic funds—indeed, the central bank can print money—it may not have the necessary foreign exchange reserves available, so the argument goes. This reasoning is erroneous. Even if the central bank cannot borrow the necessary foreign exchange funds, there is always the spot market where domestic cur-

---

[22]For a comprehensive review of the patterns of bank supervision, see Richard Dale, "Bank Supervision Around the World," New York: Group of Thirty, 1982.

rency can be sold for foreign exchange.[23] If such operations take place on a large scale, the exchange rate will depreciate, but this also happens when a domestic support operation has to be financed by printing money. Ultimately, of course, what matters is the productive capacity of an economy and the extent to which the central bank can claim output by printing money.

2. The situation is somewhat more complicated when Eurocurrency operations are carried out by foreign *branches*. Because such operations are legally part of the parent bank, they are directly subject to the home government's influence. However, the bank's operations are located in the foreign jurisdiction and do business at the *foreign government's* pleasure, at least in a legal sense, if not always in terms of economic power. We have addressed this issue at greater length in Chapter Five in the context of funding.

3. To the extent that Eurocurrency operations are "housed" on the books of (wholly owned) *foreign subsidiaries*, relationships are still more complex. Such subsidiaries are incorporated under local law and thus legal entities of the host countries. In each case, however, the equity is held abroad by a foreign parent institution which usually exercises management control. The foreign subsidiary is therefore also subject to the power of the parent institution's government, which can influence the policies of the subsidiary by putting pressure, legal or otherwise, on the parent. Many national laws and regulations indeed look through the separate legal entity completely when dealing with "controlled foreign corporations," to use the American concept as an example.

4. The overlapping relationships multiply when we deal with what have become known as **consortium banks**. These are joint ventures of parent banks with headquarters usually in a number of countries, often without participation of an institution from the Euromarket center in which the respective consortium bank is incorporated. As with subsidiaries, they are obviously subject to the regulatory framework of the jurisdiction under which they operate, but are much less susceptible to influence from the individual governments of their parents.[24] *In extremis*, a government can, of course, force a parent to sell its shares, or withdraw from management, but this will have little effect on the venture per se. In particular, the instrument of moral

---

[23]It is not even necessary that the central bank itself purchase the foreign exchange required for support operations; the bank itself can do so, provided that it is supplied with sufficient domestic-currency funds.

[24]By way of example, many of the countries where external intermediation takes place have stringent laws regarding bank secrecy, and they take a dim view of bank examiners of other governments wishing to rummage through the books of what are often legally national entities.

Country	Established	Condition of membership	Administration	How funded
America	1933	voluntary	official	contributions from participating institutions
Belgium	1985	voluntary	official	calls on participating insitutions in event of loss
Britain	1982	compulsory	official	contributions from participating institutions. Fund ceiling is £6m
France	1980	compulsory	private	calls on participating institutions in event of loss
Holland	1979	compulsory	official	calls on participating institutions in event of loss
Ireland	1989	compulsory	official	contributions from participating institutions
Italy	1987	voluntary	private	calls on participating institution in event of loss. Fund ceiling is 4 billion lire
Japan	1971	compulsory	semi-official	contributions from participating institutions
Spain	1977	voluntary	official	contributions from participating institutions
W. Germany	1966	voluntary	private	contributions from participating institutions

Sources: Bank of England, FDIC, Central Bank of Ireland, Japanese Ministry of Finance

Figure 7–6. How Bank Deposit Insurance Is Done Around the World.

Banks' annual contribution	Deposits covered	Accumulated Interest covered	Level of protection
0.083% of insured deposits (0.15% from 1991)	all	yes	$100,000
0.2% of Belgian franc liabilities	BFr only	yes	BFr 0.5m per depositor (but overall limit to assets available in Fund)
minimum initial contribution of £10,000; further calls when necessary up to £300,000; ceiling of 0.3% of bank's deposit base	£ only	yes	75% of deposits up to £20,000 per depositor
depends on losses; annual maximum for small banks 1% of deposits	FFr only	yes	FFr 0.4m per depositor
based on % of loss to be met; individual annual contributions not to exceed 10% of own funds	all	yes	35,000 guilders per depositor
0.2% of deposits; a minimum of IR £20,000 (no maximum)	IR£ (but provision to extend to other currencies)	yes	80% of first IR£5,000 70% of next IR£5,000 50% of next IR£5,000
total amount fund set at 1% ot total deposits of participating banks	all	yes	100% of claims to 200m lire 90% between 200m lire and 1.0 billion lire 80% between 1.0 billion and 3.0 billion
0.012% of deposits at year end annually	¥ only	yes	up to ¥10m per depositor
0.2% of deposits; central bank contributes equivalent to half banks contributions	all	yes	Ptas 1.5m per depositor
0.03% of deposits	all	yes	maximum of 30% of bank's liable capital per depositor

suasion by the supervisory authorities, a popular tool of banking regulators, is largely blunted when operations are carried out abroad in the form of joint ventures.

In summary, the specific problems of supervising the activities of external financial intermediaries (Eurobanks) stem from the fact that for the most part they are subject to overlapping jurisdiction and power relationships. This has led to attempts at achieving cooperation between regulators.[25] The pattern that has slowly emerged, and which was given impetus by the international banking turmoil during 1974, has been characterized as follows:

> Although the precise nature of these arrangements varies from case to case to take account of differences in national legislation, the broad principle on which the arguments are based is that of *parental responsibility* [emphasis added]. This is to say that it is accepted that parent banks have a responsibility, not merely to their overseas branches, but towards all overseas banking operations in which they have a direct stake—and further, that the central bank of the parent bank also has an indirect responsibility for such overseas operations.[26]

This statement well describes the informal understanding among the major central bankers who meet monthly at the Bank for International Settlements in Basle, Switzerland. If, say, the London branch or subsidiary of a bank headquartered in Germany gets into trouble, it reflects primarily on the German bank involved and secondarily on German banks in general, and only to a minor extent, if at all, on London as a financial center. It is up to the *national* authorities to deal with failures of their banks, and it is up to them to make distinctions between problems originating in the domestic and the external business of the institutions concerned.

The rules on parental responsibility presaged the emergence of a regulator's cartel, better known as the Basle Accord on capital adequacy, described in the accompanying box. Extending Kane's view to the international arena, this phenomenon can be seen as a defensive move of regulators to safeguard their share of the market for regulatory services in the face of technological changes, permitting financial institutions to extend their reach geographically and across different product lines.

---

[25]This section draws on C. W. McMahon, "Controlling the Euromarkets," *The Banker*, March 1976, pp. 267–272; personal interviews conducted by one of the authors; and on selected newspaper reports. Major reports are cited in the reference section at the end of the chapter.
[26]McMahon, *op. cit.*, p. 269.

SUMMARY OF THE BASLE ACCORD ON CAPITAL REQUIREMENTS

- Each balance sheet asset and off-balance-sheet equivalent is assigned a risk-weight. These are either 0%, 20%, 50%, or 100%. The risk-weight is determined by the type of counterparty or collateral.
- Multiplying the balance sheet conversion factor by the risk-weight gives the effective risk-weighted asset for each off-balance sheet item.
- Total risk-weighted assets are represented by the sum of each balance sheet asset and off-balance-sheet equivalent multiplied by its effective risk weight.
- Interest and exchange rate products (e.g., swaps, options, and futures) are treated differently as the bank's liability is not for the full face amount. An approach called the "current exposure (or replacement cost) method" has been chosen by the Committee. In this method the current replacement of the individual transaction is calculated by marking to market and adding a factor to reflect potential exposure over the remaining life of the contract.

The total risk-weighted assets figure is the base against which capital adequacy will be measured. The BIS framework also defines capital for the capital adequacy measurement.

Under the guidelines, capital is grouped into two tiers:

- Tier I or Core Capital, which is defined as:
  a) Equity capital including retained earnings
  b) Minority interests
  less (c) goodwill
- Tier II, or Supplementary Capital (comprised of all other capital elements), which is defined as follows:
  a) Hybrid capital, i.e., capital instruments combining characteristics of debt and of equity capital, such as permanent preferred shares and 99 year debentures.
  b) Subordinated term debt which includes conventional subordinated debt with an original fixed term to maturity of over five years and limited life redeemable preference shares. However, this form of capital is limited to a maximum of 50 percent of Core Capital.
  Less c) Amortization—preferred shares and subordinated debt during the last five years to maturity are to be amortized at the cumulative rate of 20 percent per year.

The background of the Basle rules on capital adequacy is by now well-known: Regulators in all major countries became concerned in the 1970s and 1980s that the volatility in the banking system, brought about by the ups and downs of energy prices and the LDC debt problems, would raise the cost of the put options that they had written in the form of guaranteeing the deposit liabilities of major and not-so-major financial institutions under their control. In order to create an incentive for management to pursue low risk strategies, the shareholders' stake in the institutions should be raised. Thus, the regulators' intention was to compel banks to increase capital ratios. Unilateral action to this effect, however, would result in a loss of market share of their particular clientele, and therefore, the regulators' market share and revenues. The rapid, if temporary, ascendance of Japanese financial institutions in international financial markets provided further cause for concern[27] as did the contingent commitments by banks in general.

In December 1987 the Committee on Banking Regulations and Supervisory Practices, representing the central banks from the world's ten major economies, known as the Group of Ten[28] or G 10 for short, met under the auspices of the Bank for International Settlements (BIS) in Basle, Switzerland, and decided, after lengthy negotiations, to adopt some fundamental principles of coordinated bank supervision:

1. A common minimum standard for capital adequacy involving a ratio of 8 percent of eligible capital to the aggregate weighted risk exposure inherent in a bank's business.
2. A common definition of capital resources of a bank.

While countries retain some aspects of their traditional regulatory standards, the transition to the new capital adequacy standard and related capital definitions was phased in by the end of 1992.

We can conclude by saying that the Eurocurrency system is at least as stable as individual domestic financial systems. A flight into primary monetary assets can occur only in the national market because of the nature of the Eurocurrency markets as systems of financial intermediaries; and disintermediation is less likely to occur and is in any case most probably without the consequences in terms of reallocation of credit which seems to be the major concern when this phenomenon manifests itself in the national markets.

---

[27]G. Dufey, "The Role of Japanese Financial Institutions Abroad," in *Japanese Financial Growth*, Charles Goodhart & George Sutija, eds., London: LSE Press, 1990.

[28]There are actually twelve countries in the Committee: Belgium, Canada, France, Germany, Italy, Japan, Luxembourg, Netherlands, Sweden, Switzerland, the United Kingdom, and the United States.

THE NEED FOR CONTROLS: ALLOCATION OF CREDIT

Any analysis of banking regulation would be incomplete were it to neglect governments' attempts to influence how credit is allocated. Indeed, the ability to influence credit allocation represents an inherent element in the microeconomic approach to analyzing the regulatory framework. Our concern in this section is with attempts to alter the availability and costs of funds among various borrowers and purposes from the patterns that would prevail if the allocation were left to a market process governed by expected profit and risk perceptions of individuals. It is also necessary to distinguish between the attempt to reallocate credit and the actual achievement of such an objective. Policy measures frequently affect only the channels through which credit flows, while the ultimate outcome may not differ very much from the allocation pattern caused by market forces, apart from losses in efficiency.

There are two distinct forms of **credit allocation**. One is **direct**, i.e., by collecting funds through taxation and lending them to borrowers judged to be deserving of special consideration. A similar direct way would be to pay an interest subsidy to certain borrowers that would allow them to obtain credit from the market. A third method is to establish public financial institutions, which, armed with a full faith and credit of the government for their liabilities and perhaps a little operating subsidy, enter the credit markets, borrow funds at market rates, and make loans to special groups for preferred purposes, usually at lower-than-market rates. The Eximbank of the United States is a typical example; another is the International Bank for Reconstruction and Development (World Bank). Finally, a program of government guarantees for certain borrowers to be subsidized is a form of direct credit allocation, although this is less open to scrutiny by the political processes than are others.

In the context of external intermediation, however, the type of credit allocation that is relevant is the **indirect** type. Since credit allocation is, almost by definition, highly political, the direct and open approach is avoided whenever possible. Instead, existing private financial institutions are induced, by various means and pressures, to take into consideration reasons other than expected return and risk when deciding where to invest funds. Thus, indirect credit allocation always tends to make the composition of the portfolio of a financial institution inferior to that which its management might choose; otherwise, it would not be necessary to apply pressure.

Examples of such indirect policies are common but often unrecognized because they have been built into the system. In the United States, for example, banks are expected to channel funds into local businesses, particularly small ones, and into community institutions such as school authorities and municipalities. Likewise, the provision of cheap credit to home buyers, farmers, and "disadvantaged minorities" has also been a preferred objective for U.S. bank regulation. The Community Reinvestment Act most clearly reflects such objectives.

In Western European countries such policies are even more widespread, although different criteria prevail,[29] and in developing countries the financial system often appears to be completely paralyzed by an extensive system of credit allocation.[30]

Apart from the fact that many of these policies have become embedded in bank policy, what makes them so obscure is that the dividing line between the objectives of credit allocation and of prudential banking supervision becomes blurred. What investment policy might better appear to promote the stability and soundness of financial institutions than that of keeping a large proportion of their assets in government paper?

The effect of indirect credit allocation is quite obvious. In an environment in which banks themselves must compete for equity capital, it is necessary that they offer their shareholders a competitive rate of return. When certain portions of their portfolio are subject to credit allocation, which means being inferior in terms of risk and/or return, both deposits and assets (loans) must be priced so as to compensate for the shortfall in profits. Domestic banks so constrained are therefore at a competitive disadvantage vis-à-vis Eurobanks, which are not subject to credit allocation. Consequently, credit tends to be rerouted through the external markets whenever credit allocation reduces the relative competitiveness of domestic intermediation. Just as the increasing incidence of credit allocation contributes to the growth of the Eurocurrency markets, the existence of these markets tends to frustrate attempts at indirect credit allocation. Countries that seek to channel funds to favored sectors by means of domestic financial institutions are increasingly discovering that the funds to be reallocated largely disappear into the external market and that the additional costs are simply borne by those who do not have access to these markets. As a result, the customers that end up with the higher-cost loans and lower-yielding deposits tend to be smaller domestic businesses and less affluent investors. The primary beneficiaries are usually the larger business units from whose reach funds are supposed to be allocated away.

Over the long run, the result appears to be an unstable equilibrium that (1) either leads to a frustrated government imposing exchange and capital controls to "keep domestic savings at home" (and which assuredly will keep foreign savings at bay), or (2) leads to relatively mild forms of credit allocation supported by tax or regulatory subsidies, constrained

---

[29]See Donald R. Hidgman, *Selected Credit Controls in Western Europe*, Banking Research Fund, Association of Reserve City Bankers, Chicago, 1976.

[30]Ronald I. McKinnon, *Money and Capital in Economic Development*, Washington, D.C.: Brookings Institution, 1973.

only by precarious segmentation between wholesale and retail markets which is constantly under attack from advances in technology and financial innovation.[31]

Could governments influence the allocation of credit by Eurobank branches of parent banks under their jurisdiction? While the institutions who perform the external intermediation are subject to the control and supervision of the home government, the function of credit allocation effectively escapes governmental control. The reason is simply diversity and competition. This can best be explained by way of illustration. The government of country X, whose banks are active in external intermediation through their foreign affiliates, puts pressure on the parent banks to instruct their foreign affiliates to contribute to a worthy cause by committing a certain proportion of their assets to it. While the home government does ultimately have the power to impose its will on the unhappy bankers, the results will not be worth the effort. The foreign affiliates of banks from country X will simply become noncompetitive, and banks based in other countries will eagerly step in and enlarge their market share. Similarly, should the government of a Eurocenter suggest too strongly that Eurobanks operating there should make a contribution to local development projects, for example, it would soon find these institutions shifting their operations elsewhere.

We can summarize this issue by stating that the Euromarkets do indeed frustrate attempts at allocating credit indirectly within a country, and if this is accepted as a legitimate task for government policy, a case can be made for control of the Euromarkets in some form. An analysis of the possible methods of doing so appears later in this chapter.

In an international context, the Euromarkets facilitate market-induced credit allocation at the expense of government-induced allocation even more dramatically. Indeed, probably no other single force has made such a great contribution to the efficient international allocation of credit as have the Eurocurrency markets. Quite apart from the operational efficiency resulting from the narrow margins on which Eurobanks operate, they increase international capital market efficiency in two ways:

1. The Euromarkets increase international capital market integration in general.
2. As a highly developed system of financial intermediaries, they achieve effective liquidity, size, and credit transformation that contribute on a worldwide scale to the level of savings and investment.

---

[31]An illustration is money market mutual funds that invest in large Eurodeposits.

The first effect is succinctly summarized in the following classic passage[32]:

> The main justification for international capital movement is that it shifts savings from locations where they are abundant and cheap relative to investment opportunities to places where they are scarce and expensive. The argument holds for all theories of interest, whether the movement equalizes the marginal efficiency of capital, differences in time preference (for consumption), or differences in preference for liquidity. Where capital is more productive in one country than another, it should be moved from the country where it is less to the country where it is more productive. Total output is increased by such movement. Where savers in one country have lesser preference for current consumption than those in another, total welfare is increased by shifting the consumption of one into the future and the other into the present. And even if there can be no difference in the efficiency of capital or in time preference, gross capital movements, though not net, will increase overall world welfare under circumstances of different preferences for liquidity, if long-term capital moves from the country with low liquidity preference to that with high, and short-term capital moves in the other direction.

The second effect arises from the role of savings intermediaries, which perform the function of matching the asset (and maturity) preferences of savers with the liability preferences of borrowers. The better this function is performed, the more it will foster efficiency in the capital market where savings are transformed and channeled into those real investments that are most productive. This is because a *money market* provides standby facilities for the financial and nonfinancial organizations that participate in the *capital market*. In short, the existence of a broad, deep, and resilient market in which liabilities and/or assets of financial intermediaries can be negotiated is a necessary ingredient for an efficient market for long-term capital.

Few financial markets perform this maturity and liquidity transformation function more effectively than does the Eurocurrency market. The great bulk of deposits in the market are of very short-term (less than six months) maturity, while the Eurobanks have dominated the provision of large medium-term and long-term revolving credit facilities for the exploitation of natural resources and for other capital investment projects. They mitigate detrimental effects of an excessive bias toward liquidity by financial investors, a bias that is particularly pronounced in periods of financial instability. The Euromarkets have, in effect, consolidated the more limited capacities of domestic capital markets by internationalizing the savings-investment process and by adding the liquidity transformation capacities of the financial sector of the world economy. And if one adds the rate risk man-

---

[32]C. P. Kindleberger, "The Pros and Cons of an International Capital Market," *Zeitschrift für die gesamte Staatswissenschaft*, October 1967, pp. 600–617.

agement capabilities associated with these markets as shown in Chapter 4, the capital risk transformation capabilities of the offshore markets become very visible.

DISTRIBUTIONAL EFFECTS

Which countries gain the most from the increased international efficiency of financial markets? The starting assumption is that the performance of the international intermediation function in a particular country (such as the United States) introduces a bias into the allocation of funds toward investment projects in that country or at least toward projects controlled by firms based in that country. This is because of familiarity and reduced risk as perceived by lenders. Thus countries that are capital importers with structurally weak domestic financial markets will gain most; countries with relatively efficient financial markets that are capital exporters may come out less well off. But all share in the general increase in efficiency of the international markets. As Kindleberger put it long ago:

> In my judgment, the economists have underestimated the contribution to *national* development of an international capital market. The visible hand of foreign aid and even of international loan funds may be a less sure road to development than the arms-length bargaining power between borrowers who have to establish their credit worthiness and lenders who have to be convinced.[33]

THE ABILITY OF GOVERNMENTS TO CONTROL THE EUROMARKETS

In this section we analyze how the Euromarkets could be controlled, and which specific measures might be instituted. The feasibility of such measures might be roughly indicative of the probability of restrictions being imposed.

In order to see exactly where restrictions might be applied, let us review the preconditions for a functioning system of external financial intermediation:

1. There must be jurisdictions that permit financial institutions to accept, or bid for, deposits denominated in a currency other than that which is used as a means of payment in the Euromarket center itself and, by the same token, make loans denominated in such a foreign currency.

---

[33]C. P. Kindleberger and A. Shonfield (eds.), *North American and Western European Economic Policies*, London: MacMillan-St. Martin's Press, 1971, p. 495.

2. It is necessary that the Eurobanks be permitted to keep working balances (demand deposits) in banks of countries whose currencies are being used to denominate the credit transactions undertaken by the Eurobanks, and that there are no restrictions on the transfer of such balances, at least among parties who are nonresidents of the country whose currency is involved.

3. There must be a sufficient number of borrowers and lenders able and willing to take up loans from, and to invest funds with, Eurobanks.

Each of these necessary (but not sufficient) conditions could provide a point of leverage for government policy to control the Euromarkets. How might such control be implemented?

The Eurocenters

The Eurocenters, the major meeting places of demand and supply for internationally mobile funds, have been the main focus of the early attempts to control the markets. If only the governments of the jurisdiction where external intermediation takes place could be persuaded to impose uniform reserve requirements on such activities, some have argued, the Euromarkets could be brought under control. There can be no doubt about the effectiveness of such measures; with sufficiently high reserve requirements, the growth of the Eurocurrency market could not only be halted but reversed, by making external intermediation uncompetitive with domestic intermediation.

The history of the Euromarkets has also shown that attempts to this effect have been fruitless because the governments where such activities take place have consistently refused to cooperate. It is simply not in their interests to do so. This can be clearly illustrated with the example of the City of London, the largest single center for Eurocurrency activities. The British authorities have primary responsibility for money and credit conditions in the sterling area, now limited to the United Kingdom proper. Monetary policy in the United Kingdom, however, is affected by the activities of the Eurobanks in London only to the extent that they accept foreign currency deposits from and make loans to U.K. residents. British exchange controls, however, severely restrict such activities. The business of London-based Eurobanks is almost exclusively with entities that are nonresidents from a British point of view.

On the other hand, this "offshore" business provides employment for skilled people and gives rise to ancillary services. Eurobanks, moreover, make profits on which they pay taxes to the British government. In addition, all these earnings are in foreign currency, contributing substantially to Britain's foreign exchange earnings. Thus the British government incurs few, if any, costs and disadvantages, but profits handsomely from such activities. And Britain receives the prestige associated with being an international financial center.

Thus it is not surprising that there are always jurisdictions that either have succeeded in or have ambitions of playing host to Eurocurrency activities. Unless a worldwide agreement is reached, any restrictions imposed on one or two centers would simply cause such business to shift to more hospitable places.

Reserve requirements can also be imposed on the Eurobanking activities of foreign branches by the governments of the parent banks. But here, too, for such policies to succeed at all, a comprehensive international agreement is necessary, not only by the major powers but by each and every country with a reasonably well-developed banking system. Since reserve requirements—unlike capital adequacy—are much more controversial, the probabilities to reach such agreement among, say the G 10, are negligible.[34]

Access to Working Balances

The removal of nonresident convertibility would be a more direct means of control. It would also be a highly effective one: Eurobanks' access to working balances, and the ability to transfer them freely, is an absolute prerequisite of any money market that is to serve nonresidents.

The Japanese yen serves as an example of the fact that without free transfer of such balances an external money market cannot survive even if all the other preconditions for a large and buoyant "Euroyen" market are present. The Japanese economy is huge, and its external links extensive; furthermore, the domestic banking system is highly regulated, and spreads between borrowing and lending rates are wide by international standards. Its money markets are thin and inefficient, even after years of piecemeal liberalization. And Singapore as well as Hong Kong provide regional centers with an infrastructure already in place to take up the business. Yet until 1981 external credit transactions in yen were few and far between, and have been always done on the basis of a swap: Eurodollars covered with a forward yen contract.[35] This is simply because Japan had not really adopted nonresident convertibility for the yen until 1980 when that country's basic control system was fundamentally altered.

---

[34]A perfect example of the failure of such a policy is Regulation M in the United States. This imposes reserve requirements on Euroloans made by foreign branches of U.S. banks to U.S. entities. The problem, of course, is that the Federal Reserve Board has no control over foreign banks outside the United States. As a result, all hat has been accomplished is to provide foreign banks with an artificial advantage when it comes to lending to U.S. corporations for domestic purposes. Even if a corporation prefers to continue to borrow from U.S. banks, it can avoid Regulation M by channeling the funds to a foreign affiliate of the corporation, say, in the Netherlands Antilles; the affiliate, in turn, lends the funds to the U.S. Parent.

[35]This mechanism is described in Chapter Four.

The removal or severe restriction of nonresident convertibility once granted is a very drastic step. Few countries are willing to bear the economic costs of such controls. If foreigners are prevented from freely transferring bank balances, investment from abroad will be deterred and international trade inhibited. Not only does the country lose what are, in effect, interest-free loans from foreigners, but residents of the country must build up balances abroad because trade and investment must go on, international payments have to be made, and these require the existence of working balances, either held in the country by nonresidents ("nostro accounts") or by residents abroad ("vostro accounts").

It is not surprising, therefore, that in the postwar period no major country has restricted nonresident convertibility; it is not sufficient merely to restrict certain transactions. Dollar accounts in New York, for example, are used not only to clear Eurodollar credit transactions, but for all kinds of international payments. To require the U.S. authorities to request documentation on each transaction would be administratively impossible. It would also end the role of the dollar as a vehicle currency, which is surely not in the interest of the United States. After all, foreigners either have paid in goods and services, or they continue to pay interest in order to hold something that costs the United States very little to produce, i.e., dollar demand balances in U.S. banks.

Control of Demand and Supply

It is important to recognize the legal nature of Eurocurrency transactions: they are international financial transactions, because they involve either a credit relationship among entities in different countries (international *credit* flow, or an international *payment*, or both). To illustrate: a Eurobank in London can make a Eurodollar loan to a corporation (a) in the United States, (b) in Britain (U.K. controls notwithstanding), or (c) in France. The first case establishes an international credit relationship, but the payment of the loan proceeds takes place in the United States, the country of the borrower. In the second case, the credit relationship is a domestic one, but the British borrower receives the loan proceeds in the United States, in a currency other than his own (i.e., an international payment is involved). In the last case, both the credit and the payment are international transactions from a French regulatory point of view.

Therefore, all Eurocurrency transactions are ultimately subject to national controls over international financial transactions, in short, exchange controls. However, exchange controls are never total, so the effectiveness of such controls varies with the precise nature of the transaction.

How do exchange controls affect the movement of funds between the national and international money markets? The answer depends on who is controlled and what the authorities seek to achieve.[36]

Controls on Banks. Financial institutions are invariably the first to be affected by policy measures regulating international fund flows. This is not only because they are the most obvious conduits for internationally mobile funds, but also because the regulatory system is usually well-developed and all that has to be done is to tailor the existing instruments to the specific task of reducing the flow of funds out of or into the particular country.

Frequently, problems as perceived by the regulatory authorities can be dealt with effectively without formal rules because financial institutions, being extensively regulated, cannot usually afford to go against the wishes of the authorities. This moral suasion proves to be quite effective as long as competition among banks from various countries is limited. In the United States, for example, commercial banks have for years refused to accommodate private individuals seeking to take positions in foreign currencies because the Fed frowned upon such activities. Likewise, they have been asked to actively discourage their (corporate) clients from switching funds from domestic (time) deposits into Eurodollar deposits.[37]

In the category of formal regulations, the traditional tools of reserve requirements have been used extensively. Special reserve requirements on (1) gross external liabilities, (2) net external liabilities, (3) the level of external liabilities or assets, and (4) changes in the level of such items have all been used at various times by various countries, to encourage banks to move funds into or out of a national market.[38]

When such measures appear to be ineffective, reserve requirements are "tightened" in one or more of the following ways:

1. Reserve requirements on external liabilities up to 100 percent.
2. Prohibition on acceptance of deposits in foreign currency.
3. Prohibition on acceptance of deposits from nonresidents.
4. Ceilings on gross or net external liabilities.
5. Obligatory matching of external assets and liabilities.
6. Control of the term structure of external liabilities.
7. Freeze on external liabilities.

[36]This section follows an outline presented by David T. Llewellyn, "How To Control Capital Flows?" *The Banker*, July 1973, pp. 764–768.

[37]See the comments on page 20 of *Improving Monetary Aggregates*, Report of the Advisory Committee on Monetary Statistics, Washington, D.C.: Federal Reserve Board, June 1976.

[38]Rodney H. Mills, Jr., "Regulations on Short-Term Capital Movements: Recent Techniques in Selected Industrial Countries," *Federal Reserve Board Discussion Paper*, Washington, D.C., November 1972.

Controls on Nonbanks. The increasing circumvention of controls on banks experienced by Germany and other countries led, in the late 1960s, to experiments with controls on nonbanks. The following are some of the more frequently employed methods of restricting the international financial transactions of nonbanks:

1. Reserve requirements on external borrowing ("bardepot").
2. Withholding taxes on interest and dividends paid to nonresidents.
3. Prohibition on foreign currency borrowing for internal use.
4. Prohibition on advance payments for imports/exports.
5. Control over access of foreign firms to domestic money markets.
6. Prohibition of foreign purchases of domestic money market assets, securities, and real estate.
7. Restrictions on holding foreign money market investments.

To the extent that it is public or quasi-public entities, such as local authorities, that are involved in undesired foreign borrowing or investing, the government's influence is relatively direct. The private sector proves to be much more difficult to handle, simply because funds can be moved internationally by means of each and every international transaction that a firm undertakes. If outright foreign borrowing or lending is restricted, funds can be moved through leading or lagging of payments, inventories can be sold to or bought from foreign affiliates, and trade receivables can be carried on the domestic books of foreign "captive" finance companies or sold to financial institutions abroad. In addition, there are the time-honored strategies of fiddling with transfer prices, dividend payments or nonpayments, and fees for technical services, patents, and overhead allocations. While these possibilities are not without limitations, if the incentives are felt to be sufficient and given enough time, a large volume of funds can be moved.

Obviously, government regulators are aware of these practices, but the authorities face a fundamental dilemma. Precisely because funds can be moved by firms in so many ways, an airtight system of controls would necessitate scrutinizing each and every transaction that a firm undertakes. This is administratively very difficult to accomplish and prohibitively costly, not only in the sense of enforcement cost but also as a result of damage done to business activity and economic efficiency.

However, without being total and comprehensive, all measures regulating the access of nonbanks to the external money market remain piecemeal. The end result is usually that the economy incurs the cost of enforcement and suffers the loss of efficiency caused by the controls that have been imposed, and yet the desired effect remains elusive because funds flow through alternative channels.

Interestingly, recognition of the fact that controls on nonbanks are either ineffective, or too costly if comprehensive, has strengthened the hand of those in the political arena who argue against controls. Indeed, in developed countries at least, the pressure from the Euromarkets has moved authorities worldwide to liberalize financial markets to such an extent that the efficient linkages gave rise to the notion of "globalization."

Open Market-Type Operations[39]

One category of policy tools is special in that it seeks to exert influence on the supply and price of funds not directly through regulation but rather by means of the supply-and-demand mechanism itself. In the money markets, such action is called "open-market operation"; in the foreign exchange markets, it is called "intervention." In the domestic financial system the central bank can influence the supply of credit by buying or selling financial instruments. Surely central banks, individually or in concert, should be able in a similar fashion to influence interest rates and the supply of credit in the Eurocurrency markets simply by depositing or withdrawing funds from the markets?

The answer to this question is "no," as we shall see shortly. Nevertheless, central banks have, from time to time, sought to increase or decrease availability in the Euromarkets by borrowing or depositing funds directly or through the services of the Bank for International Settlements. Why are such attempts doomed to failure? Simply because as long as funds can move relatively freely between the domestic money market and the corresponding external market, operations that raise or lower interest rates in the external market will result immediately in an offsetting flow of funds out of or into the domestic market. For example, if central banks borrow funds in the Euromarket to "sterilize" them, interest rates will rise relative to national markets and depositors will find incentives increased and shift funds into the external market. On the other hand, private borrowers will find the Euromarket marginally less attractive and reduce their takings accordingly. The mistake is to treat the Eurodollar market, for example, as a self-contained money market and not as merely part of the total dollar money market, domestic and international. On the other hand, the integration of domestic and international money markets implies that actions influencing the domestic supply or price of credit will be promptly felt in the external market. In other words, all that is necessary to influence the supply of credit or interest rates in the external market is normal open-market operation in the domestic market.[40]

---

[39]The contents of this section parallel the analysis found in Carl H. Stem, "Some Eurocurrency Problems" in Carl H. Stem, John H. Makin, and Dennis E. Logue (eds.), *Eurocurrencies and the International Monetary System*, Washington, D.C.: American Enterprise Institute, 1976, p. 308.

[40]Central banks' attempts to intervene in the markets for *forward foreign exchange* give rise to arbitrage operations and will fail in the absence of controls on international capital flows.

SUMMARY AND CONCLUSIONS

This chapter has addressed the issue of why and how governmental control could be exerted over the Eurocurrency market. Early in this chapter we identified three possible motives for regulation of the market:

1. To properly execute monetary and exchange-rate policy.
2. To maintain the soundness of the financial system.
3. To influence the allocation of credit.

Our conclusions were (1) that the growth of external financial markets may, to a limited extent, add to aggregate liquidity primarily through the circumvention of reserve requirements; (2) that the monetary authorities nevertheless retain control over monetary aggregates and interest rates and can influence credit growth in the Euromarket as they can in other nonbank segments of the credit system; (3) that the growth of the external segment of the money market necessitates the revision of traditional estimates of monetary aggregates; (4) that there is no serious cause for concern either about a run on all Eurobanks, or about runs on particular Eurobanks, since maintaining the soundness of the major domestic banks ensures that the soundness of their Eurobanking activities is maintained; and hence (5) no lender of last resort for the Eurocurrency market per se is necessary.

Thus the first two objectives of banking regulation are not seriously thwarted by the existence of the Euromarkets. The third, however, clearly is: The Eurocurrency market significantly affects both the international and the domestic allocation of credit and hence hinders national governments' attempts at domestic credit allocation.

Whatever the motive, any government's attempts to control the market face the reality of the fungibility of money and the footloose nature of international banking activities. In the absence of worldwide agreement, direct controls on Eurobanks themselves would result in Eurobanking business shifting either to a different jurisdiction or to a different group of Eurobanks. Exchange controls, affecting either the Eurobanks' working balances or the access of borrowers or depositors, could certainly constrain segments of the market. But such restrictions, to be effective, must be so comprehensive as to diminish the gains from international trade and investment.

From the point of view of a banker or corporate treasurer, it becomes clear that the probability of direct controls imposed by Euromarket centers (say, by the United Kingdom) or through restrictions on nonresident convertibility (by the United States, for example) is virtually nil. National controls on international financial transactions, on the other hand, are problems with to which firms and individual institutions will, given sufficient flexibility, continue to adjust.

The only types of policies that would reverse the shift of depositing and lending activities to the Euromarket are those that would make domestic intermediation more competitive with the external markets. The payment of market rates of interest on required reserves on time deposits, a reduction in indirect credit allocation, a reduction in the cost of domestic banking in general, and similar measures would contribute to returning much of the intermediation activity into the regulatory fold of the domestic authorities. But as long as countries maintain a reasonable degree of freedom for international financial transactions while continuing to restrict and control the domestic money markets, the Euromarkets will thrive and grow on the basis of freedom from such restrictions.

SELECTED REFERENCES

Balbach, Anatol B. and David H. Resler, "Eurodollars and the U.S. Money Supply," *Federal Reserve Bank of St. Louis Review*, June/July 1980, Vol. 62, No. 6, pp. 2–12.

Batten, Dallas S. and R.W. Hafer, "Currency Substitution: A Test of Its Importance," *Economic Review*, Federal Reserve Bank of St. Lewis, Aug/Sept 1984, pp. 5–11.

Dale, Richard, "Bank Supervision Around the World," New York: Group of Thirty, 1982.

Dufey, Gunter, "The Role of Japanese Financial Institutions Abroad," in *Japanese Financial Growth*, Charles Goodhart & George Sutija (eds.), London: LSE Press, 1990.

Dufey, Gunter and Otmar Issing, "Mindestreserve-politik, Geldmengensteuerung, und Euromarket," *Geld, Banken, und Versicherungen*, Hermann Goppelts und Rudolph Henn, eds. Band I, West Germany: Athenäum, 1981, pp. 100–119.

Giddy, Ian H., "Domestic Regulation vs. International Competition in Banking," *Kredit und Kapital*, August 1984, pp. 195–209.

Giovanni, Alberto and Colin Mayer (eds.), *European Financial Regulation*, Cambridge University Press, 1991.

Goodfriend, Marvin and Monica Hargraves, "A Historical Assessment of the Rationales and Functions of Reserve Requirements," *Economic Review*, Federal Reserve Bank of Richmond, March/April 1983, pp. 3–21.

Hidgman, Donald R., *Selected Credit Controls in Western Europe*, Banking Research Fund, Association of Reserve City Bankers, Chicago, 1976.

Improving Monetary Aggregates, Report of the Advisory Committee on Monetary Statistics, Washington, D.C.: Federal Reserve Board, June 1976.

"Intervention in Foreign Exchange Markets: A Summary of Ten Staff Studies," *Federal Reserve Bulletin*, November 1983, pp. 830–836.

Kane, Edward J., "How Market Forces Influence the Structure of Financial Regulation," in William S. Haraf and Rose Marie Kushmeider (eds.), *Restructuring Banking and Financial Services in America*, Washington, D.C.: American Enterprise Institute, 1988.

Kindleberger, C.P., "The Pros and Cons of an International Capital Market," *Zeitschrift für die gesamte Staatswissenschaft*, October 1967, pp. 600–617.

Kindleberger, C.P., and A. Shonfield (eds.), *North American and Western European Economic Policies*, London: Macmillan-St. Martin's Press, 1971, p. 495.

Kormendi, Roger, et al., "The Origins and Resolution of the Thrift Crisis," *Journal of Applied Corporate Finance*, April 1989.

Llewellyn, David T., "How to Control Capital Flows?" *The Banker*, July 1973, pp. 764–768.

Mader, Richard "Die Mindestreservepolitik im Internationalen Vergleich," *Die Bank*, March 1989, pp. 128–133.

McClam, Warren D., "U.S. Monetary Aggregates, Income Velocity and the Euro-dollar Market," Basle: Monetary and Economic Department, Bank for International Settlements, BIS Economic Papers, No. 2, April 1980.

McKinnon, Ronald I., "Currency Substitution and Instability in the World Dollar Standard," *Ameican Economic Review*, June 1982, pp. 320–333.

McKinnon, Ronald I., *Money and Capital in Economic Development*, Washington, D.C.: Brookings Institution, 1973.

McMahon, C.W., "Controlling the Euromarkets," *The Banker*, March 1976, pp. 267–272.

Merton, Robert C., "An Analytic Derivation of the Cost of Deposit Insurance and Loan Guarantees: An Application of Modern Option Pricing Theory," *Journal of Banking and Finance*, Vol. 1, No. 1, 1977.

Miles, Marc A., "Currency Substitution, Flexible Exchange Rates as Monetary Independence," *American Economic Review*, June 1978, pp. 428–436.

Mills, Rodney H. Jr., "Regulations on Short-Term Capital Movements: Recent Techniques in Selected Industrial Countries," *Federal Reserve Board Discussion Paper*, Washington, D.C., November 1972.

Mussa, Michael, "The Role of Official Intervention," Occasional Papers 6, New York: Group of Thirty, 1981.

Niehans, Jürg and John Hewson, "The Eurodollar Market and Monetary Theory," *Journal of Money, Credit and Banking*, February 1976, pp. 1–27.

Quinn, Terence, "The Economics of Financial Regulation: A Survey," *Central Bank of Ireland Bulletin*, Autumn 1992, pp. 55–70.

Stem, Carl H., "Some Eurocurrency Problems," in Carl H. Stem, John H. Makin, and Dennis E. Logue (eds.), *Eurocurrencies and the International Monetary System*, Washington, D.C.: American Enterprise Institute, 1976.

Swoboda, Alexander K., "Credit Creation in the Euromarket: Alternative Theories and Implications for Control," Occasional Papers 2, New York: Group of Thirty, 1980.

Willms, Manfred, "Money Creation in the Euro-Currency Market," *Weltwirtschaftliches Archiv*, Vol. 112, 1976, pp. 201–230.

Wood, John H., "Two Notes on the Uniqueness of Commercial Banks," *Journal of Finance*, March 1970, p. 90–91.

Chapter Eight

THE INTERNATIONAL MONEY MARKET: PERSPECTIVE AND PROGNOSIS

Contents: *What's So Special About the Eurocurrency Markets?   Domestic and External Credit Markets and the International Financial System   The Euromarkets and Economic Welfare   Bank Regulation and the External Credit Market   Conditions for the External Credit Markets to Continue to Exist and Thrive   The Globalization of Banks and Markets The Future*

WHAT'S SO SPECIAL ABOUT THE EUROCURRENCY MARKETS?

The objective of this book has been to explain the nature, workings, and implications of the international money market in terms of a clear and consistent conceptual framework. We have shown, in Chapter Two, how the success of the Eurocurrency market has spurred the growth in competitiveness and variety of a number of domestic money markets, while the conflicting roles of money market instruments and institutions provide a continuing rationale for the existence of the external money market. We have looked in depth at such issues as the interest rate interdependence of the external and internal markets (Chapter Three); the growth of the external markets compared with national markets, including the multiplier problem (Chapter One, Appendix); the impact on international liquidity and the safety of the banking system and other public policy issues (Chapter Seven). We have also undertaken an analysis of borrowing and lending practices (Chapters Five and Six). The intent throughout was to explain as many theoretical, practical, and public policy issues in the framework of a few unified ideas. One conclusion should be clear: there are few important aspects about the international money market that cannot be explained with reference to certain fundamental ideas. These are:

1. The external (Eurocurrency) and internal (domestic) money markets are merely competing segments of the larger markets for the assets and liabilities of financial intermediaries.

2. Domestic money markets are becoming far more efficient and diverse than they used to be, but almost all domestic money markets and banking systems serve public as well as private roles. Financial institutions in the external market, in contrast, are largely free of both informal constraints (such as pressures to allocate credit to certain borrowers) and formal regulations (such as reserve requirements). Eurobanks, typically the offshore branches of major domestic banks, can therefore operate on narrower margins than can domestic banks.

3. On the other hand, from the point of view of the depositor or borrower, deposits in and loans from Eurobanks are generally riskier, because transactions with Eurobanks are subject to restrictions on funds transfers and for credit extension by two political jurisdictions, whereas domestic transactions are subject to the political risk of only one government. Therefore Eurobanks—as a rule—offer more attractive deposit and (perhaps) loan rates than do domestic banks.

4. While entry to virtually all national banking systems is restricted, in effect if not *de jure,* there are few limits to participation by any financial institution in external financial intermediation.

5. The close links between the domestic and external credit markets in a particular currency may be partially broken when capital controls restrict transfers of funds into and out of the country of that currency.

6. The links between segments of the Eurocurrency markets denominated in different currencies are governed by exchange-rate factors. Arbitrage within the Eurocurrency market occurs through the foreign exchange markets, where the interest differentials equal the forward exchange premium or discount.

The Eurocurrency markets do differ from domestic markets in ways other than those summarized above. In most cases, however, these differences can be explained as the result of one or another of the basic features noted or can be dismissed as not being fundamental features of the external markets per se. *In all other respects, therefore, there is nothing special about the Eurocurrency markets per se.*

One can explain most aspects of the external market by analogy with a particular segment of the domestic banking market. In both systems economic units in need of funds must compete for them on the basis of the expected return paid, and financial institutions compete for the business of intermediating this credit. There are many aspects of the international money market that we have, by intent or omission, neglected to discuss. We have nevertheless sought to provide the reader with the tools with which to dissect virtually any problem relating to the market. The basic rule is this: If one cannot interpret the problem by analogy with the domestic market, it must be the result of one of the six distinguishing characteristics listed previously. We have found this to be a remarkably powerful principle.

DOMESTIC AND EXTERNAL CREDIT MARKETS AND THE INTERNATIONAL FINANCIAL SYSTEM

The international money markets involve few concepts that are not already familiar to students of money or banking. Yet this fact does not reduce their central role in the modern international financial system. The Euromarkets serve as the bridge between the financial markets of countries and currencies. They enable, for the first time, the *currency of denomination* of an asset to be separated from the *country of jurisdiction*. Stated differently, they enable borrowers and lenders to systematically separate the *currency risk* from the *political risk* of an asset or liability.

It is therefore instructive to examine precisely how the domestic and external markets for credit and the foreign exchange markets fit into the international financial system in general. The table following provides a schematic summary of the issues arising from the existence of international payments, capital flows, and financial markets. Let us explore some of these questions.

ROLE OF THE EXTERNAL MARKETS IN THE INTERNATIONAL FINANCIAL SYSTEM

PHENOMENON	FUNCTION
Existence of financial assets	Satisfies intertemporal preferences
Existence of money balances	Minimizes uncertainty and cost associated with future payments
Use of a vehicle currency	Reduces the costs and uncertainties involved in international payments
Currency denomination of financial assets and liabilities	Guards the international purchasing power and stability of portfolios
Extent of financial intermediation	Reconciles different risk and maturity preferences of borrowers and lenders
Degree of external versus internal intermediation	Reflects relative cost and risk perceptions
Market for spot and forward foreign exchange	Reconciles currency preferences and expectations
Eurocurrency market	Enables transactors to transform jurisdiction without transforming currency or institution
Arbitrage between domestic and external markets and among Eurocurrency markets	Assures equality of effective interest rates in the absence of controls

In a fundamental sense the financial system performs two functions: (1) the collection of savings and the allocation of resources into real investments, and (2) the facilitation of payment for transactions. Efficient performance of both functions requires financial assets and money balances, serving as convenient stores of value and means of payments, respectively. Internationally, there exists a need for the same services. Differences in the intertemporal preferences of economic transactors in different countries can be efficiently evened out through the international exchange of financial assets (international capital flows). And the working balances that financial institutions hold in other countries make possible an efficient transfer of funds to settle various kinds of international transactions. However, nearly all money balances are of a strictly national character, reinforced by national monopolies on issuance of currency and buttressed by legal tender laws.

If companies conducted trade and payments only bilaterally, using only the currency of the transactors, every international company or bank would be forced to hold money balances in all countries where they might have to make payments. Therefore the use of a common vehicle currency considerably improves the efficiency of the system for international payments. It permits transactors to economize on the number and amount of foreign money balances held. The choice of a national currency as a vehicle currency depends largely on these factors: (1) the relative number of "natural transactions" favoring large countries; (2) the availability of an efficient money market that permits transactors to adjust their liquidity positions at a low incremental cost; and (3) a strong expectation that the authorities will not restrict nonresidents in their use of working balances (technically this is known as the maintenance of nonresident convertibility).

Although the existence of money balances in a certain foreign currency will also promote the denomination of financial assets in that currency because transactions costs (conversion costs) will be minimized, in a world of uncertainty of exchange rates and international consumption, it is considerations of portfolio diversification that decide the currency denomination of financial assets and liabilities.

Such assets and liabilities are issued either (1) directly by (ultimate) investors to obtain funds for productive assets, or (2) by financial intermediaries who perform risk and maturity transformation by interjecting themselves between savers and investors. The extent of financial intermediation in the total savings-investment process depends largely on the ability of such institutions to better reconcile different risk and maturity preferences of borrowers and lenders than would be possible through organized securities markets. Given the institutional barriers involved in international capital flows, it is not surprising that financial intermediaries play a dominant role in the international flow of credit.

International capital flows, however, do not explain the existence and growth of extensive external ("Euro-") financial intermediation sectors; these phenomena are explained by different cost structures and risk perceptions relative to domestic financial intermediation. However, because of the special operating conditions, external financial intermediaries play an important role in the collection of savings and the allocation of credit, both internationally and in respect to the national financial market, of which they represent the external sector.

It is the special operating characteristics of the Eurocurrency markets that make them the integrating mechanism of what are different, and to a certain extent independent, functions: the international transmission of credit and payments. To the extent that payments are made in the future, markets for foreign means of payments and international credit markets are linked through arbitrage: the foreign exchange market, where currency preferences and expectations are reconciled, determines the relationship among various segments of the external markets, which, in turn, tie together national financial systems. How close these links are depends largely on the extent of governmental controls on international payments and credit transactions.

THE EUROMARKETS
AND ECONOMIC WELFARE

In Chapter One we argued that the development of large, competitive financial markets facilitates the transfer of resources from ultimate savers to ultimate investors at low cost, and so promotes economic growth. As broad, competitive, and liquid financial markets, the Eurocurrency markets contribute to the efficient transfer and allocation of resources to their most productive use. The Eurobanks enlarge the financial sector of those countries whose currencies are used in Euro instruments. As a result of their diversity of geographical location and national origin, Eurobanks may have a less domestically oriented bias in seeking out borrowers and depositors. Thus there is a strong presumption that they may contribute more to the efficient *international* allocation of credit than would the growth of an equal volume of intermediation in purely domestic markets.

Is there anything about the fundamental nature of the Eurocurrency system that suggests that its effect on economic growth and its distribution might differ from that of domestic markets? The answer is "yes," and the basis for that answer is grounded in two facts: (1) Eurobanks are not subject to pressures and legal constraints on investment behavior, and (2) they allow both international investors and borrowers to separate their choice of political risk from the choice of currency in which the asset or liability is to be denominated.

How do these features affect the growth and distribution of output? Consider first the effect on the distribution of credit, and therefore of

income, in a purely domestic context. Domestic banks are almost univer-
sally expected to allocate part of their loan and bond portfolios to "socially
preferred" borrowers who are less able to compete for funds in the open
credit market. In addition, domestic banks are required to hold noninterest-
bearing reserves, which are obligations of the government (in effect, a free
loan to the public). Each of these constraints means that banks earn less on
their portfolios, given the level of risk, than they would otherwise choose to
do. Each constraint, therefore, implies (1) a transfer of income to preferred
borrowers (including the government itself) from the bank's shareholders
and depositors, and (2) a suboptimal allocation of credit, in the sense that
the bank is prevented from allocating funds to their most profitable and productive uses.[1] By conducting their business in the external rather than the
domestic market, banks escape such constraints, so that there is a redistribution of credit away from privileged borrowers and in favor of more productive borrowers and therefore in favor of economic growth.

Similar reasoning applies to the international as opposed to the domestic allocation of credit through the external markets. Since the class of privileged borrowers (whose credit needs are perforce favored by domestic
banks) seldom extends to foreign borrowers, the latter are, when creditworthy and productive, favored by the effective removal of political constraints
on bank portfolios. The redistribution and growth-promoting effects of the
Euromarkets occur on an international as well as on a domestic scale.

It would be a mistake to deduce from this argument that the growth of
Eurocurrency banking is necessarily accompanied by a capital flow from countries with an external market to those without one. Although this may occur—
developing countries, for example, now have freer access to dollar credit than
might otherwise have been the case—the flow of loans to such countries may
well be offset by a flow of deposits from the same countries to the Euromarkets.
Such flows are even more likely now that savers can invest in dollar assets, for
example, without necessarily placing their funds in the United States. And in
the 1990s, the flow of bank loans to developing economies has been replaced by
a flow of equity capital and arm's length bond investments.

This brings us to our second point. International capital flows tend to
increase total (world) welfare by equalizing the marginal efficiency of capital, differences in preferences for present as opposed to future consumption,
and differences in preferences for liquidity. One may argue, as we have done
in Chapter Seven, that the Eurocurrency markets increase the international
mobility of capital and therefore enhance economic welfare and growth. The
reason lies partly in the institutional mechanism (it is easier to switch currencies in a single institution, place, and time zone), but also in the separation of

[1]Of course, domestic banking regulations often protect banks from competition too; so the final
effect of being subject to domestic regulations on a particular bank's profitability cannot be
stated unequivocally.

currency risk from political risk. An individual may respond to an attractive yield differential by switching his deposit or loan from one currency to another without altering the nature of the jurisdiction in which he books his deposit or loan; the same would not be true lacking the Euromarket.

Thus far, we have emphasized the *allocational efficiency* benefits of the relatively free Euromarkets. More and more, one can point to two additional effects: domestic market discipline, and financial innovation.

Financial markets allow companies to maintain temporary imbalances between their receipts and payments but this function is undermined unless they exert discipline to keep some entities from turning temporary into permanent—such as borrowing without the means or even the intention of repaying. Without discipline, resources are wasted, inefficient and perhaps corrupt financial institutions are perpetuated, and investors sooner or later lose confidence and desert the market. Market discipline on borrowers requires *open banking markets*, that is, lenders (and depositors) must have the freedom not to lend to risky borrowers, or to charge them a rational return on risk. Lenders must have access to *information*, so that discipline can be exerted in a timely fashion. Finally, there must be *no bailouts*, nor must lenders have any reason to believe that borrowers (and their creditors) will be rescued from their mistakes. These conditions have long been absent in a number of countries, developed as well as developing. What the external markets have done is to set a standard for market-based, as opposed to regulatory, discipline. When the boundaries to national banking markets erode, good banking tends to drive out lax banking.

In addition, international banks gaining access to domestic markets do not merely offer more competitive terms on loans and deposits. They bring an entirely new range of financial services. The reason is that in order to keep one's head above water in the global money and capital market, one must be able to offer newer, more valuable, more innovative products than plain vanilla deposits and loans. Today, many of these risk management products such as swaps, caps, and options. In the international markets, however, the imitation lag is increasingly short and so banks are eager to offer an innovative product range in a market where the product has not yet become commoditized. Hence one of the greatest benefits of the integration of domestic banking systems with the international banking market is the wider range of product choice and the stimulus to domestic innovation in financial services.

BANK REGULATION AND THE EXTERNAL CREDIT MARKET

If it is true that the external market enables banks to bypass the government's efforts to allocate credit by way of the private financial system, what can we conclude about the need for, and nature of, a response by the regulatory authorities? For although the Euromarkets may redistribute credit in a way that promotes economic growth, one cannot be sure that such redistribution is in the social interest of any particular country. A redistribution that increases total output does not necessarily increase total welfare. All one can say is that if a government is to tax some citizens to improve the income of others, the tax should not be levied in such a way as to discourage efficient use of resources.

The simple answer, then, to the dilemma posed by unregulated external markets is for the government to impose a *direct* tax and provide a *direct* subsidy to favored sectors or institutions. In this way the transfer of income would be effected without additional distortions in financial markets occurring. Instead, however, the usual method is to increase the burden of credit allocation on those institutions that remain subject to domestic regulatory influences, thus distorting domestic financial markets even further. But there is a limit to the extent to which authorities, such as the U.S. government, can increase the burden of indirect credit allocation on domestic institutions without forcing them into the external market. This limit may be stated in terms of **the law of maximum distortion:** *For a given level of restrictions on international capital flows, there is a limit on the extent to which a government can distort domestic financial markets.*

The reasoning behind this statement is quite simple. A government can force financial markets and institutions to allocate credit in a suboptimal fashion to a certain degree, even if an external market exists and capital inflows and outflows are relatively unrestricted. If the manipulation of banks' portfolios or investment decisions is carried too far, however, depositors and other investors will find themselves receiving returns insufficiently high for the level of risk involved. Therefore, either the financial markets and institutions themselves will shill to the external market (taking borrowers and depositors with them), or they will lose intermediation business to the external markets. Taking the United States as an example, let us assume that there is a given volume of credit intermediated in dollars. Part of the dollar credit system is external: the Eurodollar market. The more the U.S. authorities impose restraints and regulations on the rates that domestic banks can pay for deposits or obtain on assets, the greater the proportion of credit that will be intermediated externally. And the more dollar credit intermediation occurs outside the U.S. authorities' jurisdiction, the more difficult it will be to allocate credit domestically. The only recourse for the U.S. government is to accept the limits to market distortion, or to impose restrictions on investing or borrowing abroad—that is, to raise the level of capital controls. And a policy of financial isolationism has its own costs, which we need not discuss here.

What can we conclude? Since, as was argued in Chapter Seven, there is little that the U.S. government or even the major industrial countries' governments in concert can do about controlling the Eurodollar market directly, domestic financial institutions will continue to bear a disproportionate burden of regulation. Reserve requirements and other nonmarket constraints on banks' asset or liability decisions can be regarded as an indirect tax.[2] The existence of external markets means that this tax falls more heavily on domestic banks, their owners and depositors, than would be the case in the absence of external markets. This is not necessarily "unfair," because many domestic banks benefit from protected markets that result solely from regulation-related barriers to entry. But it does suggest that such a tax might be more equitably and efficiently collected by some means other than the distortion of credit markets.

Indeed, some observers have suggested that the only way for the U.S. authorities to regain controls over financial markets is to allow domestic institutions to be sufficiently competitive to attract credit intermediation business back to the United States. This could be done, for example, (1) by removing reserve requirements on bank time deposits, (2) by paying a competitive interest rate on the required reserves, and (3) by eliminating most of the explicit and informal constraints on portfolio choices that banks face. Under this scheme, both domestic banks and Eurobanks could, for a fee, buy deposit insurance such as that offered by a deposit insurance restitution such as the FDIC in the United States, and be subject to examination. But these higher costs would mean that depositors who favored such banks would have to accept a slightly lower interest rate.

CONDITIONS FOR THE EXTERNAL CREDIT MARKETS TO CONTINUE TO EXIST AND THRIVE

The Eurocurrency market is a creature of regulation and as such depends largely for its existence on the nature and degree of banking regulations and capital controls. Of course, it is not regulation per se that matters, only regulation that imposes a greater cost than it provides benefits. The banking authorities of many countries provide supervision and examination of domestic banks that are regarded as useful services by the consumers of banking services. And the test of such effects of regulation is when both borrowers and depositors are willing to accept less favorable interest rates in return for the assurance that the bank's books are subject to regular review by competent and objective authorities. The most successful of the Eurobanks, then, tend to be those that are subject to such review.

But domestic banking regulation that imposes a cost without any associated benefits provides an incentive for the banking public to avoid this cost, and it does so by means of the external money market. We conclude that, other things being equal,

---

[2]This tax is akin to a sales tax rather than a tax on income or profits. Some economists suggest that such a tax might be more equitably and efficiently collected by some means other than the distortion of credit markets.

Size of external credit market relative to total credit market in that currency	is a function of	Costs of domestic banking regulation minus Benefits of domestic banking regulation

It follows that if domestic banking regulation were to disappear, there would be little incentive for the Eurocurrency markets to exist. Yet we need not go so far. Even in the presence of banking regulation, most of the external market would shift back to the domestic market if banking regulation were such that it did not distort financial decisions.[3]

This raises a related question: If the size and existence of external markets are largely a function of the burden of domestic regulation, why is it that external credit markets have not developed in the many currencies whose countries distort banks' decisions to a much greater degree than does the United States? Why is there not a large Eurocurrency market in Brazilian cruzeiros, Indian rupees, or even Japanese yen? The answer lies in the mechanism of the market. Every transfer of funds into, out of, or between Eurobanks is made by means of a transfer in domestic banks; hence the ability to undertake such transfers is an absolute prerequisite for the existence of a Euromarket in a particular currency. To the extent that financial transactions between domestic residents and nonresidents are restricted, it becomes more difficult to establish and maintain an active external credit market. Thus it is a mistake to suppose that the Eurodollar market grew during the 1960s because of the U.S. capital controls; more accurately, it grew in spite of them. At no time, however, did the United States restrict *nonresident convertibility*—that is, foreigners were always free to increase or decrease their balances in U.S. domestic banks. The same was not true of Japan until relatively recently, hence the slow development of a market in Euroyen.[4]

There is another reason for the absence of external credit markets in most of the world's currencies. This reason is that, paradoxically, one can obtain Euroloans or Eurodeposits in any particular currency without there actually being a Euromarket in that currency. How can this be? The answer lies in the fact that an asset or liability in, say, dollars, can be effectively converted into any other currency by buying or selling that currency m the forward market. (The reader who has forgotten how this is done is referred back to Chapter Three.) Assume, for example, that a Mexican resident wishes to hold a Europeso deposit in London but discovers that no

---

[3]Even in the absence of costly regulations, however, some credit business would continue to be intermediated externally as a result *of fear* of the later imposition of restrictions on domestic banks.

[4]In Japan, yen balances in Japanese banks can be held only if they remit from authorized transactions; these become "free yen." And the short-term capital transactions that are required for Eurocurrency borrowing and lending do not fall into that category.

Europeso market exists and that even if it did, it would be narrow, illiquid, and inefficient. What he can do, instead, is sell his pesos for dollars in the spot foreign exchange market, deposit the dollars in a Eurobank, and simultaneously buy Mexican pesos forward. He will now effectively own a peso-denominated asset earning an interest rate that equals the Eurodollar rate plus the forward discount on the Mexican peso.[5]

Taken to its logical extreme, this argument implies that when an external market in one currency (such as the U.S. dollar) exists, there is no need for parallel deposit markets in any other currency, since Eurodollars can be "swapped" into any given currency as long as a forward market exists for that currency. Alternatively, since transactions in external deposit markets are perfect substitutes for forward foreign exchange transactions, the depth and liquidity of the market for forward foreign exchange is greatly enhanced by the existence of the Euromarkets.

THE GLOBALIZATION OF BANKS AND MARKETS

Thanks initially to the phenomenal growth of the Eurocurrency market, banking, many have observed, is becoming truly global. That fact in itself is not new, for the likes of Citibank, Barclays Bank, Royal Bank of Canada, and Banque Indosuez have had worldwide branching networks for decades. Yet the *character* of globalization has changed: from global institutions to global markets. What is different is the manner in which international banking and capital markets operate. Once upon a time, a Japanese corporation like Toyota which required yen debt had to borrow from a Japanese bank in Japan. To capture a share of this business, Credit Suisse would have to establish a full-fledged banking operation in Tokyo, one that conducted business in the framework of the domestic banking system. Nowadays Toyota would be just as likely to achieve the same objective by borrowing Deutsche marks from Credit Suisse in London, and converting the mark debt into effective yen debt by means of a currency swap. The Euromarkets in conjunction with the derivative markets have achieved a globalized of *choice* in lieu of the erstwhile, more cumbersome, globalization of financial institutions. This has not happened everywhere, nor at the same pace in different currencies. From the point of view of banks, it may make sense to defend a domestic franchise as long as possible. Domestic banks are therefore often in accord with some governments who fear that their authority is being undermined.

In our view, their fears are justified. There is a trend at work that would be difficult to reverse. In country after country, borrowers' and depositors' choices are being widened by the separation of currency of jurisdiction from

---

[5]Note, however, that this example or any similar transaction presupposes some degree of freedom for capital transfers into and out of the country in question.

country of jurisdiction and from the nationality of the intermediating institution. With more institutions and locations competing for once-captive business, excess profits that were previously taxed away (or that cushioned banks from the costs of regulation) are no longer available. Of course the liberalization of financial markets has not taken place everywhere, or at the same pace in different countries. What we are claiming is that there is a tendency, worldwide, toward the separation of currency of jurisdiction from country of denomination, and from nationality of financial institution.

Moreover, competition often comes from unexpected places. New financial risk management techniques are replacing the old, especially when risk management can be separated from financial assets and liabilities and from credit risk impediments. And new financial service firms are increasingly challenging even the biggest of the global commercial banks. Jettisoning traditional banking relationships, countries, companies, and individuals are turning to institutions that specialize in managing investments or to those that originate, underwrite, and distribute securities. Risk management can be separated from asset management, and purchased from specialized trading firms. Major corporations have developed highly sophisticated financial groups, and some have gone so far as to sell financial services in competition with their erstwhile financiers.

THE FUTURE

The international money market is a stable phenomenon with an evolving form. It consists of domestic money markets linked to one another through the Eurocurrency and foreign exchange markets. As long as the Euromarkets continue to thrive as a key element of the international money market, we will be able to employ the framework laid out in the first section to reinterpret any issues that arise.

The greatest strength of the international financial markets, and of the institutions that participate in them, is their ability to adapt. Like biological species that have evolved in a sheltered environment, many state owned or supported banks in national markets are having great difficulty surviving in the new environment of eroding market barriers. The challenge for banks, and for those that observe them, is to understand what it takes to succeed in different product markets.

The markets in which international banks compete are by no means homogenous. Some products, such as deposit taking and syndicated lending, are commodity-like: They have many of the attributes of efficient markets—intense competition, ease of entry and exit, low transaction and information costs, rapid adjustment to change, and very thin profit margins. Others, such as M&A advisory services, involve high degrees of product differentiation, substantial monopoly elements, natural barriers to entry, and substantial market power on the part of individual firms. Indeed the institutions of the international money market are not simply commercial banks, but complex financial service firms dealing in a host of different markets, each with its own competitive dynamics.

Some banks seem able to sustain a gap between themselves and their competitors, either by delivering financial services at a more competitive price (and cost), or through product differentiation. Naturally product differentiation is only relative in the open international money market; it means that imitation and homogenization is merely slower than in other banking products. Many banks try to create temporary monopolies through financial innovation. The more differentiated and valuable in the innovation, the greater the excess return that can be earned by the innovator. There is often a positive relationship between the complexity and uncertainty of the innovation and the imitation lag. On the other hand the more complex the product, and the more uncertain its result, the fewer the clients likely to adopt it. In any case, there is little or no patent protection or financial engineering, so it is essential for some firms to maintain a constant stream of innovations. Others, unable to reap the revenues necessary to sustain the human capital and research and development costs required, must specialize in efficient imitation.

In this and in other areas, the challenge for financial service firms is to identify their sources of competitive advantage, and to match these with the products, markets, and client groups that allow these advantages to be applied, to add value and to be sustainable. Clearly, it is not sufficient to join the crowd in the Eurocurrency market, for sustainable market power has long ago been eroded. Yet a basic capability in the global money and foreign exchange market offers essential building blocks for many of the more complex and differentiated products of the future. The goal must be to understand the competitive conditions in each market segment, and to use the money market building blocks to create value for clients—value that means helping them to manage risks or gain access to funding or investments, making them better off, in a risk-return sense, than they were before. All this, and still leave something on the table for the financial institution itself. This is no small task, and the next decade will certainly see many banks fail or become merged because they turned a blind eye to the changes being wrought by their more aggressive international rivals. The international financial markets have become complex, fast-moving, innovative, and above all, fiercely competitive.

INDEX